Building Citizenship: Civics and Economics

READING ESSENTIALS & STUDY GUIDE

Student Workbook

Bothell, WA • Chicago, IL • Columbus, OH • New York, NY

Cover Photo Credit:
Romy Vandenberg/Wesend61/Corbis

www.mheonline.com/networks

Send all inquiries to:
McGraw-Hill Education
8787 Orion Place
Columbus, OH 43240

ISBN: 978-0-07-660008-3
MHID: 0-07-660008-4

Printed in the United States of America.

12 13 14 15 16 17 18 19 RHR 20 19 18 17

The McGraw·Hill Companies

Table of Contents

The Judicial Branch

Political Parties

Voting and Elections

Public Opinion and Government

State Government

Local Government

Dealing with Community Issues

Citizens and the Law

Civil and Criminal Law

To the Student

Dear Student,

We know that taking notes, using graphic organizers, and developing critical-thinking skills are vital to achieve academic success. Organizing solid study materials can be an overwhelming task. McGraw-Hill has developed this workbook to help you master content and develop those skills necessary for academic success.

This workbook includes all core content found in the *Building Citizenship: Civics and Economics* program. The note-taking, graphic organizer, and Foldables activities will help you learn to organize content for improved comprehension and testing.

Note-Taking System

You will notice that the pages in the *Reading Essentials and Study Guide* are arranged in two columns. The large column on the page contains running text and graphics that summarize each lesson of the chapter. The smaller column will help you use information in various ways and develop note-taking skills.

Graphic Organizers

Many graphic organizers appear in this workbook. Graphic organizers allow you to see the lesson's important information in a visual format. In addition, they help you summarize information and remember the content.

Notebook FOLDABLES®

Notebook Foldables®, invented by Dinah Zike, M.Ed., show you how to make interactive graphic organizers based upon skills. Foldables are easy to create. Every Notebook Foldable® is placed directly within the content pages, helping you with your note-taking skills. Making a Foldable® gives you a fast way to organize and retain information. Each Notebook Foldable® is designed as a study guide for the main ideas and key points presented in lessons of the chapter.

The *Reading Essentials and Study Guide* is a thoroughly interactive workbook that will help you learn social studies content. You will master the content while learning important critical-thinking and note-taking skills that you will use throughout your life.

Notebook Foldable Basics

Notebook Foldables® are an easy, unique way to enhance learning. Instructions are located where the Foldable® is used and every template is provided at the back of the this workbook. You will cut out the appropriate Foldable® template and place it into the workbook as instructed. This quickly turns a workbook into a study guide.

Using Notebook Foldables®

You will write information such as titles, vocabulary words, concepts, questions, main ideas, summaries, definitions, and dates on the tabs of the Foldables®. This will help you easily recognize main ideas and important concepts as you read the content.

In the back of this workbook are several pages with four different Foldable® style templates – one-tab, two-tab, three-tab, and Venn diagram. Each style has an instruction page followed by the templates. Cutting and using the different templates is very simple to master.

Anchor Tab – Glue the back of the Foldable to the workbook with the anchor tab. A dotted line is provided on the workbook page to guide you to proper placement.

Information Tab – Write information on the front and reverse of the information tab.

This tab may be cut again after gluing if it is a two-, three-, or Venn diagram style.

Reverse Information Tab

Folding Instructions

1. **Cut** out the appropriate Foldable® template.
2. **Fold** the anchor tab over the information tab.
3. **Glue** the anchor tab to the workbook page according to the instructions. *(Just a dab is needed!)*

Multiple Foldables® can be glued on top of each other by gluing anchor tabs on top of anchor tabs. This would make a small book on the page.

FOLDABLES®

Supplies

The only supplies needed to utilize Notebook Foldables® are scissors and glue. All paper templates are in the back of the workbook. Consider using crayons and colored pencils, a stapler, clear tape, and anything else you think students might make your Foldables more interesting.

Who is Dinah Zike?

Dinah Zike, M.Ed., is an award-winning author, educator, and inventor known for designing three-dimensional hands-on manipulatives and graphic organizers known as Foldables®. Foldables are used nationally and internationally by teachers, parents, and educational publishing companies. Dinah has developed more than 150 supplemental educational books and materials. Her two latest books, *Notebook Foldables®* and *Foldables®, Notebook Foldables®, & VKV®s for Spelling and Vocabulary 4th-12th* were each awarded *Learning* Magazine's Teachers' Choice Award for 2011. In 2004, Dinah was honored with the Council for Elementary Science International (CESI) Science Advocacy Award. Dinah received her M.Ed. from Texas A&M, College Station, Texas. Dinah has been a valued contributing editor to the McGraw-Hill K-12 education programs for many years.

NAME ______________________ DATE ____________ CLASS __________

networks

Americans, Citizenship, and Governments

Lesson 1: Being an American

ESSENTIAL QUESTION

What are the characteristics that make up a culture?

GUIDING QUESTIONS

1. ***From what areas did early Americans come?***
2. ***What do Americans value?***

Terms to Know

immigrant a person who moves permanently to a new country
distinct separate
ethnic group people who have the same national, cultural, or racial background
values general beliefs people use to make decisions
institution a key practice, relationship, or organization in a society
arbitrary unrestrained
popular sovereignty idea that government gets its power from the people

What Do You Know?

In the first column, answer the question based on what you know before you study. After this lesson, complete the last column.

Now...		Later...
	What shared values unite Americans?	

Explaining

1. Explain why the United States is known as a nation of immigrants.

____

____

Identifying

2. Where did Native Americans come to North America from?

____

A Diverse Population

Almost all of the people in the United States come from families who once lived in another country. This is why the United States is called a nation of **immigrants** (IH•muh•gruhnts). Immigrants are people who come from other lands to live in a new country.

The first people to live in North America came from Asia thousands of years ago. They slowly spread across the land. These early Americans developed many different languages and **distinct** cultures. Today they are called Native Americans.

Other people began moving to North America, beginning in the 1500s. The first European settlers were Spanish. They settled in what is now Florida, the Southwest, Texas, and California. In the 1600s, the French settled in Canada, and the English came to live on the Atlantic coast. They were soon joined by other Europeans.

The Dutch were the first Europeans to settle in what is now New York. People from Sweden and other parts of northern Europe came to live in Delaware.

Lesson 1: Being an American, *Continued*

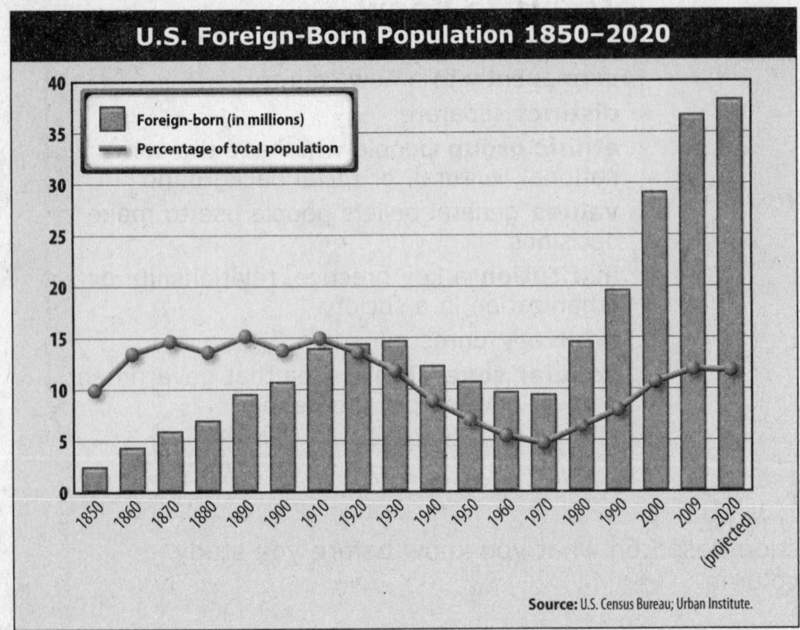

Some people did not come to North America of their own free will. Many Africans were captured in their homelands and sold into slavery. Hundreds of thousands were brought to the United States. Congress ended the slave trade in 1807. By then, there were about 500,000 enslaved Africans in this country.

Between 1830 and 1930 about 40 million immigrants came to the United States. During the 1800s many came from northern and western Europe. They were trying to escape hardship and disease. Then gold was discovered in California in 1848. Many immigrants came hoping to get rich. Thousands were from China.

Immigration changed in the late 1800s. From 1890 to 1924 new immigrants came from a different part of Europe. They came from countries in southern and eastern Europe, including Italy, Greece, Poland, and Russia.

Immigration changed again in the later 1900s. Most immigrants came from Asia and Latin America.

People have also moved around within the United States. In the mid-1800s, people began moving from the country to the city. After the Civil War, many African Americans moved to cities in the North. They hoped to find jobs and a better life.

By the 1920s, more than half of all Americans lived in towns or cities. Many were blue-collar workers. This meant they worked in factories. People who worked in offices and other businesses were called white-collar workers.

Use the Graphic

3. In what year was the *percentage of total population* the lowest in the United States?

____

In what year was it the highest?

____

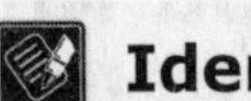

Identifying

4. What group of people was brought to the United States against their will?

____

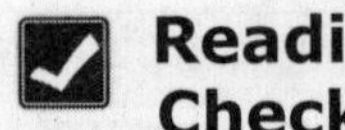

Reading Check

5. Describing How did immigration begin to change in the 1890s?

____

____

Explaining

6. Starting in the mid-1800s many Americans began moving from the countryside to cities and towns. Why?

____

____

Lesson 1: Being an American, *Continued*

Vocabulary

7. Latinos are an example of a(n) (circle one)
blue-collar group.
ethnic group.
European group.

Analyzing Visuals

8. According to the circle graph, what was the largest non-white ethnic group in the United States in 2010?

____

What was the smallest?

____

Locating

9. What is the second largest ethnic group shown on the graph?

____

Explaining

10. In your own words, explain the importance of values.

____

____

Today, work has changed. More women work jobs than ever before. Many people work from home. Also the number of factory jobs has decreased. More people earn a living by providing services, rather than by working in factories. This means they do things such as provide health care, teach, or offer other services to people.

The people who make up the United States today come from many different ethnic groups. An **ethnic** (EHTH•nihk) **group** is a group of people who share the traits of a race, culture, or national background. Latinos, or people of Hispanic origin, are one ethnic group. Their heritage traces back to Latin America. African Americans are another ethnic group. The graph below shows different ethnic groups in the United States. White Americans form the largest group. The others are said to be minority groups.

Americans also practice many different religions. About 173 million Americans belong to a Christian church, but millions follow other religions or practice no religion at all.

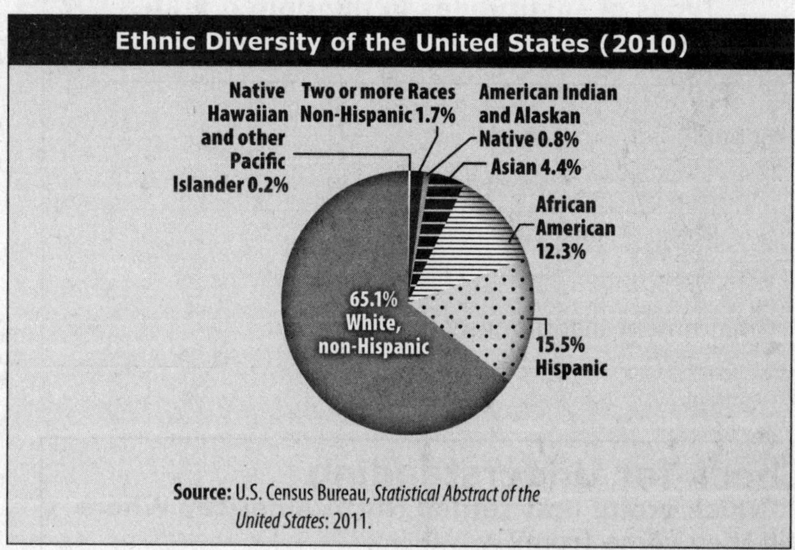

Source: U.S. Census Bureau, *Statistical Abstract of the United States*: 2011.

Values and Institutions

Each American has his or her own values. **Values** are beliefs about what is good or bad that people use to make decisions. The people of the United States have many shared values. Some examples of the common values that help unite the American people are freedom and democracy.

The Declaration of Independence states some of these values. It says that everyone is equal and has a right to freedom. It also says that everyone has the right to life and to seek happiness.

Lesson 1: Being an American, *Continued*

People express their values through their institutions. An **institution** can be many things. It can be an important custom, relationship, or an organization. The family is the most important institution. It is the center of social life. Families teach values. Schools and religions also teach values. Clubs and volunteer groups bring together people with shared values.

U.S. government institutions are also based on values. These values protect our freedom to live without **arbitrary** meddling from the government. They are also based on the idea of **popular sovereignty** (PAH•pyuh•luhr SAH•vuhr•uhn•tee). This is the idea that the government gets its power from the people.

The Constitution is also based on American values. One important idea is that the power of government should be limited. To achieve this the government is divided into three parts. No one part can have more power than the others.

Types of Institutions in the United States
1. _______________
2. Schools
3. _______________
4. _______________
5. Government institutions

/ / / / / / / / / / / / / Glue Foldable here / / / / / / / / / / / / /

Check for Understanding

Which group first settled North America? Where did they come from?

1. _______________ 2. _______________

How are Americans' values reflected in their government institutions?

3. _______________

____

Reading Check

11. Why is the family an important institution?

____

____

Listing

12. Which two American documents reflect important American values?

____

____

Examining Details

13. Fill in the chart at left with types of U.S. institutions.

FOLDABLES®

14. Place a three-tab Foldable along the line. Label the tabs *First Americans, Other Immigrants,* and *Forming America*. On the back, write a sentence about each group and how America formed.

NAME ______________________ DATE ____________ CLASS ________

networks

Americans, Citizenship, and Governments

Lesson 2: Becoming a Citizen

ESSENTIAL QUESTION
What is a citizen?

GUIDING QUESTIONS
1. ***How does a person become a citizen of the United States?***
2. ***In what ways can a foreign person enter the United States?***

Terms to Know
citizen a person who is loyal to a government and is protected by that government
government the ruling authority for a community
civics the study of the rights and duties of citizens
citizenship the rights and duties of citizens
naturalization a legal process to become a citizen
deny to take away a right or privilege
alien a foreign-born resident of the United States who has not been naturalized
refugee a person who flees his or her home to escape danger such as war
priority highest ranking

What Do You Know?
In the first column, answer the questions based on what you know before you study. After this lesson, complete the last column.

Now...		Later...
	What does it mean to be a citizen?	
	What is meant by the term *illegal alien*?	

Reading Check
1. Why do we study civics?

____

____

____

____

What Is Civics?
A **citizen** (SIH•tuh•zuhn) is a person who is loyal to a government and is protected by that government. **Government** is the ruling power for a group of people. For government to work well, citizens must understand their rights and duties.The study of the rights and duties of citizens is called **civics** (SIH•vihks).

The idea of citizenship is very old. **Citizenship** (SIH•tuh•zuhn•SHIP) is the rights and duties of citizens. It began in ancient Greece and Rome. At that time, citizenship was only for men who owned property. Their duties included paying taxes and serving in the armed forces.

In the 1700s, new ideas arose about citizenship and government. Citizenship came to mean belonging to a nation. People came to believe that governments got their power from the people. This idea is known as "consent of the governed."

Lesson 2: Becoming a Citizen, *Continued*

The Growth of American Citizenship	
1776	Only white men who owned property could vote
1868	African American men could vote with the passing of the the 14th Amendment
1920	Women win voting rights in the 19th Amendment
1924	All Native Americans are granted full United States citizenship

Today citizenship in the United States is not based on how much land a person owns. It is also not based on gender, race, or religion. Instead it is based on birth. People who are citizens because they were born in the United States or have U.S.-born parents are called natural-born citizens.

A person is an American citizen if he or she was born in any one of these places:

- in any of the 50 states or in the District of Columbia
- in an American territory
- on a U.S. military base in another country

Even if a person's parents are not citizens of the United States, he or she is still a citizen if born on American soil.

There are two ways a person who is born in another country can be an American citizen.

1. if both parents are U.S. citizens
2. if one parent is a U.S. citizen who has lived in the United States

A person can also be a citizen of both the United States and another country. This is known as dual citizenship.

A person can become an American citizen even if he or she is not a natural-born citizen. He or she must complete the naturalization process. **Naturalization** (NA•chuh•ruh•luh•ZAY•shuhn) is a legal process to become a citizen.

Immigrants who want to become citizens must meet five requirements. They must

1. be at least 18 years old
2. have been a legal permanent resident for five years
3. be able to read, write, and speak English
4. be of good moral character
5. show that they understand U.S. civics

Visualizing

2. On the bottom of this page, draw a timeline of the events shown in the chart.

Mark the Text

3. Find and circle the amendments to the Constitution that grant citizenship and full rights to various groups of people in the United States over the course of the last 150 years.

Mark the Text

4. Find and underline the phrase in the text that explains what citizenship is based on today.

Identifying

5. Is a person who was born on a U.S. military base in another country a U.S. citizen? What kind of citizen is such a person considered to be?

____

____

____

Lesson 2: Becoming a Citizen, *Continued*

Summarizing

6. Summarize the five requirements for immigrants who want to become citizens.

____

____

____

____

Identifying

7. What is USCIS?

____

____

Prior Knowledge

8. What is an oath? How is it related to the naturalization process?

____

____

____

Explaining

9. Explain what could cause a person to lose her or his citizenship. Give specific examples.

____

____

____

There are four main steps to the naturalization process. They are shown in the box below.

Steps in the Naturalization Process
1. Fill out an application with U.S. Citizenship and Immigration Services (USCIS).
2. Talk with a USCIS official.
3. Pass a citizenship exam.
4. Attend a citizenship ceremony.

When the applicant meets with a USCIS official, the official makes sure the person meets all the requirements. The exam tests whether the applicant can read, write, and speak English. It also asks questions about U.S. history and government. At the citizenship ceremony, applicants swear their loyalty to the United States. They promise to obey the Constitution and the laws. After taking this oath and signing a paper, they are citizens.

A person can lose his or her citizenship. This can happen in three ways.

1. **Expatriation.** If a person gives allegiance to another country, such as by becoming a naturalized citizen of another country.
2. **Denaturalization.** If a person is found to have lied on his or her citizenship application, he or she loses citizenship and can be deported. To be deported is to be sent out of the country.
3. **Being convicted of certain crimes.** If a person is convicted of treason, rebelling against the government, or using violence to try to overthrow the government he or she can lose citizenship.

Only the federal government can grant citizenship or take it away. The states can **deny,** or take away, some privileges of citizenship. They can prevent a person from voting, for example. But they cannot take away citizenship itself.

Foreign-Born Residents

Many people who live in the United States are not citizens. People who were born in another country and who have not been naturalized are called **aliens** (AY•lee•uhnz). There are three kinds of aliens: legal aliens, refugees, and illegal aliens.

Legal aliens can be either resident aliens or nonresident aliens. A resident alien is a person who lives permanently in the United States. They may stay as long as they wish. A nonresident alien is a person who is planning to stay for only a certain length of time. A reporter from Mexico who is covering a U.S. election would be a nonresident alien.

Legal aliens have some rights. They can hold jobs, own property, and attend public schools. They have some duties, such as paying taxes. They do not have the right to vote or hold public office. They also cannot work in government jobs or serve on juries.

A **refugee** (REH•fyoo•JEE) is a person who leaves his or her country to escape danger, such as an earthquake or a war. Our government protects some refugees.

The United States allows only about one million people to enter the country each year. Top **priority** goes to relatives of U.S. citizens and people with job skills that are needed. Another million people enter the country illegally each year. Some come as visitors and then never leave. Others cross the borders from Canada or Mexico. Close to 12 million people live in the United States illegally today. Most came in search of a better life. But living as an illegal alien is hard. It is against the law to hire illegal aliens, so most end up working for low pay and without benefits. They live in fear that they will be discovered and sent out of the country.

/ / / / / / / / / / / / / Glue Foldable here / / / / / / / / / / / / / /

Check for Understanding

A person must be 18 years old to become a naturalized citizen. List two other requirements.

1. ______________________________

2. ______________________________

Why do most illegal aliens come to the United States?

3. ______________________________

Comparing and Contrasting

10. What is the difference between a resident alien and a nonresident alien?

____

____

Reading Check

11. How do the rights of legal aliens differ from those of U.S. citizens?

____

____

____

____

FOLDABLES®

12. Place a three-tab Foldable along the line. Label the anchor *Residents of U.S.* Label the first tab *Citizen by Birth,* and the second *Citizen by Naturalization,* and the last tab *Aliens.* On both sides, record facts about these groups and what they have in common.

Lesson 3: Duties and Responsibilities of American Citizens

ESSENTIAL QUESTION

What is a citizen?

GUIDING QUESTIONS

1. ***What are the duties of American citizens?***
2. ***What are American citizens' responsibilities?***
3. ***How can citizens make their community a better place to live?***

Terms to Know

responsibility an obligation that we meet of our own free will
duty an action we are required to do
register to record or enroll formally
draft to call for military service
tolerance respecting and accepting others
welfare the health, prosperity, and happiness of the members of a community
volunteerism giving your time and services to others without expecting payment

What Do You Know?

In the first column, answer the questions based on what you know before you study. After this lesson, complete the last column.

Now...		Later...
	Why must we pay taxes?	
	What does it mean to be *tolerant* of others?	
	Why is volunteering important?	

Vocabulary

1. What is the difference between a *duty* and a *responsibility*?

____

____

____

Duties of Citizens

A community can be a neighborhood, town, school, workplace, state, country, or even the world. We all play a part in making our communities safe and successful. We all have responsibilities. **Responsibilities** (rih•SPAHN•suh •BIH•luh•teez) are things we should do. They are obligations we meet of our own free will. No law requires us to meet our responsibilities. Duties are different from responsibilities. **Duties** are things that we have to do. If we ignore or forget our duties, we may have to pay a fine or even go to jail. The chart below shows the duties of citizens.

Major Duties of American Citizens
• obey the law • pay taxes • defend the nation • serve in court • attend school

Lesson 3: Duties and Responsibilities of American Citizens, *Continued*

Citizens have many duties. The most important is to obey the law. Laws are rules that help people live together in peace. Laws keep order in society by letting people know which actions are acceptable and which are not. It is important for people to obey the law so that communities can keep order and protect our health, safety, and property.

Citizens are also required to pay taxes. Taxes keep the government running. They allow the federal government to pay its employees, defend the country, and help those in need. Taxes allow state governments to run the schools, pave roads, and hire firefighters. There are different kinds of taxes. The main kinds are income, property, and sales taxes.

Most male citizens aged 18 to 25 must **register** with the Selective Service System (SSS). In the case of a war or a major national emergency, the government may draft men from the SSS list. To **draft** means to call into military service. No draft has happened in this country since 1973 because we have enough volunteers to meet our needs.

Another duty is serving in court. The Constitution guarantees any person accused of a crime the right to trial by jury. A jury is a group of citizens who listen to the facts of a case and decide whether the accused person is innocent or guilty. Every adult citizen must be prepared to serve on a jury. An accused person also has the right to call witnesses. If a citizen is called as a witness, he or she has a duty to respond.

Attending school is also a duty. Most states require children aged 7 to 16 to go to school. Schools teach the knowledge needed to be good citizens. They also prepare students to be skilled workers.

Responsibilities of Citizens

For society to work, every citizen must do his or her part. The chart below lists a citizen's major responsibilities.

Major Responsibilities of American Citizens
• be informed and vote • participate in government and your community • respect the rights and property of others • respect different opinions and ways of life

Reading Check

2. Why must we obey laws?

____

____

____

Listing

3. List things that the federal government uses taxes for, and things state governments use taxes for.

____

____

____

Vocabulary

4. If the U.S. military did not have enough volunteers to fight a war, what would the government do?

____

____

Explaining

5. Why is attending school a duty?

____

____

____

Lesson 3: Duties and Responsibilities of American Citizens, *Continued*

Describing

6. Why is it important to stay informed about what the government does?

____

____

Reading Check

7. Why is voting important?

____

____

Paraphrasing

8. Why is tolerance important in the United States?

____

____

____

____

Reading Check

9. What is volunteerism?

____

____

____

The first responsibility of citizens is to be informed and active. Government decisions affect your life. You will have less money to spend if the state legislature decides to raise the sales tax. You will have to get up earlier if the local school board decides to extend the school day. You have a responsibility to know what the government is doing so that you can voice your opinion about these matters.

Remember that government in this country gets its power from the people. This means that you have a responsibility to make sure the government is working properly. You can do this by contacting elected officials and by voting.

All citizens who are at least 18 years old have the right to vote. Voting gives you the chance to help shape the future of your community, state, and nation. To vote well you must study the candidates and the issues. You must also keep track of what your elected officials are doing. If you do not like how they are performing, you can vote against them in the next election. Voting is a peaceful way to hand power from one group to another.

Society runs smoothly when people respect one another's rights and property. Respecting others' opinions and ways of life is also important. The United States is nation of many diverse people. Everyone has a right to his or her own opinions and beliefs. For all these different people to get along, citizens must respect and accept others. This is called **tolerance.**

Being Involved

Good citizens care about the welfare of others. **Welfare** includes people's health, wealth, and happiness. One way to help others is to volunteer. Volunteering makes our communities better places to live. It also helps us learn useful skills.

Giving your time and services to others without expecting payment is called **volunteerism** (VAH•luhn•TIHR•IH•zuhm). Millions of people in this country volunteer. Without their help, the needs of many people would not be met.

Some people choose to support causes by giving money. Americans give more than $300 billion to charities every year. Much of this money comes from small donations from ordinary citizens.

Lesson 3: Duties and Responsibilities of American Citizens, *Continued*

More than one million charities are registered with the federal government. Some are small and local. Others are national and help thousands of people.

The federal government supports volunteerism through many agencies. The chart bellows outlines some of the more important ones.

Government Agency	Purpose
Corporation for National and Community Service	• provides money, training, and other help for volunteer groups • manages AmeriCorps, Senior Corps, Learn and Serve America
AmeriCorps	• provides work in education, public safety, health, and the environment. • gives members money to pay for college in return for a year of service.
Senior Corps	• provides Americans aged 55 or older a chance to help their communities by serving as foster grandparents, assisting the disabled, and more.
Learn and Serve America	• promotes service learning in schools by linking community service with classroom work

/ / / / / / / / / / / / / Glue Foldable here / / / / / / / / / / / / /

Check for Understanding

List two major duties of American citizens.

1. ______________________

2. ______________________

List two major responsibilities of American citizens.

3. ______________________

4. ______________________

How can you make your community a better place to live?

5. ______________________

Mark the Text

10. Find evidence in this paragraph that volunteerism is important in the United States. Underline the sentence that proves this point.

Examining Details

11. Which government agency benefits communities while at the same time helping young adults pay for college?

____

FOLDABLES®

12. Place a two-tab Foldable along the dotted line. Label the anchor tab *U.S. Citizens*. Label the first tab *Responsibilities* and the second tab *Duties*. On the reverse tabs write the definition of each.

Americans, Citizenship, and Governments

Lesson 4: Forms of Government

ESSENTIAL QUESTION

Why do people create, structure, and change governments?

GUIDING QUESTIONS

1. ***What is the purpose of government?***
2. ***What are the types of government?***

Terms to Know

resolve to find a solution to a disagreement

public policy the decisions and actions a government takes to solve problems

representative democracy government in which people choose leaders to govern for them

constitutional monarchy monarchy in which the power of the hereditary ruler is limited by the country's constitution and laws

majority rule political principle that says a majority of the people has the power to make laws binding upon all the people

regime the government in power

authoritarian regime a government in which one leader or group holds all the power

totalitarian describes a system in which government controls almost all aspects of people's lives

ideology a set of ideas about life and society

socialism system in which society, sometimes through the government, controls the economy

What Do You Know?

In the first column, answer the questions based on what you know before you study. After this lesson, complete the last column.

Now...		Later...
	What do governments do?	
	Which type of government is found most often in the world?	

Reading Check

1. How do governments keep order in society?

______

______

The Importance of Government

A government is the ruling power for a community. Any group that can make and carry out laws and decisions for those living in a community is a government.

Government helps people to live together peacefully. Governments do many things. The most important purpose is to make rules, or laws. Laws help prevent conflict. They also help resolve conflict when it does occur. To **resolve** means to find a solution. Governments use police officers and courts to enforce the law.

Governments also keep the nation safe. They set up armed forces to guard the people from enemies.

Lesson 4: Forms of Government, *Continued*

FUNCTIONS OF GOVERNMENT	
KEEP ORDER	**PROVIDE SECURITY**
Pass and enforce laws to deter crime	Establish armed forces
Establish courts	Protect citizens from foreign attacks
PROVIDE SERVICES	**GUIDE THE COMMUNITY**
Protect public health	Develop public policy
Protect public safety	Manage the economy
Provide public welfare	Conduct foreign relations

Governments provide many services. They run libraries, schools, hospitals, and parks. They build and repair streets and bridges. They collect garbage and deliver the mail. Some services are meant to keep people healthy and safe. These services include police and fire protection and the licensing of doctors. The government ensures the safety of food, medicines, and a long list of other products.

Governments also help the poor and those who are out of work. They supply housing, health care, and special programs for people with disabilities.

Governments guide the community by making public policy. **Public policy** means the decisions and actions a government takes to solve problems. Putting public policies to work takes money. Since governments have limited funds, they must plan carefully.

Governments also guide the community by working with other nations. Trade and travel are two areas where governments must work together to help their citizens.

The United States has a federal system of government. This means that power is divided between the national government and the states. The states then give some power to local governments.

The national government makes and enforces laws for the entire country. It also sets the rules for citizenship. State and local laws cannot go against national laws.

Each state has its own government. These governments make laws and create public policy for the people of their state. States do things such as make marriage laws, run schools, and hold elections. They protect health and safety.

Listing

2. What three types of services do governments provide according to the chart?

____

____

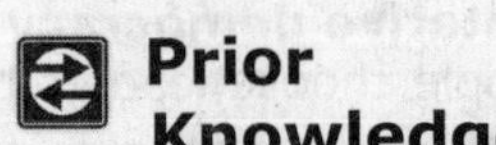

Prior Knowledge

3. Name three types of leaders that the people of the United States elect to represent them.

____

____

Explaining

4. Explain how power is divided in a federal system of government.

____

____

Contrasting

5. How do state governments differ from the national government?

____

____

Lesson 4: Forms of Government, *Continued*

Identifying

6. What do local governments do?

____

____

FOLDABLES®

7. Place a Venn Diagram Foldable along the dotted line to cover the text. Write *Democracies* on the anchor tab. Label the first tab *Representative Democracies,* the middle tab *Both,* and the last tab *Constitutional Monarchies*. On both sides of the tabs, record two facts you learned about each and explain what they have in common on the middle tab.

Vocabulary

8. Explain what *majority rule* is. What type of government uses it?

____

____

____

____

They build roads and bridges. States also can set up local governments.

Local governments are found in counties, cities, and towns. They help the local community by setting up police and fire departments and local courts. They light the streets and remove snow. Like state governments, local governments cannot do anything that goes against the federal government.

The Types of Government

/ / / / / / / / / / / / / Glue Foldable here / / / / / / / / / / / / /

Nations have different forms of government. Not all nations are governed like the United States. Many countries, however, do have a detailed, written plan of government called a constitution.

Democracy began in ancient Greece more than 2,500 years ago. The Greek city of Athens had a direct democracy. This meant that all citizens met to discuss and vote on issues.

Today's nations are too large for direct democracy to work. Instead, many countries have **representative democracies** (REH•pree•ZEHN•tuh•tiv dih•MAH•kruh•seez). In this type of government, the people choose leaders to represent them. The United States is the world's oldest representative democracy. The key principles of democracy are found in the chart on the next page.

There are two types of representative democracies. They are republics and constitutional monarchies. The United States is a republic. In a republic, citizens play a part in choosing the head of government.

The second type is a **constitutional monarchy** (kahn•stuh•TOO•shnuhl MAH•nuhr•kee). In a monarchy, the head of government is not chosen by the people. Instead, a king or queen inherits this position. The power of most monarchs today is limited by a constitution. For this reason, these governments are called constitutional monarchies. The monarch has only ceremonial and social duties. Real power is found in an elected lawmaking body. The members of that body choose a leader called a prime minister.

Democracy works on the principle of **majority rule** (muh•JAWR•uh•tee ROOL). This means that citizens agree that they will abide by what most people want. At the same time, members of the minority keep their rights as citizens.

Lesson 4: Forms of Government, *Continued*

PRINCIPLES OF AMERICAN DEMOCRACY	
RULE OF LAW	All people, including those who govern, are bound by the law.
LIMITED GOVERNMENT	Government is not all-powerful. It may do only those things that the people have given it the power to do.
CONSENT OF THE GOVERNED	American citizens are the source of all government power.
INDIVIDUAL RIGHTS	In American democracy, individual rights are protected by government.
REPRESENTATIVE GOVERNMENT	People elect government leaders to make the laws and govern on their behalf.
FREE, FAIR, AND COMPETITIVE ELECTIONS	Every citizen's vote has equal value. They choose between candidates and parties. They vote by secret ballot free from government interference.
MAJORITY RULE	A majority of the members of a community has the power to make laws binding upon all the people.

The government in power is called a **regime.** In a democracy, the people rule. In **authoritarian regimes** (aw•THAHR•uh•TEHR•ee•uhn ray•ZHEEMZ), one person or a small group holds all the power. They do not answer to the people. Though uncommon now, some monarchies are authoritarian. For this reason they are called absolute monarchies. The king of Saudi Arabia and the emir of Qatar might still be seen as absolute monarchs. Their power is officially without limits.

An authoritarian regime can be a dictatorship. Dictators usually seize power by force. To stay in power, they often rely on the army. Elections usually are not allowed. People do not have freedoms. They cannot criticize the government.

Many dictators force the people to accept **totalitarian** (toh•TA•luh•TEHR•ee•uhn) rule. This means that the government controls people's lives. They decide what factories and farms will produce. They tell people what they can believe and what groups they can join.

Totalitarian leaders often have an **ideology** (EYE•dee•AH•luh•jee) that they expect people to obey. An ideology is a strict idea about life and society. To enforce their ideas, totalitarian leaders control the media. They use fear, violence, and propaganda. Propaganda is information used to support a cause or to damage someone else's cause.

Identifying

9. Study the chart. List three principles of U.S. democracy. Next to each principle, explain how an authoritarian regime differs.

____

____

Identifying

10. Name two types of authoritarian regimes.

____

____

Reading Check

11. How does an absolute monarchy differ from a constitutional monarchy?

____

____

____

Lesson 4: Forms of Government, *Continued*

Contrasting

12. What is the difference between a federal system of government and a unitary system of government?

____

____

____

____

FOLDABLES®

13. Place a two-tab Foldable along the line. Label the anchor *Government*. Label the tabs *Purpose* and *Types*. On both sides of the tabs, write what you remember about the purpose and types of government.

Some totalitarian states practice the system of **socialism.** In such a state, society, or the people, control the economy. Sometimes this control is through the government. The government, rather than private owners, decides what factories will make. It also decides what jobs people will have. Under socialism, it was hoped that a nation's wealth would be more evenly divided among its people. In totalitarian states, this did not happen.

Nations also differ in how they share—or do not share—power between levels of government. The United States has a federal system of government. In a federal system, power is divided between a central government and smaller political units, such as states. Germany, Brazil, and India also have federal systems.

Most nations do not divide governmental power this way. They have unitary systems of government. In a unitary system, all power is held by the central government. France, Japan, and Great Britain have unitary systems.

The United States did not always have a federal system. When it first formed, the United States was governed under a confederal system of government. A confederal system is made of member states that have agreed to join together. The states create a common body to carry out certain functions. They keep their separate powers, however.

/ / / / / / / / / / / / / / Glue Foldable here / / / / / / / / / / / / / /

Check for Understanding

Why is government important?

1. ______________________________

In today's democracies why is representative democracy practiced, rather than direct democracy?

2. ______________________________

____

The American Colonies and Their Government

Lesson 1: Influences on American Colonial Government

ESSENTIAL QUESTIONS

How does geography influence the development of communities?

Why do people create, structure, and change governments?

GUIDING QUESTIONS

1. ***What ancient principles, traditions, and events have shaped the system of government we have today?***
2. ***How did Europe's Enlightenment influence ideas about government in what became the United States?***
3. ***How were the first English colonies in America shaped by earlier ideas about democracy and government?***

Terms to Know

democracy rule by the people
direct democracy a system in which the people govern themselves
representative democracy a system in which the people choose leaders to govern for them
republic a country with a representative democracy
document an official paper or form that is a record of something
limited government the idea that the power of a ruler or government can be limited
legislature a group of representatives that makes laws
natural rights rights that government cannot take away, such as the right to life, the right to freedom, and the right to own property
social contract an agreement between the people and their government in which the people agree to give up some freedom and the government agrees to protect the people's rights
compact a written agreement

What Do You Know?

In the first column, answer the questions based on what you know before you study. After this lesson, complete the last column.

Now...		Later...
	Why do people need government?	

Mark the Text

1. Underline the definition of a democracy.

The Foundations of Democracy

A **democracy** is a government in which the people rule. This is different from a government in which one person has all the power. This type of ruler is called a monarch.

The Jewish religion gave the world some of its first democratic ideas. Since ancient times, Judaism has taught that every person has worth. This belief is one of the basic ideas of democracy.

Lesson 1: Influences on American Colonial Government, *Continued*

Our government today was influenced by ancient Greece and Rome. In ancient Greece, the people of Athens created the world's first direct democracy in the 400s B.C.

In a **direct democracy,** the people govern themselves. This works when the population is small. In Athens, all free men over 18 years old were citizens. They could take part in the assembly. The assembly made decisions for the whole community. In places with large populations, an assembly of all citizens would be too big. In those places, people would choose leaders to govern for them. This is called **representative democracy.**

When a country has a representative democracy, it is called a republic. In 509 B.C., the Romans overthrew their king and set up a republic. It was the world's first republic. A senate ran the government. Its members were chosen from Rome's wealthy upper class. The United States is a **republic.** The Roman republic helped shape the American government today.

After the Roman Empire ended, kings and lords ruled most of Europe for 700 years. Lords were noblemen that usually inherited land and wealth. As the kings became more powerful, some nobles rebelled. In England they made King John sign a **document** called the Magna Carta (Latin term for "Great Charter"). The graphic organizer below lists important points from the Magna Carta.

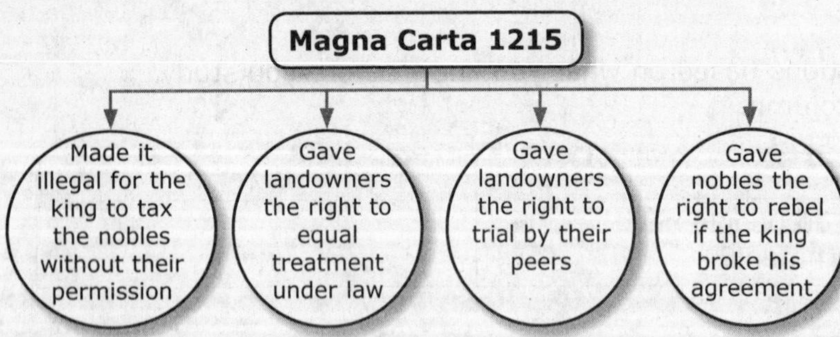

The Magna Carta put forth the idea of **limited government.** This meant that a ruler or government was no longer all-powerful.

By the late 1300s, England had a group of nobles that advised the king. It was called Parliament. In addition to giving the king advice, Parliament made laws. A group of representatives that makes laws is called a **legislature.** So Parliament was a legislature.

Glue Foldable here

FOLDABLES®

2. Glue a one-tab on top of a two-tab Foldable to create a book. Place the book along the line. Title the top Foldable *Democracy* and define the word. On the second Foldable, label the tabs *Direct Democracy-Greece* and *Representative Democracy-Rome.* Use the back of the tabs to describe the importance of each to the growth of democracy.

Explaining

3. What rights did the Magna Carta give landowners?

____

____

____

Reading Check

4. How did the Magna Carta establish the principle of limited government?

____

____

Lesson 1: Influences on American Colonial Government, *Continued*

Explaining

5. What did the Petition of Right do?

Identifying

6. What was the Glorious Revolution?

Mark the Text

7. Circle the sentences that help you understand what the Enlightenment was.

Reading Check

8. What natural rights did John Locke believe all people had?

Many kings did not want Parliament's help. In 1625, King Charles I dismissed Parliament and ruled alone. In 1628, he called Parliament back and its members forced him to sign the Petition of Right. The Petition of Right limited the power of England's kings.

The English Parliament decided to make changes to their government. In 1688, Parliament forced King James II from the throne. It asked James's daughter Mary and her husband William to rule instead. This change became known as the Glorious Revolution.

Parliament created a set of rules for the government called the English Bill of Rights. William and Mary had to accept the English Bill of Rights before they took power.

These rules listed certain rights of English citizens and said that kings could not take them away. The Glorious Revolution and the English Bill of Rights changed English government forever. The events also received much notice in the English colonies in North America.

Influence of the Enlightenment

The problems between the monarchy and Parliament created new ideas about government. These ideas were part of a movement in Europe known as the Enlightenment.

New discoveries in science also led to the Enlightenment movement. Some came to believe that God had created a universe governed by laws. These laws of nature could be discovered using human reason, or careful thought.

Enlightenment Thinkers

NAME	YEARS LIVED	BELIEFS
Thomas Hobbes	1588–1679	People agree to be ruled because their ruler pledges to protect their rights.
John Locke	1632–1704	People have rights to life, liberty, and property that the government must protect for the common good.
Baron de Montesquieu	1689–1755	Separate the parts of government so no one part can become too powerful.
Voltaire	1694–1778	People have the right to speak freely, and this right should be defended by everyone.
Jean-Jacques Rousseau	1712–1778	The legislative power belongs to the people.

Lesson 1: Influences on American Colonial Government, *Continued*

Enlightenment thinkers wanted to apply the laws of nature to people and societies. These ideas changed how people thought of government in Europe and in the Americas. The chart shows some important Enlightenment thinkers.

The Glorious Revolution also let Enlightenment thinkers share their ideas more freely. One important Enlightenment thinker was John Locke. Locke influenced how the settlers in North America thought of government. Locke said that people form governments to protect their natural rights. **Natural rights** are rights that everyone should have. These include the right to life, the right to freedom, and the right to own property.

Also, Locke argued that an agreement existed between government and the people. Locke called this agreement the **social contract**. According to the social contract, the people agreed to give up some freedom and be ruled by government. In return, the government agreed to protect the people's rights. If it did not do that, the contract was broken. If the contract was broken, then the people could choose new leaders.

The First Colonial Governments

During the 1600s, people from England traveled to North America and set up colonies. A *colony* is a settlement controlled by another country. The early colonists were loyal to England. They had a strong belief in democracy and representative government. They brought these ideas to America.

Early Settlement Governments

Year, Group	Place	Government
1607, Virginia Company	Jamestown, Virginia	**Representative government:** Elected *House of Burgesses* in 1619
1620, Pilgrims	Plymouth, Massachusetts	**Direct democracy:** *Mayflower Compact* established direct democracy

The first permanent English settlement in North America was Jamestown. The Virginia Company set it up in 1607. At first, the Virginia Company appointed officials to run Jamestown. To convince more people to come to Jamestown, the company began to let the colonists make their own laws.

Summarizing

9. Circle Locke's ideas about natural rights. Then underline his ideas about the social contract.

Defining

10. Explain what a contract is. Use context clues from the text.

____

____

____

Listing

11. What were the first two permanent English settlements in North America?

____

____

Mark the Text

12. Study the chart. Underline the type of government Plymouth had.

Lesson 1: Influences on American Colonial Government, *Continued*

Reading Check

13. Summarizing What beliefs about government did early English colonists bring to America?

____

____

FOLDABLES

14. Place a one-tab Foldable along the line. Draw a circle in the center of the tab and write *Colonist Values*. Draw five lines from the circle. On each line write an idea or right that the colonists valued.

Beginning in 1619 the colonists elected leaders called *burgesses* to represent them. This group was called the House of Burgesses. Jamestown's House of Burgesses was the first representative government in the colonies.

In 1620, another group of people from England called Pilgrims sailed to North America. The pilgrims wanted the freedom to practice their religion. Their small ship was called the *Mayflower*. The ship landed in what is now Massachusetts. There was no English government in this part of North America. The men on the ship decided to make a list of rules for the colony. It was called the Mayflower Compact. A **compact** is a written agreement. The Mayflower Compact set up a direct democracy in the new colony of Plymouth.

/ / / / / / / / / / / / / Glue Foldable here / / / / / / / / / / / / /

Check for Understanding

What are three ideas that the English colonists brought with them to North America?

1. _______________

2. _______________

3. _______________

NAME ______________________ DATE ______________ CLASS ____________

Lesson 2: Settlement, Culture, and Government of the Colonies

ESSENTIAL QUESTIONS

How does geography influence the development of communities?

Why do people create, structure, and change governments?

GUIDING QUESTIONS

1. ***Why did people settle in England's colonies in America?***
2. ***How was life in the colonies shaped by where people lived?***
3. ***What factors weakened the ties between England and its colonies?***

Terms to Know

indentured servant a person who agreed to work for someone else for a certain length of time, in return for passage on a ship, food, shelter, and clothing

dissenter someone who does not agree with official or common views

economy way of using wealth and resources

cash crop crops grown in large amounts to be sold

plantation large farms where crops are grown for sale

benefit to be useful, or profitable to

What Do You Know?

In the first column, answer the questions based on what you know before you study. After this lesson, complete the last column.

Now...		Later...
	Why did settlers come to America?	
	What was life like in the colonies?	

Settling the English Colonies

Colonists came to North America from many parts of Europe. Settlers traveled across the ocean from England, Scotland, Ireland, and Wales. The Dutch and the Swedes also started colonies along the Atlantic Coast.

People came to America for many reasons. Most of the colonists came to America for land or jobs. Even those who could not afford the cost of the trip to America could come by agreeing to be indentured servants. An **indentured servant** had to work for another colonist for a certain length of time. In return, the colonist paid for the indentured servant's trip to the colonies. They were also given food, shelter, and clothing when they reached America. The servants worked from four to seven years, and after that they were free to work for themselves.

In Europe, some people were being treated harshly because of their religious beliefs. Many of these people came to America for the right to worship in their own way.

Reading Check

1. Why did some people come to the colonies as indentured servants?

____

____

____

____

Lesson 2: Settlement, Culture, and Government of the Colonies, *Continued*

Listing

2. Name the two major reasons that people came to America.

____

____

Vocabulary

3. Were the founders of Rhode Island *dissenters*? Why or why not?

____

____

____

Comparing and Contrasting

4. How were the Pilgrims and the Puritans different? How were they the same?

____

____

____

Describing

5. Describe what life was like for farmers in the New England colonies.

____

____

____

That is why the Pilgrims left England. Another group started the Massachusetts Bay Colony near Plymouth. They were called Puritans. The Puritans were dissenters. A **dissenter** is a person who is against official or common views.

The Puritans wanted freedom to worship in their own way, but they did not allow others to do so. Some people were forced to leave the Massachusetts Bay Colony because of their religious views. These people started the colonies of Rhode Island and Connecticut. In 1639, the people of Connecticut produced America's first written constitution. They called it the Fundamental Orders of Connecticut. It created an assembly of elected representatives from each town. These leaders passed laws for the colony. The colonists also elected their own governor and judges.

Colonial Life

By 1733, England had 13 colonies along the Atlantic Coast of North America. The land and the climate, or weather, was different among the colonies from north to south. These differences affected each colony's **economy**, or way of producing goods, as well as their way of life.

Reasons for Settling the Colonies	
Economic Opportunity	**Religious Freedom**
• People came as indentured servants to work for passage to the colonies, food, and shelter. • People came for a chance to earn a better living than where they came from. • People came for farmland.	• Puritans came to worship as they pleased. They were dissenters in England. • Pilgrims came for religious freedom. They founded Plymouth.

In New England, most people lived in towns. The cold climate and rocky soil made it hard to farm. Farms were small and were located near towns. Many New Englanders worked as shopkeepers or in other small businesses. The region's forests provided wood for shipbuilding. Fishers worked on boats in the Atlantic Ocean. Others hunted and trapped. They sold the furs to Native Americans and also shipped furs overseas.

NAME ______________________ DATE ____________ CLASS ____________

networks

Lesson 2: Settlement, Culture, and Government of the Colonies, *Continued*

The New England states were far north, which was why the climate was cold. The Middle Colonies were between the New England and Southern Colonies. The climate was pleasant and warm. The map below shows where the colonies were located.

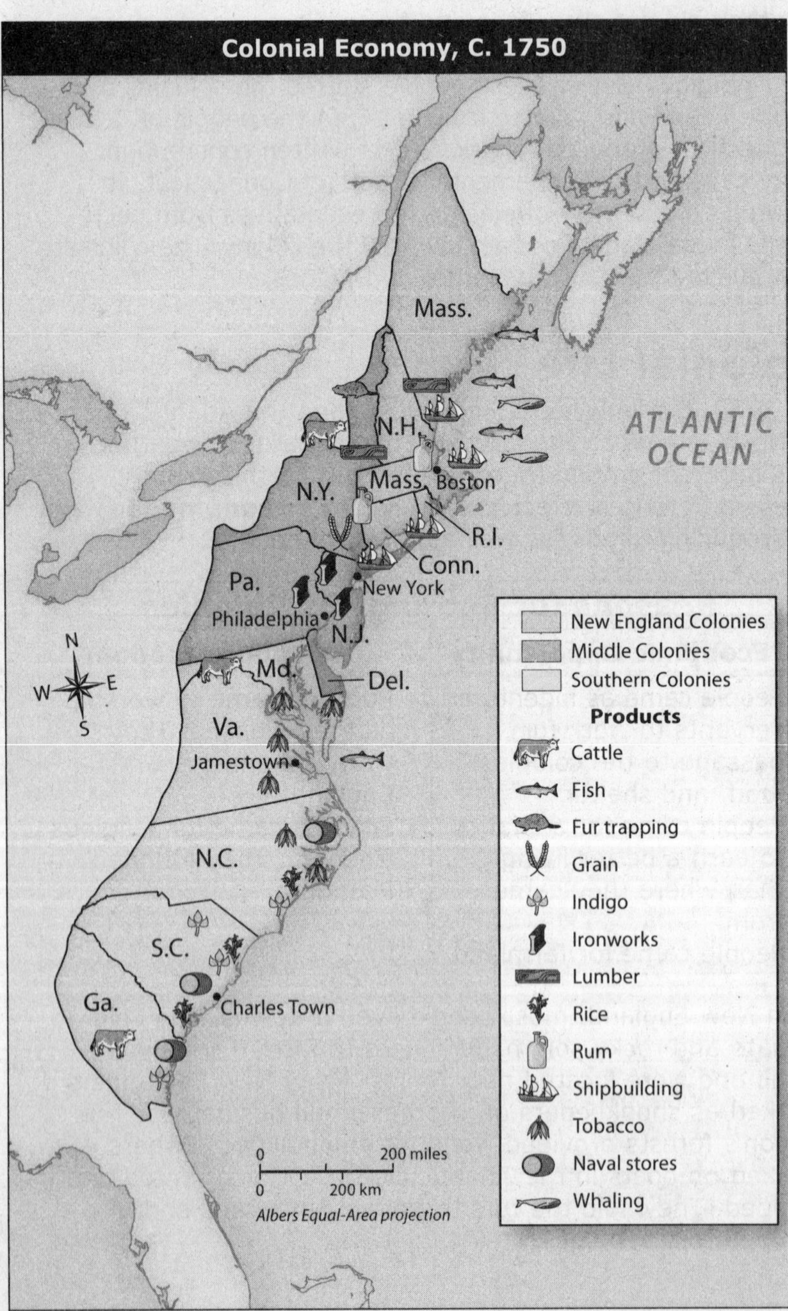

Visualizing

6. What industries helped build New York and Philadelphia into busy port cities?

____

____

____

Identifying

7. Use the symbols on the map to identify important export crops in the Southern colonies.

____

____

____

Making Connections

8. In the New England and Middle colonies, the map shows related industries clustered together. Identify and explain some of these connections.

____

____

____

____

The American Colonies and Their Government

Lesson 2: Settlement, Culture, and Government of the Colonies, *Continued*

Identifying

9. Fill in the missing details in the chart about natural resources and industry in the colonies.

Comparing and Contrasting

10. How did the farms of the Southern colonies compare to those of the New England colonies?

____

____

____

____

Reading Check

11. Who controlled the elected assemblies in the Southern Colonies and why?

____

____

____

____

Natural Resources and Industry in the Colonies

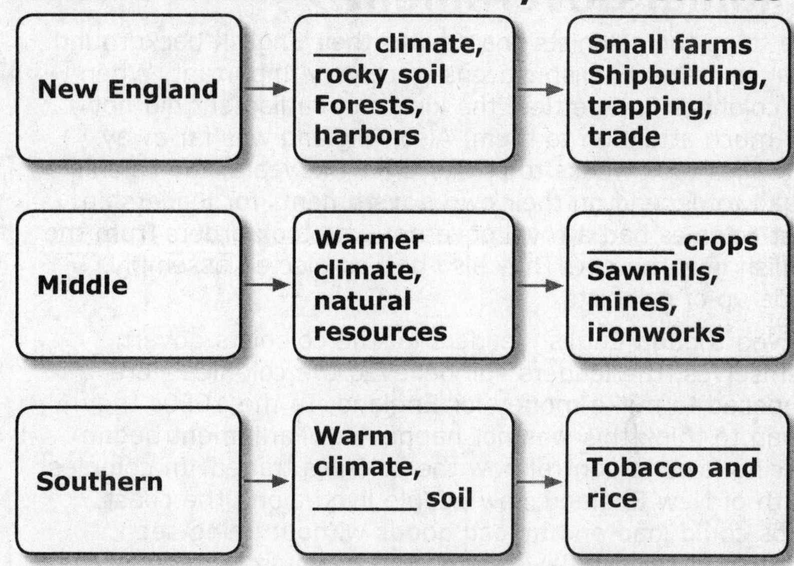

In the Middle Colonies, the climate and soil were better for farming. Farmers raised wheat and other **cash crops.** Cash crops are crops that are grown in large amounts. They were sold instead of being saved to feed the farmers' families. Cash crops were often sold overseas. This trade helped make New York City and Philadelphia busy port cities. The Middle Colonies were also rich in natural resources such as lumber, metals, and harbors. Because of this sawmills, mines, ironworks, and other businesses grew.

The Southern Colonies had warm weather, a long growing season, and rich soil. This meant that crops grew well in these colonies. Tobacco and rice, especially, grew well along the coast. They were the cash crops of the region. Large farms called **plantations** developed. Many workers were needed on these plantations. At first indentured servants did the work. Over time, however, plantation owners came to depend on the labor of enslaved Africans.

Plantation owners were very rich and powerful. They controlled the government and the economy in the region. They had so much control that few towns and industries developed there.

The American Colonies and Their Government

Lesson 2: Settlement, Culture, and Government of the Colonies, *Continued*

Colonial Government

One thing the colonists shared was their English background. Their rights as English citizens were very important. When the colonists first settled, the king and Parliament did not pay much attention to them. Also, England was far away. Messages took weeks to arrive. Over the years, the colonists began to depend on their own governments for leadership. Most colonies had a royal governor who took orders from the English government. They also had an elected assembly made up of colonists.

Even though English leaders let the colonists govern themselves, the leaders still believed the colonies were supposed to make money for England. In the 1650s they began to think this was not happening. Parliament began passing laws to control how the colonies traded. In colonies south of New England, few people lived along the coast. Ships could load and unload goods without being seen. Because of this the laws were hard to enforce, and the colonists often ignored them.

As time went on, the colonial assemblies grew strong. The assemblies made local laws. They could also tax the colonists and decide how that tax money would be spent. They used these powers to make the royal governor weaker.

By the mid-1700s, the colonists were used to governing themselves. Most agreed with John Locke's idea that government should protect the people's rights. The colonists thought it was unfair when the royal governors did things to **benefit**, or help, England instead of the colonies. Many colonists also began to think that they did not have as many rights as people in England did. Over time, the colonists came to see themselves as Americans rather than as English citizens.

Check for Understanding

List the colonial regions and one fact about each.

1. ______ ______

2. ______ ______

3. ______ ______

List two strengths of the colonial assemblies.

4. ______ 5. ______

Glue Foldable here

Reading Check

12. How did the distance between England and America influence colonists' ideas about leadership?

______

______

______

Contrasting

13. How did the approach of the English government toward its colonies change from the early to mid-1600s?

______

______

FOLDABLES®

14. Place a three-tab Foldable along the line. Label the tabs *New England Colonies*, *Middle Colonies*, and *Southern Colonies*. On the front tabs list the colonies located in each area. On the back, list facts about the regions.

The American Colonies and Their Government

Lesson 3: Disagreements With Great Britain

ESSENTIAL QUESTION

Why do people create, structure, and change governments?

GUIDING QUESTIONS

1. ***What events and movements affected colonial attitudes?***
2. ***What events increased colonists' anger toward British rule?***
3. ***What ideas about government influenced the Declaration of Independence?***

Terms to Know

authority the power to make others obey
liberty personal freedom
proclamation official announcement
boycott refuse to buy or use
repeal to cancel
duty a tax on imported goods
smuggling moving goods illegally in or out of a country
delegate representative
debate to talk about or argue

What Do You Know?

In the first column, answer the questions based on what you know before you study. After this lesson, complete the last column.

Now...		Later...
	What changed the colonists' ideas about Britain?	
	Why were colonists angry with the British?	
	Why was the Declaration of Independence written?	

Vocabulary

1. Define the word *authority*. Underline the words in the paragraph that help you determine its meaning.

____

____

____

____

Social and Political Changes in the Colonies

In the 1740s, a religious movement called the Great Awakening began in the colonies. Colonists began to question the traditional religious **authority** of the church. Enlightenment thinkers urged people to question political authority. The Great Awakening and the Enlightenment made people in the colonies want more **liberty,** or personal freedom. More and more colonists believed that they should have the same rights as people in Great Britain.

The colonists thought that Parliament should protect the rights of British people from the king. Yet the king and Parliament made the laws for the colonists. The colonists thought they should be able to choose their own leaders. The royal governors did what the king wanted, not what the colonists wanted.

Lesson 3: Disagreements With Great Britain, *Continued*

The colonies began to get bigger. By the 1750s, British colonists were moving west into places that France said it already owned. Soon people from Great Britain and France began to fight over the land. In 1754, French soldiers joined with some Native American groups. Together, they tried to make the British colonists leave the land west of the Appalachian Mountains. Britain sent troops to the colonies. The conflict was called the French and Indian War.

The British won the French and Indian War in 1763. Now the British controlled French lands as far west as the Mississippi River. The colonists wanted to move onto those lands. The shaded area on the map below shows the land that the British won from France.

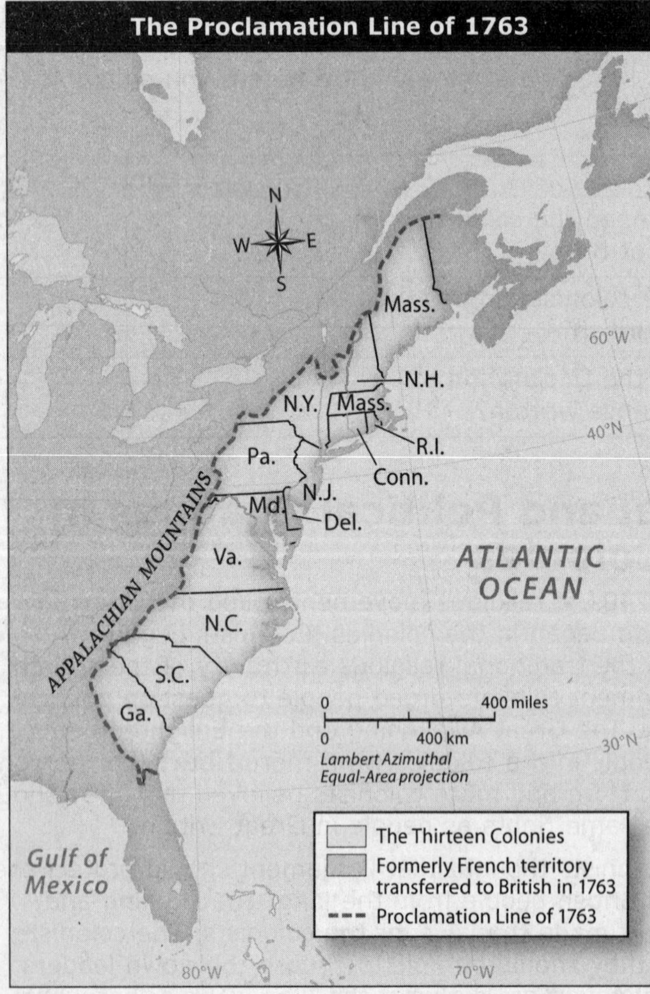

Glue Foldable here.

FOLDABLES®

2. Place a two-tab Foldable along the dotted line. Label the top tab *The Great Awakening* and the bottom tab *The French and Indian War*. On the front of the tabs identify the dates of each event. On the back of the tabs, describe how the events changed the way that colonists viewed English rule.

Drawing Conclusions

3. Was the land Britain won from France in the French and Indian War large enough to meet the colonists' needs for expansion? Explain your answer.

____
____
____
____

Lesson 3: Disagreements With Great Britain, *Continued*

Explaining

4. Why did the British pass the Stamp Act?

____

____

Reading Check

5. Why were the colonists angered by the Proclamation of 1763?

____

____

Explaining

6. Which British law was related to the housing of soldiers?

____

____

Identifying

7. Fill in the blanks on the chart to identify what the various British laws did.

Paraphrasing

8. Why did the colonists dislike the Tea Act?

____

____

King George did not want the colonists to move onto the lands won from France because he did not want fighting with Native Americans to start again. He made it against the law to move there. He let the colonists know about this in a new law called the Proclamation of 1763. A **proclamation** is an official announcement. The colonists were angry; they thought that Great Britain was trying to limit their growth.

King George also decided that the colonists should help pay for the war. Fighting the French and Indian War had cost a lot of money and Great Britain was in debt. In 1765, Parliament passed the Stamp Act to raise money to help pay for the war. This law made the colonists buy and place tax stamps on all official documents. These stamps had to be put on many kinds of documents, even on newspapers.

The colonists were angry about the new law. The colonists did not think Parliament had the right to tax them. To show this, they **boycotted** British goods. This meant that they refused to buy them. Colonial leaders organized a Stamp Act Congress to write a protest to Parliament and the king. Finally Parliament **repealed**, or canceled, the Stamp Act.

Colonial Dissatisfaction Grows

A year later, Parliament began to tax the colonists again. One type of tax was a duty. A **duty** is a tax on imported goods. The chart below shows some of the taxed goods.

Great Britain Angers the Colonies

Act	Year Passed	What It Did
Sugar Act	1764	Set duties on sugar imports from countries other than Great Britain
Stamp Act	1765	____________________legal papers, newspapers, and other documents
Townshend Acts	1767	Placed duties on goods the colonists imported to the colonies
Tea Act	1773	Made British ___________other tea sold in the colonies. British tea grown in India did not have to pay the import duty, but other tea did.
Coercive Acts	1774	Included several laws to punish the colonists for resisting British authority
Quartering Act	1774	Required the colonists to give food, housing, and help to ___________

Lesson 3: Disagreements With Great Britain, *Continued*

One of the Townshend Acts gave British officials the power to search any business or home. Officers searched for goods on which the import duty had not been paid. The searches were meant to stop smuggling by the colonists. **Smuggling** is moving goods illegally in or out of a country.

These searches angered the colonists. Nearly 20 years later, Americans remembered them when they added a protection against "unreasonable searches and seizures" to the United States Constitution.

The Tea Act also angered the colonists. It hurt the business of colonial tea merchants. The colonists responded to the act by boarding British ships in Boston harbor. They dumped the ships' cargoes of tea into the water. This came to be called the Boston Tea Party.

Parliament passed laws called the Coercive Acts to punish the colonists for the Boston Tea Party. These acts took away some of the colonists' basic rights. They were so harsh that the colonists called them the Intolerable Acts. Some of these laws violated the English Bill of Rights—rights that the colonists believed in strongly.

Steps Toward Independence

Discussing Independence

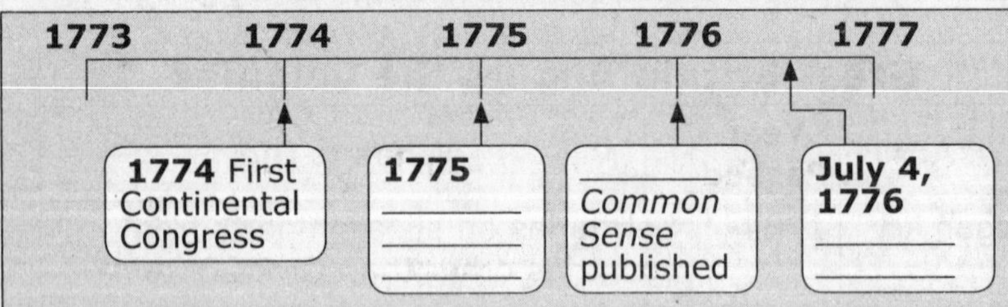

Anger about the Coercive Acts made the colonies join together. They wanted the British government to change the laws. In 1774, **delegates**, or representatives, from 12 colonies met in Philadelphia. This meeting was called the First Continental Congress. The delegates decided to send a letter to the king asking him to change the laws. They also agreed to boycott British goods and stop all trade with Great Britain.

King George refused to do as the colonists asked. He sent more soldiers to the colonies. In 1775, fighting broke out in Massachusetts between British soldiers and colonists.

Identifying

9. Why did British officials search people's homes and businesses using one of the Townshend Acts?

____

____

Reading Check

10. Why did the colonists call the Coercive Acts the Intolerable Acts?

____

____

____

Vocabulary

11. The colonists' refusal to buy British goods was called a _______.

Sequencing

12. Fill in the blanks on the time line as you read about moving toward independence.

NAME ______________________ DATE ____________ CLASS ________

networks

The American Colonies and Their Government

Lesson 3: Disagreements With Great Britain, *Continued*

Vocabulary

13. Define the word *debate*. Underline the words in the paragraph that help you determine its meaning.

____

____

Reading Check

14. How did Thomas Paine use John Locke's ideas in his pamphlet *Common Sense?*

____

____

Making Connections

15. Underline the Enlightenment thinkers mentioned on this page. How did they influence Jefferson when he wrote the Declaration of Independence?

____

____

____

Delegates from the colonies met again to **debate** what to do next. This meeting was called the Second Continental Congress. The discussion lasted for months. Some delegates wanted independence, but others did not.

Support for independence was growing. In January 1776, Thomas Paine published a pamphlet called *Common Sense*. In it, he explained why he felt that America needed to be independent. Paine used some of John Locke's ideas to make his case.

Common Sense was so popular that 500,000 copies were sold. By the spring of 1776, more than half of the delegates to the Second Continental Congress also wanted independence.

The Congress decided it was time to tell the world why the colonies wanted to be free. A group of delegates worked together on an announcement. Thomas Jefferson, a delegate from Virginia, did most of the writing. The document was called the Declaration of Independence.

Enlightenment thinking, along with ancient Greek ideas about democracy, influenced Jefferson's writing. The Enlightenment thinker Voltaire believed that people had a right to liberty. Jean-Jacques Rousseau wrote that if a government did not protect its people's freedom, it should not exist.

John Locke's ideas about natural rights and the social contract were Jefferson's main guide. In the Declaration of Independence, Thomas Jefferson wrote, "all men are created equal." He also said that they had God-given rights. Jefferson pointed out that Great Britain had broken the social contract. This gave the colonists the right to rebel.

The Second Continental Congress approved the Declaration on July 4, 1776. No other government in the world was based on the ideas of natural rights and the social contract. Since 1776, many nations have used the Declaration as an example to follow.

Check for Understanding

List two events that changed the way colonists viewed English rule.

1. ______________ **2.** ______________

List two reasons why the colonists became angry with Parliament and the king.

3. ______________________________

4. ______________________________

The Constitution

Lesson 1: The Country's First Governments

ESSENTIAL QUESTION

Why do people create, structure, and change governments?

GUIDING QUESTIONS

1. ***How did citizens set up governments as they transitioned from colonies to states?***
2. ***How did the Articles of Confederation create problems for the United States?***

Terms to Know

constitution a detailed, written plan for government
bicameral divided into two parts, or houses
confederation a group that comes together for a common purpose
Articles of Confederation the first plan of government for the United States
ratify to approve
ordinance a law
area a region
Ordinance of 1785 law that set rules for surveying and selling land in the Northwest Territory
Northwest Ordinance law that set rules for governing the new territory
impact an effect
Shays's Rebellion armed uprising in which farmers attacked a federal building in Massachusetts

What Do You Know?

In the first column, answer the questions based on what you know before you study. After this lesson, complete the last column.

Now...		Later...
	How were state governments different from colonies?	
	Why did the Articles of Confederation not work?	

State Constitutions

By 1776, American colonists were planning for independence. They knew that freedom from Great Britain would mean an end to colonial charters. The colonists would need to form new governments. New Hampshire led the way. In January 1776, its leaders wrote the first state constitution. A **constitution** is a detailed, written plan for government. Within a few years the other states had done the same.

The state governments were all very much alike. Each one had a legislature to make laws. Most of the state legislatures were **bicameral.** This means they were divided into two parts, called houses. Each state had a governor.

Explaining

1. Why did the colonies write state constitutions, beginning in 1776?

____

____

____

Lesson 1: The Country's First Governments, *Continued*

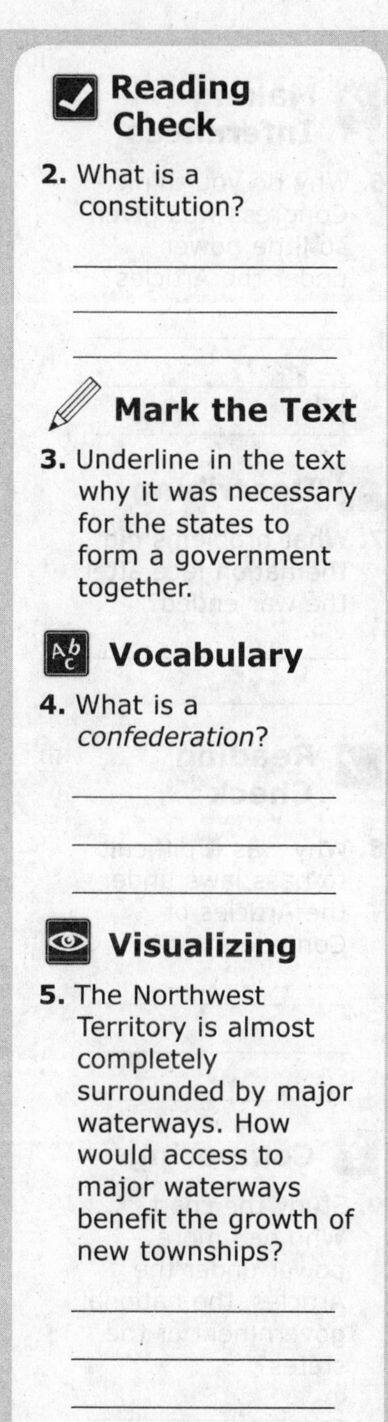

The governor's job was to carry out the laws. Each state also had courts. Court judges decided how to apply the laws in cases of lawbreaking.

Most state constitutions also included a bill of rights. This is a list of the basic freedoms that belong to every citizen. A bill of rights guarantees that the government will protect the rights of its citizens. Some of these rights can be traced back to the Magna Carta and the English Bill of Rights.

The Articles of Confederation

Each state was ready to govern itself when independence was declared. However, the states also needed to join together. They could not win a war against Britain with thirteen small armies. They needed one strong army under a single command.

In 1777, the Second Continental Congress wrote a plan to unite the states. It called for the states to form a confederation. A **confederation** is a group that comes together for a common purpose. The plan was called the **Articles of Confederation.** It set up a "league of friendship" among the independent states. By 1781, all 13 states had ratified the Articles. To **ratify** means to approve. The Articles of Confederation became the first constitution of the United States.

The Articles of Confederation set up a national legislature. It had one house, and each state had one vote. The legislature was known as the Confederation Congress. It controlled the army and had the power to deal with foreign countries for the United States.

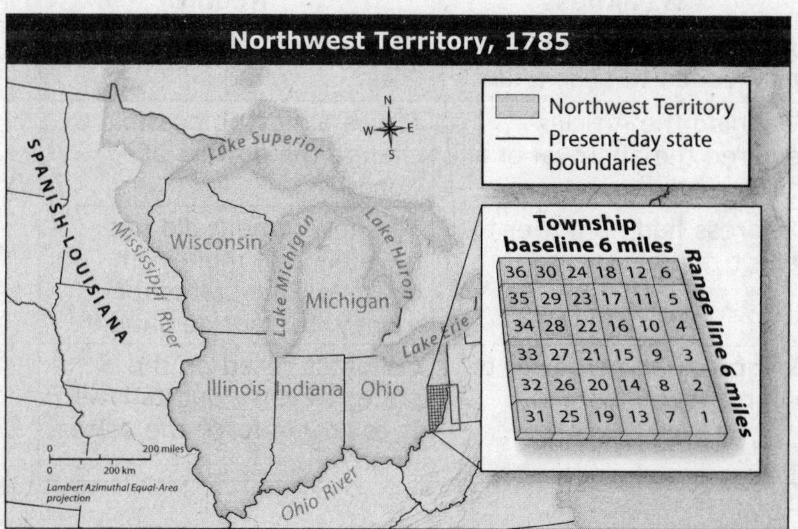

Lesson 1: The Country's First Governments, *Continued*

The Confederation Congress passed two important laws, called **ordinances.** These laws helped settle the Northwest Territory. This was an **area,** or region, that would later become Ohio, Indiana, Illinois, Michigan, Wisconsin, and part of Minnesota.

The first law was the **Ordinance of 1785.** It set up rules for measuring and selling the land. It divided land into townships six miles square. This is shown on the map found on the previous page. The second law was called the **Northwest Ordinance**, passed in 1787. This ordinance set up a plan for governing the new territory. It created a way for new states to join the Union. It also made slavery against the law in the Northwest Territory. These ordinances would have a major **impact,** or effect, on the future settlement of the West.

However, the Articles of Confederation also withheld some important powers from Congress. Congress could not enforce its own laws. It did not have the power to tax. Its voting rules made it hard to get anything done. As a result, Congress was weak and states could ignore its laws.

The powers in the Articles helped the United States become a nation. However, the new nation was in trouble. Congress was in debt and it could not collect taxes. The state governments were also in debt. They taxed the people heavily. They also taxed goods imported from other states and countries. These taxes hurt trade. As trade slowed, merchants, workers, and farmers all suffered.

Weaknesses of the Articles of Confederation

Weakness	Result
The approval of nine states was needed to pass a law.	It was very hard to pass laws.
Changing the Articles required the approval of all thirteen states.	It was almost impossible to change the powers of Congress.
Congress had no power to collect taxes.	The government did not have enough money. It could ask the states for money, but not demand it.
Congress had no power to enforce laws.	Congress relied on the states to carry out its laws. It could not force the states to do so.

Making Inferences

6. Why do you think Congress was given so little power under the Articles?

____

____

____

Describing

7. What problems did the nation face after the war ended?

____

____

Reading Check

8. Why was it difficult to pass laws under the Articles of Confederation?

____

____

____

Comparing

9. Study the chart. Who had more power under the Articles, the national government or the states?

____

____

Lesson 1: The Country's First Governments, *Continued*

Explaining

10. Why was the Confederation Congress unable to solve the country's problems?

______

Determining Cause and Effect

11. Fill in the effect of Shays's rebellion in the chart on the right.

FOLDABLES®

12. Create a four-tab Foldable using a two-tab and cutting each tab in half up to the anchor tab. Place it along the dotted line. Write *State Governments* on the anchor tab. Then label the first tab *Constitution,* the second *Bicameral Legislature,* the third *Governor,* and the last *Court System*. Write the definition of each on the reverse tabs.

The Confederation Congress did not have the power to fix these problems. Americans became fearful that the government could not protect them. In Massachusetts, a farmer named Daniel Shays owed money because of heavy taxes. The state court threatened to take his farm away. In response, Shays led an army of farmers in an attack on a federal building that held weapons. The uprising became known as **Shays's Rebellion.**

Shays's Rebellion scared the whole country. People started to wonder if the government was too weak to keep law and order. Leaders began to call for a stronger national government. In 1787, twelve states sent delegates to a meeting in Philadelphia. A delegate is someone who represents others. The task of the delegates was to change the Articles of Confederation and make them stronger.

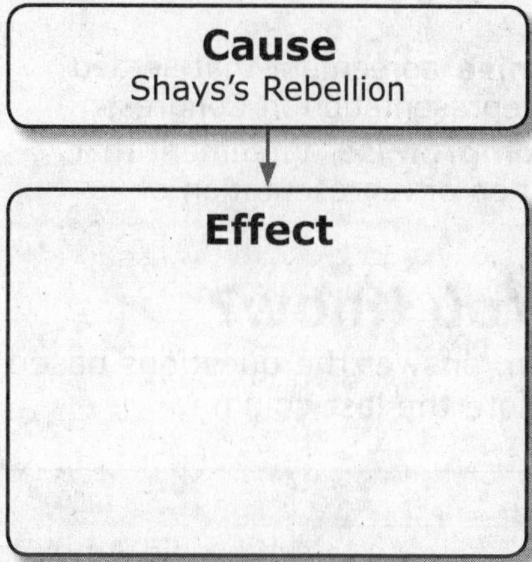

/ / / / / / / / / / / / / / Glue Foldable here / / / / / / / / / / / / / /

Check for Understanding

Name two things that the colonies did so that they would be ready to create a new government.

1. ______

2. ______

Name two weaknesses in the Articles of Confederation that made it hard for the new government to get anything done.

3. ______

4. ______

The Constitution

Lesson 2: Creating a New Constitution

ESSENTIAL QUESTION

Why do people create, structure, and change governments?

GUIDING QUESTIONS

1. ***Why did American leaders decide to create a new plan of government?***
2. ***Why were compromises made at the Constitutional Convention?***
3. ***How did Federalist and Anti-Federalist viewpoints differ?***

Terms to Know

process a series of steps taken to achieve something
despite regardless of, in spite of
Constitutional Convention meeting at which the United States Constitution was written
Great Compromise agreement that settled the question of representation in Congress
Three-Fifths Compromise agreement that settled the question of representation of enslaved people in Congress
Electoral College group of electors who choose the president and vice-president
Federalist person who wanted to ratify the Constitution
federalism system in which power is divided between the federal and state governments
The Federalist Papers essays supporting the Constitution
Anti-Federalist person who was against ratifying the Constitution

What Do You Know?

In the first column, answer the questions based on what you know before you study. After this lesson, complete the last column.

Now...		Later...
	Why did America need a new government?	

The Constitutional Convention

On May 25, 1787, a convention began in Philadelphia. The purpose of this convention was to change the Articles of Confederation to make the national government stronger.

Fifty-five delegates attended. Many of them had been leaders in government. Most were well educated and wealthy. They included lawyers, merchants, and planters. Only Rhode Island did not send delegates. That state did not want a stronger central government. Also, there were no women, African Americans, or Native Americans at the convention. These groups were not allowed to have a part in politics at that time.

At the beginning of the convention **process**, the delegates chose General George Washington to lead them.

Defining

1. Use the context clues to write a sentence using the word *convention*.

____

____

____

Lesson 2: Creating a New Constitution, *Continued*

Making Connections

2. Why do you think it would be important for the delegates to talk freely?

Reading Check

3. Why did the delegates want a new plan instead of making changes to the Articles of Confederation?

Identifying

4. Which proposed plan for government favored states with large populations?

Defining

5. What is a *compromise*?

He was greatly respected for his leadership during the American Revolution.

The public would not be allowed at the meeting. The doors were guarded and the windows were kept shut, **despite** the hot weather. This would allow delegates to talk freely. James Madison of Virginia kept a journal, however. This is how we know today what went on at the convention.

The delegates also decided that the Articles of Confederation could not be fixed. The Articles were too weak and flawed. They decided to write a whole new plan of government. The United States Constitution was the result of their work. The meeting came to be known as the **Constitutional Convention.**

Compromising for a Constitution

When the delegates began their work, the Virginia delegates introduced a plan. It was called the Virginia Plan, and it was written by James Madison.

The Virginia Plan called for a government with a president, a congress with two houses, and courts. It was very similar to our government today. The number of representatives in both houses of congress would be based on each state's population. This would give large states more votes—and more power—than small states.

Delegates from smaller states did not like the Virginia Plan. They thought that a congress controlled by large states would ignore their interests. The small states introduced a plan called the New Jersey Plan. It called for a congress with one house. Each state would have one vote so all states had equal power. This plan thought a committee, not a president, should carry out the laws.

There was much debate. Large and small states could not agree. Finally, Roger Sherman of Connecticut came up with a compromise. A compromise is an agreement between opposing sides. Each side gives up something but gains something else.

Sherman's plan called for two houses of congress—a Senate and a House of Representatives. In the Senate, each state would have two members. The small states liked this. It gave them equal power in the Senate. In the House, the number of members for each state would be based on population. The large states liked this. It gave them more power in the House. The plan was one that both sides could accept. It is known as the **Great Compromise.**

Lesson 2: Creating a New Constitution, *Continued*

Glue Foldable here

Plans for a Constitution

Virginia Plan
Two houses of Congress, representation in both houses by population

Great Compromise
Two houses of Congress, equal representation in the Senate, representation by population in the House of Representatives

New Jersey Plan
One house of Congress, equal representation

Disagreements came up between Northern and Southern delegates also. They disagreed about representation in Congress. More than 550,000 enslaved people lived in the South. The Southern states wanted to count them as part of their populations. This would give them more seats in the House and more power. The Northern states were against this. In Congress, a member has a "seat" so the number of members are counted as seats.

The delegates came up with a plan called the **Three-Fifths Compromise.** They decided that every five enslaved people would equal three free people. This meant that three-fifths of the enslaved population of a state would count toward seats in Congress.

Northern and Southern delegates also compromised on trade. They agreed to give Congress the power to make laws regulating trade. This included trade between states and trade with other countries. This pleased the Northern delegates because trade was important to their economy.

However, the delegates did not allow Congress to tax exports. Exports are goods sold to other countries. Nor could Congress try to end the slave trade before 1808. This pleased the Southern delegates. Their economy depended on exports of crops grown by enslaved laborers.

Another compromise settled a debate over how to choose the president. Some delegates thought the state legislatures should elect the president. Others thought the people should. The convention decided on an **Electoral College.** This is a special group of electors. They would be chosen by state legislatures to elect the president and vice-president. The Electoral College is still in use today. However, the voters of each state now choose the electors.

FOLDABLES®

6. Place a three-tab Foldable along the dotted line. Label the anchor tab *Constitutional Convention*. Write *New Jersey Plan*, *Great Compromise*, and *Virginia Plan* on the tabs. On the front, explain what small states thought of the plans. On the back, explain what large states thought of the plans.

Explaining

7. In the Great Compromise, what did small states and large states give up?

____

____

Reading Check

8. What does the Three-Fifths Compromise show about how most free Americans viewed enslaved people?

____

____

____

Lesson 2: Creating a New Constitution, *Continued*

Reading Check

9. Describe the views of the Federalists. How did they feel about ratifying the Constitution?

____

____

Vocabulary

10. In the text, underline the definition of *federalism*.

Comparing

11. In each column of the chart, write the side's central view.

FOLDABLES®

12. Place a one-tab Foldable along the dotted line. Write *Compromise* on the anchor tab. Write the definition on the front tab. On the reverse explain why compromising is important.

Federalists and Anti-Federalists

The delegates signed the finished document on September 17, 1787. Now it was up to the states to approve it. At least nine states had to ratify the Constitution for it to become the law of the land.

Americans had differing views of the Constitution. Those who supported it were known as **Federalists.** They believed the Constitution would create a system in which power is divided between the federal, or national, government and the states. This is called **federalism.**

James Madison, Alexander Hamilton, and John Jay were leaders of the Federalists. They argued that the nation needed a strong central government to survive. They wrote essays in defense of the Constitution. These essays are known as the **Federalist Papers.**

People who opposed the Constitution were called **Anti-Federalists.** They argued that a strong central government would ignore the rights of the states. They also thought it would favor wealthy people. They pointed out that the Constitution had no bill of rights to protect citizens. Many states said they would not ratify it without a bill of rights.

Federalists	Anti-Federalists

Federalist leaders promised to add a bill of rights if the Constitution was adopted. In June of 1788, New Hampshire became the ninth state to ratify, and the Constitution took effect. By May of 1790, the other four states had also ratified. The thirteen states were now a nation.

/ / / / / / / / / / / / / / Glue Foldable here / / / / / / / / / / / / / /

Check for Understanding

Name two compromises that were made in order to create the Constitution.

1. ______________________

2. ______________________

The Constitution

Lesson 3: The Structure of the Constitution

ESSENTIAL QUESTION

Why do people create, structure, and change governments?

GUIDING QUESTIONS

1. ***How does the U.S. Constitution organize the government?***
2. ***In what ways can the Constitution be changed?***

Terms to Know

Preamble introduction to the U.S. Constitution

article section of the Constitution describing the structure of government

legislative branch the part of government that makes laws

executive branch the part of government that enforces the law

judicial branch the part of government that applies the law

interpret to decide what something means

amendment any change in the Constitution

assume to take on or accept a role or responsibility

What Do You Know?

In the first column, answer the questions based on what you know before you study. After this lesson, complete the last column.

Now...		Later...
	Why does the Constitution organize the government?	
	Can the Constitution be changed?	

The Parts of the Constitution

The U.S. Constitution is more than a plan of government. It is the highest law of the land. It is a symbol of our nation and its values of freedom and fairness.

The Constitution has three main parts. It has a preamble, articles, and amendments.

The first part is the **Preamble** (PREE•am•buhl). The Preamble states the purposes of the Constitution. It is one sentence long. It begins with these famous words: "We the People of the United States . . . ." It ends with these words: ". . . do ordain and establish this Constitution for the United States of America." These words make clear that the power of government comes from the people.

Identifying

1. Which part of the Constitution states the purposes of government?

____

Mark the Text

2. Highlight the three main parts of the Constitution.

Lesson 3: The Structure of the Constitution, *Continued*

Identifying

3. Which part of the Constitution outlines the structure of government?

____

____

Mark the Text

4. Underline the sentences that explain the purpose of the articles of the Constitution.

Reading Check

5. What branches of government does the Constitution establish?

____

____

____

Describing

6. Complete the graphic organizer. Write a sentence in each box describing the powers of each branch.

The second part of the Preamble lists six purposes of the government. They are:

- to unite the states
- to make sure people are treated equally
- to keep peace and order and protect citizens
- to defend the country from attack
- to help the people live healthy and happy lives
- to guarantee people's basic rights

The second part of the Constitution is made up of the articles. There are seven **articles,** or sections. They describe how the government is to be set up. The government is divided into three parts called branches. Each branch has different powers.

Article I describes the **legislative branch,** or Congress. This branch has the power to make laws. It describes how members will be chosen and what rules Congress has to follow when making laws.

Article II describes the **executive branch.** This branch carries out the laws and makes sure laws are obeyed. The president and vice president lead the executive branch. This article explains how these leaders are elected and how they can be removed from office. It also lists the president's powers, which includes leading the armed forces.

Article III describes the **judicial branch.** This branch is made up of the Supreme Court and lower courts. The Supreme Court is the head of the judicial branch. The courts **interpret** laws, or decide what laws mean, and make sure laws are enforced fairly. This article also describes the kind of cases the courts may hear.

The Three Branches of Government

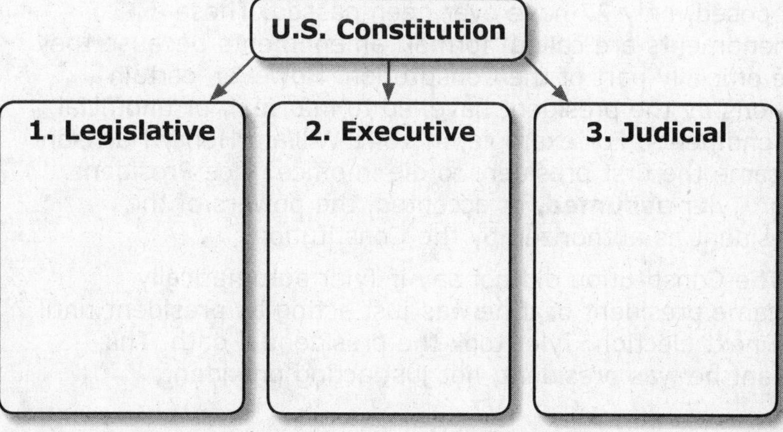

The rest of the articles explain the relationship between the states and the federal government. They also tell how the Constitution can be changed.

The last part of the Constitution is made up of the **amendments.** These are changes that have been added over time. There are 27 amendments. The first ten amendments are the Bill of Rights. They were added soon after ratification.

Amending and Interpreting the Constitution

The writers of the Constitution knew that changing even a small detail of the Constitution would have a major effect on the government. They wanted to make sure it could be changed when the people demanded it. They did not want change to be too easy, but they did want it to be possible.

They created a process for amending, or changing, the Constitution. The process has two steps. First, an amendment must be proposed. Then it must be ratified.

The Formal Amendment Process

Two-thirds of Congress votes to propose an amendment. → Three-fourths of states vote to approve the amendment. → New amendment to the Constitution

An amendment may be proposed either by a two-thirds vote of Congress, or by a national convention called by two-thirds of state governments.

To ratify an amendment, three-fourths of the states must vote to approve it. Of the thousands of amendments proposed, only 27 have ever been passed. These amendments are called "formal" amendments because they are officially part of the Constitution. However, certain actions by the president have led to informal, or unofficial, amendments. For example, in 1841 William Henry Harrison became the first president to die in office. Vice President John Tyler **assumed,** or accepted, the powers of the president as authorized by the Constitution.

The Constitution did not say if Tyler automatically became president or if he was just acting as president until the next election. Tyler took the presidential oath. This meant he was president, not just acting president.

Vocabulary

7. What is an *amendment*?

____

____

____

____

Drawing Conclusions

8. Why do you think the writers of the Constitution made it hard to amend it?

____

____

____

Identifying

9. How many states must approve an amendment in order for it to be ratified?

____

Contrasting

10. What is the difference between a formal and an informal amendment?

____

____

____

____

Lesson 3: The Structure of the Constitution, *Continued*

Listing

11. List three ways our interpretations of the Constitution can change.

____

____

____

Reading Check

12. How can Congress change the Constitution? Are these types of changes formal or informal?

____

____

____

FOLDABLES®

13. Place a one-tab Foldable along the dotted line. Write *U.S. Constitution* on the anchor tab. On the front of the tab, answer this question: **Why is the U.S. Constitution important?** On the reverse, list facts about the Constitution.

His action became an informal amendment. It was the way things were done for more than a hundred years. In 1967, the Twenty-fifth Amendment was ratified. It made Tyler's action a formal part of the Constitution.

The writers of the Constitution knew that the world would change. So, they wanted the Constitution to be as general as possible. They were very specific about some things but left others open to interpretation. That is, people have to decide what certain things mean. For example, the Constitution gives Congress the power to make all laws that are "necessary and proper." This allows Congress to use powers that are not directly written in the Constitution. These are called "implied powers." Regulating, or controlling, air pollution is an example of an implied power.

The Supreme Court is the final judge of what the Constitution means. However, the Court's interpretations can change. As new judges come on to the court, interpretations can vary. Congress and the president also sometimes change the way they interpret their powers. Changing customs and values can also bring about new interpretations of the Constitution. Though interpretations can change how the Constitution is applied, the basic principles and organization of our government will remain the same.

/ / / / / / / / / / / / / Glue Foldable here / / / / / / / / / / / / /

Check for Understanding

Name two of the three branches of the federal government that were organized by the Constitution.

1. _______________

2. _______________

Name two ways in which a change to the Constitution can be proposed.

3. _______________

4. _______________

Lesson 4: Principles of the Constitution

ESSENTIAL QUESTION

How do societies balance individual and community rights?
How does social change influence government?

GUIDING QUESTIONS

1. ***What are the principles of United States government?***
2. ***How is power distributed under federalism?***

Terms to Know

popular sovereignty the people's right to rule

ensure to make sure of or protect

limited government the idea that the government can only do what the people allow it to do

rule of law the idea that the law applies to everyone

separation of powers the division of the government into three branches

checks and balances the ways that each branch of government limits the power of the other two branches

assign to give

enumerated powers the powers given to the federal government under the Constitution

reserved powers the powers set aside for the states

concurrent powers the powers that both federal and state governments may exercise

supremacy clause the part of the Constitution that puts federal law over state law, and the Constitution over both

What Do You Know?

In the first column, answer the questions based on what you know before you study. After this lesson, complete the last column.

Now...		Later...
	What ideas are important to the United States government?	
	What is federalism?	

Major Principles of Government

Principles are basic beliefs that guide people's lives. Principles can also guide governments. The United States Constitution contains five basic principles. They are the base on which our government is built.

These five principles are:

- Popular sovereignty
- Limited government and the rule of law

Mark the Text

1. Underline the text that defines *principles.*

Lesson 4: Principles of the Constitution, *Continued*

Mark the Text

2. As you read, underline the definition of each principle of government.

Reading Check

3. How is the will of the people, or popular sovereignty, most strongly expressed according to the Constitution?

____

____

Making Connections

4. How does the idea of limited government ensure that the power of government comes from the people?

____

____

____

Explaining

5. Why did the writers of the Constitution create checks and balances?

____

____

____

- Separation of powers
- Checks and balances
- Federalism

Popular sovereignty (SAH•vuhrn•tee) is the idea that the power of government comes from the people. *Sovereignty* means "the right to rule." *Popular* means "of the people." So popular sovereignty is "the people's right to rule."

The Constitution **ensures,** or guarantees, popular sovereignty by giving citizens the right to vote. The will of the people, or what they want, is shown in whom they elect. The people elect members of Congress to represent them. The people vote for a president to lead them. All elected officials have to answer to the people who put them in positions of power. Otherwise, the people will vote for someone else next time.

Limited government is the idea that the government can do only what the people allow it to do. The writers of the Constitution did not want the government to have too much power. So they put specific limits in the Constitution. The Constitution states what the federal government and the states may and may not do.

Under the Constitution, the government is also limited by the **rule of law.** This means that the law applies to everyone. It applies even to those who govern. No one, even the president, is above the law.

The Constitution limits power in another way, too. It divides the government into three branches. This is called **separation of powers.** The Constitution assigns each branch its own tasks. Each branch has some power, but no branch has all the power.

Even so, the writers of the Constitution feared that one branch could still control the other two. So they put **checks and balances** into the Constitution. Different tasks are **assigned** to different branches of government. These are ways that each branch can limit the power of the other two branches.

A good example of checks and balances is how laws are made. The Constitution says that a bill passed by Congress must be signed by the president to become law. The president can also veto, or refuse, to sign, a bill. This veto is a check on legislative power. However, Congress can override the veto if two-thirds of its members vote to do so. This is a check on executive power. There are many checks and balances in the Constitution. They allow the branches of government to challenge each other's power.

Lesson 4: Principles of the Constitution, *Continued*

Five Principles of American Government

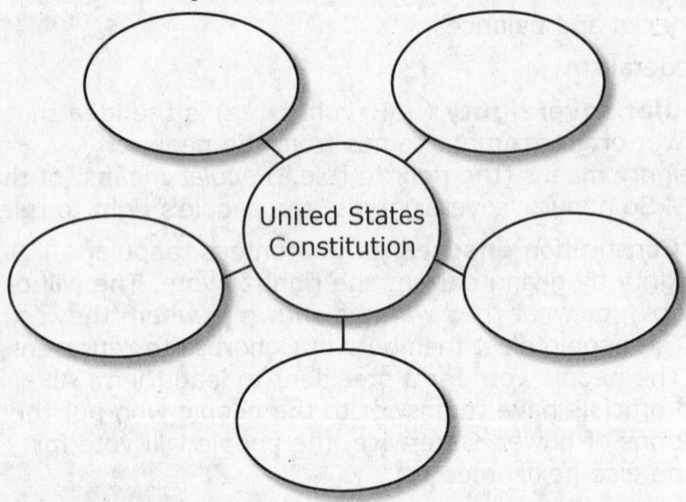

Federalism

Our federal system also limits the power of government. Under this system, power is divided between the national government and the states. Some powers are also shared.

Federal and State Powers

NATIONAL GOVERNMENT
- Coin money
- Maintain army and navy
- Declare war
- Regulate trade between states and with foreign nations
- Carry out all expressed powers

NATIONAL AND STATE GOVERNMENTS
- Establish courts
- Enforce laws
- Collect taxes
- Borrow money
- Provide for general welfare

STATE GOVERNMENTS
- Regulate trade within a state
- Protect public welfare and safety
- Conduct elections
- Establish local governments

The Constitution gives certain powers to the national government. These are called **enumerated powers.** *Enumerated* means "listed" or "spelled out." The national government can set up post offices and print money because of these powers.

Other powers are set aside, or reserved, for the states. These are called **reserved powers.** For example, the states can set up and oversee school systems.

Identifying

6. Fill in the diagram with the five principles of government in the U.S. Constitution.

Vocabulary

7. What are *enumerated powers*?

____

____

____

8. What are *reserved powers*?

____

____

Reading Check

9. What are two examples of concurrent powers?

____

____

____

____

Lesson 4: Principles of the Constitution, *Continued*

Comparing

10. Which has the highest authority—state law, federal law, or the Constitution?

____

FOLDABLES®

11. Place a one-tab Foldable along the dotted line. Label the anchor tab *Five Principles of U.S. Government.* List the principles on the front of the tabs and then write what each means on the reverse.

Glue Foldable here

Some powers belong to both levels of government. These are called **concurrent powers.** They include the power to collect taxes and to set up courts and prisons.

In a federal system, a state may sometimes pass a law that conflicts with, or is different from, a federal law. The writers of the Constitution knew this might happen. So they included a statement called the **supremacy clause.** It says that the Constitution and other laws and treaties made by the national government "shall be the supreme Law of the Land." This means that federal law has authority over state law. The Constitution has authority over both.

Check for Understanding

Name two of the five principles that guide the United States government.

1. ______________________

2. ______________________

Name two ways that the Constitution divides the powers of the federal government.

3. ______________________

4. ______________________

The Bill of Rights

Lesson 1: The First Amendment

ESSENTIAL QUESTION

How do societies balance individual and community rights?

GUIDING QUESTIONS

1. ***Which individual rights are protected by the First Amendment?***
2. ***Why are limits placed on individual rights?***

Terms to Know

civil liberty the freedom to think and act without government interference
civil having to do with citizens
free speech the right to say our ideas in public or private, without fear of punishment by the government
censorship banning printed materials or films due to offensive ideas they contain
petition a formal request for action
slander spoken lies about someone
libel printing lies about someone
restriction limit placed on something

What Do You Know?

In the first column, answer the questions based on what you know before you study. After this lesson, complete the last column.

Now...		Later...
	What are some First Amendment rights?	
	Should there be limits on individual rights?	

Paraphrasing

1. In your own words, explain why civil liberties are important.

____
____
____

Mark the Text

2. As you read this section, underline the five civil liberties protected by the First Amendment.

Guaranteeing Civil Liberties

The first 10 amendments to the Constitution are known as the Bill of Rights. The Bill of Rights lists the basic freedoms that all citizens of the United States have. These freedoms are also called **civil liberties.** The word **civil** means "relating to citizens." So civil liberties are those liberties relating to people. Protecting civil liberties is one of the most important parts of a democracy. Having civil liberties gives citizens the power to have their own beliefs. These liberties also give citizens the power to express themselves to others and to the government. The Bill of Rights states that the government may not take away our civil liberties.

The First Amendment in the Bill of Rights protects five basic freedoms.

1. **Freedom of Religion** The First Amendment protects religious freedom in two ways. It says that the government may not set up or support an official religion for the country. It also says that people are free to worship in any way they choose.

The Bill of Rights

Lesson 1: The First Amendment, *Continued*

2. **Freedom of Speech** *Free speech* means being able to say what we think without fear of being punished by the government. The First Amendment gives us the right to express ideas even if they offend other people. Not all free speech is expressed in words. The first amendment also protects the right to express yourself in music, art, and dress.
3. **Freedom of the Press** The *press* means sources of news and information. It includes books, newspapers, and magazines. It also includes radio, television, and the Internet. The First Amendment forbids government **censorship** of the press. This means that the government cannot tell the press what it can or cannot print or broadcast. A free press is important in a democracy. It helps keep the government honest by telling the people about mistakes or misuse of power.
4. **Freedom of Assembly** This is the right to gather in groups. Meetings, parades, and protests are all forms of assembly. We have the right to assemble for any reason, as long as the assemblies are peaceful. We also have the right to associate with any group we want. So you can start or join any group you want.
5. **Freedom to Petition the Government** A **petition** is a formal request for the government to act. It may be a statement signed by many people. It may also be a simple letter from one person. A petition is a way to tell the government what you think.

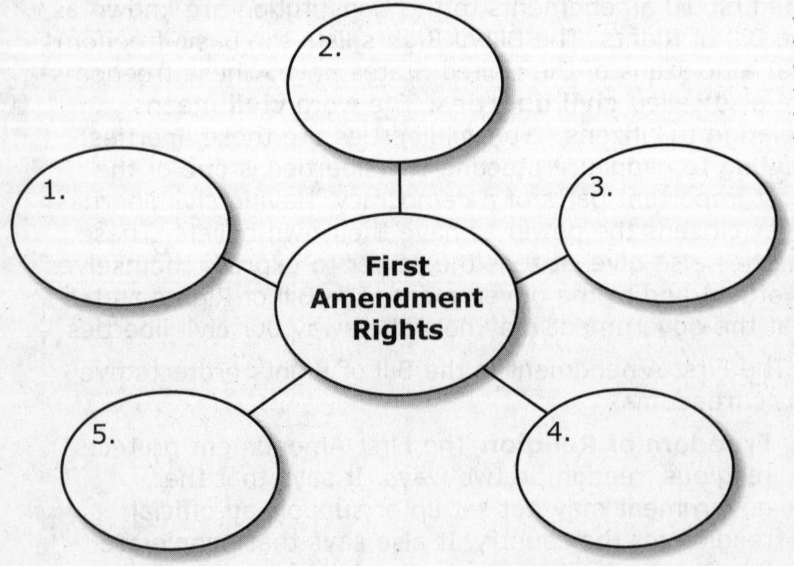

Glue Foldable here

Reading Check

3. How are Americans' rights to express themselves protected by the First Amendment?

____

____

Explaining

4. How is a free press a check on government power?

____

____

Identifying

5. Fill in the diagram with the five freedoms protected by the First Amendment.

FOLDABLES®

6. Make a five-tab Foldable by cutting a one-tab into five tabs up to the anchor. Label the anchor *The First Amendment*. Label the tabs: *Religion, Speech, Press, Assembly,* and *Petition.* Explain each right on the reverse sides.

NAME _______________ DATE _______________ CLASS _______________

networks

Vocabulary

7. What is the difference between *slander* and *libel*?

____

____

____

Hypothesizing

8. Study the chart. What do you think might happen if there were no limits on civil liberties?

____

____

____

____

Making Connections

9. Give an example of a situation where it is justified to limit a person's civil liberties. Explain the reason for limiting the person's rights.

____

____

____

____

____

____

Limits on Civil Liberty

The First Amendment contains rights given to all Americans, but that does not allow citizens to do and say whatever they want. Each person's rights must be balanced against the rights of others. That means that acting on your rights should not harm others or the community. Communities also have rights. In order to protect the rights of everyone, the government places limits on our civil liberties.

Citizens are expected to use their rights responsibly. This means that in using their individual rights they should not interfere with the rights of others. For example, free speech gives you the right to criticize public figures. It does not give you the right to tell lies about them. Spreading lies that hurt someone's reputation is a crime. If the lies are spoken, the crime is called **slander.** If the lies are printed, the crime is called **libel.**

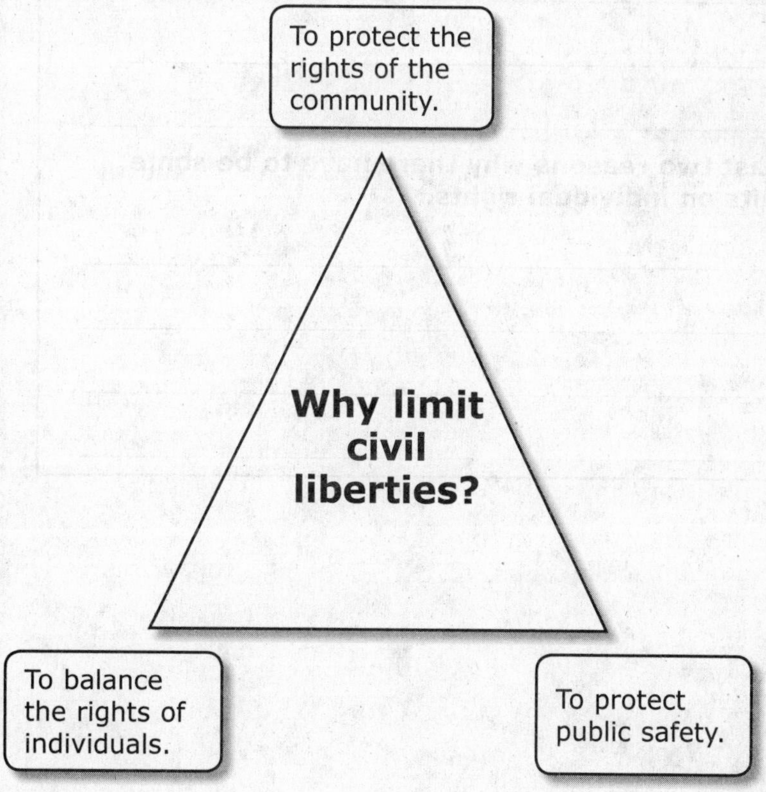

To protect the rights of the community.

Why limit civil liberties?

To balance the rights of individuals.

To protect public safety.

Lesson 1: The First Amendment, *Continued*

Other **restrictions,** or limits, on civil liberties protect public safety. For example, no one has the right to say or write anything that directly leads someone to commit a crime. Another example is that people have the right to march in protest, but not to riot.

Communities also have rights. As a result, individual rights have to be balanced against the rights of the community. When these are in conflict the rights of the community come first. If that were not the case, society would fail apart.

/ / / / / / / / / / / / / / Glue Foldable here / / / / / / / / / / / / / /

Check for Understanding

Name three of your basic rights that are protected under the First Amendment.

1. ______________________

2. ______________________

3. ______________________

List two reasons why there have to be some limits on individual rights.

4. ______________________

____

5. ______________________

____

Reading Check

10. Do Americans enjoy unlimited civil liberties? Explain.

____

____

____

FOLDABLES®

11. Place a one-tab Foldable along the dotted line. Label the anchor tab *First Amendment.* On the tab list five words or phrases about the First Amendment. On the reverse, explain why it is important to protect civil liberties.

NAME _______________ DATE _______________ CLASS _______________

networks

The Bill of Rights

Lesson 2: Other Bill of Rights Protections

ESSENTIAL QUESTION

How do societies balance individual and community rights?

GUIDING QUESTIONS

1. ***How does the Bill of Rights protect the rights of the accused?***
2. ***Which other protections does the Bill of Rights offer?***

Terms to Know

accused officially charged with a crime
search warrant court order allowing police to search a suspect's property and seize evidence
probable cause strong reason to think a person or property was involved in a crime
due process legal steps that must be followed
eminent domain the government's right to take private property for public use
indictment formal charge by a grand jury
double jeopardy being tried twice for the same crime
self-incrimination testifying against oneself
bail money paid as a deposit to make sure someone returns for their trial
license a document that gives the holder permission to do something
retain to keep or hold on to

What Do You Know?

In the first column, answer the questions based on what you know before you study. After this lesson, complete the last column.

Now...		Later...
	What rights does someone accused of a crime have?	
	How does the Bill of Rights protect people?	

Defining

1. What is a *crime* according to the courts?

____

____

____

Rights of the Accused

An important part of democracy is protecting the rights of people accused of crimes. The Fourth, Fifth, Sixth, and Eighth Amendments protect the rights of the **accused.** These amendments guarantee their right to fair legal treatment.

The Fourth Amendment has to do with searches. It says that no law officer can search a person's home or property without a search warrant. A **search warrant** is a court order. It allows the police to search a suspect's home, business, or other property and seize, or take, evidence. To get a search warrant, the police must convince a judge that they have **probable cause** to suspect a person of a crime. Probable cause means to have a valid reason.

Lesson 2: Other Bill of Rights Protections, *Continued*

The Fifth Amendment protects many rights. It protects every citizen's right to due process of the law, for example.

Due process refers to the legal steps that must be followed before the government can take away a person's life, freedom, or property. For example, the government cannot take a person's house without paying a fair price it.

The government has the power to take away property to be used for the public if it pays for the property. This power is called **eminent domain** (EH•mih•nehnt doh•MAYN). The Fifth Amendment limits this power. It also says:

- No one can be tried for a serious crime without an indictment. An **indictment** (ihn•DITE•muhnt) is a formal charge from a grand jury. This is a group of citizens that looks at evidence to decide if a person may have carried out a crime.
- No one can put on trial twice for the same crime. This is called **double jeopardy.**
- No one can be forced to testify against himself or herself. This is called **self-incrimination.**

The Sixth Amendment guarantees other rights to accused people. The accused

- must be told the charges against them.
- must be allowed a speedy and fair trial.
- have the right to a public trial by a jury, or to be tried by a judge if they wish.
- have the right to hear, question, and call witnesses.
- have the right to a lawyer.

The Eighth Amendment says that bail may not be set too high. **Bail** is a type of security deposit. It is money that an accused person pays to remain free while waiting for trial. The Eighth Amendment also forbids "cruel and unusual" punishment. The question of what punishments are cruel and unusual is a matter of debate.

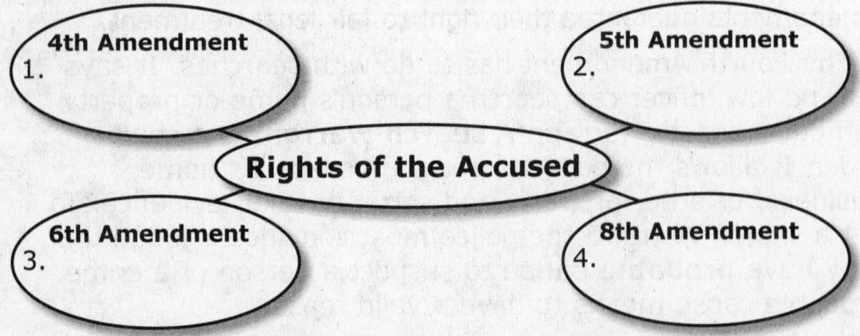

Identifying

2. Which amendment protects people from having to testify against themselves?

____

Summarizing

3. What four rights are protected by the Sixth Amendment?

____

____

____

____

Reading Check

4. Which of the Fourth, Fifth, Sixth, and Eighth Amendments applies to the police? Which applies to the courts?

____

____

____

Identifying

5. In each circle of the diagram, write the protections that each amendment provides.

Explaining

6. How have the courts interpreted the Second Amendment?

____

____

____

____

Mark the Text

7. The writers of the Bill of Rights wanted to limit the power of government to protect the rights of citizens. Underline the words and phrases that talk about this.

Drawing Conclusions

8. In what way does the Ninth Amendment protect civil liberties?

____

____

____

Additional Protections

When the Founders wrote the Bill of Rights they remembered the events that led to the American Revolution. They felt that certain actions by the British government were wrong. The Founders wanted to prevent the new American government from taking some of these actions. As a result, the Second, Third, Seventh, Ninth, and Tenth Amendments were written to protect other rights of American citizens.

The Second Amendment states that people have the right to "keep and bear arms." People do not agree about the exact meaning of that phrase. The courts have ruled that the government cannot stop people from owning guns. The government can pass laws to control how guns are sold and who can have a **license,** or permission to own guns.

The Third Amendment says that in peacetime soldiers may not move into people's homes without the home owner's permission. This was important to early American colonists. They were forced to house and feed British soldiers.

The Seventh Amendment talks about the rights of people involved in lawsuits. Lawsuits are also called civil cases. Civil cases are about disagreements between people rather than crimes. Civil cases are tried in the courts. The amendment guarantees the right to a trial jury in most of these cases.

The Ninth Amendment says that people's rights are not limited to what is in the Bill of Rights. People **retain,** or hold on to, other rights as well. The government may not deny those rights just because they are not spelled out in the Constitution.

Lesson 2: Other Bill of Rights Protections, *Continued*

The Tenth Amendment says that any powers not given to the federal government belong to the states or to the people. This is meant to keep the president and Congress from becoming too strong. The government of the United States can have only the powers the people give it.

Amendment	Right It Protects
__________	states that citizens have rights beyond those listed in the Constitution that cannot be taken away
Tenth	__________ the power of the national government
__________	provides for juries in civil cases
Third	protects people from having to house __________ during peacetime
__________	lets the government __________, but not prevent, gun ownership

/ / / / / / / / / / / / / Glue Foldable here / / / / / / / / / / / / /

Check for Understanding

Name three ways that the Bill of Rights protects someone accused of a crime.

1. ______________________________

2. ______________________________

3. ______________________________

List two other ways that the Bill of Rights protects individual freedoms.

4. ______________________________

____

5. ______________________________

____

Reading Check

9. In what ways do the Ninth and Tenth Amendments protect citizens?

____

____

____

Mark the Text

10. Fill in the blanks in the list of constitutional amendments.

FOLDABLES®

11. Place a two-tab Foldable along the dotted line. Title the first tab *Rights of the Accused* and the second tab *Rights of Citizens.* Write facts about each on both sides of the tabs.

NAME _______________ DATE _______________ CLASS _______________

networks

The Bill of Rights

Lesson 3: Furthering Civil Liberties

ESSENTIAL QUESTION

How do societies balance individual and community rights?

GUIDING QUESTIONS

1. ***How were civil rights extended following the Civil War?***
2. ***In what ways have twentieth-century amendments affected voting rights and changed elections?***

Terms to Know

black codes laws made after the Civil War that kept African Americans from holding certain jobs, gave them few property rights, and limited their rights in other ways
suffrage the right to vote
conduct to carry out
eliminate to take away or to end
poll tax money that voters have to pay before they are allowed to vote

What Do You Know?

In the first column, answer the questions based on what you know before you study. After this lesson, complete the last column.

Now...		Later...
	How did civil rights change after the Civil War?	

Prior Knowledge

1. What is the Bill of Rights and what is it meant to do?

____
____
____
____

Explaining

2. Why was the Fourteenth Amendment needed?

____
____
____

Civil War Amendments

The Bill of Rights was meant to protect citizens from the power of the federal government. It did not apply to state governments. Because of this, states could and often did pass laws that denied people's rights. For example, women and African Americans could not vote in most states. Slavery was legal in Southern states. Enslaved African Americans had almost no rights at all and were often treated as property.

After the Civil War, three new amendments were added to the Constitution. They extended civil liberties to African Americans. The first was the Thirteenth Amendment. It made slavery against the law.

Though slavery was against the law, many states still would not give African Americans basic rights. Many Southern states passed laws called **black codes.** Black codes put strict limits on where freed slaves could live and what jobs they could do. The Fourteenth Amendment was passed to help with this problem. The amendment protected the rights of the newly freed slaves.

The Fourteenth Amendment struck down the black codes. It said that all people "born or naturalized in the United States" were citizens. That included most African Americans. It said the states had to give all citizens "equal protection of the laws." It also said that the states must guarantee due process to all citizens.

Lesson 3: Furthering Civil Liberties, *Continued*

Since that time, the "equal protection" part of the Fourteenth Amendment has helped women and other groups gain equal rights. The Supreme Court has also said that the "due process" part of the amendment makes the Bill of Rights binding on the states. It means that American citizens in every state have the same basic rights.

The last Civil War amendment was the Fifteenth Amendment. It extended **suffrage,** or the right to vote, to African Americans. However, it applied only to men. State laws still kept women from voting in most elections.

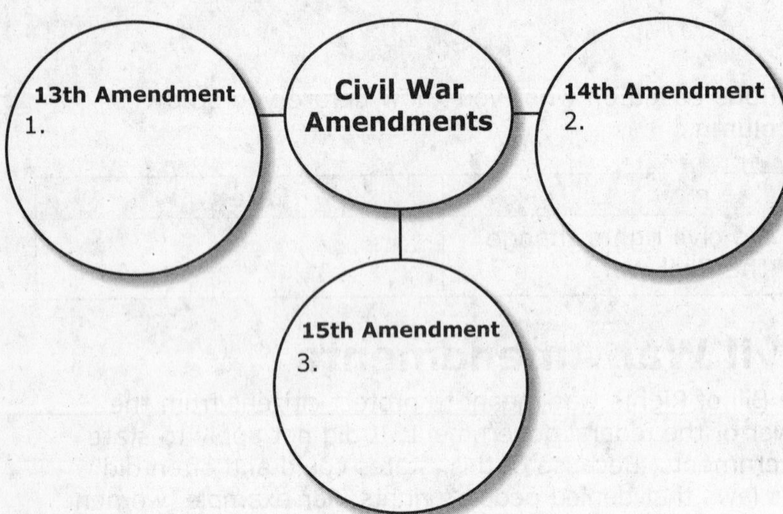

Electoral Process and Voting Rights

The Constitution was amended several more times in the 1900s. Some new amendments extended the right to vote to more people. Others changed the way elections were **conducted,** or carried out. These changes helped put more power in the hands of the people.

The Seventeenth Amendment changed the way U.S. senators are chosen. It was passed in 1913. Up until then, members of the Senate were chosen by the legislatures of their states. The Seventeenth Amendment says that people will elect their senators directly.

The Nineteenth Amendment gave women the right to vote. The question of woman's suffrage had always been left up to the states. Most states did not allow it. This changed in 1920 when the Nineteenth Amendment passed. It gives women the right to vote in all elections.

Defining

3. How is due process related to the idea of equal protection?

____

____

Vocabulary

4. What is *suffrage*?

____

Summarizing

5. Complete the organizer. Write a sentence in each circle summarizing the importance of each amendment.

Reading Check

6. What was the purpose of the Civil War amendments?

____

____

Analyzing

7. How did the Seventeenth Amendment put more power in the hands of the people?

____

____

NAME ______________________ DATE ______________ CLASS ________

networks

Lesson 3: Furthering Civil Liberties, *Continued*

Identifying

8. What groups gained the right to vote by constitutional amendment in the 1900s?

____

____

Reading Check

9. How did eliminating the poll tax affect voting rights?

____

____

Categorizing

10. For each amendment, check the column that shows whether it extended voting rights or changed the electoral process.

FOLDABLES®

11. Place a two-tab Foldable on the line. Label the anchor *Increased Rights.* Label the tabs *Civil Rights* and *Voting Rights.* Explain on each how rights were extended through the new amendments.

The Twenty-third Amendment was added in 1961. It gave voting rights to people living in Washington, D.C. "D.C." stands for the District of Columbia. Because this area is not part of any state, its residents could not vote in national elections. The Twenty-third Amendment gave them the right to vote for president and vice president. But even today they do not have representatives in Congress.

The Twenty-fourth Amendment was added in 1964. It **eliminated** poll taxes. A **poll tax** is a fee that is charged for voting. Southern states used poll taxes to keep poor people from voting. Fees were charged for the current year and previous years. Many people could not pay them. This kept most African Americans away from the polls. The fees also affected poor whites.

In 1971, the Twenty-sixth Amendment lowered the voting age to 18 years of age. Before then, most states had set the minimum age for voting at 21.

Amendment	Voting Rights	Electoral Process
Seventeenth Amendment		√
Nineteenth Amendment		
Twenty-third Amendment		
Twenty-fourth Amendment		
Twenty-sixth Amendment		

/ / / / / / / / / / / / / Glue Foldable here / / / / / / / / / / / / / /

Check for Understanding

Name two ways that the Civil War amendments added to individual freedoms.

1. ______________________

2. ______________________

List three ways that amendments made to the U.S. Constitution in the 1900s changed the voting process.

1. ______________________

2. ______________________

3. ______________________

NAME ______________________ DATE ______________ CLASS __________

networks

The Bill of Rights

Lesson 4: The Civil Rights Movement

ESSENTIAL QUESTIONS

How do societies balance individual and community rights?
How does social change influence government?

GUIDING QUESTIONS

1. ***Why did the civil rights movement occur?***
2. ***What other groups of citizens have struggled to win civil rights?***

Terms to Know

discrimination unfair treatment based on prejudice against a certain group
"Jim Crow" law Southern segregation law
segregation the social separation of the races
persist to last or to continue
civil rights the rights of full citizenship and equality under the law
nonviolent resistance peaceful protest against unfair laws
sit-in the act of occupying seats or sitting down on the floor of an establishment as a form of organized protest
exploit to use unfairly for someone else's gain
hate crime a violent act against a person attack because of their race, color, gender, national origin, or disability

What Do You Know?

In the first column, answer the questions based on what you know before you study. After this lesson, complete the last column.

Now...		Later...
	What was happening in our country before the civil rights movement?	

Origins of the Civil Rights Movement

For many years African Americans faced **discrimination,** or unfair treatment because of prejudice. The Civil War amendments were meant to help African Americans gain equal rights. The amendments did not do enough. Southern states passed laws to keep the races separate in public places. This practice is called **segregation.** The laws were called **"Jim Crow" laws.**

These laws **persisted,** or lasted, for decades. The laws said that African Americans had to go to separate schools. They had to ride in the backs of buses and trains. They had to use separate public restrooms and swimming pools.

Mark the Text

1. As you read this section, circle important dates in the civil rights movement and underline why they are important.

Lesson 4: The Civil Rights Movement, *Continued*

Describing

2. Describe the idea of "separate but equal" that allowed segregation to continue.

______

______

______

Identfying

3. Who was Rosa Parks?

______

______

Reading Check

4. What are some of the methods African Americans used to secure their civil rights?

______

______

______

Comparing

5. How are boycotts and sit-ins alike?

______

______

It took a long time for African Americans to win their civil rights. **Civil rights** are the rights of full citizenship and equality under the law. African Americans started a movement to win their civil rights.

The courts had ruled that segregation could continue as long as African Americans, though separate, were treated equally. As early as the 1930s, African Americans began to challenge this idea of "separate but equal." In *Brown v. Board of Education of Topeka, Kansas, (1954)*, they won a major victory. An African American family took the city of Topeka to court because their daughter was not allowed to go to an all-white school. The case made it to the Supreme Court. The Supreme Court struck down "separate but equal." It ruled that segregation in public schools was against the Constitution. Segregation, the Court said, went against the call for equal protection found in the Fourteenth Amendment.

In 1955, an African American woman named Rosa Parks refused to move to the back of a bus in Montgomery, Alabama. She was arrested. African Americans responded by boycotting the public buses. A boycott is a refusal to buy or use something. The Montgomery bus boycott led the Supreme Court to strike down laws that segregated the public buses. An important leader of the boycott was Dr. Martin Luther King, Jr.

King believed in **nonviolent resistance.** This is the peaceful protest of unfair laws. King led thousands of people in the push for equality. African Americans and other supporters of civil rights marched in protest. They carried signs and held boycotts. African Americans also held protests called **sit-ins.** They would sit at lunch counters that served only whites. They would refuse to leave until they were served. Some protestors traveled together by bus across the South to spread their message. These groups were called "Freedom Riders."

A high point of the civil rights movement was the March on Washington in 1963. More than 200,000 people gathered in the nation's capital.

Lesson 4: The Civil Rights Movement, *Continued*

They came to support a new civil rights bill. Dr. Martin Luther King, Jr., was there also. He gave his now-famous "I Have A Dream" speech.

The civil rights movement pushed the government to take action. In 1964, Congress passed the Civil Rights Act. This law banned segregation in public places. It also outlawed discrimination in job hiring. It was followed by the Voting Rights Act of 1965. This law removed state voting requirements that kept African Americans from the polls. It ensured that no citizen could be denied the right to vote.

Key Events of the Civil Rights Movement

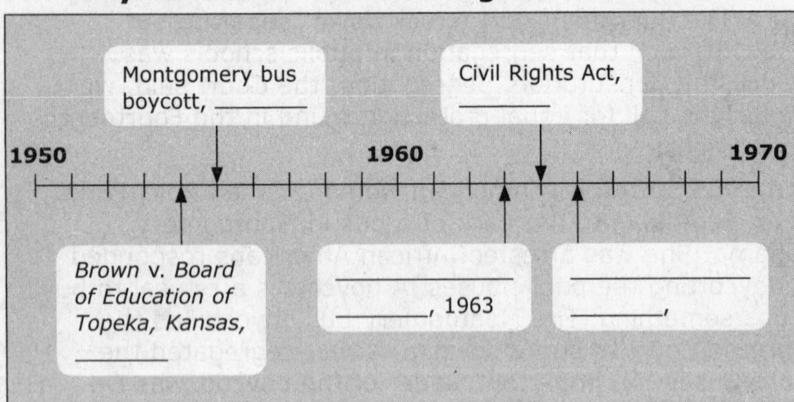

The Struggle Continues

The Civil Rights Act did not just benefit African Americans. It also outlawed discrimination based on gender, religion, and national origin. As a result, other groups also made gains in the fight for equal rights and fair treatment. They included women, Mexican Americans, Native Americans, and the disabled.

The struggle for equal rights is still going on. Many people still face discrimination in the workplace. Racial profiling is another concern. This occurs when law officers single out people as suspects based on the way they look. **Hate crimes** are also a problem. Hate crimes are attacks on people because of their race, religion, gender, national origin, or disability.

In 1961 President John F. Kennedy began a new policy called affirmative action. Its goal is to increase the hiring of women and minorities in business. Affirmative action also helps women and minority students get into college.

Sequencing

6. Review the years you circled in the text. Use them to mark and label five key events on the time line.

Visualizing

7. How many years passed between the Montgomery bus boycott and the passage of the Civil Rights Act?

____

Reading Check

8. What other groups were inspired by the civil rights movement to work for equality for themselves?

____

____

Making Inferences

9. In what way might affirmative action be seen as unfair?

____

____

____

The Bill of Rights

Lesson 4: The Civil Rights Movement, *Continued*

Making Connections

10. The groups that gained rights were all different, but also had much in common. Explain what they were trying to change. What were they trying to gain?

____

____

____

____

Describing

11. What was the Equal Rights Amendment?

____

____

____

FOLDABLES®

11. Place a two-tab Foldable along the dotted line. Title the tabs *Civil Rights Movement* and *Civil Rights Act.* Write the events and decisions that affected human rights in the United States.

Some people do not think affirmative action is good. They say that it is reverse discrimination and is unfair to whites and to men.

Other groups raised their voices in hopes of gaining rights. In 1968 several Native Americans formed a group called the American Indian Movement. Its goal was to improve the lives of Native Americans. It worked to protect the rights granted to Native American peoples by treaties. It has also tried to keep native culture alive.

The Chicano Movement was formed by Mexican Americans. It tried to fight segregation against this group in the Southwest. Other Mexican American leaders worked for fair treatment of farm workers. Most farm workers were Mexican American. They were **exploited,** or used unfairly, by the companies they worked for. César Chávez and Dolores Huerta used strikes and boycotts to gain better working conditions and pay for these workers.

The National Organization for Women formed in 1966. It gave the movement for women's rights new energy. The group worked to end on-the-job discrimination against women. It worked to pass laws against domestic violence. Many people worked hard to get an Equal Rights Amendment, or ERA, added to the Constitution. The ERA said that no state could deny any person equal rights because of gender. In 1972 Congress approved the ERA. It did not become an amendment because it was never ratified by enough states.

People who have disabilities have also won rights. In 1990, Congress passed the Americans with Disabilities Act. This law protects the rights of people with disabilities.

/ / / / / / / / / / / / / / Glue Foldable here / / / / / / / / / / / / / /

Check for Understanding

Name three events that led to the rapid growth of the civil rights movement.

1. ______________________

2. ______________________

3. ______________________

Name two other groups of people who have benefited from the passage of the Civil Rights Act.

4. ____________ **5.** ____________

NAME ______________________ DATE ____________ CLASS ________

networks

The Legislative Branch

Lesson 1: Structure of Congress

ESSENTIAL QUESTION

Why do people create, structure, and change governments?

GUIDING QUESTIONS

1. Why is Congress composed of a House of Representatives and a Senate?

2. Why are members of Congress assigned to work on committees?

Terms to Know

Senate the upper house of the United States Congress

House of Representatives the lower house of the United States Congress

constituent a voter that a member of Congress represents

occur to happen or take place

census a count of the population

adjust to change or modify

gerrymander to draw congressional district lines to favor one party

majority party party that holds the most seats

minority party party that does not hold the majority

seniority years of service

What Do You Know?

In the first column, answer the questions based on what you know before you study. After this lesson, complete the last column.

Now...		Later...
	How big is Congress?	
	How does Congress do its work?	

? Contrasting

1. What is one difference between the two houses of Congress?

____

____

____

____

The Two Houses of Congress

Article I of the Constitution describes the United States Congress. It says that Congress should have two parts. These parts are called the **Senate** and the House of Representatives. The Senate has equal representation, two senators for each state. The **House of Representatives** has proportional representation. Each state has one or more representatives, depending on its population.

Each member of Congress is elected by his or her constituents to make laws for the country. A **constituent** (kuhn•STIHCH•wuhnt) is a person represented by a legislator.

Members of Congress gather in the U.S. Capitol, in Washington, D.C. A Congress lasts for a term, or time period, of two years. Each Congress is numbered.

Lesson 1: Structure of Congress, *Continued*

The First Congress met from 1789 to 1791, and the 112th Congress met from 2011 to 2013.

Each term of Congress is divided into two meetings called sessions. A joint session **occurs** when the House and Senate meet together. Congress may also hold a special session during times of crisis.

Representatives serve for two years. They can be re-elected at the end of that time and can serve an unlimited number of terms. Today, there are 435 members in the House of Representatives. The number of representatives for each state is based on how many people live in that state. To find this number, a **census,** or population count, is taken every ten years. Congress uses the count to **adjust** the number of representatives each state has in the House.

Each state is divided into congressional districts. One representative is elected from each district. The law says that each district must include about the same number of voters. Sometimes state lawmakers **gerrymander** districts, however. That means the district lines are drawn to help one party gain voting strength. If most of a state's representatives are Republican, they can draw the lines to make oddly shaped districts that have more Republican than Democratic voters.

Gerrymandering after a census often leads to oddly shaped districts such as this one, shown in an 1812 cartoon.

There are 100 members, two from each of the 50 states, in the Senate. Each senator represents the entire state, not just one district. Senators serve a six-year term. Like representatives, they can be reelected when their term ends.

Glue Foldable here

FOLDABLES®

2. Place a two-tab Foldable along the dotted line. Label the top tab *Senate (upper house)* and the bottom tab *House of Representatives (lower house)*. On the front, list the number of members in each part of Congress. On the reverse, explain what that number represents.

? Analyzing Visuals

3. In your own words, what opinion about gerrymandering is expressed in the cartoon?

____

____

____

✓ Reading Check

4. How many members are there in the House? The Senate?

____

____

Lesson 1: Structure of Congress, *Continued*

Vocabulary

5. Explain the difference between the *majority party* and the *minority party*.

Identifying

6. What title is given to the leader of the House of Representatives?

Mark the Text

7. Underline the words that tell you what *pro tempore* means.

Defining

8. What is a party *whip*?

What is the *minority leader*?

In both the House and the Senate, the **majority party** is the party that holds more than half the seats. The other party is called the **minority party.** When a term begins, the House and the Senate each choose leaders. They play a large role in getting bills, or drafts of new laws, passed. The majority and minority leaders in each house push bills along and try to win votes. This table shows the most important leaders in Congress.

Congressional Leaders	
House of Representatives	**Senate**
Speaker of the House	Majority leader
Majority leader	Vice president, President pro tempore
Minority leader	Minority leader
Party whips	Party whips

Both houses have a presiding officer. In the House this is the Speaker. The Speaker of the House has great power. She or he leads House sessions and heads the majority party. The Speaker also guides proposed laws through the House and leads debates. If anything happens to both the president and vice president, the Speaker is next in line to become president.

The Senate's presiding officer is the vice president. He or she, unlike the Speaker of the House, can vote only to break a tie. The president pro tempore (proh•TEHM•puh•ree) leads the Senate when the vice president is absent. He or she is from the majority party and is usually the member who has served the longest. *Pro tempore* means "for the time being."

Party "whips," or assistant leaders, help the majority and minority leaders. They make sure legislators are present for key votes.

The Committee System

In each session, Congress looks at thousands of bills. It is a huge job. To make it easier, the work is shared among many small groups called committees. Committees do most of the work of Congress. The table on the next page shows the three types of committees in Congress.

Lesson 1: Structure of Congress, *Continued*

Types of Committees	
Type	**Definition**
Standing committee	A permanent committee, such as those dealing with agriculture, commerce, and veterans' affairs
Select committee	A temporary committee that deals with special issues; meets until it completes the assigned task
Joint committee	A committee that includes members of both houses; meets to work on specific problems

Newly elected senators and representatives try to get on committees that are important to the people they serve. Senators from a farming area might want to be on the agriculture committee. Those who have many factories in their districts might want to be on the labor committee.

Party leaders decide who should be on which committee. They look at members' preferences and skills. They also look at **seniority,** or years of service. Members who have served the longest usually get to sit on the most interesting committees.

The longest-serving majority committee member usually becomes the chairperson. The committee chairperson has an important job with a lot of power. Chairpersons decide when and if a committee will meet. They also decide which bills will be studied and who will serve on each subcommittee. The longest-serving committee member from the minority party leads the members of that party. He or she is called the ranking minority member.

/ / / / / / / / / / / / / Glue Foldable here / / / / / / / / / / / / / /

Check for Understanding

Name the two houses of Congress.

1. ______________________

2. ______________________

List three kinds of congressional committees.

3. ______________________

4. ______________________

5. ______________________

Reading Check

9. What are the three types of committees?

____

____

____

Identifying

10. Study the chart. Which type of committee would be formed to investigate possible causes of the financial crisis in 2008?

____

Explaining

11. Explain the seniority system in Congress.

____

____

____

FOLDABLES®

12. Place a two-tab Foldable along the line. Title the tabs *Congress* and *Committees*. Write five or more facts about each on both sides of the tabs.

NAME ______________ DATE ______________ CLASS ______________

networks

The Legislative Branch

Lesson 2: Powers of Congress

ESSENTIAL QUESTION

Why do people create, structure, and change governments?

GUIDING QUESTIONS

1. ***What kinds of lawmaking powers were given to Congress by the Constitution?***
2. ***What powers does Congress have to check the powers of the other branches of government?***

Terms to Know

expressed power a power of Congress that is listed in the Constitution

enumerated power another name for a power of Congress that is listed in the Constitution

implied power a power of Congress that the expressed powers point to

elastic clause part of the Constitution that says Congress has implied powers

nonlegislative power a power that is not related to making laws

impeach to accuse officials of wrongdoing

writ of habeas corpus an order that makes sure prisoners are told why they are being held

bill of attainder a law that punishes a person without a trial

ex post facto law a law that makes an act a crime after the act has been committed

regulate to manage or control

What Do You Know?

In the first column, answer the questions based on what you know before you study. After this lesson, complete the last column.

Now...		Later...
	How is congressional power limited?	
	How can Congress act as a check on the power of the president?	

Listing

1. List two legislative powers of Congress.

____

____

Legislative Powers

The Constitution gave Congress the power to make laws for the United States government. These lawmaking powers include the power to coin money and **regulate,** or manage, commerce. Commerce is the buying and selling of goods. All of Congress's duties that are actually listed in the Constitution are called **expressed powers** or **enumerated powers.** In Article I, Section 8, Clause 18, the Constitution also says that Congress has **implied powers.** These are powers that are not written in the Constitution. Instead they are implied, or pointed to, by the expressed powers.

Lesson 2: Powers of Congress, *Continued*

They are things that Congress needs to do to carry out its expressed powers.

Clause 18 is also called the **elastic clause.** It allows Congress to stretch its powers or do whatever is "necessary and proper" to use its expressed powers. For example, the Constitution does not say that Congress can create an air force. However, the elastic clause lets Congress do so as part of its expressed power to support an army and a navy.

Congress has many expressed and implied powers. The graphic organizer below lists some of the expressed powers.

Other Powers and Limits

The most important job of Congress is to make laws, but it also has other duties. To do these other jobs, Congress has **nonlegislative powers.** The most important nonlegislative powers are the ones that allow Congress to check other branches of the government. Some nonlegislative powers include

- suggesting amendments to the Constitution.
- approving or rejecting the president's choices for Supreme Court justices, federal judges, and ambassadors. This is done only by the Senate.
- impeaching federal officials.

Comparing and Contrasting

2. What is the difference between expressed and implied powers?

______

______

Making Connections

3. Study the graphic. Which power of Congress deals with taxes?

______

______

Reading Check

4. Why is the "necessary and proper" clause also called the elastic clause?

______

______

Identifying

5. What is one nonlegislative power of Congress?

______

______

Lesson 2: Powers of Congress, *Continued*

Reading Check

6. Why do you think the Constitution forbids Congress from passing ex post facto laws?

____

____

____

____

Listing

7. The Constitution limits Congress's power over the states. List the three ways.

____

____

____

____

FOLDABLES®

8. Place a three-tab Foldable along the dotted line. Label the tabs: *expressed powers, implied powers,* and *checks and balances*. Write an explanation of each on the reverse side of the tabs.

To **impeach** means to accuse a person of doing something wrong. The House may impeach any federal official, even the president. The Senate then decides whether that person is guilty. If two-thirds of senators agree the official is guilty, he or she must leave office.

Only two presidents have been impeached: Andrew Johnson in 1868 and Bill Clinton in 1998. The Senate did not find them guilty, so they were not removed from office.

The Constitution also lists the things that Congress may not do. Congress may not

- pass laws that go against the Constitution. A law that does not allow freedom of religion would go against the Constitution, for example.
- favor one state over another.
- tax exports.
- tax business between states.
- block the **writ of habeas corpus** (HAY•bee•uhs KAWR•puhs). This is an order that makes sure prisoners are told why they are being held.
- pass **bills of attainder.** These are laws that punish a person without a trial.
- pass **ex post facto laws.** These laws make an act a crime after the act has been committed.

Congress cannot override certain powers set aside for the states. For example, states control their own school systems.

Congress is also part of the system of checks and balances. For example, Congress makes laws, but the Supreme Court can decide whether those laws go against the Constitution. The president can veto bills passed by Congress. On the other hand, Congress can override a president's veto.

/ / / / / / / / / / / / / Glue Foldable here / / / / / / / / / / / / /

Check for Understanding

Name two of the powers given to Congress by the Constitution.

1. ______________________

2. ______________________

Name two ways that Congress's powers are checked by other branches of government.

3. ______________________

4. ______________________

The Legislative Branch

Lesson 3: How Congress Works

ESSENTIAL QUESTION

Why do people create, structure, and change governments?

GUIDING QUESTIONS

1. ***What are the qualifications for becoming a member of Congress?***
2. ***How do members of Congress exercise their responsibilities?***

Terms to Know

franking privilege the special right members of Congress have to send job-related mail without paying postage

lobbyist a person hired to influence government decisions

draft to make a rough version or outline

estimate to judge the approximate value or amount of a thing

casework the work of helping people deal with the federal government

pork-barrel project when a representative gets government money for projects in one district or state

What Do You Know?

In the first column, answer the questions based on what you know before you study. After this lesson, complete the last column.

Now...		Later...
	Who can become a member of Congress?	
	What else does Congress do besides make laws?	

Qualifications and Staffing

To become a member of Congress, a person must meet certain requirements. These requirements are listed in the Constitution. They are different for members of the House and Senate. The chart below shows what they are.

Qualifications for Congress		
Requirement	**Senate**	**House**
Age	30 years old	25 years old
Residency	Live in the state you plan to represent	Live in the state you plan to represent
U.S. Citizenship	9 years	7 years

Listing

1. What three requirements must a person meet to be a member of the Senate or the House of Representatives?

____

____

____

NAME ______________________ DATE ______________ CLASS __________

networks

The Legislative Branch

Lesson 3: How Congress Works, *Continued*

Reading Check

2. Why might the franking privilege help a member of Congress get reelected?

____

____

____

Mark the Text

3. Underline the definition of *immunity* in the text.

Vocabulary

4. Fill in the blank with the correct word to complete the sentence.

______________________ *represent interest groups. They meet with congressional staff members to try to influence policy.*

Explaining

5. What might a personal staff member do at the Library of Congress?

____

____

____

Once a person is elected to Congress, he or she has many benefits. In addition to their salary, representatives and senators also enjoy

- free office space, free parking, and free trips home.
- the **franking privilege:** members can send job-related mail at no cost.

Members of Congress also have immunity, or legal protection in certain situations. This is not meant to allow members of Congress to break the law. It allows them to debate and talk freely without fear.

Members of Congress have a huge workload. To get everything done, they hire people to help them. Members of a congressperson's personal staff include:

- clerks
- administrative assistants
- research assistants

Personal staffs work both in Washington and in the congressperson's home state. They answer questions from voters and help them deal with federal government agencies. They also research bills and talk to reporters. Another job of staff members is to meet with lobbyists. **Lobbyists** are people who represent interest groups. They contact government officials to try to influence, or shape, policy making.

Some assistants are students. They are usually from the member's district and volunteer their time. They get to learn about Congress as they help with research, deliver messages, and do other office tasks.

Committee staff members are assistants who help keep committee work running smoothly. They schedule committee hearings. They **draft,** or outline, bills.

Congress also has several agencies to help with its work. These agencies include the Library of Congress, the Government Accountability Office (GAO), and the Congressional Budget Office (CBO).

The Library of Congress has a copy of every book published in the United States. Members of Congress and their staffs use these books for research. The GAO looks at federal programs and suggests ways to improve how the government spends money. The CBO helps plan the nation's budget. When Congress or the president has an idea for a new program, this office **estimates,** or tries to figure out, how much the program will cost.

Congress at Work

Congress is best-known for making laws. That is why members of Congress are called "lawmakers." But our lawmakers also do other work. A great deal of time is spent on **casework,** or helping people deal with the federal government. Members of Congress get many requests from the voters. Voters ask for help with all sorts of things, from understanding laws to finding a late Social Security check.

Staff members spend hours each day on casework. If they cannot find answers or get results, the senator or representative will step in. Lawmakers want to help people. They know that casework does other good things, such as:

- helping them build public support for reelection
- allowing them to see how well the executive branch handles programs like Social Security
- providing help to citizens dealing with the government

Members of Congress have another important job. They try to make sure that their state or district gets some federal money. The federal government distributes public-works money to states to use on projects such as highways, dams, and military bases. These projects create jobs and boost the local economy.

Only the executive branch can decide where federal money goes. But members of Congress try to sway those decisions. They also ask the voters to tell agency officials about their needs.

When a representative gets federal money that is mainly for one district or state, it is called a **pork-barrel project.** To understand this term, think of members of Congress dipping into the "pork barrel" (federal treasury, or money) and pulling out a piece of "fat" (a federal project for his or her district). Critics say that this is a waste of taxpayers' money. Lawmakers believe that bringing money to their state helps their voters.

/ / / / / / / / / / / / / / Glue Foldable here / / / / / / / / / / / / / /

Check for Understanding

List two things that members of Congress do as part of their job.

1. ______________

2. ______________

Drawing Conclusions

6. Give an example of casework. Why is it important for legislators to do casework such as the example you gave?

____

____

Reading Check

7. Do you think pork-barrel projects are a good idea? Or should such projects be distributed evenly among states and districts?

____

____

FOLDABLES®

8. Place a one-tab Foldable along the line. Label the anchor tab *Congress's Benefits and Qualifications.* Write five benefits and qualifications. Then choose one and explain on the back why Congress should have that benefit.

The Legislative Branch

Lesson 4: How a Bill Becomes a Law

ESSENTIAL QUESTION

Why do people create, structure, and change governments?

GUIDING QUESTIONS

1. ***What kinds of bills come before Congress?***
2. ***How does a bill become a law?***

Terms to Know

submit to offer for consideration

joint resolution a resolution passed by both houses of Congress that has the force of law if signed by the president

special-interest group a group of people who work together for a common cause

rider amendment to a bill that is unrelated to the subject matter of the bill

filibuster to talk a bill to death

cloture a vote by three-fifths of the Senate to limit debate on a bill

voice vote a voting method in which those in favor say 'Aye' and those against say 'No'

standing vote a vote in which members stand to be counted for or against a bill

roll-call vote a vote in the Senate in which senators give their vote as their name is called

pocket veto the president's power to kill a bill, if Congress is not in session, by not signing it for ten days.

What Do You Know?

In the first column, answer the questions based on what you know before you study. After this lesson, complete the last column.

Now...		Later...
	What kinds of laws does Congress vote on?	
	What is a congressional bill?	

Reading Check

1. What are the two types of bills?

____

____

Types of Bills

During each term of Congress, more than 10,000 bills are often **submitted,** or offered for consideration. Only a few hundred of them actually become laws. This should tell you that it is not easy to pass a law!

There are two kinds of bills. One is called a private bill. A private bill deals with one person or place. The other type of bill is called a public bill. It applies to the whole nation. A bill about taxes would be a public bill.

Congress also considers resolutions. These are formal statements of lawmakers' opinions or decisions. Many resolutions do not have the power of law. A **joint resolution** is an exception, however. This type of resolution must pass both houses of Congress. If the president signs the resolution, it becomes a law. Joint resolutions can be used to propose amendments to the Constitution. They can also be used to fund special projects, like natural disaster aid.

Defining

2. What is a *resolution?*

____

____

____

Listing

3. List the two actions a standing committee can take on a bill.

____

____

Comparing and Contrasting

4. How are the House and Senate debates similar? How are they different?

____

____

____

Summarizing

5. What four main steps are involved in passing a bill in Congress?

____

____

____

____

From Bill to Law

Every bill starts with an idea. Ideas for bills come from citizens, the president, and special-interest groups. A **special-interest group** is a group of people who work together for a common cause.

Only a member of Congress can introduce a bill. When a bill is first read, it is given a title and a number. These show which house proposed the bill and when it was introduced. The first bill in the Senate is labeled S.1. The first bill in the House is labeled H.R.1.

Next, the bill is sent to the correct standing committee. The committee decides if the bill should be passed on to the full House or Senate for a vote. The committee can take five actions on the bill:

- pass the bill
- make changes in the bill and suggest that it be passed
- replace it with a new bill on the same subject
- ignore the bill and let it die, also called "pigeonholing"
- kill the bill by a majority vote

If a bill makes it through committee, it will be debated by the full House or Senate. Members will argue its pros and cons and amendments will be considered. The House allows amendments only if they are directly related to the subject of the bill. The Senate allows its members to attach **riders,** or completely unrelated amendments, to a bill.

In the House there is a time limit set for how long a representative can talk about a bill. This limit is necessary because the House has so many members. Senators, however, can speak for as long as they wish. Senators sometimes use this freedom to **filibuster** a bill. To filibuster means to talk a bill to death. Senators can stop a filibuster with cloture. **Cloture** (KLOH•chuhr) is when three-fifths of the members vote to limit the time for debate to one hour for each speaker.

The Legislative Branch

Lesson 4: How a Bill Becomes a Law, *Continued*

Vocabulary

6. What is a *voice vote*?

____

____

Reading Check

7. Why do you think senators attach riders to bills?

____

____

FOLDABLES®

8. Make a two-tab Foldable into a four-tab by cutting each tab in half up to the anchor. Place the Foldable along the dotted line. Label the anchor tab *How a Bill Becomes a Law.* Then starting with the top tab label the tabs: *bill is introduced, bill goes to a committee for approval, approved bill goes to Congress for debate,* and *Congress votes on the bill.* On the reverse side of the tabs, explain what each step means.

Glue Foldable here

After debate, it is time to vote. A majority of members must vote for a bill for it to pass. The chart below shows the different ways votes are taken in each house.

Voting in Congress	
House	**Senate**
voice vote—members say "Aye" or "No" to a bill	
standing vote—members stand to be counted for or against a bill	
recorded vote—members' votes are recorded electronically	**roll-call vote**—senators say "Aye" or "No" as their names are called

If a bill passes in one house, it is sent to the other. If a bill is defeated in either house, it dies. If both houses pass a different form of the same bill, a conference committee is formed. In this committee, members of both houses come up with one bill that everyone can agree on.

The approved bill is then sent to the president. The president can do one of three things:

1. sign the bill into law
2. veto, or refuse to sign, the bill
3. ignore the bill

An ignored bill becomes law after 10 days if Congress is in session. If Congress has adjourned, the bill dies. This is called a **pocket veto.**

Congress can pass a bill over a president's veto. To do so, two-thirds of each house must vote to override the veto. This does not happen very often.

Check for Understanding

Name two places ideas for new bills come from.

1. ______________________

2. ______________________

Name two things that could happen to a bill when it goes to a committee for study.

3. ______________________

4. ______________________

NAME ______________________ DATE ______________ CLASS ________

networks

The Executive Branch

Lesson 1: The President and Vice President

ESSENTIAL QUESTION

What is required of leaders?

GUIDING QUESTIONS

1. ***How does a citizen become president?***
2. ***What happens if the president must step down from office?***

Terms to Know

elector member of the Electoral College that chooses the president

outcome a result or consequence

resign to give up one's office or position

display to show or list

What Do You Know?

In the first column, answer the questions based on what you know before you study. After this lesson, complete the last column.

Now...		Later...
	Can any U.S. citizen be president?	
	Can the president be replaced before the end of a term?	

Making Inferences

1. What is the purpose of the Constitution's rules about who can be president?

____

____

Prior Knowledge

2. List three U.S. presidents.

____

____

____

Office of the President

The President of the United States heads the executive branch of the national government. Because of America's strong influence around the world, the president may hold the most important job in the world.

The Constitution lists three rules about who can become president. A person must be at least 35 years old and have been born in the United States. He or she must also have lived in the country for at least 14 years.

Most past presidents have been white male Protestant Christians and many were lawyers. In the past 60 years, candidates from a wider group of Americans have had a chance to be elected. In 1960, John F. Kennedy became the first Roman Catholic elected as president. In 2008, Barack Obama became the first African American president. In addition, two women have run for vice president with a major party, Geraldine Ferraro and Sarah Palin. Joseph Lieberman was the first Jewish candidate for vice president.

The election for president is held every four years. The people, however, do not directly choose the president Instead, a group called the Electoral College elects him or her.

Lesson 1: The President and Vice President, *Continued*

When people vote for a president, they are actually choosing **electors.** Electors are members of the Electoral College who are selected to vote for presidential candidates in elections. The electors meet to vote for the president in December.

Each state has the same number of electors as it has members of Congress. There are 538 electors in the Electoral College today. In most states, the candidate who gets more than half of the people's votes wins all of that state's electoral votes. This is called the "winner takes all" rule. This is true even if the candidate wins by only a few votes. So a small number of votes can make a big difference in the **outcome,** or result, of an election.

To win the national election, a person must get at least half of the 538 electoral votes. This means the person must get at least 270 votes. If no one person gets 270 votes, the House of Representatives must decide the election. This has only happened twice, in 1800 and in 1824. If the House votes, each state has only one vote.

The president serves a four-year term. At first, the Constitution did not limit the number of terms a president could serve. George Washington served for two terms. He set an example by refusing to run for a third term. Many years later, Franklin Roosevelt ran for president four times. He won all four elections.

Many people worried that if the number of presidential terms were not limited that one person could become too powerful. So Congress passed the Twenty-second Amendment. It was ratified in 1951. It said that a president could only serve two terms in office.

The president receives pay and other benefits while in office. Those are shown in the chart below.

President's Salary and Benefits
Paid a salary of $400,000 per year
Receives money for personal costs and travel
Lives and works in the White House
Staff of more than 80 people takes care of the president's family
Has use of Camp David
Has use of special fleet of cars, helicopters, and airplanes *Air Force One,* for example

Glue Foldable here

FOLDABLES®

3. Glue a one-tab on top of a two-tab Foldable at the anchor. Place the book along the line to cover the text. Title the top Foldable *Electoral College.* Label the tabs of the two-tab Foldable *President* and *Vice President.* Write facts about each on the tabs.

Reading Check

4. How many votes are needed to win in the Electoral College?

____

Identifying

5. Why did Congress pass the Twenty-second Amendment?

____

____

Prior Knowledge

6. Why would people be concerned about the president having too much power?

____

Lesson 1: The President and Vice President, *Continued*

Analyzing

7. Why is it important for the nation to know the order of succession in the government?

Explaining

8. When a vice president becomes president, how is the next vice president chosen?

Identifying

9. Study the chart. Which officer becomes president if the vice president, Speaker of the House, and president pro tempore are unable to serve?

The Electoral College also chooses the vice president. The rules for becoming vice president are the same as those for the president.

The Constitution does not give the vice president much power. It says that the vice president will lead the Senate but can only vote to break a tie. It also says that the vice president becomes president if the president dies, is removed from office, falls seriously ill, or **resigns.**

Presidential Succession

President William Henry Harrison died in 1841. He was the first president to die in office. The Constitution says that the vice president should take on "the powers and duties" of the presidency. But no one was sure what that meant. Should the vice president stay in office as the vice president but do the president's job? Vice President John Tyler decided that he should declare himself president and take the oath of as acting office. Then he served out the rest of Harrison's term.

In 1947, Congress passed a law called the Presidential Succession Act. *Succession* means "to follow." The law spelled out who would become president and in what order. The vice president is first, followed by the Speaker of the House, and then the president *pro tempore* of the Senate. If none of these three people can serve, the job falls to the secretary of state. The list provides 18 possible replacements for the president. The chart below **displays,** or shows, the first ten.

Order of Succession	
1	Vice President
2	Speaker of the House
3	President *pro tempore* of the Senate
4	Secretary of State
5	Secretary of the Treasury
6	Secretary of Defense
7	Attorney General
8	Secretary of the Interior
9	Secretary of Agriculture
10	Secretary of Commerce

Lesson 1: The President and Vice President, *Continued*

In 1967, Congress passed the Twenty-fifth Amendment. This amendment gives the procedures to be followed if it becomes necessary for the vice president to assume the president's job. It also solved another problem.

In the past, when a vice president became president, the office of vice president was left empty. The Twenty-fifth Amendment states the following:

- If the president dies or leaves office, the vice president becomes the president.
- The new president then chooses a vice president. Congress must approve this choice.
- If the president becomes disabled and cannot do the job, the vice president serves as acting president until the president is able to go back to work. This could happen because of an event such as a heart attack or surgery.

For the vice president to step in as acting president, the vice president and a majority of the cabinet members must agree and report to Congress that the president is unable to do the job.

Check for Understanding

Name two of the qualifications that a person must have to become President of the United States.

1. ______________________________

2. ______________________________

If a president dies and the vice president takes over, name the two things that must happen before a new vice president can take office.

3. ______________________________

4. ______________________________

Glue Foldable here

Mark the Text

10. Circle an example of what might cause the vice president to assume the duties of acting president.

Reading Check

11. What problem with the vice presidency was the Twenty-fifth Amendment meant to solve?

____

____

FOLDABLES®

12. Place a three-tab Foldable along the dotted line. Write the title *Executive Office* on the anchor tab. Label the top tab *President,* the middle tab *Vice President,* and the bottom tab *Presidential Successor.* Write the qualifications for each office on the front and reverse tabs.

Lesson 2: The President's Powers and Roles

ESSENTIAL QUESTION
What is required of leaders?

GUIDING QUESTIONS
1. ***What are the duties of the president?***
2. ***What roles does the president have?***

Terms to Know

require to order or to have a need for
executive order an order given by the president that has the same force as a law
pardon presidential order that forgives a crime
reprieve presidential order that delays punishment
amnesty pardon for a group of people
ambassador a person who represents the U.S. government in another country

What Do You Know?

In the first column, answer the questions based on what you know before you study. After this lesson, complete the last column.

Now...		Later...
	What is the president's job?	
	What roles does the president play when fulfilling his or her duties?	

Defining

1. What is the veto power?

____

____

Listing

2. List two powers of the president.

____

____

____

____

Presidential Powers

The role of the president of the United States is a symbol of the federal government and the nation. The president is the most powerful public official in the country. The president's main job is to execute, or carry out, the laws passed by Congress. The Constitution also gives the president other powers. They are the power to:

- veto, or reject, bills passed by Congress
- call special sessions of Congress
- serve as commander in chief of the armed forces
- receive leaders and other officials of foreign countries
- make treaties with other countries
- appoint judges to the federal court and other top government offices
- pardon or reduce the sentences of people convicted of federal crimes

The legislative branch can check the president's powers. The Senate must approve treaties and many appointments made by the president.

Lesson 2: The President's Powers and Roles, *Continued*

The judicial branch can also check the president's powers. The Supreme Court has ruled that the president is not above the law, which means the president must obey the same laws as everyone else.

The Constitution also **requires,** or orders, the president to tell Congress how the country is doing. The president does this is by presenting the annual State of the Union message. This is a speech in which the president talks about the important issues facing the country.

Explaining

3. What is the purpose of the State of the Union speech?

____

____

Reading Check

4. What are two powers of the president as stated in the Constitution?

____

____

____

____

Describing

5. Describe the president's main role and how he or she carries it out.

____

____

____

____

____

Presidential Roles

The president's main role is to carry out the nation's laws. When performing this role, the president is called the chief executive. As chief executive, the president is in charge of 15 cabinet departments and many agencies.

Presidents use executive orders to spell out the details of the laws and to put them into use. An **executive order** is a command that has the same force as a law. Presidents also use executive orders so that they can act quickly in some situations. In 1948, for example, President Harry S. Truman used an executive order to end the separation of races in the nation's military.

As chief executive, the president appoints, or chooses, justices to serve on the Supreme Court. This power is important because Supreme Court justices serve for life.

Lesson 2: The President's Powers and Roles, *Continued*

Mark the Text

6. Underline the sentence that explains a president's goal for choosing judges.

Vocabulary

7. What is a *pardon*?

____

____

Contrasting

8. What is the difference between a pardon and amnesty?

____

____

____

____

Examining Details

9. Why is it difficult for the president and Congress to agree when making new laws?

____

____

____

____

____

____

That is why presidents try to choose judges who share views similar to their own. The president also chooses judges to serve on federal courts throughout the country.

The president also has the power to grant pardons to people found guilty of federal crimes. A **pardon** forgives a crime and ends punishment. The president can also grant reprieves and amnesty. A **reprieve** delays punishment. **Amnesty** is pardon for a group of people.

The president is the country's chief diplomat. In this role, the president represents the United States government in its dealings with other countries. The president also appoints ambassadors. An **ambassador** is a person who represents the U.S. government to foreign governments.

Another role of the president is that of the head of state. As head of state, he or she represents the American people. The president greets visiting leaders from other countries. Giving out medals at ceremonies is another job of the head of state.

The president is commander in chief of the armed forces. This allows presidents to back up foreign policy decisions with force when they need to. The president and Congress share the power to make war. Only Congress can declare war. Only the president has the power to order troops into battle. The War Powers Resolution puts limits on the president's power to send troops into battle. Congress passed the resolution in 1973 after the Vietnam War.

The president tries to help the economy do well. People expect the president to find solutions to problems such as unemployment, high taxes, and rising prices.

The president is a legislative leader. The president often gives Congress ideas for new laws. He or she then works with members of Congress to get those laws passed. The president also makes speeches around the country to get citizens to support the new laws being passed.

Congress and the president do not always agree about which laws should be passed. This is because the president represents the interests of the whole nation. Members of Congress represent the interests of their states or congressional districts. Those interests are not always the same as the national interests.

The president must plan the federal budget each year. He or she meets with budget officials and members of Congress to decide which programs to support and which to cut. These decisions can have a big effect on the economy.

Lesson 2: The President's Powers and Roles, *Continued*

The president is also the party leader of his or her political party. The president supports other party members that are running for office. He or she also helps the party raise money.

The President's Roles
A. Chief Executive
1. carries out the nation's laws
2. grants pardons, reprieves, and amnesty
B. Chief Diplomat
1.
2.
C. Head of State
1.
2.
D. Commander in Chief
1.
2.
E. Economic Leader
1.
2.
F. Legislative Leader
1.
2.
G. Party Leader
1.
2.

Check for Understanding

Name three powers given to the president.

1. ____________
2. ____________
3. ____________

Name two roles given to the president.

4. ____________ 5. ____________

Glue Foldable here

Comparing

10. Which of the presidents' roles do you think is most important? Why?

Mark the Text

11. Complete the outline about the roles of the president. Give two details about each job. The first one has been done for you.

Reading Check

12. Why is the War Powers Resolution important?

FOLDABLES®

13. Place a two-tab Foldable along the line. Write *President of the United States* on the anchor tab. Label the other tabs *Powers* and *Roles*. Write a sentence about each on the reverse tabs.

The Executive Branch

Lesson 3: Making Foreign Policy

ESSENTIAL QUESTION

What is required of leaders?
Why do nations interact with each other?

GUIDING QUESTIONS

1. ***What are the goals of foreign policy?***
2. ***What are the tools the president uses to carry out U.S. foreign policy?***

Terms to Know

foreign policy the plan a nation follows when dealing with other nations
target a goal or aim
national security keeping the nation safe from attack
treaty a formal agreement with another nation
executive agreement an agreement between the president and the leader of another country
method a procedure or process of doing something
trade sanctions stopping or slowing trade between the United States and another country
embargo an agreement among nations to refuse to trade with a nation

What Do You Know?

In the first column, answer the questions based on what you know before you study. After this lesson, complete the last column.

Now...		Later...
	What is foreign policy?	
	Why does the government make foreign policy?	

Explaining

1. Why is trade so important in today's economy?

____

____

____

The President and Foreign Policy

Foreign policy is the plan a nation follows when it deals with other nations. The United States has four main foreign policy **targets,** or goals. The most important one is **national security.** This means keeping the nation safe from attack. The second goal is to encourage trade with other countries. This is very important in today's world. Trade builds markets for U.S. goods. It also creates jobs.

A third foreign policy goal is to promote world peace. Any war, in any part of the world, can harm trade. It can also put the nation's security at risk. The fourth goal is to advance democracy around the world. Supporting basic human rights and democratic governments encourages peace.

Lesson 3: Making Foreign Policy, *Continued*

The Big Four: U.S. Foreign Policy Goals	
1 national security	**3** peace
2 trade	**4** democracy

The president directs U.S. foreign policy through the roles of commander in chief and chief diplomat. A large team of experts helps the president. These experts include people in the following executive branch agencies:

- State Department
- Defense Department
- National Security Council
- Office of the Director of National Intelligence (ODNI)
- Central Intelligence Agency (CIA)

These agencies supply the president with information for making decisions. They also help carry out American foreign policy decisions around the world.

Congress also plays a part in foreign policy. Only Congress can declare war. Congress can block some military actions through the War Powers Act. Congress also has the power to decide how much money the country should spend on defense.

Who Plays a Part in U.S. Foreign Policy?

President	
State Department	ODNI
Defense Department	CIA
National Security Council	Congress

The Constitution is not clear about how these branches of government should work together or which branch controls the war powers. So at various times in our country's history, control over the war powers has shifted back and forth between Congress and the president.

Identifying

2. What is the most important goal of U.S. foreign policy?

____

____

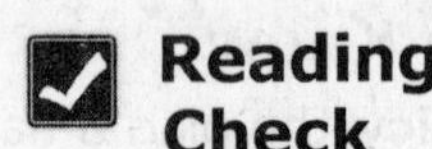

Reading Check

3. What executive agencies help the president in making and carrying out foreign policy?

____

____

____

____

____

Paraphrasing

4. Paraphrase the last paragraph on this page.

____

____

____

____

____

Reading Check

5. What is an executive agreement?

____

____

Mark the Text

6. Underline the sentences that explain how an ambassador is chosen.

Examining Details

7. Which form of foreign policy tool is being used when the United States sends food to a country that has been hit by a hurricane?

____

____

Describing

8. What are three ways that the United States uses trade as a foreign policy tool?

____

____

____

The Tools of Foreign Policy

The president and Congress have many tools they can use to conduct foreign policy. One such tool is a treaty. A **treaty** is a formal agreement between the governments of two or more nations. The president can make a treaty, but the Senate must approve the treaty.

Another tool for making foreign policy is an executive agreement. An **executive agreement** is an agreement between the president and the leader of another country. It does not require Senate approval.

The United States also sends ambassadors to other countries. They represent the United States government. The president appoints ambassadors, but the appointments must be approved, or confirmed, by the Senate. Ambassadors are sent only to those governments the United States recognizes. The president can refuse to recognize, or accept, the government of another country.

Foreign aid is another useful tool in making foreign policy. Foreign aid is help the United States government gives to other countries. The help these countries receive can be in the form of money, food, military assistance, or supplies. The Marshall Plan is one of the nation's greatest examples of foreign aid. It was a program that helped Western Europe rebuild after World War II. The United States also sends foreign aid to countries after natural disasters.

The president can use economic **methods,** or approaches, to conduct foreign policy. One method is to order trade sanctions. **Trade sanctions** stop or slow trade between the United States and another country. Another choice is for the United States to join an embargo. An **embargo** is an agreement among a number of nations who refuse to trade with a nation.

Congress also has a role in economic areas. It can set tariffs. Tariffs are taxes placed on goods imported from other countries. This makes the price of these goods the same as or higher than the price of similar U.S. goods. Congress also decides whether the United States should join international trade groups.

As commander in chief, the president has the power to use military force to carry out foreign policy decisions. The president and Congress share the power to make war. Congress has the power to declare war.

Lesson 3: Making Foreign Policy, *Continued*

The president has the power to order troops to battle. At times, the president has used this power even when Congress has not declared war. The Vietnam War is an example of this type of foreign policy.

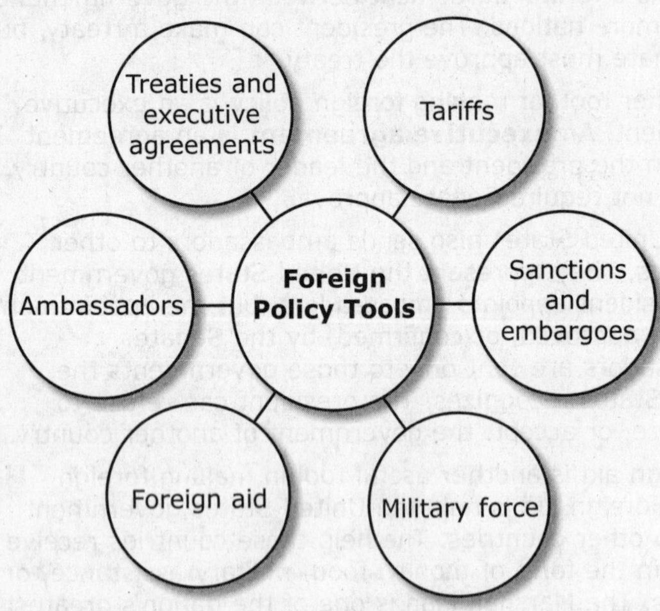

FOLDABLES®

9. Glue a one-tab Foldable on top of a two-tab Foldable at the anchor tab to create a book. Place it along the dotted line. Label the one-tab Foldable *Foreign Policy*. Define the term on the front of the tab. List the U.S. foreign policy goals on the reverse. Now turn to the second Foldable. Label the top tab *President: Foreign Policy Tools* and the bottom tab *Congress: Foreign Policy Tools*. On the tabs, write the tools each uses to direct foreign policy.

Glue Foldable here

Check for Understanding

Name two goals of America's foreign policy.

1. _______________

2. _______________

List three tools the president uses to carry out America's foreign policy.

3. _______________

4. _______________

5. _______________

NAME ______________________ DATE ______________ CLASS __________

networks

The Executive Branch

Lesson 4: How the Executive Branch Works

ESSENTIAL QUESTION

What is required of leaders?

GUIDING QUESTIONS

1. ***What offices make up the Executive Office of the President?***
2. ***What role does the president's cabinet play in the government?***
3. ***What is the federal bureaucracy?***

Terms to Know

role the job or function of a person or thing

cabinet the heads of the 15 executive departments

federal bureaucracy the agencies below the cabinet departments in the executive branch

specific exact or detailed

executive agency a type of independent agency that deals with specific government programs

government corporation a business operated by the government

regulatory commission a type of independent agency that makes rules that businesses must follow

spoils system system in which workers are given jobs in return for their political support

civil service system system the government uses to hire workers

merit system system in which workers are hired based on their skills and test scores

political appointee a person appointed to a federal job by the president

What Do You Know?

In the first column, answer the questions based on what you know before you study. After this lesson, complete the last column.

Now...		Later...
	What does the Executive Office of the President do?	
	What does the president's cabinet do?	

Mark the Text

1. Circle the name of the person who created the EOP.

Executive Office Agencies

In the early days of the nation, only a few people worked in the executive branch. Today thousands of people do. Many of them work in the Executive Office of the President (EOP).

The EOP was created by President Franklin D. Roosevelt in 1939. The EOP has grown over the years and now has many different offices. The White House Office works directly for the president. It includes the president's closest advisers, called the White House staff.

Lesson 4: How the Executive Branch Works, *Continued*

The most powerful member of the White House staff is the chief of staff. This person directs the White House staff and handles the president's schedule.

The Office of Management and Budget (OMB) is another EOP agency. It works closely with the president to prepare the federal budget. It also monitors, or watches, how hundreds of government agencies spend their money.

The National Security Council (NSC) helps the president with defense and security. NSC officials include the vice president, the secretary of state, the secretary of defense, the chairman of the Joint Chiefs of Staff, the Director of National Intelligence, and the National Security Advisor.

Several other offices in the EOP help the president carry out the responsibilities of the executive branch. The Council of Economic Advisers (CEA) helps the president in his **role,** or job, as economic leader. The CEA is responsible for giving the president advice on economic matters, such as jobs, inflation, and trade.

Selected Executive Offices of the President

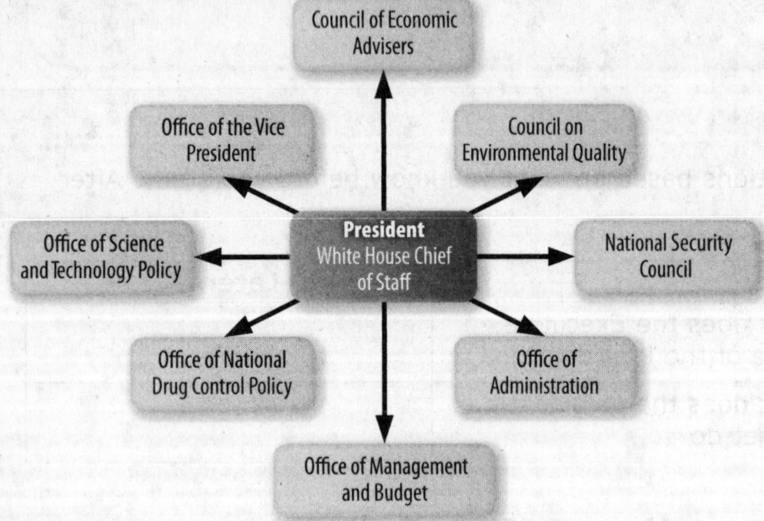

Reading Check

2. Which officials make up the National Security Council?

____

____

Making Inferences

3. Why do you think the Secretary of State is a member of the National Security Council?

____

____

Identifying

4. Choose three of the offices in the chart. Circle each one and write a brief description of what it does.

____

____

____

____

Lesson 4: How the Executive Branch Works, *Continued*

Reading Check

5. When does the cabinet meet?

Prior Knowledge

6. What do you think caused Congress to create the Department of Homeland Security?

Critical Thinking

7. Study the chart with the cabinet departments. List the three cabinet departments that you think are the most important. Explain your choices.

The President's Cabinet

The executive branch also includes 15 executive departments. The president chooses the heads of these departments with the Senate's consent. This group of advisors is called the **cabinet.** The president decides when it is necessary for the cabinet to meet.

The head of the Department of Justice is called the attorney general. The other cabinet members are called secretaries. Each secretary advises the president and manages the work of his or her department. For example, the secretary of the interior manages and protects the nation's national parks.

The Department of Homeland Security is the newest cabinet department. It was created in 2002. It is responsible for keeping the nation safe from terrorist attacks.

The Constitution does not mention the cabinet. The cabinet developed when George Washington started meeting regularly with the heads of the first four executive departments in the new government.

The Cabinet Departments	
Department of Agriculture	Department of the Interior
Department of Commerce	Department of Justice
Department of Defense	Department of Labor
Department of Education	Department of State
Department of Energy	Department of Transportation
Department of Health and Human Services	Department of the Treasury
Department of Homeland Security	Department of Veteran's Affairs
Department of Housing and Urban Development	

You may wonder how the vice president fits into the executive branch. Some vice presidents have not had much authority. Others have played key roles. This has become especially true in recent years. Some active vice presidents include Al Gore, Dick Cheney, and Joe Biden.

The Federal Bureaucracy

The executive branch has hundreds of agencies below the cabinet departments. Together, these agencies are called the **federal bureaucracy** (byu•RAH•kruh•see). The agencies of the federal bureaucracy have three main jobs. As they do these jobs, they help shape government policy.

First, the agencies must make new laws work. Congress passes laws, but it does not say how to make them work in the real world. This is the job of the executive agencies. They write **specific** rules so that businesses and people can follow the law.

Second, the agencies carry out the government's daily work. The federal workers deliver the mail, collect taxes, take care of the national parks, and do thousands of other jobs.

Third, the agencies regulate various kinds of businesses, services, and public utilities. These include banking, the airlines, nuclear power plants, and many others. For example, the Food and Drug Administration makes sure that food and medicine are safe for consumers.

The executive branch includes hundreds of independent agencies. These agencies are independent because they are not part of the cabinet. There are three types:

1. **Executive agencies** work with special government programs. The National Aeronautics and Space Administration (NASA) is an independent executive agency.
2. **Government corporations** are businesses that are owned and run by the government. The United States Postal Service (USPS) is an example of a government corporation.
3. **Regulatory commissions** make rules that businesses must follow. For example, the Federal Communications Commission (FCC) sets rules for broadcasters. Regulatory commissions are the only independent agencies that do not have to report to the president. The president appoints their members but only Congress can remove them.

Visualizing

8. What do you think the secretary of commerce would advise the president about?

______

Vocabulary

9. What is the *federal bureaucracy?*

______

______

Explaining

10. What do federal agencies do?

______

______

Listing

11. List the three types of independent agencies in the executive branch.

______

______

______

Mark the Text

12. Underline the sentence that explains what makes the regulatory commissions different than the other independent agencies.

The Executive Branch

Lesson 4: How the Executive Branch Works, *Continued*

Vocabulary

13. Explain what the *merit system* is in your own words.

____

Reading Check

14. Which jobs go to political appointees today?

____

____

____

FOLDABLES

15. Place a two-tab Foldable along the line. Label anchor tab *Executive Offices*. Label the tabs *Executive Office of the President* and *Cabinet*. Write the definition of each on the tabs. On the reverse tabs make a list of the purposes of each.

The executive branch has many workers. Early in our nation's history the government used the **spoils system** to hire workers. Under the spoils system, each new president filled jobs only with his with supporters.

In 1883, Congress passed the Civil Service Reform Act. This act changed the way the government hired workers. The new system is called the **civil service system.** It is a **merit system.** *Merit* means "ability." In this system people have to take tests and are hired based on their skills. The people who are hired become civil service workers. About 90 percent of government workers are civil service workers. Civil service workers usually have permanent jobs.

Today only the top government jobs are awarded to **political appointees.** Political appointees are people chosen by the president. People in these jobs usually leave office when the president does.

/ / / / / / / / / / / / / Glue Foldable here / / / / / / / / / / / / / /

Check for Understanding

Name two government agencies that are part of the Executive Office of the President.

1. ______________________

2. ______________________

Name two ways that the work of the president's cabinet affects how the government runs.

3. ______________________

4. ______________________

NAME _________________________ DATE _____________ CLASS ___________

networks

The Judicial Branch

Lesson 1: Federal Courts

ESSENTIAL QUESTION

How can governments ensure citizens are treated fairly?

GUIDING QUESTIONS

1. ***What is the role of the federal courts?***
2. ***What kinds of cases are heard in federal courts?***

Terms to Know

dual court system a system with both federal and state courts
presume to assume to be true without proof
jurisdiction the authority to hear and decide a case
exclusive jurisdiction authority of federal courts alone to hear and decide cases
concurrent jurisdiction authority of both federal and state courts to hear and decide cases

What Do You Know?

In the first column, answer the questions based on what you know before you study. After this lesson, complete the last column.

Now...		Later...
	What do the federal courts do?	
	What kinds of cases do they try?	

Role of the Federal Courts

The judicial branch is the third branch of the federal government. The branch's two main jobs are to make sure the laws are enforced fairly and to interpret the law. Courts hear two kinds of cases, criminal and civil.

In criminal cases, people accused of crimes appear in court for trial. In a criminal trial, witnesses present evidence. A jury or judge decides whether the accused person is innocent or guilty.

In civil cases, courts use the law to settle civil disputes. In a civil dispute, both sides come before a court. Each side lays out its view. The court applies the law to the facts that have been presented. Then it decides in favor of one side or the other. A civil dispute is a conflict between:

- two private parties (people, companies, or organizations)
- a private party and the government
- the U.S. government and a state or local government

Federal courts decide criminal and civil cases that involve federal laws.

Identifying

1. What are the two main jobs of the judicial branch?

____

____

Listing

2. A civil dispute is a conflict between two sides who feel harmed. List two types.

____

____

Lesson 1: Federal Courts, *Continued*

Reading Check

3. Why did the Framers of the Constitution create a federal judiciary?

____

____

Contrasting

4. What was the difference between the types of cases heard by district and circuit courts?

____

____

Vocabulary

5. What is a *dual court system*?

____

____

____

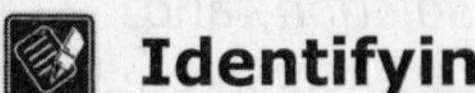

Mark the Text

6. Underline the sentence that states the main goal of the federal courts.

Identifying

7. Fill in the diagram to show the three levels of the federal courts.

The power of the federal courts comes from the Constitution. Under the Articles of Confederation, the country had no national court system. Each state had its own laws and courts. Citizens were not guaranteed equal justice in all the states. To solve these problems the Founders decided to create a federal judiciary. Article III of the Constitution created a national Supreme Court. It gave Congress the power to set up a system of lower courts.

Congress set up two kinds of lower federal courts: district courts and circuit courts. District courts heard minor civil and criminal cases. They served as the trial courts for specific geographic areas. Circuit courts took more serious cases and heard appeals from the district courts. An appeal is when a person asks a higher court to review a case. In 1891, Congress made circuit courts solely courts of appeals.

The district courts at the lower level are trial courts. The circuit courts in the middle are appeals courts. The Supreme Court, the court of final appeal, is at the top.

Each state also has laws and a court system. The state courts and federal courts exist side by side. This gives our country a **dual court system.** The federal courts get their powers from laws passed by Congress. The state courts get their powers from state constitutions and laws.

The federal courts make sure citizens in every state are treated the same. Each person is **presumed,** or thought to be, innocent until proven guilty. To make sure all citizens have equal justice, the Constitution gives every accused person the right to a public trial. If the accused cannot pay for a lawyer, the court will provide one.

U.S. Courts

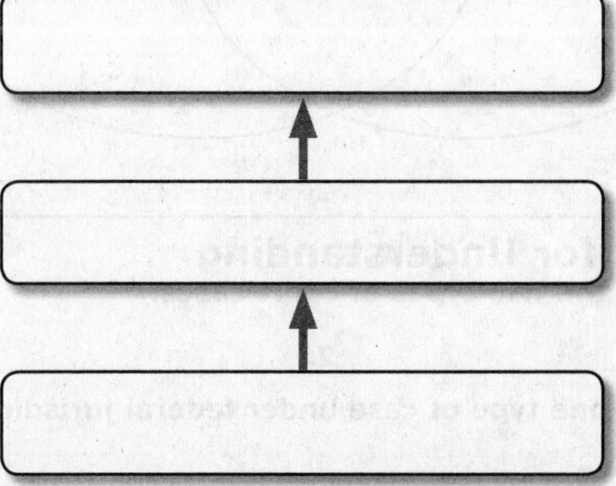

Federal Court Jurisdiction

Most court cases involve state laws and are tried in state courts. The Constitution gives federal courts the power to hear certain kinds of cases, however. The authority to hear and decide a case is called **jurisdiction.** Federal courts have jurisdiction in cases that have to do with the following:

- the Constitution and federal laws
- disputes between the states
- disputes between citizens of different states
- disputes that involve the federal government
- accidents or crimes that happen at sea
- disputes between U.S. and foreign governments

In most of these areas, federal courts have **exclusive jurisdiction.** Only federal courts can decide on these cases. Other cases are under the state court jurisdiction.

In some cases, both federal and state courts have jurisdiction. This is called **concurrent jurisdiction.** For example, this occurs when a crime breaks both federal and state laws. When this happens, either court may hold a trial.

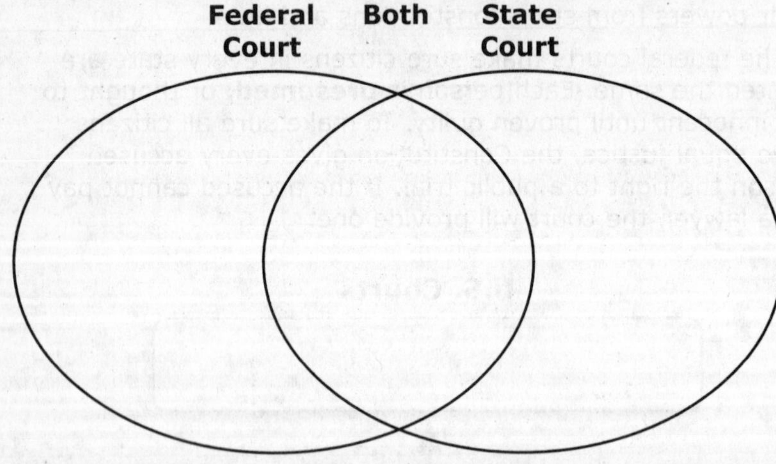

/ / / / / / / / / / / / / / Glue Foldable here / / / / / / / / / / / / / /

Check for Understanding

Name the two types of court cases.

1. ______________ **2.** ______________

Name one type of case under federal jurisdiction.

3. ______________

Vocabulary

8. What is *jurisdiction*?

____

Reading Check

9. What are two examples of cases where the federal courts would have exclusive jurisdiction?

____

Mark the Text

10. Fill in the diagram. List a federal court case, a state court case, and a case that might be heard in both.

FOLDABLES®

11. Place a three-tab Foldable along the line. Label the tabs *Federal Exclusive Jurisdiction*, *Concurrent Jurisdiction*, and *State Exclusive Jurisdiction*. Write facts about each on the reverse tabs.

Lesson 2: The Federal Court System

ESSENTIAL QUESTIONS

How can governments ensure citizens are treated fairly?
Why do people create, structure, and change governments?

GUIDING QUESTIONS

1. ***How are the federal courts organized?***
2. ***What is the selection process for federal judges?***

Terms to Know

original jurisdiction the authority to hear cases for the first time
appellate jurisdiction the authority to hear a case appealed from a lower court
ruling an official decision
opinion a detailed explanation of the legal thinking behind a court's decision in a case
precedent a legal ruling that is used as a basis for a decision in a later, similar case
litigant a person engaged in a lawsuit
consent approval
tenure the right to hold an office once a person is confirmed
preliminary coming before the main part; introductory
subpoena a court order requiring someone to appear in court

What Do You Know?

In the first column, answer the questions based on what you know before you study. After this lesson, complete the last column.

Now...		Later...
	What courts are in the federal court system?	
	How are federal judges picked?	

? Contrasting

1. How does jurisdiction differ between district courts and courts of appeals?

____
____
____
____

The Lower Courts

You have learned that the federal court system has three levels. District courts are at the lowest level. These courts have what is called **original jurisdiction.** This is the authority to hear cases for the first time. Most federal cases begin in a U.S. district court.

There are 94 district courts. Every state has at least one. District courts hold both civil and criminal trials. Juries listen to witnesses and decide guilt or innocence based on evidence.

People who lose a case in district court may appeal it to a federal appeals court. This means they can ask a higher court to review and possibly change the result of the trial.

The authority to review the fairness of a case appealed from a lower court is called **appellate** (uh•PEH•luht) **jurisdiction.**

People appeal cases for different reasons. Usually a lawyer thinks that a district court judge has made a mistake. Other times, new evidence becomes available that might have changed the original outcome of the trial.

There are 12 federal appeals courts. Each court has jurisdiction over an area called a circuit. These courts are also called circuit courts of appeals. There is also a thirteenth appeals court. It is called the Court of Appeals for the Federal Circuit. It has nationwide jurisdiction to hear special cases. These cases include patent law, international trade, and other civil cases of the U.S. government.

Appeals courts do not have trials. Judges make the decisions. Their decisions are called **rulings.** Three or more judges review each case. They listen to the lawyers' arguments. Then they meet and vote on how to rule. They can choose to do the following:

- uphold, or keep the original decision made by the district court
- reverse the district court's decision
- remand the case

To remand the case means to send the case back to the lower court to be tried again.

Appeals court judges do not decide guilt or innocence. Rather, they rule only on whether the trial was fair. Appeals court rulings may be appealed only to the Supreme Court.

When an appeals court makes a ruling, one judge writes an opinion for the court. The **opinion** explains the legal thinking behind the court's decision. The opinion is also an example to be followed by other judges. Such an example is called a **precedent.** A precedent does not have the force of law, but it is a powerful legal argument.

Since early in the nation's history, the federal courts have followed certain guiding ideas, or principles. One is that judges or justices cannot decide a question of law by seeking out a lawsuit. They have to wait for litigants to file lawsuits. **Litigants** are people involved in a lawsuit. The principle of precedent is another guiding idea.

Federal Judges

Federal judges make the final decisions in the federal court system. There are more than 650 federal judges in the district courts. Each district court has at least two judges.

Reading Check

2. What kinds of rulings do appeals courts make?

______

______

______

______

Mark the Text

3. Underline the text that defines an *opinion.*

Paraphrasing

4. In your own words, explain why a precedent is important.

______

______

______

______

______

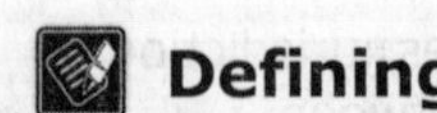

5. What is a lawsuit?

______

______

______

Lesson 2: The Federal Court System, *Continued*

Explaining

6. How are federal judges chosen?

____

____

Analyzing

7. Why do you think the Senate must give consent to presidential appointments?

____

Reading Check

8. What are the duties of a magistrate judge?

____

____

FOLDABLES®

9. Place a one-tab Foldable on the line. Label the anchor *Federal Judge*. Write two sentences that summarize facts about federal judges.

Each appeals court may have between 6 and 28 judges. The U.S. Supreme Court has nine judges, called justices.

The Constitution gives the president the power to appoint federal judges. However, the Senate must give **consent,** or approval, to all appointments. This limits the president's power. When presidents appoint judges to district courts, they follow a practice called senatorial courtesy. This means they tell the senators from the nominee's home state about their choice first. If the senators do not like the nominee, the president will usually choose a different person.

Federal judges have their jobs for life. They can be removed only through a process called impeachment. This kind of job security is called **tenure.** Judges who have tenure cannot be fired. This keeps them from being pressured when they have to make difficult decisions.

District courts also have magistrate judges who help judges with the workload. They do much of the routine work. They issue search and arrest warrants. They hear **preliminary,** or introductory, evidence to decide whether a case should be tried. They may also try minor cases.

Each district court has a U.S. attorney. These lawyers prosecute people accused of breaking federal laws. They also represent the United States in civil cases. They are appointed by the president and approved by the Senate.

Each district also has a U.S. marshal. Marshals keep order in the court. They make arrests and take convicted people to prison. They also serve, or deliver, subpoenas. A **subpoena** (suh•PEE•nuh) is a court order requiring someone to appear in court.

/ / / / / / / / / / / / / Glue Foldable here / / / / / / / / / / / / / /

Check for Understanding

List the three levels of federal courts.

1. ______________ 2. ______________

3. ______________

Name the two steps every person must go through before becoming a federal judge.

4. ______________

5. ______________

The Judicial Branch

Lesson 3: The Supreme Court

ESSENTIAL QUESTION

How can governments ensure citizens are treated fairly?

GUIDING QUESTIONS

1. ***What is the jurisdiction of the Supreme Court?***
2. ***What powers are given to the Supreme Court?***

Terms to Know

judicial review the power to review any federal, state, or local law or action to see if it is constitutional

constitutional allowed by the U.S. Constitution

nullify to cancel

challenge to object to a decision

What Do You Know?

In the first column, answer the questions based on what you know before you study. After this lesson, complete the last column.

Now...		Later...
	What cases does the Supreme Court hear?	
	What kind of powers does the Supreme Court have?	

Jurisdiction and Duties

The United States Supreme Court is the highest court in the land. All other courts must follow its decisions. The Supreme Court has eight justices and one chief justice. The justices' main job is to decide whether laws are allowed under the U.S. Constitution. The Supreme Court is also the final authority in all cases involving the Constitution, acts of Congress, and treaties with other countries.

The Supreme Court has original jurisdiction in only two kinds of cases. It can hear cases that involve diplomats from other countries. It can also hear cases that involve disputes between states. In all other cases, the Supreme Court hears appeals from lower courts.

Each year thousands of cases are appealed to the Supreme Court. The justices choose the ones they will hear. After deciding a case, the Court issues a written opinion. When the Court refuses to hear a case the decision of the lower court stands.

The Constitution does not list any specific requirements for a Supreme Court justice. Before joining the Court, many justices were lawyers, educators, or lower court judges. Supreme Court justices have their jobs for life.

Identifying

1. What kinds of cases does the Supreme Court mainly hear?

____

Reading Check

2. What happens if the Supreme Court refuses to hear a case?

____

____

____

Lesson 3: The Supreme Court, *Continued*

FOLDABLES

3. Place a one-tab on top of a two-tab Foldable to create a book. Place the book on the line. Title the one-tab *The Supreme Court* and explain the job of the Supreme Court. Then label the top tab of the two-tab Foldable *Judicial Review* and the bottom tab *Opinion*. Explain each on the reverse.

Identifying

4. What branch of government organized the federal courts?

____

Explaining

5. What does it mean to say that a law is unconstitutional?

____

Describing

6. In the diagram, write how each law or decision contributed to the Supreme Court's power of judicial review.

Glue Foldable here

Powers and Limits

The Constitution gave Congress the power to decide how the Supreme Court should be organized and what its powers should be. Congress set the number of justices at nine.

A key power of the Supreme Court is the power of **judicial review.** This is the power to review any federal, state, or local law or action to see if it is constitutional. **Constitutional** means allowed by the Constitution. The Court may decide that a law or action is unconstitutional. That is, the law or action goes against what is written in the Constitution. In that case the Court has the power to **nullify,** or cancel, that law or action.

The Constitution did not give the Supreme Court the power of judicial review. That power came from the Judiciary Act of 1789, which gave the Supreme Court the power of judicial review over the acts of state governments. Later, the case of *Marbury* v. *Madison* in 1803 established the Court's power of judicial review over laws passed by Congress. This power gives the court a check on the other two branches of government.

The other branches check the Supreme Court's power. Congress can get around a ruling by passing a new law. It can change a law that has been ruled unconstitutional. Congress and the states can also try to undo Court rulings by amending the Constitution.

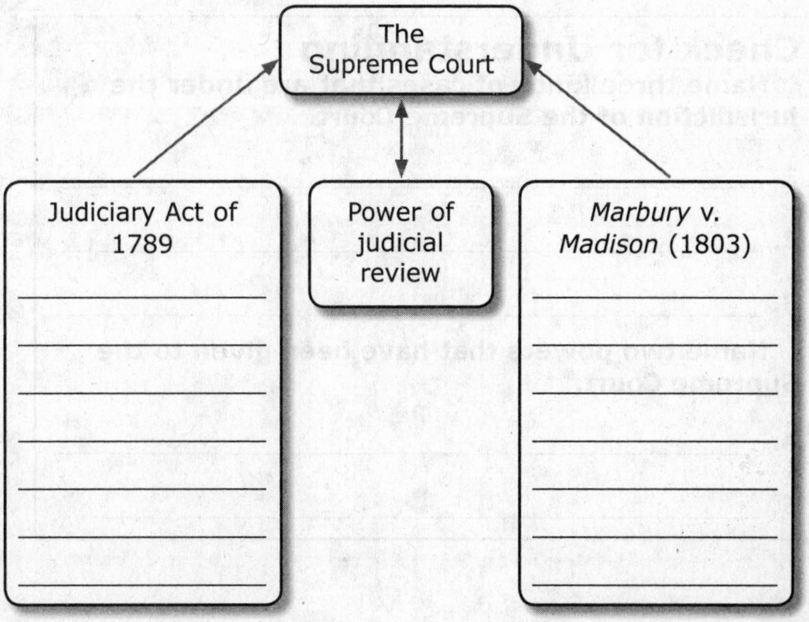

The Supreme Court

Judiciary Act of 1789	Power of judicial review	*Marbury* v. *Madison* (1803)
______________________		______________________

Lesson 3: The Supreme Court, *Continued*

The Supreme Court's power is limited in other ways as well. The Court can only hear and rule on cases that come to it through the lower courts. A person cannot simply ask the Supreme Court to decide if a law is constitutional. The Court will only rule on a law that has been **challenged,** or objected to, on appeal. It can only take cases that concern a federal question.

The Supreme Court does not have the power to enforce its rulings. It relies on the executive branch and on the states to do this. The executive branch usually enforces Supreme Court rulings, but not always. In 1832, the Supreme Court ruled in *Worcester* v. *Georgia* that the state of Georgia had to stop ignoring federal land treaties with the Cherokee Nation. President Andrew Jackson refused to enforce the ruling. Most people agreed with the president. As a result, he felt no pressure to take action.

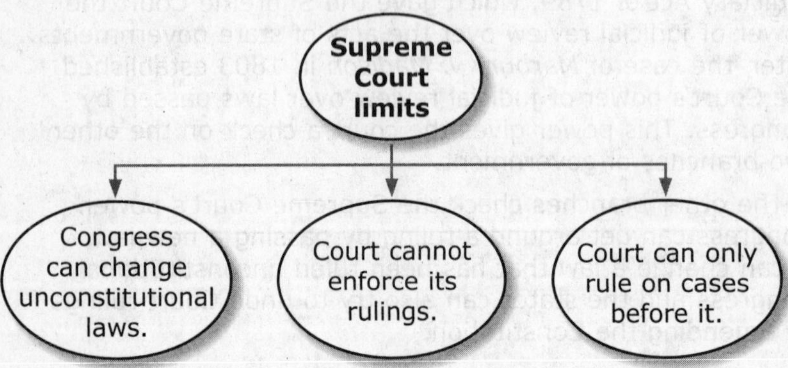

Check for Understanding

Name three kinds of cases that are under the jurisdiction of the Supreme Court.

1. ______________________

2. ______________________

3. ______________________

Name two powers that have been given to the Supreme Court.

4. ______________________

5. ______________________

Glue Foldable here

Explaining

7. What can Congress do if the Supreme Court rules a law unconstitutional?

____

Describing

8. How does the Supreme Court depend on the other branches?

____

Reading Check

9. How is judicial review a part of our federal system of government?

____

FOLDABLES®

10. Place a three-tab Foldable on the line. Write *U.S. Supreme Court* on the anchor. Label the tabs *Kinds of Cases, Powers,* and *Limits*. Describe each on the reverse.

NAME ______________________ DATE ______________ CLASS __________

networks

The Judicial Branch

Lesson 4: Supreme Court Procedures and Decisions

ESSENTIAL QUESTION

How can governments ensure citizens are treated fairly?

GUIDING QUESTIONS

1. ***What kinds of cases does the Supreme Court decide to hear?***
2. ***What factors affect the Court's decisions?***

Terms to Know

writ of certiorari an order from a higher court to see the records from a lower court case

docket a court's calendar

caseload the number of cases handled in a court term

brief a written document explaining one side of a case

concurring opinion a statement written by a justice who votes with the majority but for different reasons

dissenting opinion a statement written by a justice who disagrees with the majority opinion

unanimous opinion a ruling on which all the justices agree

draft to write a document in its first form

stare decisis the practice of using earlier rulings as a basis for deciding cases

What Do You Know?

In the first column, answer the questions based on what you know before you study. After this lesson, complete the last column.

Now...		Later...
	Why is the Supreme Court important to our legal system?	
	How does the Supreme Court make its decisions?	

Reading Check

1. How do the justices decide which cases to hear? Underline three factors that help their decisions.

____

____

Court Procedures

The Supreme Court meets each year for about nine months. Each term begins the first Monday in October and ends in the summer. So, the 2012 term began in October 2012. Sometimes special sessions are called to handle a serious matter.

The Supreme Court carefully chooses the cases it will hear. The justices look for cases that raise constitutional questions. These are questions about issues such as freedom of speech, equal protection of the laws, and the right to a fair trial. The justices also look for cases that deal with real people and events. They look for cases that affect the whole country, rather than one person or group.

Lesson 4: Supreme Court Procedures and Decisions, *Continued*

Almost all cases reach the Supreme Court on appeal from a lower court. Most appeals come to the Court as a petition, or request, for a writ of certiorari. A **writ of certiorari** (SUHR•sheeuh•REHR•ee) orders a lower court to send its case records to the Supreme Court for review.

The justices receive about 10,000 petitions, or requests, for writ of certiorari each term. Of these, the Court accepts 75 to 80 cases. The Court accepts a case when four of the nine justices agree to do so. The accepted cases go on the Court **docket,** or calendar of cases to be heard. The number of cases handled in a period of time is called the **caseload.**

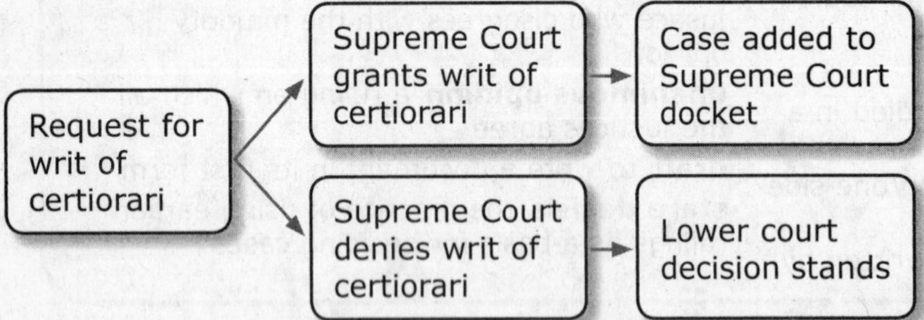

How the Court's Rulings Are Made

First, the lawyers for each side in a case write a brief. A **brief** is a written document that explains one side's position, or point of view, on the case. The two parties study each other's briefs and then give a second brief to the Court. The second brief is shorter and answers the arguments made in the first brief by the other side.

The justices study the briefs and ask questions. Next, each side is given 30 minutes to present oral arguments before the Court. The justices then meet to make decisions about the cases. The meetings are secret. No official records are kept. At least six justices must be present to vote on a ruling. A majority vote decides a case.

When the Court has reached a decision, one justice writes the opinion for the majority. The opinion states the facts of the case and gives the ruling. It explains the reasoning that led to the decision. The Court's written opinion sets a precedent for the lower courts to follow.

Sometimes a justice agrees with the majority decision but for different reasons. They write a **concurring opinion.** Justices might also disagree with the majority decision. They write a **dissenting opinion.** Sometimes all the justices vote the same way. Then the Court issues a **unanimous opinion.** These decisions have special force.

Examining Details

2. Study the diagram. What is the outcome when a request for a writ of certiorari is denied?

____

Explaining

3. How is the Court's caseload determined?

____

____

Classifying

4. Explain what each type of opinion expresses.

majority opinion

____

____

dissenting opinion

____

____

concurring opinion

____

____

unanimous opinion

____

____

Lesson 4: Supreme Court Procedures and Decisions, *Continued*

Vocabulary

5. Write a sentence using the vocabulary word *drafted* in the same context as the text.

____

____

____

____

____

Mark the Text

6. Study the table. Circle the cases that related to public school students.

Making Connections

7. Which landmark Supreme Court case do you think had the greatest impact on everyday life in the United States? Explain your answer.

____

____

____

____

____

____

After the opinions are **drafted,** or written in their first form, the justices review it. They comment on the draft. The justice writing the opinion takes their comments into account as he or she revises the opinion. Once the draft is final the Court announces its decision.

Landmark Supreme Court Decisions
***Marbury* v. *Madison* (1803)** established the Supreme Court's power of judicial review.
***Plessy* v. *Ferguson* (1896)** upheld the "separate but equal" doctrine of public segregation.
***Brown* v. *Board of Education* (1954)** overturned *Plessy* v. *Ferguson* and started public school integration.
***Gideon* v. *Wainwright* (1963)** said that a person accused of a major crime had the right to a lawyer.
***Miranda* v. *Arizona* (1966)** ruled that suspects must be informed of their rights before questioning.
***Tinker* v. *Des Moines* (1969)** ruled that freedom of speech applies to students in public schools.
***United States* v. *Nixon* (1974)** ruled that the president cannot use executive privilege to withhold evidence.
***Hazelwood* v. *Kuhlmeier* (1988)** said that public school officials may impose some limits on student newspapers.
***Bush* v. *Gore* (2000)** ruled that Florida's recount of presidential votes violated the Fourteenth Amendment.

Lesson 4: Supreme Court Procedures and Decisions, *Continued*

The justices consider many factors when deciding a case. One important factor is precedent. Justices are guided by a principle called **stare decisis** (STEHR•ee• dih•SY•suhs). In Latin this means "let the decision stand." In other words, follow precedent.

However, the law must also be able to change with the times. The Supreme Court has the power to overturn outdated decisions. For example, in *Brown* v. *Board of Education*, the Court overturned an earlier decision that supported segregation laws. In that case, the Supreme Court changed its interpretation of the law to reflect changes in society.

Check for Understanding

Name three kinds of cases that Supreme Court justices could choose to hear.

1. ____________________

2. ____________________

3. ____________________

Name three types of written opinions that Supreme Court justices can issue.

4. ____________________

5. ____________________

6. ____________________

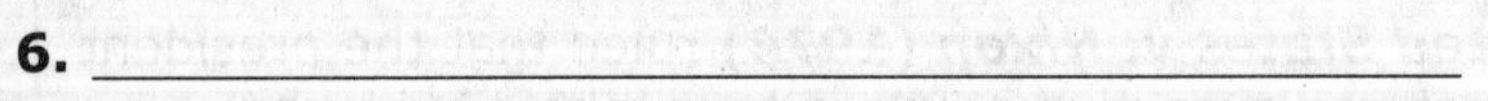

Glue Foldable here

Paraphrasing

8. In your own words, why is *stare decisis* important?

____

____

Reading Check

9. What role do changing social conditions play in court rulings?

____

____

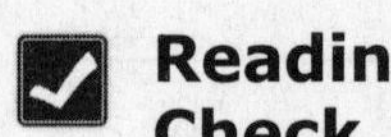

10. Place a two-tab Foldable on the line. Write *Supreme Court Justices* on the anchor. Label the tabs *Types of cases heard* and *Types of written opinions.* List them on the reverse.

Political Parties

Lesson 1: History of Political Parties

ESSENTIAL QUESTION

How do citizens, both individually and collectively, influence government policy?

GUIDING QUESTIONS

1. ***Why did political parties develop in the United States?***
2. ***What is the importance of third parties in American politics?***
3. ***How do America's major modern political parties differ?***

Terms to Know

political party a group of voters with common interests who want to influence decision making in government by electing the party's candidates to public office

two-party system a system of government in which two political parties try to win power

stress to give special importance to

third party a political party that challenges the two major parties

promote to advance a cause or idea

platform a series of statements that state a party's beliefs and positions on election issues

What Do You Know?

In the first column, answer the questions based on what you know before you study. After this lesson, complete the last column.

Now...		Later...
	Why do we need political parties?	
	How are the political parties different?	

Identifying

1. What are the names of the two major parties in the United States today?

____

____

Mark the Text

2. Underline in the text the reason why political parties formed.

Growth of American Parties

A **political party** is a group of people with general common interests about government. They work together to help the candidates they support win elections. They also try to help shape government policy. The United States has a **two-party system.** The names and makeup of the two main parties have changed over the years. Today's major parties are the Democratic and the Republican parties.

The Constitution did not mention political parties. Still, political parties have been around for a long time. Not all of the Founders wanted them, however. They were afraid that political parties would divide and weaken the new nation. Despite this, by the late 1790s, political parties formed because people had different ideas about what the government should do.

Lesson 1: History of Political Parties, *Continued*

Formation of Early Political Parties

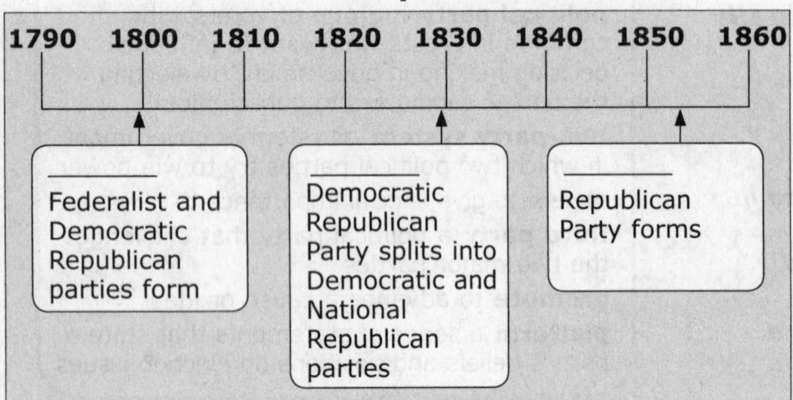

The first political parties formed in the late 1790s. Alexander Hamilton was the Secretary of the Treasury. He thought that the national government should have most of the power. He believed that the national government needed to be strong to protect people's rights. People who agreed with Hamilton's ideas formed the Federalist Party.

Thomas Jefferson was the Secretary of State. He thought that state governments should have most of the power in order to protect people's rights. Those who agreed with Jefferson's ideas formed the Democratic-Republican Party. Slowly Jefferson's party grew stronger and Hamilton's party grew weaker. Soon, the Federalist Party was gone.

In 1828, the Democratic-Republicans split into two parties. People who supported Andrew Jackson for president called themselves the Democratic Party. They used that name because they wanted to **stress** their connection to the common people. Those who opposed Jackson were called the National Republicans. The National Republican Party did not last long.

The Whig Party was the main competition of the Democratic Party. The Whigs and the Democrats were the two major parties in the United States until the 1850s. They tried to avoid the issue of slavery. The Whig Party broke up when slavery became a major political issue.

In 1854, people who were against slavery got together to form a new party. They named it the Republican Party. Some Republicans believed slavery should be abolished in Southern states. Others did not agree, but they did believe that slavery should not spread to the territories controlled by the U.S. government. Since the late 1850s, the Republicans and the Democrats have been the nation's major parties.

Sequencing

3. Use the time line to help you see how America's early political parties developed. As you read the material, place the correct dates next to the events shown on the time line.

Listing

4. What were the two major American political parties until the 1850s?

____

____

Reading Check

5. How did Federalists view the power of the national government?

____

____

____

Identifying

6. Who formed the Republican party?

____

____

Lesson 1: History of Political Parties, *Continued*

Vocabulary

7. What are *third parties*?

Comparing

8. Study the chart. What do the Prohibitionist Party and the Green Party have in common?

Identifying

9. In the chart, who organized the Populist Party? Why?

Listing

10. List three reasons why third parties do not win national elections.

Third Parties

Sometimes small parties form to compete with the Democratic and Republican parties. These parties are called **third parties.** They usually do not get much support from voters, but they often make people aware of special issues. Some of those issues later become important to the major parties. Third parties form for many reasons.

Third parties form:

- to **promote** ideas that are new or unpopular with the major parties.
- to support a single issue.
- to promote their beliefs about government.
- to support an independent candidate.

The following chart shows roles third parties have played.

Name of Party	Reason	Influence on America
Populist Party Year - 1892	promote ideas	Organized by farmers and laborers who wanted the direct election of senators and eight-hour work day
Progressive Party Year - 1952	promote ideas	Wanted a direct primary election to give people more power in selecting general election candidates
Prohibitionist Party Year - 1920	single issue	Wanted to outlaw the sale of alcohol
Communist Party USA Year - 1919	beliefs	Wants more government and worker ownership of all resources and businesses
Tea Party Year - 2009	beliefs	Opposes Democrats and Republicans; does not want any government control over business
Green Party Year - 2000	single issue	Wants more attention put on the environment

Third parties usually lose major elections. There are many reasons for this. Candidates from the major parties get their names put on the general election ballot automatically. Third-party candidates have to get on the ballot by petition. A petition is a long process of collecting a large number of signatures from voters.

Lesson 1: History of Political Parties, *Continued*

Third parties usually do not have very much money. They usually do not have strong networks. Networks are groups of people who work together. The major parties have strong local, state, and national networks.

Most countries have political parties, but not two-party systems. Many democracies have multiparty systems. Countries with multiparty systems might have three or more major parties competing for power. Canada has three major parties. Germany has five major parties. Israel has more than 20 major parties. The People's Republic of China only has one political party.

Party Differences

The Democrats and the Republicans both want to win as many elections as they can. They avoid taking extreme positions on most issues because most Americans are political moderates and generally agree on many social and political issues. So the parties also take moderate positions. *Moderate* means being opposed to major social changes or making changes too quickly. One major difference between the two parties is over how much the government should be involved in people's lives. Democrats think that government should help fix society's problems. Republicans think that government should not get involved in fixing those problems. Both parties think that economic growth will give poor people a better chance to find jobs on their own.

One way to find out what each party believes about an issue is to read the party **platform.** The platform is written for each party's national convention. The convention is held every four years. The platform gives the party's positions on important issues. It also states the party's basic beliefs. Each party also chooses its candidates for president and vice president at the convention.

/ / / / / / / / / / / / / Glue Foldable here / / / / / / / / / / / / / /

Check for Understanding

List the two political parties that developed in America in the 1790s.

1. _______________ 2. _______________

Name two reasons people form third parties.

3. _______________

4. _______________

Reading Check

11. Name three types of third parties and explain why they form.

____

____

____

Mark the Text

12. Underline the text that describes a platform.

Reading Check

13. Why do the two major parties often seem similar?

____

____

____

14. Place a three-tab Foldable along the line. Label the tabs *Democrats*, *Republicans*, and *Third Parties*. List facts about each on the reverse tabs.

Political Parties

Lesson 2: Political Parties Today

ESSENTIAL QUESTION

How do citizens, both individually and collectively, influence government policy?

GUIDING QUESTIONS

1. ***How are political parties organized?***
2. ***How do political parties nominate candidates?***
3. ***What other roles do political parties play?***

Terms to Know

national committee Representatives from the 50 state party organiztions who run a political party

caucus meeting of political party members to conduct party business

precinct a geographic area that contains a specific number of voters

adjacent located next to

political machine a strong party organization that controls political decisons

direct primary election in which voters choose candidates to run in a general election

closed primary election in which only members of a political party can vote

open primary election in which voters do not have to state their party preference

plurality the most votes among those running for office

majority a number that is more than 50% of the total

What Do You Know?

In the first column, answer the questions based on what you know before you study. After this lesson, complete the last column.

Now...		Later...
	How do political parties work?	
	How do candidates get nominated?	

Explaining

1. Who makes up a national committee?

____

____

____

Organization of Political Parties

Political parties have local, state, and national organizations. A **national committee** is in charge of each party. This committee includes people from every state. These people are called representatives, or delegates. The committee's most important job is to organize the national convention. The convention happens once every four years. Delegates at the convention choose the party's candidates for president and vice president. The delegates to the convention are chosen through presidential primary elections or by **caucuses** (KAW•kuhs•uhz). Caucuses are special meetings of state and local party organizations.

Lesson 2: Political Parties Today, *Continued*

The convention is an important time to build party unity. It also starts the election campaign.

The major parties also have campaign committees for the candidates running for Congress. The committees help raise money for the candidates and give them advice and support.

Each party also has state and local organizations. They choose and help candidates run for state and local offices. They also support their party's candidates for president and vice president. Cities and counties are divided into small districts, or areas, called **precincts** (PREE•sihngts). Precincts are areas that have a certain number of voters. Therefore, a precinct might be a whole town or a group of **adjacent** neighborhoods in a larger city. Everyone in a precinct votes at the same place. County committees are the largest political units within the state. They are headed by a county chairperson. This person usually has a great deal of political power.

Precincts appoint a captain. The captains build support for the party at the local level. Captains also organize volunteers and register voters. Local leaders also make sure party members vote on Election Day.

Glue Foldable here

Organization of Political Parties

Sometimes a local party organization becomes too strong and it wins almost every election. Then it is called a **political machine.** In the late 1800s and early 1900s, political machines ran many cities. At that time, political machines gave immigrants and poor people food and fuel and helped them find jobs. The political machines gained votes by doing this. Unfortunately, some members of political machines hurt the cities. One example of a political machine is Tammany Hall in New York City. Tammany Hall was led by William "Boss" Tweed. They cheated the city by taking bribes (illegal money payments) from people doing business with the city. Today, cities avoid political machines.

Selecting Party Candidates

Political parties are important in the government. Political parties are active all the time, but their busiest time is during an election. They nominate, or choose, the candidates who run for public office. Parties generally use primary elections to nominate candidates for office.

Vocabulary

2. Define the terms:
caucus

____

precinct

____

FOLDABLES®

3. Place a two-tab Foldable along the line. Write *Political Party Organizations* on the anchor tab. Label the tabs *National* and *State, County, Local*. On the reverse tabs describe what the organizations do.

Reading Check

4. How do higher-level party leaders depend on precinct leaders?

____

____

Critical Thinking

5. Why could a political machine in a county be dangerous?

____

____

Lesson 2: Political Parties Today, *Continued*

Defining

6. What does it mean to nominate someone to a political office?

____

____

Prior Knowledge

7. What are the two major political parties in the United States?

____

____

Reading Check

8. What is the difference between an open and a closed primary?

____

____

____

Listing

9. What are two ways that political parties help government?

____

____

Closed Primary
Voters have to choose a party in order to vote for that party's nominees.

Open Primary
Voters do not need to choose a party in order to vote for the party's nominees.

Petition
Candidates who are not members of either major party make a petition. They must have a certain number of voter signatures to get their name on the general election ballot.

GENERAL ELECTION BALLOT

- **John Diaz** Republican Party
- **Janet Jones** Democratic Party
- **Jackie Smith** Green Party

The chart above describes the different ways that candidates get on the ballot for the general election.

The candidate who wins the primary is the one who gets a **plurality,** or the most votes. A candidate with the most votes wins even if his or her share is less than 50 percent of the total votes.

In a few states, the winner must have a **majority.** This means the winner must get more than 50 percent of the total votes. Sometimes no candidate gets a majority. Then the party holds another primary called a *runoff*. The winner becomes the party's candidate in the general election.

Most offices have only one officeholder; for example, there is only one mayor in a city. Sometimes more than one type of position is vacant, or empty, in the same election. For example, a city might have many council members. In this case, the party can nominate more than one candidate. The party chooses the top vote-getters in the primary.

Other Political Party Functions

Political parties do more than get candidates elected. They help citizens practice self-government. This means they help people communicate with the government. Political parties also make sure government listens to the people.

Lesson 2: Political Parties Today, *Continued*

Government
Political parties tell government about citizens' concerns.

Political parties

Citizens
Political parties tell citizens what the issues are and what government is doing.

Political parties also:

- **support candidates.** They help raise money for the campaigns. They also register citizens to vote and make sure supporters get to the polls on Election Day.
- **run different parts of the government.** Congress and most state legislatures are organized by party. Leaders make sure that all the lawmakers in the party support the party position when making laws.
- **link different parts of the government.** Political parties make it easier for different levels of government to work together. Senators, governors, and others who are members of a major party usually know each other. This makes it easier for them to work together to solve problems.
- **act as a watchdog for citizens.** Between elections one party is out of power. This is the party that lost the elections. It is often called the opposition party. The opposition party acts as a watchdog over the party in power. It gives a voice to people who disagree with the party in power. This makes sure the party in power listens to all views.

/ / / / / / / / / / / / Glue Foldable here / / / / / / / / / / / /

Check for Understanding

Name three ways that national political parties are broken down into smaller groups.

1. ____________ 2. ____________

3. ____________

List two ways that a candidate can be nominated to run for office.

4. ____________

5. ____________

Explaining

10. What do political parties do to help people vote?

____

Critical Thinking

11. Why do you think it is important for political parties to act as watchdogs?

____

____

Reading Check

12. How do political parties help the American people practice self-government?

____

____

13. Place a one-tab Foldable on the line. Write *The Importance of Political Parties* on the front. On the back, write a paragraph about why political parties are important.

NAME ______________________ DATE ____________ CLASS ________

Voting and Elections

Lesson 1: Who Can Vote?

ESSENTIAL QUESTION

What are the rights and responsibilities of citizens?

GUIDING QUESTIONS

1. ***What are the requirements to vote?***
2. ***What steps must you follow to vote?***
3. ***Why is it important to vote?***

Terms to Know

principle basic belief
suffrage the right to vote
register to sign up to vote
polling place location where a person goes to vote
ballot a list of candidates who are running for each office
voter turnout rate the percentage of people allowed to vote who actually do vote
apathy a lack of interest

What Do You Know?

In the first column, answer the questions based on what you know before you study. After this lesson, complete the last column.

Now...		Later...
	How do you vote?	
	Why does voting matter?	

Prior Knowledge

1. What is an amendment?

____

Reading Check

2. Which amendment to the Constitution gave suffrage to women?

____

Qualifying to Vote

For most of history, countries were ruled by kings and queens. People did not have a say in how they were governed. Even in the United States, **suffrage,** or the right to vote, was limited to white men who owned land. The **principle,** or basic belief, that "all men are created equal" had not yet been achieved. Individuals and the government worked for many years to give more people the right to vote. Over time, all American citizens over the age of eighteen were granted the right to vote.

Most voting rights in the United States were granted through amendments to the Constitution. The graphic organizer below shows these amendments.

15th Amendment Ratified in 1870; Allowed African Americans to vote → **19th Amendment** Ratified in 1920; Allowed women to vote → **26th Amendment** Ratified in 1971; Lowered voting age to 18

Voting and Elections

Lesson 1: Who Can Vote?, *continued*

Even after the Fifteenth Amendment passed, some states did not let African Americans vote. This lasted for another hundred years. Women who fought for the right to vote were called suffragists. Famous suffragists included Alice Paul and Susan B. Anthony.

Millions of people are eligible, or allowed, to vote in the nation today. To be eligible to vote, a citizen must

- be 18 years old and
- be a U.S. citizen.

Some people are not eligible to vote. People who have committed serious crimes are not able to vote while in prison. Also, people who suffer from certain mental illnesses may lose their eligibility to vote. Most citizens in the United States can vote. Each time you vote, you are helping to run your government.

Steps in the Voting Process

Voting requires three steps. First you must **register** to vote. To register means to sign up. Most states require voters to register 25 days before the election. Some let you register on Election Day. Registering to vote is easy. You just fill out a form with your name, address, and age. You might also list your political party. You will need to show your driver's license, birth certificate, or another valid form of identification to prove your age and citizenship.

There are many ways you can register to vote, including

- using the mail,
- using the Web,
- visiting the library,
- visiting government offices, and
- visiting agencies that serve people with disabilities.

In addition, the National Voter Registration Act says that people are allowed to register to vote when they renew their driver's licenses. Some people call this the "Motor Voter" law.

After you register, your second step is to prepare to vote. You must be informed about current issues because your vote will affect the lives of many people. You also need to find out about the candidates before you can decide which one to vote for.

Defining

3. What does it mean to be *eligible* to vote?

____

Identifying

4. What are the requirements for a person to vote?

____

____

Mark the Text

5. Circle the document(s) you will need to bring with you when you register to vote.

Making Inferences

6. What do you think the purpose of the National Voter Registration Act is? What effect do you think it had on voter registration?

____

____

____

____

Lesson 1: Who Can Vote?, *Continued*

Reading Check

7. What are the three steps in the voting process?

____

____

Describing

8. Describe what happens when you go to cast your vote in an election.

____

____

____

Making Inferences

9. Think about the information in the chart. What type of ballot has probably been in use longest in the United States?

____

____

Paraphrasing

10. How did the Supreme Court influence the 2000 presidential election?

____

____

____

Preparing to Vote
Does the candidate stand for the issues I think are important?
Is the candidate reliable and honest?
Does the candidate have experience?
Will the candidate be effective in office?

Watching the news, reading the newspaper, using the Internet, listening to the radio, and reading books and magazines help you become an informed voter. You must be careful to separate facts from opinions as you gather information. Some people use bias in their materials. They try to tell you only their opinion instead of fact.

The third step is casting your vote. This is done at a **polling place.** Polling places are usually set up in schools, fire stations, or other public buildings. There is one polling place in each precinct, or voting district. Many states allow early voting. This means that citizens can vote before Election Day. This can be done by mail in some states and at certain locations in others.

When you get to your polling place, you will be asked to show identification. You will then enter a voting booth. The booth may have a curtain. It may have some other way to make sure your vote is secret.

A **ballot** is a list of candidates who are running for each office. The table below shows the different types of ballots.

Types of Ballots Used Today	
Paper ballot	Vote is marked using a special pen.
Absentee ballot	Vote is mailed in by people who know they cannot get to the polls on Election Day.
Touch-screen ballot	Vote is marked by touching a computer screen.

In the 2000 presidential election, ballots became a source of major conflict. Some of the ballots were not marked clearly. This made it hard for election officials to read them properly. In the end, the U.S. Supreme Court had to make a decision. In the U.S. Supreme Court case *Bush* v. *Gore,* the Court said that the votes should not be recounted. The decision meant that George W. Bush won the election.

Some people cannot get to the polls on Election Day. They may be traveling or they may be serving in the military. These voters can send in an absentee ballot. You must get an absentee ballot before Election Day.

Why Your Vote Counts

Have you ever heard the phrase "every vote counts"? It is true. The United States is committed to the ideal of equality. When you vote, your vote will be counted exactly the same way, and be given the same value, as everyone else's vote.

Voting is a right. It is also a responsibility. There are many good reasons to vote.

- You can help choose government leaders.
- You can vote to keep leaders that you like.
- You can vote to remove leaders whose work you dislike.
- You will have a say in how your community, state, and nation are run.

The people who vote each Election Day know that every vote counts. They also know that they have no right to complain about things if they have not voted. They believe in the democratic process.

But many people do not vote. **Voter turnout rate** is the measure of how many people actually vote. In the United States, this number is often under 50 percent. There are many reasons for this. Some people say they are too busy to vote. Others suffer from voter apathy. **Apathy** is a lack of interest. Still others forget to register to vote. Some others do not know that moving requires them to register again. If they wait too long, they will not meet the deadline.

/ / / / / / / / / / / / / Glue Foldable here / / / / / / / / / / / / / /

Check for Understanding

Name the requirements people must meet in order to vote.

1. ____________________

2. ____________________

Name three things you need to do before you can vote.

3. ____________________

4. ____________________

5. ____________________

Reading Check

11. What does the saying "every vote counts" mean?

____

____

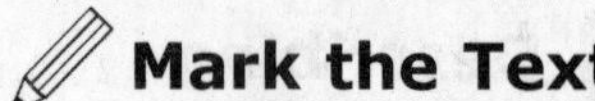

Mark the Text

12. Circle the reason for voting that is most important to you.

Paraphrasing

13. What does it mean to say that voter turnout is often less than 50 percent?

____

____

____

FOLDABLES®

14. Place a one-tab Foldable along the dotted line. Label the front *Voting Rights* and explain why it is important. Label the reverse *Voting Requirements* and explain U.S. voting requirements.

NAME ______________________ DATE ______________ CLASS __________

networks

Lesson 2: Elections and Campaigns

ESSENTIAL QUESTION

Why do people create, structure, and change governments?

GUIDING QUESTIONS

1. ***Why are there different types of elections in the American political system?***
2. ***How are presidents elected?***
3. ***How do candidates run for political office?***

Terms to Know

issue matter of public concern

initiative process that lets voters propose new laws or amendments to state constitutions

referendum process that allows voters to accept or reject a law passed by the state legislature

recall election in which voters can remove a person from office

Electoral College group of electors that chooses the president

popular vote the votes cast by the people in the general election

winner-take-all system Electoral College system in which the winner of a state's popular vote gets all of that state's electoral votes

pursue to reach or attain

canvass to go from door to door to gather support for a candidate

political action committee (PAC) organization set up by interest groups to raise money for candidates

What Do You Know?

In the first column, answer the questions based on what you know before you study. After this lesson, complete the last column.

Now...		Later...
	What are the types of elections?	

FOLDABLES®

1. Place a one-tab Foldable on the line. Use both sides to list the kinds of elections and a definition of each.

Types of Elections

/ / / / / / / / / / / / / / Glue Foldable here / / / / / / / / / / / / / /

There are more than a half-million elected officials in the United States today. All of these people had to run for office. To do so, they had to understand the election process. The basic steps of that process are fairly simple.

The first step in most states is to win the primary election. A primary is usually held in the spring or summer. The purpose of the primary is to pick candidates for the general election in November.

There are times when no candidate wins a majority of votes in the primary. In this case, a runoff primary is held. The winner of the runoff goes on to run in the general election.

Lesson 2: Elections and Campaigns, *Continued*

The general election is held on the same day across the country. This day is always the first Tuesday after the first Monday in November. National elections are held in even-numbered years. Elections for the entire House of Representatives and one-third of the Senate are held every two years. Elections for president are held every four years. State and local officials are usually elected at the same time.

During an election, people are also asked to vote on issues. An **issue** is a matter of public interest. For example, if a city council wants to build a new school, the council will put that issue on a ballot. The voters decide if the school gets built or not.

There are two ways that voters can have a direct voice in government. The chart below explains these methods.

Direct Voice Methods for Voters	
Initiative	process that lets voters propose new laws or amendments to state constitutions
Referendum	process that allows voters to accept or reject a law passed by the state legislature

In an initiative, a certain number of voters must sign a petition. The petition asks for a new law. If enough people sign the petition, the proposal is put on the ballot.

Some states also allow **recall** elections. These are elections in which voters can remove a person from office. A recall begins with a petition. If enough people sign the petition, a recall vote is held. If the people vote to remove the official, another special election is held to find a replacement. Special elections are also held to fill an office if an elected official has died or resigned.

Presidential Elections

The election of the president is different from other elections. The president is not elected directly by the people. When people vote for president, they are really voting for electors. These electors make up the **Electoral College.** The Electoral College actually chooses the president and vice president. People vote for the electors through a **popular vote.** This is when citizens tell the electors which candidate they want elected. The diagram on the next page will help you understand how this works.

Making Inferences

2. Why do you think only one-third of senators are up for election every two years?

____

____

Explaining

3. What can voters do in some states if they want to change their state constitution?

____

____

Reading Check

4. What is the difference between a recall election and a special election?

____

____

____

Reading Check

5. When people vote for the president of the United States, for whom are they actually voting?

____

Lesson 2: Elections and Campaigns, *Continued*

Examining Details

6. If one million voters choose Candidate A for president and one million five hundred choose Candidate B in a state, which candidate would win all of that state's electoral votes?

____

Defining

7. Explain what a *campaign* is.

____

____

____

____

Prior Knowledge

8. Think about a public election or a school election that you remember. How did the candidates run their campaigns?

____

____

____

____

Some people do not like the Electoral College system. They especially dislike that it is a **winner-take-all system.** In most states, the winner of the popular vote gets all of that state's electoral votes. This is true even if the candidate wins by only a few votes.

Sometimes the person who wins the popular vote in a presidential election still might not get enough electoral votes to become president. This has happened four times.

The Electoral College Process

1. The general election for president takes place in **November.** In most states, the candidate who wins the most popular votes in the general election wins all of that state's electoral votes.

2. In **December,** the electors meet and cast their ballots. They send the results to the Senate.

3. In **January,** the House and Senate meet in joint session to officially count the votes.

4. The candidate who wins a majority of the electoral votes (at least 270 of 538) wins the election.

Running for Office

When a person tries to win an election, his or her efforts are called a *campaign*. A campaign begins when someone decides to run for office. The person must first make sure they meet the requirements for the office. Most offices require a person to be a certain age and a U. S. citizen. If someone wants to run for president, the candidate will form an exploratory committee. The committee's job is to find out how many people support the candidate.

If there is enough support, the candidate announces that he or she is running for office. Usually several people from each party decide to run for president. The party picks one of these people as their candidate at the national convention. The conventions are huge events that get a lot of attention from the media.

Lesson 2: Elections and Campaigns, *Continued*

No matter what office candidates are running for, they must make many public appearances before the election. They give speeches and interviews. They hold debates. They try to appeal to as many voters as possible.

Candidates usually have staff to help them. Volunteers help candidates **pursue** voters in many ways. Volunteers **canvass** neighborhoods. This means they go from door to door to gather support. They also make telephone calls and send e-mails to tell people about their candidate.

People running for office also try to get endorsements, or support, from important people or groups. They hope that voters who like these people or groups will vote for them. Some examples of this kind of support are celebrities, politicians, newspapers, and unions. Candidates also spend a great deal of money on ads in newspapers, on the radio, and on TV.

Campaigns cost a lot of money. The race for president costs each candidate hundreds of millions of dollars. Most of this money comes from donations. Donations are made by individuals, businesses, unions, and political action committees (PACs). **Political action committees (PACs)** are set up by interest groups to raise money for candidates.

The Federal Election Commission (FEC) makes rules about how much money candidates can spend. But many Americans still worry that campaigns cost too much. They also worry that elected officials will try to please big donors rather than the people.

Check for Understanding

Name two kinds of elections that are held in the United States.

1. ______________ **2.** ______________

Write the reason that the president has to be officially elected by the Electoral College.

3. ______________

Name two things that a candidate running for office must do.

4. ______________

5. ______________

Glue Foldable here

Mark the Text

9. Underline the words that tell you what *canvass* means.

Reading Check

10. Why do candidates want endorsements?

____

____

Identifying

11. What is the purpose of a PAC?

____

____

Describing

12. What is the job of the FEC?

____

____

FOLDABLES®

13. Place a one-tab Foldable along the dotted line. Label the anchor *Electoral College*. Write three sentences that describe the Electoral College.

Public Opinion and Government

Lesson 1: Forming Public Opinion

ESSENTIAL QUESTION

How do citizens, both individually and collectively, influence government policy?

GUIDING QUESTIONS

1. ***What is public opinion?***
2. ***How is public opinion measured?***

Terms to Know

public opinion the ideas and views that people have about elected officials, candidates, government, and political issues

gender whether a person is male or female

mass media mass communication, including television, radio, the Internet, print resources, recordings, and movies

interest group group of people who share the same opinion about an issue and unite to promote their beliefs

public opinion poll a survey in which individuals are asked to answer questions about a particular issue or person

pollster a specialists whose job is to conduct polls regularly

random by chance

What Do You Know?

In the first column, answer the questions based on what you know before you study. After this lesson, complete the last column.

Now...		Later...
	What do you think public opinion includes?	
	Can public opinion be measured?	

Prior Knowledge

1. What is an opinion?

____

Vocabulary

2. What is meant by *public opinion?*

____

____

Public Opinion

Government leaders often talk about "the public." Who do they mean? Did you know that you are part of "the public?" The public is all of the people in our nation.

Many people want to know what the public thinks. Businesses and government leaders are especially interested in **public opinion.** Public opinion means the ideas and views of the people about an issue or a person. Public opinion is important in a democracy. Officials need to understand what the people they represent want them to do. Presidents often try to judge public opinion. This tells them when the public is ready for a new idea. It also helps them propose programs that people will support.

Lesson 1: Forming Public Opinion, *Continued*

Opinions are shaped by experiences. Many things affect the kinds of experiences people have. One is a person's **gender.** Gender means whether a person is male or female. The diagram below shows other things that shape people's opinions.

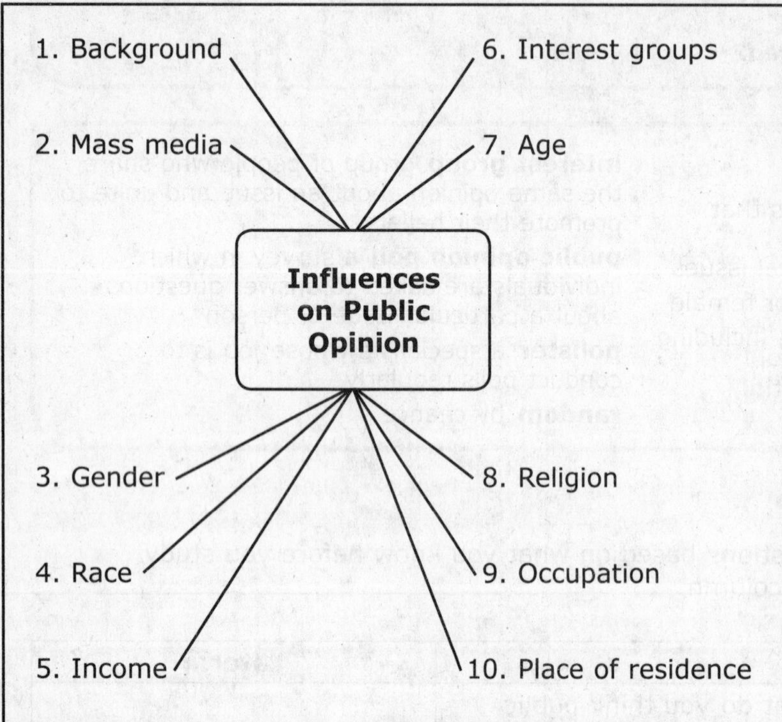

People need information to form their opinions. A major factor shaping public opinion is the mass media. The **mass media** are all the types of communication that can reach a large number of people. These media include television, radio, the Internet, newspapers, books, recordings, and movies.

Interest groups also try to shape public opinion. An interest group is a group of people who share the same opinion about an issue. They come together to support their beliefs. They try to persuade others to agree with them. This includes people in government as well as other citizens. Interest groups can put political pressure on government leaders to act a certain way, such as passing a law. Because of this, interest groups are sometimes called pressure groups.

Glue Foldable here

Reading Check

3. What factors influence public opinion?

____

____

Mark the Text

4. Circle the type of mass media that you use most often.

FOLDABLES®

5. Glue a two-tab Foldable on top of a one-tab Foldable to make a book. Place it along the dotted line. Label the anchor tab *Public Opinion,* the top tab *Three Features,* and bottom tab *Polls.* Explain on each how public opinion influences government policy. Then label the top of the one-tab Foldable *Public Opinion.* On the reverse explain why it is important in a democracy.

Paraphrasing

6. Write the paragraph explaining the features of public opinion in your own words.

Reading Check

7. Besides elections, what is another way to measure public opinion?

Identifying

8. What is a good sample for a poll?

Mark the Text

9. Underline the definition of *random* and circle the definition of *pollster.*

Public Opinion has Three Features

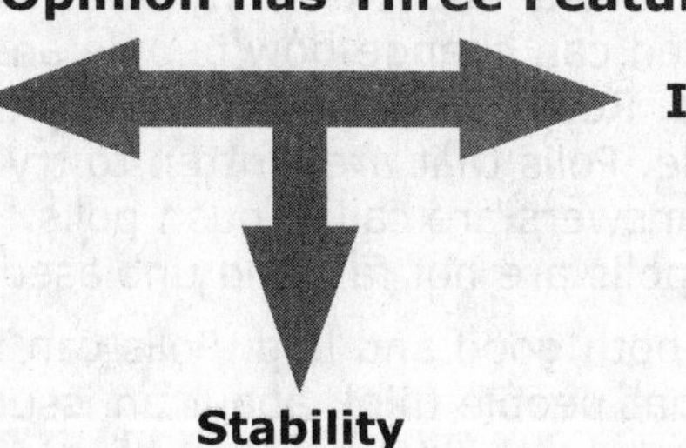

Direction tells whether the public's opinion agrees or disagrees with an issue or a person. Do people agree or disagree with a tax cut? In most cases, the direction is mixed, but one side can be stronger than the other. *Intensity* shows the strength of a person's or group's opinion. When people feel strongly about an issue, they may take action. Actions include voting, joining an interest group, or working on a campaign. *Stability* tells how firmly people hold their opinions. In other words, are they likely to change their minds? Opinions based on a strong belief are generally very stable. For example, most people's opinions about civil rights are more stable than their views about candidates.

Public Opinion Polls

Public opinion can be measured. One way is to look at election results. However, elections give only a general idea of public opinion. This is because people vote for many reasons. For example, they may not support all of a candidate's views, yet still vote for that person.

A better way to measure public opinion is to ask many people questions about issues. This is called a survey, or **public opinion poll.** Such polls put many people's answers together to measure public opinion.

Political leaders use polls to know public opinion. They also use polls to help them create programs or make laws that fit the people's needs.

A person who conducts polls is called a **pollster.** Pollsters have different ways of selecting people to survey. One way is to choose people at **random,** or by chance. A good random group, or sample, is a smaller version of the whole population. It reflects the opinions of people all over the United States.

Lesson 1: Forming Public Opinion, *Continued*

Pollsters are careful about wording questions. The way a question is asked can change how people answer. A good poll is unbiased. Responsible pollsters do not want to influence people. Polls that are written to try to influence, or shape, the answers are called push polls. The questions asked in push polls are not fair and unbiased.

Polls can be both good and bad. Polls can help leaders by telling them what people think about an issue. They can also distract leaders or unfairly affect election results. Some say that polls can make people decide not to vote. If a poll shows that a candidate is far behind, people may think he or she has already lost, and so they will not bother to vote.

Glue Foldable here

Check for Understanding

Name two ways citizens can influence public policy.

1. ______

2. ______

List two reasons why public opinion is important.

3. ______

4. ______

Explaining

10. How can you recognize a push poll?

______

Comparing and Contrasting

11. In what ways are polls helpful? In what ways can polls be harmful?

______

FOLDABLES®

12. Place a two-tab Foldable along the dotted line. Write *Policy* and *Opinion* on the tabs. Write the definitions of each term on the reverse.

Public Opinion and Government

Lesson 2: The Mass Media

ESSENTIAL QUESTION

How do citizens, both individually and collectively, influence government policy?

GUIDING QUESTIONS

1. ***How do the media influence public opinion and government?***
2. ***What are the restrictions on freedom of the press?***

Terms to Know

public agenda issues thought to be most important by government officials

leak to release secret government information by anonymous government officials to the media

acknowledge to admit

watchdog role played by the media that uncovers waste or illegal prctices

prior restraint the act of stopping information from being known before it is published

shield law a law that protects a reporter from revealing his or her sources

libel written lies about a person

malice evil intent

regulatory describing an agency that controls or directs

What Do You Know?

In the first column, answer the questions based on what you know before you study. After this lesson, complete the last column.

Now...		Later...
	What tools does the media use to influence public opinion and the government?	
	Should freedom of the press be limited?	

Reading Check

1. What are the two broad types of mass media sources?

____

____

The Influence of the Media

The mass media can affect politics and government. They also link people and their elected leaders. The two broad types of mass media, print and electronic, are shown in the chart below.

Print Media	Electronic Media
• newspapers • magazines • books	• the Internet • television • radio

Public Opinion and Government

Lesson 2: The Mass Media, *Continued*

The government deals with many problems and issues. Those that receive the most time, money, and effort from government leaders make up what is often called the **public agenda.** An agenda is a set of items that a person or group wants to address.

The media have an effect on what problems officials see as important. When the media focus on a problem, people begin to worry about it. Then they expect the government to deal with it.

The mass media can affect who runs for office. Usually candidates are experienced politicians. They spend years working in their political parties. Some candidates, though, are people who were famous for their success in another field. For instance, actor Arnold Schwarzenegger was elected governor of California in 2003. When candidates are already well known, the media cover their campaigns with interest. In this way, the candidate takes advantage of the media's desire to cover a story.

Reporters and politicians have a complex relationship. They need each other. Reporters need information to write stories. Political leaders need media coverage to get their message out. At the same time, the two groups often clash. As one presidential assistant explained, "Politicians live—and sometimes die—by the press. The press lives by politicians."

Officials try to use the media to their advantage. They may **leak,** or secretly pass, information to reporters. They may do this to test the public's response to a proposal before they openly **acknowledge,** or admit, that they are considering it. If the public reacts well, officials might act on the idea. If the public reacts negatively, officials can drop it. Politicians also use leaks to shape public opinion on an issue, or to gain favor with a reporter.

At the same time, reporters can present stories in ways that show an official in a bad light. They can ask officials tough questions about the positions that the officials take. Politicians may try to avoid this difficulty by refusing to answer their questions. That practice, though, can result in criticism from the media.

The mass media also play a crucial **watchdog** role. That means they keep a close eye on government activities. Journalists write stories that expose waste and corruption at all levels of government. These kinds of stories attract a large audience. Throughout our history the media have played this role. This has served the interests of both the media and the public by exposing wrongdoing by officials.

Explaining

2. Why do politicians and reporters need each other?

____

____

____

____

Mark the Text

3. Underline the words that tell you what *leak* means.

Explaining

4. How does the media's role as a watchdog help both the public and the media?

____

____

____

____

____

Lesson 2: The Mass Media, *Continued*

Reading Check

5. What are two ways the federal government can manage broadcast media?

____

____

____

Vocabulary

6. How are *libel* and evil intent related?

____

____

____

FOLDABLES®

7. Place a two-tab Foldable along the dotted line and label the anchor tab *Media and Public Opinion.* Write *Freedoms* on the top tab and *Restrictions* on the bottom tab.On each tab explain how the media has freedom to share information with the public and how it also has restrictions.

Glue Foldable here

Americans need to be informed. At the same time, the government keeps some secrets because of national security. The government classifies, or labels, some information as secret.

The government uses other methods to shape the news. During the first part of the war in Iraq, some journalists traveled with the troops to report on battles and on the daily life of the troops. Some critics said this practice allowed the government to control news reporting.

Protecting the Press

Our nation's founders knew that democracy needs ideas and information to be shared freely. That is why freedom of the press is one of the first in the Bill of Rights. The press refers to TV, radio, newspapers, and the Internet.

The Supreme Court has ruled that freedom of the press means that government cannot use **prior restraint.** Prior restraint is when the government censors material before it is published. To censor means to edit or stop a publication. In general, writers and editors are free to choose what they will write or say even if it is unpopular.

Sometimes people give information to the media even when doing so could cause them harm. For example, some people could lose their jobs if they share secret information about their employer. Because of this, many states have **shield laws** to allow the press to keep their sources secret.

There are some limits on freedom of the press. A person cannot publish false written information that harms someone's reputation. This is called **libel.** It is hard for public officials to prove libel. They must show that the publisher knew the information was false and published it anyway. This is called **malice,** or evil.

Check for Understanding

How do the media help shape public opinion and the government?

1. _______________

What are the restrictions on freedom of the press?

2. _______________

NAME _______________ DATE _______________ CLASS _______________

Lesson 3: Interest Groups and Lobbying

ESSENTIAL QUESTION

How do citizens, both individually and collectively, influence government policy?

GUIDING QUESTIONS

1. ***How do special-interest groups influence public policy?***
2. ***How does the government regulate interest groups?***

Terms to Know

guarantee to promise
public-interest group a group that supports causes that affect the lives of most Americans
nonpartisan free from party ties or bias
lobbyist a representative of an interest group who contacts government officials to influence their policy making
biased favoring one view

What Do You Know?

In the first column, answer the questions based on what you know before you study. After this lesson, complete the last column.

Now...		Later...
	What are special interest groups?	
	What is the relationship between interest groups and the government?	

Interest Groups

There are many ways to contact elected officials. Many have social media sites, Web sites, and email. They are interested in what you have to say. You have the right to contact them. You also have the right to join together with other people to make your voice heard. This right is **guaranteed,** or promised, in the First Amendment. It says people have a right to assemble.

When people join together on issues, they have a stronger voice. Interest groups are one way to join with others to influence the government.

There are many interest groups. They can be broken down into types. One type represents particular kinds of businesses. These groups try to get the government to act in a way that benefits their business. The National Automobile Dealers Association is one such group. It works on behalf of companies that sell cars and trucks.

Another type of interest group focuses its efforts on workers. These groups are concerned with issues such as wages and working conditions.

Paraphrasing

1. Paraphrase the paragraph about why people form interest groups.

____
____
____
____
____
____
____

Lesson 3: Interest Groups and Lobbying, *Continued*

Defining

2. What is the AFL-CIO?

______

______

FOLDABLES®

3. Glue a one-tab Foldable to the line. Label the anchor *My Interest Group.* On both sides, write two sentences about which group you would join and why.

Vocabulary

4. A ______ interest group is an interest group that does not work for any political party.

Reading Check

5. What tools do interest groups use to influence government and public opinion?

______

______

______

______

Glue Foldable here

The American Federation of Labor and Congress of Industrial Organizations (AFL-CIO) is the largest of these worker groups. It is a partnership of labor unions.

Some interest groups are based on shared economic goals. For example, the U.S. Chamber of Commerce works for businesses. The AMA, American Medical Association, is a group that works with and for doctors.

Another type of interest group works for people who share similar characteristics. For example, the National Association for the Advancement of Colored People (NAACP) works for the rights of African Americans. Others groups promote the rights of women and of older Americans.

Other interest groups work for special causes. The Sierra Club works to protect nature and the National Rifle Association (NRA) handles the concerns of gun owners.

Another type of group is called a **public-interest group.** A public-interest group supports causes that affect most Americans. One example is the League of Women voters. This **nonpartisan** group does not work for any political party. It informs voters about candidates and issues.

Types of Interest Groups	
Business and worker groups	*National Auto Dealers Association, AFL-CIO*
Economic/other with similar interests groups	*American Medical Association, NAACP*
Public-interest groups	*League of Women Voters*

Interest groups play an important role in the United States. Their main role is to shape government policy. They do this by working in four areas: (1) on elections, (2) through the courts, (3) with lawmakers, and (4) trying to shape public opinion.

Interest groups focus on elections. They want to get people elected who support their ideas. Many interest groups have formed political action committees (PACs). A PAC raises money from its members. It then uses the money to help their favored candidates get elected.

Interest groups affect public policy by bringing cases to court. For instance, an interest group for women might help a woman worker sue a company if it feels she was paid unfairly. A group may also argue that a law or government policy is unconstitutional.

Lesson 3: Interest Groups and Lobbying, *Continued*

One of the most important ways interest groups try to shape policy is by lobbying. Interest groups hire **lobbyists** to contact lawmakers directly on their behalf. They try to convince officials at all levels of government to support their ideas. This is called *lobbying.*

Lobbyists understand how government works. They are convincing. Good lobbyists help government leaders by giving them information about particular issues. They might suggest solutions to problems. They may also write drafts of bills and testify at hearings. Lawmakers appreciate this help. But they also know that lobbyists can be **biased.** This means the information they supply might not be neutral.

Many interest groups want to sway public opinion. They want to get new members. They want to convince people that their causes are important. Many use direct mail or e-mail to do this. They advertise in the media. They also try to get media attention by holding protests or organizing public events.

Interest groups sometimes use propaganda to get their message across. Propaganda is a way to present information to make people believe in an idea. There are many ways of spreading propaganda. The Propaganda Techniques table shows some common techniques, or methods, used during elections.

Propaganda Techniques

Technique	Explanation
Bandwagon	Join us, we're sure to win!
Name-calling	Candidate A is a dangerous extremist.
Endorsement	Movie star says, "I'm voting for Candidate A. You should, too!"
Stacked cards	Our candidate has the best record on the environment.
Glittering generalities	Our candidate will bring peace and prosperity.
Just plain folks	I'm running for office. My parents were plain, hardworking folks, and they taught me those values.
Transfer	Surround the candidate with patriotic symbols such as flags.

Explaining

6. Explain what lobbyists do for interest groups.

____

____

____

____

Visualizing

7. Briefly describe a print or television ad that might be developed by a environmental interest group. What techniques might be effective?

____

____

____

____

Identifying

8. The president and other government leaders often make speeches at campaign events for members of their parties who are seeking reelection. What kind of propaganda technique is this?

____

____

Reading Check

9. Why must former government officials wait before becoming lobbyists?

____

____

Mark the Text

10. Underline the sentence that explains why some people dislike interest groups.

FOLDABLES®

11. Place a two-tab Foldable on the line. Label the anchor *Interest Groups.* Write *Influence Public Policy* on the top tab. On the reverse, list methods interest groups use. Label the next tab *Regulation*. Use the reverse of this tab to explain the purpose of regulating interest groups.

Regulating Interest Groups

The Constitution protects the right of people to belong to interest groups. But laws do put some controls on interest groups. They limit how much money PACs can give candidates. Lobbyists must register, or sign up, with the government. They must report who they contact and how much money they spend. Former government officials must wait for a period of time after leaving office before they can become lobbyists. The delay is meant to stop them from using friendships and inside knowledge to help special-interest groups. This kind of law has not been very successful.

Some people criticize interest groups. They think these groups have too much influence. Others believe that interest groups make the government address people's concerns. They also believe that interest groups are one way that people can actively take part in government.

Glue Foldable here

Check for Understanding

List three ways that interest groups influence public policy.

1. _______________

2. _______________

3. _______________

Name two ways that the government regulates interest groups.

4. _______________

____

5. _______________

____

NAME ______________________ DATE ____________ CLASS ________

networks

State Government

Lesson 1: The Federal System

ESSENTIAL QUESTION

Why and how do people create, structure, and change governments?

GUIDING QUESTIONS

1. ***How does the federal system allow the national government and state governments to share power?***
2. ***What characteristics do all state governments share?***

Terms to Know

federal system the sharing of power between the central and state governments
reserved powers powers that the U. S. Constitution gives only to the states
concurrent powers powers that state and federal governments share
supremacy clause clause in Article VI of the Constitution that says federal laws are above state laws when there is conflict
function to serve a purpose
grants-in-aid money given to the states by the federal government
violate to fail to keep or to break, as a law

What Do You Know?

In the first column, answer the questions based on what you know before you study. After this lesson, complete the last column.

Now...		Later...
	How does federalism work?	
	In what ways are state governments alike?	

Vocabulary

1. What is a *federal system*?

____

____

Mark the Text

2. Underline the part of the text that explains why a federal system was formed.

Federal and State Powers

Earlier you learned that the Constitution gives certain powers only to the federal government. It leaves other powers to the states. Some powers are shared by both. This is known as a **federal system** of government. In a federal system, the national and the state governments share and divide powers. The two levels of government often carry out similar tasks, for example, both build highways.

In writing the Constitution, the Framers created a central government that was stronger than the central government that existed under the Articles of Confederation. However, they also thought that state governments were important. So the Framers created a federal system that divides powers between state and national governments. The Constitution limits the powers of states, but it also protects the states. The following chart shows some of the protections provided to the states in the Constitution.

Lesson 1: The Federal System, *Continued*

Constitutional Protections of States	
Article and Section of Constitution	**Example**
Article IV, Section 1 Says each state must respect legal actions taken by other states	One state accepts driver's license given by another.
Article IV, Section 2 Promises each state will treat the people of other states equally	One state cannot give people from another state tougher punishments for a crime than they would get in their own state.
Article IV, Section 3 Guarantees each state's area	Land cannot be taken from any state to make a new state without that state's approval.
Article IV, Section 4 Promises each state a republican form of government and vows to protect that government against enemy attack or revolt	Each state has control over its Army National Guard. In times of war, the federal government can call the National Guard into action to take part in federal missions.

Under the Constitution, the federal government has three kinds of powers:

- *Expressed* powers are listed in the Constitution. The power to coin money is an example.
- *Implied* powers are not listed, but are based on statements in the Constitution. For example, the Constitution says the president is commander in chief of the armed forces. This implies that the president has the power to send troops to respond to a crisis.
- *Inherent* powers are the kind of powers a government has simply because it is a government. Buying land from another country is an example.

The Framers knew that state governments were important. So they kept certain powers only for the states.

These are called **reserved powers.** Reserved powers come from the Tenth Amendment. An example of a reserved power is that states have the power to set up local governments. They also have the power to conduct elections.

Critical Thinking

3. The table gives examples of the protections for the articles shown. Can you think of another example of something that might be an Article IV, Section 1 protection?

____

Which article protects a state's borders?

____

Making Inferences

4. How are implied powers and expressed powers related?

____

____

Explaining

5. Why do you think that the federal and state governments were both given the power to tax?

____

____

Identifying

6. Study the Venn diagram. Which level of government has the power to create local government systems?

____

FOLDABLES®

7. Place a one-tab Foldable along the dotted line. Label the anchor tab *Concurrent Powers*. On the tab, write five phrases to describe powers that both the federal and state governments have.

Reading Check

8. What are two limits that the Constitution puts on the powers of state governments?

____

____

Explaining

9. How does the supremacy clause limit state power?

____

____

____

Other powers are held by both the national and state governments. These are called **concurrent powers.** They include the power to tax, borrow money, and pass laws.

They also include the power to spend money for the general good of the people. For example, both federal and state governments build highways. The following diagram shows how federalism divides powers between the national and state governments.

Glue Foldable here

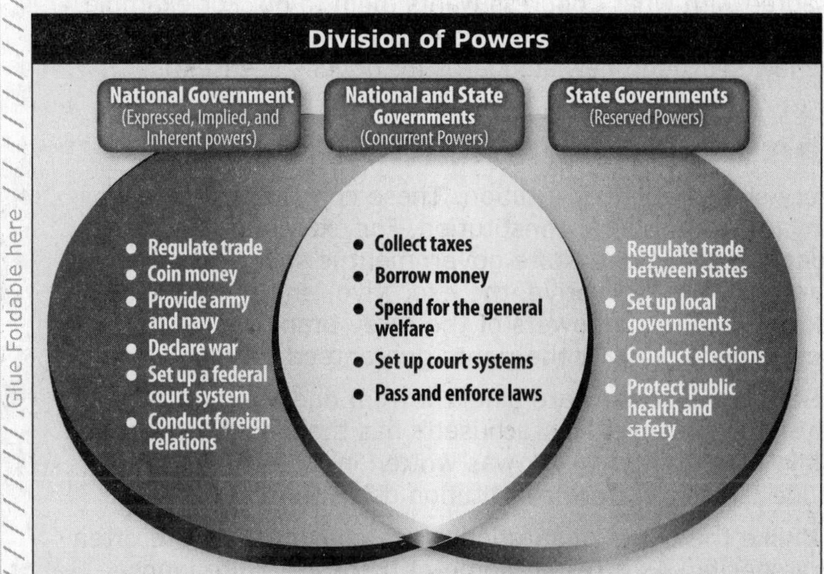

The Constitution also sets specific limits on the states. A state may not declare war. It may not enter into a treaty with another country. It cannot issue its own money. It cannot tax imports from other states or countries.

States must abide by the Bill of Rights. This is because the Fourteenth Amendment says that states must give all citizens "equal protection of the laws." States cannot take away the rights of its citizens "without due process of law."

State power is also limited by the **supremacy clause** in the Constitution. This clause puts the Constitution and federal law above state law. If a state law conflicts with the Constitution or a federal law, the state law is thrown out.

In our system, the federal and state governments work together. Each year the federal government gives large sums of money to the states.

These sums are called **grants-in-aid.** The grants are to be used to meet goals that Congress has set. For example, grants might be used for health care or education.

Lesson 1: The Federal System, *Continued*

State governments also work together. For example, several states are working as a group to design an energy policy. States often help each other with law enforcement.

The states and Congress do not always agree. Sometimes a federal law tells the states to meet certain goals, but does not give them the money to do so. Such laws are known as unfunded mandates. State officials complain that these laws **violate,** or go against, the rights of states. States may also disagree with what Congress wants them to do. For example, many states have protested the Real ID Act passed in 2005. The law set tough new standards for driver's licenses.

The State Constitutions

Every state has a constitution. These constitutions are similar to the federal constitution. For example, like the federal government, state government is split into three branches—the legislative, the executive, and the judicial. It also spells out the powers of the three branches. State constitutions also list the rights guaranteed to each citizen.

State constitutions are different from one another in some ways. For example, Massachusetts has the oldest constitution still in use. Its framework was written in 1780. In contrast, Rhode Island's current constitution dates from 1986.

Unlike the U.S. Constitution, state constitutions are often very specific. As a result, some of them are quite long. Alabama's constitution is the longest, at 365,000 words. It also has the most amendments, more than 800. Three-quarters of them affect a single county in the state. California's constitution is specific in a different way: it has a long list of resources that cannot be taxed.

State constitutions vary because state governments vary throughout the country. You will read more about these differences later in the chapter. No state constitution can include laws that go against the U. S. Constitution, though.

/ / / / / / / / / / / / / Glue Foldable here / / / / / / / / / / / / /

Check for Understanding

Name two powers that are shared between the national government and state governments.

1. ____________ **2.** ____________

Name two ways that state constitutions are alike.

3. ____________ **4.** ____________

Analyzing

10. How might a state argue that an unfunded mandate violates its rights?

____

____

____

____

Reading Check

11. Why are state constitutions often longer than the U. S. Constitution?

____

____

FOLDABLES®

12. Place a three-tab Venn diagram Foldable along the dotted line. Label the first tab *U. S. Constitution*, the middle tab *Both,* and the last tab *State Constitutions*. Write facts about each on the outer tabs. Write things that both share on the middle tab.

NAME ______________________ DATE ______________ CLASS __________

networks

Lesson 2: State Legislative Branch

ESSENTIAL QUESTION

Why and how do people create, structure, and change governments?

GUIDING QUESTIONS

1. ***What are the functions of state legislatures?***
2. ***What economic challenges do state legislatures face?***

Terms to Know

unicameral having a one-house legislature
minimum the least amount possible
redistricting redrawing the boundaries of a legislative district
malapportionment an unequal representation in a state legislature
session a meeting of a legislative or jusicial body to conduct business
special session a legislative meeting called for a specific purpose
legislative referendum a vote called by a legislature to seek voter approval of a law
popular referendum a question placed on a ballot by a citizen petition to decide if a law should be repealed
rely to depend on something or someone

What Do You Know?

In the first column, answer the questions based on what you know before you study. After this lesson, complete the last column.

Now...		Later...
	What does a state legislature do?	
	Does a state have similar economic challenges as a town, city, or county?	

? Contrasting

1. Explain the difference between unicameral and bicameral houses.

____

____

____

How Legislatures Function

In all but one state, the state legislature is bicameral. *Bicameral* means the legislature has two houses, like in the U.S. Congress. Nebraska is different. Its legislature is **unicameral** (YOO•nih•KAM•ruhl), or has only one house. In every state, the upper house is called the senate. In most states, the lower house is called the house of representatives.

How old does a person have to be to serve in a state legislature? The **minimum** age changes from state to state. To serve in the lower house, a person has to be at least 18 years old in some states, and 21 in other states. State senators have to be at least 25 in many states. However, in some states an 18-year-old can serve in the senate.

NAME ______________________ DATE ______________ CLASS ______________

networks

State Government

Lesson 2: State Legislative Branch, *Continued*

In most states, state senators serve four-year terms. House members usually serve for two years. All states pay their lawmakers. However, the pay changes from state to state.

Each house of a legislature has a leader. In the lower house, this person is called the speaker. The speaker is chosen by the members of the house. The lieutenant governor of a state usually heads the senate. The members of each party in each house also choose a leader. They are the majority leader and the minority leader. They help set the schedule for legislation and planning when bills will be discussed.

Every member of a legislature represents a district. All the districts in a state are supposed to be about equal in population. Every ten years, the federal government takes a census, or count, of all Americans. The results are used to draw the borders of the districts. The task of drawing new borders every ten years is called **redistricting** (ree•DIHS•trihkt•ihng).

In the past, states did not always draw new borders, even though district populations had changed. This meant that people were not being represented equally. Having unfair district sizes like these is called **malapportionment** (MA•luh•PAWR•shun•muhnt). The U.S. Supreme Court ended this practice in the 1962 *Baker* v. *Carr* case. In that case, the Court ruled that state legislative districts must be very close in terms of population size. This rule helps make sure that each citizen of a state has an equal voice in government.

Lawmakers meet and work together during a legislative session. A **session** usually lasts a few months. Sometimes a legislature will call a **special session.** This is a meeting held for a particular purpose, such as dealing with a natural disaster.

State legislators do many jobs. They vote to approve a governor's choices for state offices. They help the citizens in their district. Their main job, though, is to make laws.

To make a law, a lawmaker first suggests a bill. It goes to a committee for review. If this group approves the bill, it goes to the full house. If the house approves the bill, it goes to the other house. They follow the same steps. Once both houses approve a bill, it goes to the governor. If the governor signs it, the bill becomes law.

Paraphrasing

2. Summarize the paragraph about the legislatures' leaders in your own words.

____

____

____

____

____

Explaining

3. How does the federal government make sure citizens are equally represented in state legislatures?

____

____

____

____

Mark the Text

4. Underline the definition of *malapportionment* in the text.

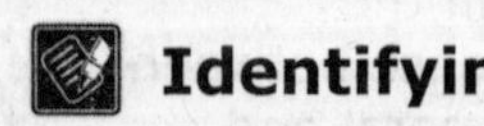

Identifying

5. What is a state legislator's most important job?

____

____

Mark the Text

6. Circle the step where a veto can be used to kill a bill.

Reading Check

7. In which state would bills not be passed by two houses before going to the governor? Why?

Describing

8. What can citizens in some states do if they do not like a state law?

Reading Check

9. What are the main sources of income for state governments?

The following chart shows the steps state legislators take to make laws.

The State Legislative Process

1. Legislator introduces a bill.
↓
2. Committee reviews and votes on bill.
↓
3. If passed by the committee, the full house reviews and votes on bill.
↓
4. Bill goes to the other house.
↓
5. Committee reviews and votes on bill.
↓
6. Full house reviews and votes on bill.
↓
7. Bill goes to governor for signature or veto.

Sometimes voters are asked to approve a new state law. This type of vote is called a **legislative referendum.** In many states, citizens can also petition, or ask, for a **popular referendum** if they do not like a law. This is a vote to decide whether to repeal, or cancel, a law that people don't like.

State Economic Issues

States face hard choices when they are preparing a budget. Almost all of them have laws that say the state budget must be balanced. This means the states cannot spend more money than they have.

States **rely** on taxes for most of their income. Sales tax and income tax are the two main types. People pay sales tax on goods that they buy. People pay income tax on the money they earn from work or other sources. States also make money by charging fees for such things as marriage and driver's licenses.

Lesson 2: State Legislative Branch, *Continued*

States spend their money on a range of services. They give aid to local governments. They pay benefits to the poor and the disabled. They pay the salaries of state workers. They pay for health care, schools, police, roads, and parks.

When times are hard, paying for all this is a challenge. Beginning in 2008, the American economy began to suffer. Many businesses had to lay off workers. People had less income and so they spent less money. The states could not collect enough taxes to meet expenses. At the same time, states faced growing demands. People needed help from the government. The federal government stepped in to give states extra money.

/ / / / / / / / / / / / Glue Foldable here / / / / / / / / / / / / / /

Check for Understanding

List three jobs state legislators perform.

1. _______________

2. _______________

3. _______________

List three services states spend money on.

4. _______________

5. _______________

6. _______________

Explaining

10. Why are hard economic times especially challenging for state governments?

____

____

____

FOLDABLES®

11. Place a three-tab Foldable along the dotted line. Label the anchor tab *State Government*. Label the first tab *Income*, the middle tab *Spending*, and the last tab *Financial Challenges*. Use the space on both sides of the tabs to list facts about state government budgets.

Lesson 3: State Executive Branch

ESSENTIAL QUESTION

Why and how do people create, structure, and change governments?

GUIDING QUESTIONS

1. ***What are the powers and duties of a governor?***
2. ***What is the role of the executives who head a state's administrative departments?***

Terms to Know

tradition a custom; the long-followed way of doing things

line-item veto to veto only a specific part of a bill

specific clearly specified or spelled out, precise, or exact

commute to decrease a criminal's sentence

parole to give a prisoner an early release from prison, with certain limits

What Do You Know?

In the first column, answer the questions based on what you know before you study. After this lesson, complete the last column.

Now...		Later...
	What does a governor do?	
	What are the roles of state executive departments?	

The Governor

What does it take to become the governor of a state? In most states, a person has to be at least 30 years old and live in the state. In some states, the minimum age is 18. In a few states, the governor is not required to live there.

In most states, a governor's term lasts four years. The number of terms a governor may serve is different from state to state. Most states limit a governor to two terms. If a governor dies or leaves office, the person who fills the governor's position is the lieutenant governor.

Governors have many roles. Two of these roles are based on **tradition,** or custom, not law. For example, their ceremonial role and position as party leader are not mentioned in state constitutions.

Under the state constitution, a governor's main job is to head the executive branch. In this role, a governor is much like the president. The governor makes sure state laws are carried out. He or she heads the state's National Guard. The governor often has the power to name people to state offices. Usually the state senate has to confirm the choices.

Paraphrasing

1. Restate the third paragraph on this page in your own words.

____

____

____

____

Comparing

2. How is a governor like the president?

____

____

Lesson 3: State Executive Branch, *Continued*

The U.S. Constitution gives state governors an added power. They can choose someone to fill a seat in the U.S. Senate if it becomes vacant.

In most states the governor also writes the budget. Usually the legislature has to approve it before it goes into effect.

Governors have a role in passing laws. They can send bills to the legislature. They also have the power to veto a bill. For all but six governors, they can also use a **line-item veto.** This means they can veto **specific** parts of a bill instead of the whole law. Lawmakers can override both kinds of vetoes by voting to pass the bill again.

Governors also have a role in the judicial branch. They appoint judges. They can pardon criminals and **commute,** or decrease, a criminal's sentence. Governors can also grant prisoners an early release from jail. That early release is called **parole** (puh•ROHL).

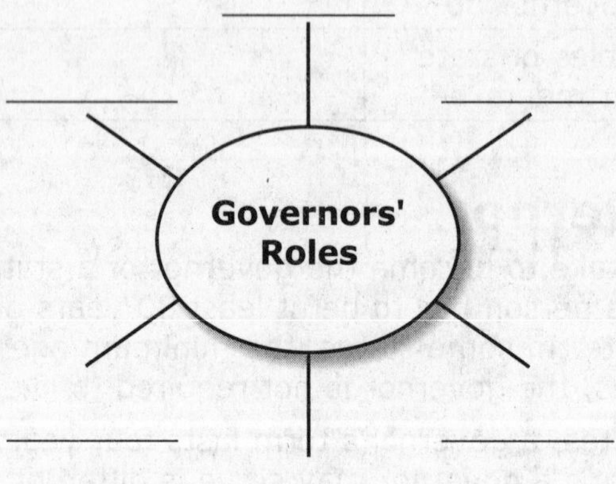

Just as with the president, it is important to know who will replace a governor who dies or leaves office before their term is over. In most states it is the lieutenant governor. Between 2000 and 2010, governors were replaced 20 times.

State Executive Departments

In the federal government, departments are run by people that the president chooses and the Senate approves. In state governments, elected officials run many departments. The governor has no role in deciding who gets these jobs. Since the governor does not choose these officials, they may not want to take direction from the governor.

Reading Check

3. What kind of check is there on the governor's power to appoint people to fill vacant offices?

Explaining

4. What kind of check does a governor have on a state legislature?

Identifying

5. Fill in the diagram with examples of different roles that governors have. Add more lines if needed.

Drawing Conclusions

6. Why might a top state official not be willing to take direction from a governor?

Lesson 3: State Executive Branch, *Continued*

Paraphrasing

7. Describe the job of the secretary of state in your own words.

____

____

____

Describing

8. What is the job of the attorney general?

____

____

____

Reading Check

9. What is the role of the cabinet?

____

____

____

FOLDABLES

10. Place a one-tab Foldable along the dotted line. Label the anchor tab *Governor*. Use both sides of the tab to write three sentences that summarize a governor's job.

It is not uncommon for a state government to have dozens of agencies, boards, and commissions. In most states, five chief executive officials carry out important tasks.

- The secretary of state oversees elections and records state laws. He or she heads the department that keeps official records. In most states, voters elect this official.
- The attorney general is the state's chief lawyer. This department represents the state in legal matters. These include legal arguments with the federal government. In most states, voters elect the attorney general.
- The state treasurer handles and keeps track of the money that the state collects and spends. In most states, voters elect the state treasurer.
- The state auditor reviews the behavior of state departments and offices. He or she makes sure work is done honestly and that tax dollars are not misused. About half the states elect auditors. In other states, the legislature or the governor chooses auditors.
- The commissioner or superintendent of education oversees the state's public school system. More often than not, this official is appointed, not elected.

In most states, the cabinet is made up of the heads of executive departments. The cabinet meets with the governor to give advice and share information. These officials from different departments each bring special knowledge when talking about issues.

/ / / / / / / / / / / / / Glue Foldable here / / / / / / / / / / / / / /

Check for Understanding

List three of the duties that are part of a governor's job.

1. ______________________

2. ______________________

3. ______________________

Name two elected officials who head departments in state government.

4. ______________________

5. ______________________

NAME ______________________ DATE ______________ CLASS ______________

networks

State Government

Lesson 4: State Judicial Branch

ESSENTIAL QUESTION

Why and how do people create, structure, and change governments?

GUIDING QUESTIONS

1. ***How is the state's judicial system organized?***
2. ***What are the usual methods for selecting judges?***

Terms to Know

complex complicated or intricate

trial court a court in which a judge or jury listens to evidence and reaches a verdict in favor of one party or another in the case

misdemeanor the least serious type of crime

civil case court case in which one party in a dispute claims to have been harmed by the other

plaintiff the person in a civil case who claims to have been harmed

defendant the person in a civil case who is said to have caused the harm

appellate court type of court in which a party who lost a case in a lower court asks judges to review that decision and reverse it

felony a type of crime more serious than a misdemeanor

bias good or bad feelings about a person or group that affect judgment

What Do You Know?

In the first column, answer the questions based on what you know before you study. After this lesson, complete the last column.

Now...		Later...
	What types of courts are in a state judicial system?	
	How do you think judges should be chosen?	

The Structure of State Courts

Each state has its own court system. These systems are all organized in a similar way. Each state has lower courts and higher courts. The cases heard in the higher courts are more serious and **complex** than the cases heard at the lower level. The chart on the next page shows the courts that make up the state judicial branch.

The lower courts are **trial courts.** In a trial court, a judge or jury listens to evidence and reaches a verdict, or decision. Lower courts have different names. They may be called justice courts, district courts, or municipal courts.

? Inferring

1. Why do you think state judicial systems have two levels of courts?

____

____

____

Identifying

2. Study the chart. What happens in appeals courts and who hears those cases?

Describing

3. What parts do the plaintiff and the defendant each play in a civil case?

Identifying

4. What kind of court would try a felony case?

Making Connections

5. Which court would hear a misdemeanor burglary case?

Which court would first hear an appeal from the general trial courts?

The State Court System

State Supreme Court
Panel of judges hears appeals from lower courts.

Intermediate Appellate Courts
Panel of judges hears appeals from lower courts.

General Trial Courts
More serious criminal and civil cases

Lower Courts
Justice, municipal, or district courts
Minor crimes
Civil cases involving little money

Lower courts handle both criminal and civil cases. In a criminal case, a person is accused of a crime. A trial is held to decide if the person is innocent or guilty. The crimes at this level are simple ones. They may be traffic violations or **misdemeanors** (MIHS•dih•MEE•nuhrz). Misdemeanors are the least serious of crimes. Punishment is usually a fine or a short stay in a local jail rather than in prison. A judge instead of a jury often decides these cases.

In a **civil case,** one party claims to have been harmed by another party. The person who claims to have been harmed is the **plaintiff.** The person said to have caused the harm is the **defendant.** Civil cases in the lower courts usually involve small amounts of money.

The higher state courts can be either trial courts or **appellate** (uh•PEH•luht) **courts.** An appellate court is one in which appeals are heard. To appeal means to ask a judge to review and reverse, or undo, an earlier court decision.

Lesson 4: State Judicial Branch, *Continued*

Higher-level trial courts handle crimes that are more serious. Such crimes are called **felonies** (FEH•luh•neez). They include robbery and murder. These courts also handle more serious civil cases. The cases often have to do with a lot of money. Either a jury or a judge may decide civil or criminal cases.

Most states have two levels of appellate courts. The first level is the intermediate appellate court. Some states with small populations do not have intermediate appellate courts. This court is often called the court of appeals. Here, a group of judges reviews each case and agrees on a decision. They may decide to accept or throw out the earlier court decision.

The top appellate court is the state supreme court. Every state has one. This court hears appeals from the intermediate appellate courts. Like the U.S. Supreme Court, state supreme courts put out written explanations of their rulings. These explanations guide state judges in future cases. State supreme court rulings are usually final. However, a state supreme court ruling may be appealed to the U.S. Supreme Court if a person thinks the decision goes against his or her rights under the U.S. Constitution.

Staffing the Courts

What qualities should a judge have? Judges must know the law. They should be free of **bias** so they can judge a case fairly. Bias is good or bad feelings about a person or group that affect judgment. They should also be independent—so they will not be swayed by political pressure. Judges in the United States serve in a representative democracy. This means that people usually vote on who holds an office. However, the way states choose judges is different from state to state.

Trial court judges are chosen in many different ways. Trial court judges may be chosen by the governor, the legislature, the state supreme court, or by city officials. Other judges are elected by the voters. In other states, judges are appointed for one term and then run for election after that. Some states use a mixture of ways to staff their courts. The length of a term for judges varies from four to ten years.

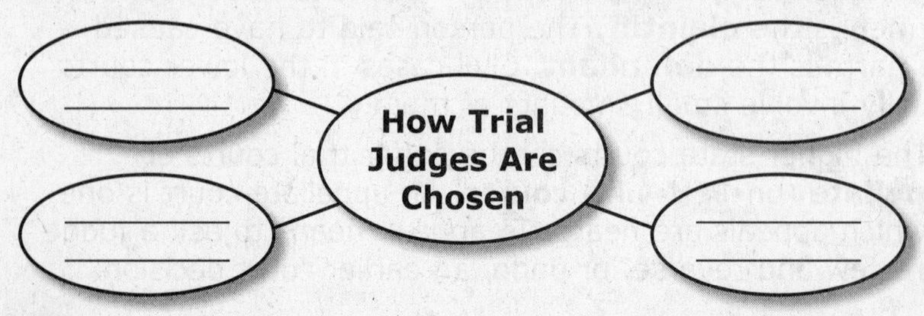

Reading Check

6. What is the role of state supreme courts?

Explaining

7. What can make it hard for a judge to make a fair decision?

Making Inferences

8. Why is it important for judges to be free from bias?

Mark the Text

9. Fill in the graphic organizer with the ways trial court judges are chosen.

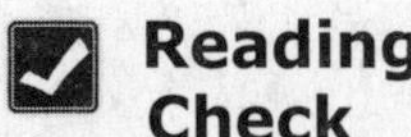

Lesson 4: State Judicial Branch, *Continued*

Reading Check

10. What are the most common ways to select appellate judges?

______

______

Paraphrasing

11. How can judges be suspended or removed?

______

______

______

FOLDABLES®

12. Place a three-tab Foldable along the dotted line. Write the title *Judges* on the anchor tab. Label the first tab *Qualifications,* the middle *Appointment or Election* and the last tab *Removal from Office*. Use both sides of the Foldable to list facts about judges.

Election systems differ too. Some states have nonpartisan elections. This means that candidates are not linked to any political party. Other states allow judges to run as members of political parties.

Choosing judges for the appellate courts is simpler. About half of the states elect them.

In the other half, the governor chooses them. In some states, judges who are chosen must be accepted by the legislature or another body.

The length of time an appellate judge serves is different from state to state. In most states, once a term is done, a judge has to be approved again for the next term. In forty-one states this is done by popular vote. In the other states, either the governor or the legislature makes the decision.

Judges can be removed from office by impeachment, but this takes a long time. Most states also have a board that looks into complaints about judges. If the board finds that the judge's actions were wrong it can make a recommendation, or suggestion, to the state supreme court. The court has the power to suspend or remove the judge.

/ / / / / / / / / / / / / Glue Foldable here / / / / / / / / / / / / / /

Check for Understanding

List the two levels of state courts. Give a brief description of each.

1. ______

2. ______

List two ways appellate judges are approved for a second term.

3. ______

4. ______

NAME ______________________ DATE ____________ CLASS __________

networks

Local Government

Lesson 1: City Governments

ESSENTIAL QUESTION

Why do people create, structure, and change governments?

GUIDING QUESTIONS

1. ***How are local governments created, funded, and organized?***
2. ***How does the mayor-council form of government operate?***
3. ***How do the council-manager and commission forms of government serve local communities?***

Terms to Know

incorporate to receive a state charter officially recognizing a local government

city charter a document granting power to a local government

home rule allows cities to write their own charters, choose their own type of government, and manage their own affairs

ordinance a law, usually of a city or county

at-large election an election for a city or other area as a whole

dominate to have great influence over

reluctant unwilling

special district a unit of government that deals with a single service, such as education, water supply, or transportation

metropolitan area a large city and its suburbs

suburb a community near a larger city

What Do You Know?

In the first column, answer the questions based on what you know before you study. After this lesson, complete the last column.

Now...		Later...
	How are local governments similar to the federal government?	
	How do local governments help their community?	

Mark the Text

1. Circle the services that local governments provide.

How City Governments Are Created

About three out of four Americans live in cities or urban areas. City governments play a big role in people's daily lives. They provide local services, such as police and fire protection, water and sewer service, schools, public transportation, and libraries. Local governments are not independent, though. Their powers and duties come from their state constitutions.

Lesson 1: City Governments, *Continued*

New cities are created when communities **incorporate**. To incorporate means to apply for and be granted a **city charter.** A city charter is a plan for city government. The city charter, granted by the state, gives power to a local government. Communities must meet certain conditions to get a city charter. Sometimes a certain number of people have to live there. Like a constitution, a city charter describes the city's type of government, how it will be set up, and its powers. An incorporated city is also known as a municipality.

Sometimes a state legislature gives a city **home rule.** This lets cities write their own charters. These cities choose their own form of government. They run their own affairs. However, they still have to follow state laws.

How City Governments Are Created

A community meets the requirements and applies to the state legislature for a city charter. → The state legislature grants the charter. The charter describes the form of government the city must have. → The community incorporates. It forms a city government based on its charter.

Local governments pay for the services they provide with money from federal and state grants. Money also comes from taxes. The rest comes from fees and fines for things like dog licenses and traffic tickets.

The Mayor-Council Form

Most American towns and cities use one of three forms of government. They are:

- the mayor-council form,
- the council-manager form, and
- the commission form.

The mayor-council form is the oldest type of city government. Most of the nation's biggest cities use it. It is based on a separation of powers. The mayor is the chief executive. He or she oversees city departments such as police and fire. Mayors often appoint people to head the departments. The council has legislative power. It passes city laws, or **ordinances**. It approves the city's budget.

Reading Check

2. How are city governments created?

____

____

____

Identifying

3. What sources of income do local governments use to pay for the services they provide?

____

____

Listing

4. List the three forms of government most U.S. towns and cities use.

____

____

____

Identifying

5. What is the basis for the mayor-council form of city government?

____

____

Lesson 1: City Governments, *Continued*

Vocabulary

6. Use the term *dominate* to describe the role of strong mayors.

Reading Check

7. Why would successful government be less likely under a weak-mayor plan?

Explaining

8. Why was the council-manager form of city government created?

Reading Check

9. How does a council-manager government differ from a commission government?

The voters elect the mayor and members of the council. In some cities, each voting district elects a representative to the city council. Other cities hold **at-large elections** for council members. This means they are elected by the whole city instead of individual districts.

There are two types of mayor-council government. One is the strong-mayor system. This system gives the mayor strong powers. The mayor can veto, or cancel, laws passed by the city council, appoint department heads, and write the budget. Strong mayors tend to **dominate**, or control, a city government.

Under the weak-mayor system, the mayor's power is limited. The council appoints department heads. It makes the key decisions. Under this plan, many people share responsibility. The mayor usually directs council meetings but only votes if there is a tie. Success in this system depends on how well the mayor and the council work together. The weak-mayor system dates back to colonial days when people were **reluctant** to give any official too much power.

Council-Manager and Commission Governments

The council-manager form of government began in the early 1900s. It was seen as a way to make city government more honest and well organized.

Under this plan, an elected city council hires a city manager. The manager oversees city departments and suggests a budget. The city council can fire the manager by a majority vote. Most city managers have special training in areas like managing money and planning.

The commission form of government also began in the 1900s. It does not separate legislative and executive powers. Instead, the government is divided into departments, such as fire, police, and health. The heads of these departments are called commissioners. The people elect them. As department heads, they have executive power, or they run the day-to-day activities of the departments they lead. The commissioners meet regularly as a body called a commission. One of the commissioners serves as chairperson. The commission meets to pass city laws. As a body, they have legislative power.

This system has some problems. No one person is in charge of a commission. Without clear leadership, a commission has trouble setting and meeting goals.

Lesson 1: City Governments, *Continued*

Commissioners will usually focus on their own individual departments. They may compete for resources like money. They may not think about what is best for the city as a whole. Only a few cities still use this form of government.

Two other types of local government are the special district and the metropolitan area. A **special district** is a unit of government formed to handle one service. This might be water supply or education. A special district is run by a board or a commission. Its members may be elected or appointed. Local school districts are the most common example of a special district.

A **metropolitan area** is a city and the **suburbs** around it. A suburb is a community near or around a city. A metropolitan area can also include the small towns outside the suburbs. Suburbs have grown since the 1950s. As a result, more people live in some suburbs than the cities they surround. Metropolitan areas are challenged in the areas of transportation, pollution, and land use. Some metropolitan areas form special councils that bring city and suburban officials together to work on common problems.

Check for Understanding

List three services that local governments provide.

1. ________ **2.** ________ **3.** ________

Name the three forms of government used by cities and towns.

4. ________ **5.** ________ **6.** ________

Name two duties performed by mayors in the strong-mayor form of government.

7. ________ **8.** ________

Explaining

10. What is the main drawback to a commission form of government?

____

____

____

Identifying

11. Fill in the diagram with the basic forms of city government.

Vocabulary

12. What is a *metropolitan area*?

____

____

FOLDABLES®

13. Place a Venn diagram Foldable along the dotted line. Cut lines up to the anchor to make three tabs. Label the tabs *Council-Manager*, *Both*, and *Commission*. On each of the outer tabs, write facts about each on both sides. On the inner tab write the facts that they have in common.

Glue Foldable here

NAME ______________________ DATE ______________ CLASS __________

networks

Local Government

Lesson 2: County Governments

ESSENTIAL QUESTION

Why do people create, structure, and change governments?

GUIDING QUESTIONS

1. ***How is county government organized?***
2. ***What functions do county governments perform?***

Terms to Know

county usually the largest land-based and political subdivision of a state

county seat the town where a county courthouse is located

levy to demand and collect a tax or other payment

estimate to form a rough or general idea of the cost, size, or value of something

What Do You Know?

In the first column, answer the questions based on what you know before you study. After this lesson, complete the last column.

Now...		Later...
	How is a county government different from a state government?	
	What problems do county governments solve?	

FOLDABLES

1. Place a one-tab Foldable on the line. Write *Counties* on the anchor. On the front and back, write facts about counties as you read this section.

Reading Check

2. How were county seats originally chosen?

____

How County Governments Are Organized

/ / / / / / / / / / / / / Glue Foldable here / / / / / / / / / / / / /

Most states are divided into smaller units of land called **counties**. There are more than 3,000 counties or county-like divisions in the nation. County government is another type of local government.

Each county is very different. One county might have millions of residents. Another county might have only a few dozen. Counties also differ in size. Some counties in the West are bigger than whole states in the East. Two states do even not use the term *county*. In Alaska, counties are called boroughs. In Louisiana, they are known as parishes.

In the 1800s, the county courthouse was the center of county government. It was where legal records were kept and trials were held. The town where the county courthouse was located was called the **county seat**. It was usually located in the center of the county because officials wanted citizens to be able to travel there and get back home in one day traveling by horse and buggy.

The Functions of County Government

Counties today play a different role than they once did. As cities have grown, many have taken over the services that counties once handled. However, some counties are stronger than ever. Many have taken on the duties of cities. These duties include sewer and water service, police and fire protection, road repairs, and public transportation.

Most counties are governed by a board of three to five elected officials. These officials are called commissioners or supervisors. The board acts as a legislature. It passes ordinances, or laws. It sets a yearly budget for the county, **levies** taxes, and oversees law enforcement.

The basic form of county government is the strong commission form. Two other forms are the commission-manager and commission-elected executive.

In the strong commission form, the county commissioners or supervisors have both legislative and executive powers. They pass and carry out the laws. They work alongside other county officials to do some executive work. They supervise other offices. People who serve in these positions come from a variety of backgrounds, but do not always have a lot of experience in government. Some states have training programs for their board members.

As public needs have grown, many counties have changed the function of the county board. In such counties, the board has legislative power only. Executive power goes to either the commission-manager or commission-elected executive. In the commission-manager form, the board names a county manager. This person is like a city manager. In the commission-elected executive form, counties create a new office. The voters elect the executive.

In both of these forms, the county manager or the executive manages the county government and carries out its laws. The county board works with this leader.

Commission-Manager	Commission-Elected Executive	Strong Commission

Explaining

3. How has the role of county government changed over time?

____

____

____

____

Vocabulary

4. What does it mean to *levy* a tax? Circle the unit within county government that levies taxes.

____

____

____

Reading Check

5. What body governs most counties in the United States?

____

____

Describing

6. In each box, write two words or phrases describing how that form of government is organized.

Lesson 2: County Governments, *Continued*

Identifying

7. How are county sheriffs and district attorneys chosen?

____

Vocabulary

8. Use the term *estimate* in a sentence about county government.

____

____

Inferring

9. What are some characteristics of a property that county assessors may consider when estimating its value?

____

____

____

____

FOLDABLES®

10. Place a one-tab Foldable along the dotted line. On the tab list ways county governments help citizens.

Glue Foldable here

Some important county officials are elected on their own to do very specific jobs. One of these is the county sheriff. He or she is in charge of law enforcement. The sheriff's department enforces court orders and runs the county jail.

Another is the district attorney (DA). The DA is the county's prosecutor. He or she looks into crimes and brings charges against people suspected of breaking the law. He or she tries to prove in court that they are guilty.

Other county officials may be appointed or elected:

- The county assessor **estimates,** or sets a rough value on, how much taxable land and buildings are worth. The county's property tax is based on the rough value he or she sets.
- The county treasurer is in charge of the county's money. The treasurer collects taxes and pays the bills.
- The auditor makes sure the county follows state and local laws when spending its money.
- A county clerk keeps official records for the government.
- A county coroner works with the police department. He or she tries to figure out the cause of death in unusual cases.

Check for Understanding

Name three ways that county government can be organized.

1. ______________________

2. ______________________

3. ______________________

List two services that county government may provide for citizens.

4. ______________________

5. ______________________

Local Government

Lesson 3: Towns, Townships, and Villages

ESSENTIAL QUESTION

Why do people create, structure, and change governments?

GUIDING QUESTIONS

1. ***How and why did town governments and meetings develop?***
2. ***How are township and village governments organized?***

Terms to Know

town a political unit that is larger than a village and smaller than a city

township a subdivision of a county that has its own government

town meeting a gathering of local citizens to discuss and vote on important issues

complex having many parts connected together

similar almost the same

village the smallest unit of local government

What Do You Know?

In the first column, answer the questions based on what you know before you study. After this lesson, complete the last column.

Now...		Later...
	Why do we need town governments?	
	How does government in towns and villages work?	

Towns and Town Meetings

Counties are often divided into smaller political units. In the New England states, units that are smaller than cities and larger than villages are called **towns**. In other states, especially in the Midwest, they are called **townships**. These governments get their powers from the state, just as county and city governments do.

In New England, town governments take care of the needs of most small communities. Elsewhere, townships and counties share powers. In the South and West, where there may be no townships, county governments are usually more important.

Many New England towns have a **town meeting** form of government. This kind of government began in the 1600s. In a town meeting, the people of a town gather once a year. They discuss local and world issues and vote on town rules, taxes, and budgets. Citizens, not elected representatives, make the decisions. This is direct democracy, one of the oldest forms of government in the country.

Vocabulary

1. Explain the difference between a *town* and a *township.*

____

____

Reading Check

2. What are town meetings?

____

____

Lesson 3: Towns, Townships, and Villages, *Continued*

Explaining

3. Why have some New England towns given up the town meeting form of government?

Analyzing

4. Give an example of a broad issue that citizens may vote on during a yearly town meeting.

Drawing Conclusions

5. Why do you think many Midwestern townships today look perfectly square on a map?

Explaining

6. How are most townships governed?

Yearly town meetings are good for making broad decisions, but not for day-to-day governing. So towns also elect people to take care of the daily work of government. These officials are called "selectmen." This is an old title. It is used today for both men and women.

As towns grew, the duties of government became more **complex.** Direct democracy did not always work. As a result, some New England towns have changed to representative town meetings. Other towns no longer hold town meetings. They elect a town council to run the local government.

How New England Town Meetings Changed Over Time

In early New England town meetings, citizens—not elected representatives—made the important decisions. →	Government business grew more complex over time. Town meetings were not able to handle all of the functions of government. →	Towns began electing representatives to carry out the daily functions of government. Yearly town meetings let citizens vote on broad issues. Some towns have replaced traditional town meetings with representative town meetings.

Townships and Villages

In New York, New Jersey, and Pennsylvania, counties are divided into townships. Township governments are to town governments.

Midwestern states also have townships. They were made when the nation was growing to the west. Congress ordered surveyors to divide the new land into square blocks. Each block was six miles wide and six miles long. As people settled the region, they set up local governments called townships.

Most townships elect a group of officials to pass laws and deal with government business. The group may be called a township committee, board of supervisors, or board of trustees. It will usually hold meetings to involve citizens in government. Often township and county governments work together to provide local services.

Local Government

Lesson 3: Towns, Townships, and Villages, *Continued*

The smallest unit of local government is the **village.** Villages are usually inside a township or county. In some communities, people grow unhappy with the county's services. For example, they may want to set up their own school system. When that happens, the people may ask the state for permission to set up a village government.

Most villages elect a board of trustees to run their government. Some villages also elect an executive, who may be called a mayor, chief burgess, or president of the board. A large village might hire a city manager. The village board has the power to collect taxes. It may spend this money on projects that help the community, such as water systems and taking care of the streets.

The people in a village usually have better services than they had before. This can attract visitors, new residents, and businesses. Becoming a village has a downside, however. Taxes may be higher to support the added layer of government. Still, many people think that the higher taxes are worth the other benefits of living in a village.

Check for Understanding

List two things that citizens may be asked to vote on in a town meeting.

1. ______________________

2. ______________________

Name two ways in which village governments may be organized.

3. ______________________

4. ______________________

Glue Foldable here

Comparing

7. How is setting up a village government like setting up a city government?

____

____

Reading Check

8. What is an advantage of setting up a village government?

____

____

____

FOLDABLES®

9. Place a two-tab Foldable along the dotted line. Write *Local Government* on the anchor tab. Write *Direct Democracy* on the first tab and *Representative Democracy* on the second. Use the front and reverse to describe the different forms of local government.

Dealing With Community Issues

Lesson 1: How a Community Handles Issues

ESSENTIAL QUESTION

How do citizens, both individually and collectively, influence government policy?

GUIDING QUESTIONS

1. ***How does public policy work to serve the needs of the community?***
2. ***How do community leaders make public policy decisions?***

Terms to Know

policy a guiding course of action

public policy the government plan to solve problems or resolve issues in the community

convince to persuade or win over

planning commission an advisory group to a community

professional a worker with much education and high-level skills

short-term plan a government policy being carried out over the next few years

long-term plan a government plan for policy that can span 10 to 50 years

infrastructure a community's system of roads, bridges, water, and sewers

resource the money, people, and materials available to accomplish a community's goals

master plan a plan that states a list of goals and explains how the government will carry them out over time

What Do You Know?

In the first column, answer the questions based on what you know before you study. After this lesson, complete the last column.

Now...		Later...
	What is public policy?	
	How do local communities make public policy?	

Mark the Text

1. Circle examples of needs communities have. Underline challenges. As you read, think of other examples.

Shaping Public Policy

All communities have needs. Some examples of these needs are transportation, clean water, and good schools. Communities also face challenges. For example, one town might lack housing for everyone who needs it. Another might have overcrowding in the schools. A third community might need more businesses.

To solve problems like these, governments develop policies. A **policy** is a course of action that a group takes to address an issue. All organizations have policies. For example, your school has a policy to deal with students who are late or absent.

Lesson 1: How a Community Handles Issues, *Continued*

A government's course of action in response to a community issue or problem is called **public policy.** Public policy may deal with a single issue, such as whether to build a road. Or it may deal with broad issues such as health care.

Ideas for public policy come from many places. People in government and the media may suggest them. Political parties often put forward policy ideas. Private citizens can also help shape public policy, especially at the local level. One person or group can often **convince,** or persuade, a local government to address their concerns.

Planning for the Future

Making public policy is not easy. Community leaders have to think about the results of their decisions. They must consider how a policy will affect people, not just now but in the long run. In other words, they must plan for the future.

Local governments often use planning commissions to do this work. A **planning commission** is a group that gives advice about future needs. It helps guide the growth of a community.

A planning commission may include leaders from government and business. It may include people who live in the community. It may also include **professionals.** These are people with a high level of education and skill in a certain field. For example, engineers and architects are types of professionals.

There are two types of public policy, short term and long term. A **short-term plan** is a policy that is meant to be carried out in a few years. For example, building a new school is a short-term plan. A **long-term plan** is a broader policy. It is meant to serve as a guide over 10, 20, or 50 years.

Community Project Planning	
Short-Term Plan	**Long-Term Plan**
Build a new school	Infrastructure planning

Reading Check

2. What is public policy?

____

____

Explaining

3. At what level are private citizens usually most effective at influencing public policy?

____

____

Analyzing

4. Why is it important to include government and business leaders, citizens, and professionals on a planning commission?

____

____

____

Identifying

5. Write examples of community projects that you think might require each type of plan in the chart.

Dealing With Community Issues

Lesson 1: How a Community Handles Issues, *Continued*

Reading Check

6. What factors should a community consider when setting priorities? Why?

____

____

____

Identifying

7. What are the two main considerations when planning for future growth?

____

____

FOLDABLES®

8. Place a three-tab Venn diagram Foldable along the dotted line. Label the first tab *Short-term Plan,* the middle tab *Both,* and the last tab *Long-term Plan*. On the reverse tabs write facts about each to compare and contrast the plans made by local governments for their communities.

Making Public Policy

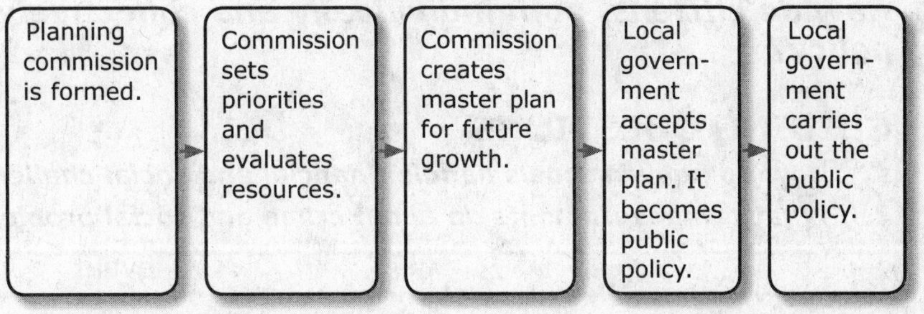

Planning commission is formed.	→	Commission sets priorities and evaluates resources.	→	Commission creates master plan for future growth.	→	Local govern-ment accepts master plan. It becomes public policy.	→	Local govern-ment carries out the public policy.

To make long-term plans, a planning commission has to consider a community's future needs. For example, a growing town will have more people using the infrastructure in years to come. **Infrastructure** is a town's system of roads, bridges, water, and sewers.

The planning commission must plan for future growth, but how? Should they build more roads to allow for more cars? Or expand the bus or train system? Whatever policy they pick, town leaders must also raise money to pay for it.

Such decisions usually depend on two things: priorities and resources. A community's priorities are its most urgent or important goals. A community must first set its goals. Then it needs to compare and rank them by importance.

Resources are the money, people, and materials on hand to reach a community's goals. Town leaders must identify existing resources. They must also find ways to increase resources to pay for the higher costs of growth.

The planning commission then creates a **master plan** that sets out specific priorities. It explains how the government will carry out the goals to meet changing needs. If the local government accepts the plan, it becomes public policy. The government is then responsible for carrying out the policy.

/ / / / / / / / / / / / / Glue Foldable here / / / / / / / / / / / / /

Check for Understanding

What type of public policy would address:

1. A need for new sidewalks? ______________________

2. A housing shortage? ______________________

3. Litter in the parks? ______________________

NAME ______________________ DATE ______________ CLASS __________

networks

Dealing With Community Issues

Lesson 2: Education and Social Issues

ESSENTIAL QUESTION

How do citizens, both individually and collectively, influence government policy?

GUIDING QUESTIONS

1. ***How do public schools handle financial and social challenges?***
2. ***What can governments do about crime and social problems?***

Terms to Know

charter school a type of school that receives state funding but is excused from meeting many public school regulations

regulation a rule

alternative other choice

tuition voucher a certificate issued by the government that provides money for education, allowing families the option of sending students to private schools

community policing local police force visibly keeping the peace and patrolling neighborhoods

What Do You Know?

In the first column, answer the questions based on what you know before you study. After this lesson, complete the last column.

Now...		Later...
	What problems do public schools face?	
	How are states trying to solve problems with schools?	

Public Education

About 50 million students today go to public schools in the United States. These schools are under the control of the states. This is because the U.S. Constitution does not mention education as an area of federal responsibility.

The first free public schools opened in colonial times. They were run and paid for by local governments. In most states today, local school districts still run elementary and secondary schools. They pay for the schools with local taxes. Local districts also receive money from the state, and they must follow rules set by the state.

The federal government also has an important role, or function, in the public schools. It provides money to the states to help fund the schools. In return, it requires schools to follow certain rules.

Identifying

1. How do local governments pay for schools?

____

____

____

____

Lesson 2: Education and Social Issues, *Continued*

Analyzing

2. In what ways does the federal government influence education?

Reading Check

3. What is the reason for the spending gap between wealthy and poor school districts?

Listing

4. List four problems facing public schools today.

Vocabulary

5. What is a *charter school*?

In recent years, the federal government has gotten more involved in public education. For example, the No Child Left Behind Act of 2001 provides money for schools. But it also requires states to test all students in grades three through eight in reading, science, and math. A 2009 law created the Race to the Top Fund. To win a share of the money in the fund, states had to meet goals set by the federal government. Some critics say that these laws overstep the limits of federal power set out in the Constitution.

The states' goal is to make sure that all public school students receive an equal, high quality education. It is a challenge. Most schools are funded by local property taxes. Wealthier districts with high property values get plenty of tax revenue. Poorer districts with low property values get very little. Many states give money to schools in poorer areas to help close the gap.

Schools also face social problems. They include low test scores and high dropout rates. Crime and violence are issues in some schools. Such problems have roots in larger social problems, such as poverty, and drug and alcohol use.

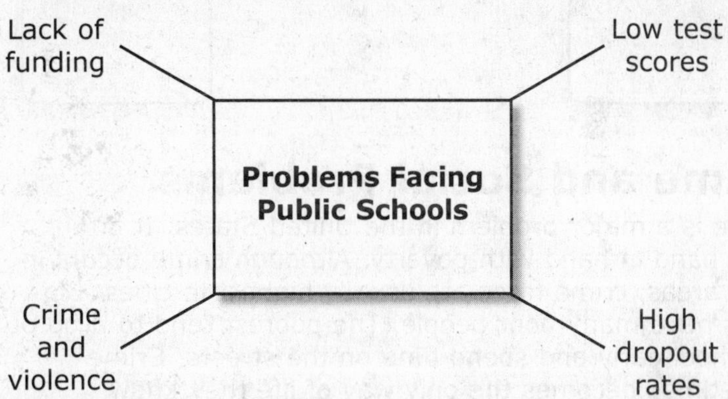

There are many ideas for how to improve low-performing public schools. One idea is more testing. The No Child Left Behind Act is based on this idea. The tests are meant to measure student learning and to show how well teachers and schools are doing their job. However, not everyone agrees that more tests lead to greater learning.

States are also trying new ways of running schools. Many states now allow **charter schools.** These schools receive state funding but do not have to meet many state **regulations,** or rules, for public schools. Some school districts have also tried bringing in private companies to run schools.

Lesson 2: Education and Social Issues, *Continued*

Another idea is to give parents an **alternative,** or other choice, with **tuition vouchers.** These are like government money orders. Some cities and states give out tuition vouchers to help parents pay for private school. Critics say that vouchers violate the First Amendment because they can be used to pay for a child to go to a religious school. However, the Supreme Court has ruled that their use is constitutional. The funds must go directly to the parents or guardians and not to the schools, however.

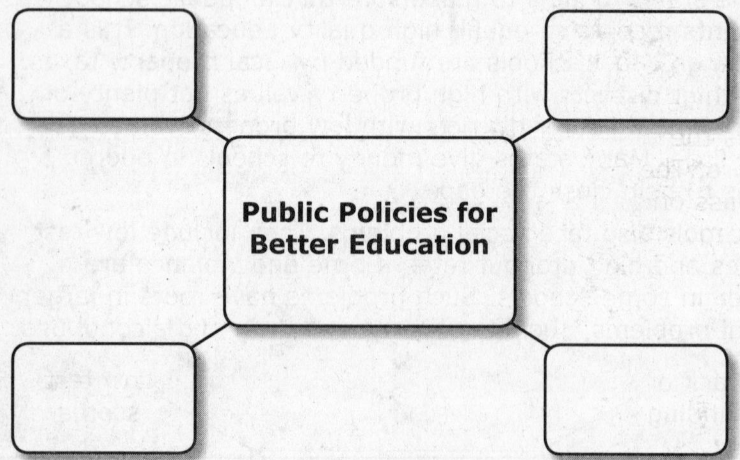

Mark the Text

6. Underline the words that tell you what *alternative* means.

Identifying

7. In the diagram, write four public policies aimed at improving education. Circle the one you think will improve education the most.

Explaining

8. In which areas is the crime rate highest? Why?

____

____

____

____

Describing

9. Describe the different police forces used in cities, rural areas, and by the states.

____

____

____

____

Crime and Social Problems

Crime is a major problem in the United States. It often goes hand in hand with poverty. Although crime occurs in rural areas, crime rates are usually highest in cities. Big cities have many poor people. The poorest tend to drop out of school early and spend time on the streets. Crime sometimes becomes the only way of life they know.

America's major cities all have large police forces. In rural areas, county sheriffs and deputies enforce the law. Every state also has either a state police department or a highway patrol to enforce state law.

Police departments do a range of jobs. They investigate crimes and capture suspects. More often, they keep the peace. They handle neighborhood disputes and direct traffic.

Lesson 2: Education and Social Issues, *Continued*

Analyzing

10. How might community policing help a local school?

____

____

Reading Check

11. What is the basic purpose of welfare programs?

____

____

____

Identifying

12. In the chart, write the public policy solution to the problems listed.

FOLDABLES®

13. Place a three-tab Foldable along the dotted line. Write *Public Education* on the anchor tab. Label the tabs *Local, State,* and *Federal Government*. On the back of each tab, write how that level of government helps public education.

Community policing is a program in which police are active in neighborhoods. Officers patrol on foot or on bikes. They get to know residents. They work with neighborhood watch groups. These groups keep an eye on the community and report suspicious activity to the police. Such programs have brought down the crime rate in many cities.

To fight poverty and other social problems, the government provides welfare programs. These programs give financial help to Americans who suffer from ill health, old age, poverty, and disabilities. Welfare programs have existed for years. They have both critics and supporters.

In 1996, Congress created a new program called Temporary Assistance for Needy Families (TANF). TANF gives the states more control over welfare than they had before. The federal government gives money to the states to pass on as welfare payments. Each state decides who gets money and how much. State programs have to meet federal rules. They also have to provide job training to help people find work and get off welfare.

Under TANF, the number of people on welfare has dropped. Some say that this is because the economy grew in the years after TANF became law. Jobs were easier to find. In 2008, the economy entered a slump. Many people lost jobs and income. However, the number of people on welfare is still less than in the past. Some say that this is a problem. They argue that hard times have now left many Americans both without jobs *and* without the welfare payments.

Social Problem	Policy Solution
Crime	
Poverty	

/ / / / / / / / / / / / / Glue Foldable here / / / / / / / / / / / / / /

Check for Understanding

What roles do local, state, and federal governments play in public education?

1. ______________________________

2. ______________________________

Dealing With Community Issues

Lesson 3: Environmental Issues

ESSENTIAL QUESTION

How do citizens, individually and collectively, influence government policy?

GUIDING QUESTIONS

1. ***Why is it important to protect and preserve the environment?***
2. ***How do local governments control pollution and deal with waste?***

Terms to Know

environmentalism movement concerned with protecting the environment
solid waste the technical name for garbage
landfill a place where garbage is dumped
attitude a feeling or way of thinking
NIMBY an acronym that stands for "not in my backyard"; attitude of opposing landfills near one's home
toxic poisonous or deadly
recycling reusing old materials to make new ones
conservation the careful preservation and protection of natural resources
generate to produce

What Do You Know?

In the first column, answer the questions based on what you know before you study. After this lesson, complete the last column.

Now...		Later...
	What environmental problems do communities face?	
	Where does most pollution come from?	

Environmental Concerns

One of the biggest problems facing communities today is pollution. Pollution is the dirtying of air, water, and land with chemicals.

Pollution is a side effect of living in an industrial society. Factories, industrial plants, and most modern forms of transportation create pollution. For example, at airports in winter, chemicals are used to remove ice from airplanes before they take off. Sometimes the chemicals end up in nearby streams. These polluted streams are white and hazy. They cannot support life.

Identifying

1. What is pollution? What causes it?

____

____

____

Dealing With Community Issues

Lesson 3: Environmental Issues, *Continued*

Mark the Text

2. Underline the main idea in the second paragraph.

Explaining

3. What problems do landfills have?

Contrasting

4. Why is it better to recycle paper, plastic, glass, and metal than throw them away?

Reading Check

5. What are some ways to practice conservation?

Environmentalism is the movement concerned with protecting the environment. For years this movement has been working to raise awareness about pollution. In 1970, Congress passed the Clean Air Act. It also set up the Environmental Protection Agency (EPA). The EPA makes rules for business and industry that require them to limit pollution. Many states also have programs that check air and water quality.

Another major problem for communities is getting rid of **solid waste,** or garbage. Americans produce hundreds of millions of tons of garbage each year. **Landfills** are places where it can be dumped. Landfills have problems, though. They are filling up fast. Also, rainwater seeping through the trash can pollute water supplies in the ground below.

It is hard to find new sites for landfills because nobody wants to live near one. This type of **attitude,** or way of thinking, has a name. It is often referred to as **NIMBY,** which stands for "not in my back yard." Citizen groups have blocked the use of many possible sites for landfills.

Some solid waste is burned in huge incinerators. However, burning pollutes the air with **toxic,** or poisonous, smoke.

Recycling is a different way of getting rid of solid waste. **Recycling** means reusing old materials to make new ones. Much of the trash that we throw away is paper. Recycling paper saves forests. It also reduces air and water pollution. Metal cans, plastic bottles and bags, and glass bottles can also be recycled.

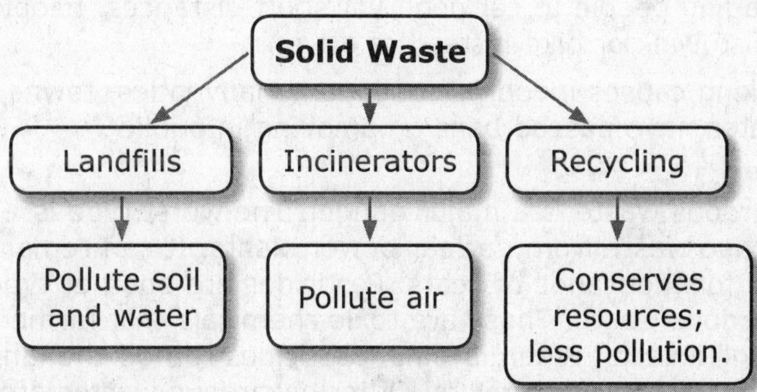

Recycling not only gets rid of waste, it conserves resources. **Conservation** means preserving and protecting natural resources. There are many ways to conserve. Use less water. Turn off lights. Use cloth bags at the store. Turn down the heat or air conditioning in your home. For many Americans, conservation has become a way of life.

Protecting the Air, Water, and Land

Pollution is caused both by industries and by individuals. Most water pollution comes from factories. They **generate,** or produce, many kinds of chemical waste. Factories once dumped this waste into waterways, or buried it in the land. Factories also pollute the air by sending toxic gases up smokestacks.

Today, federal rules limit the amount and kind of pollution factories may release. However, these rules are often not strictly enforced.

Major Sources of Pollution	
AIR	**WATER**
Factory smokestacks	Chemical waste from factories
Cars and trucks	Landfills
Solid waste incinerators	Pesticide runoff from farms

Cars and trucks are a major source of air pollution. The federal government has taken steps to reduce it. The government required that lead be removed from gasoline. It also pushed the auto industry to make cars that pollute less and use less fuel.

Getting cars off the road would also reduce air pollution. Many local governments are trying to get people to drive less. They are building mass transit systems. They are also encouraging people to car pool. For short distances, people could also walk or bike instead of drive.

Smoking causes indoor air pollution. Many cities, towns, and states have passed bans on smoking in public buildings.

Hazardous waste is a major danger. The worst type is radioactive waste from nuclear power plants. It can remain harmful for thousands of years. Pesticides are another type of hazardous waste. These are toxic chemicals that farmers use to kill insects. When it rains, pesticides run off the land and enter streams and rivers. Other hazardous wastes are batteries, motor oil, house paint, and auto engine coolant.

Identifying

6. Where does most water pollution come from?

____

____

Explaining

7. What did the federal government do to try to reduce pollution from cars and trucks?

____

____

____

____

Summarizing

8. Why is hazardous waste particularly harmful?

____

____

____

____

Listing

9. List four types of hazardous waste.

____

____

____

____

Dealing With Community Issues

Lesson 3: Environmental Issues, *Continued*

Analyzing

10. Why do you think ocean dumping has been banned?

______

______

______

Reading Check

11. What have individual citizens done to protect the environment?

______

______

______

Mark the Text

12. Underline three federal laws that protect the environment.

FOLDABLES®

13. Place a one-tab Foldable along the dotted line. At the top of the tab write *Ways local, state, and federal governments try to control pollution*. Use both sides of the Foldable to write your answer.

Getting rid of toxic waste is difficult. No method is completely safe. Leaks can occur. Toxic waste used to be sealed in metal containers, covered in concrete, and dumped in the ocean. Today ocean dumping is illegal. Toxic waste is sent to special landfills. Those sites are filling up.

Many citizen groups have formed to protect the environment and conserve natural resources. These groups often work with local governments and businesses. Their shared goal is sustainable development. This means creating economic growth without harming the environment. For example, builders can design new buildings that use less energy to heat and cool. Timber companies can plant new trees after cutting down old ones.

The federal government also plays a role. The EPA sets and enforces pollution standards. The Clean Air Act sets limits for air pollution from factories and cars. The Clean Water Act (1972) limits dumping in the nation's lakes and rivers. The Endangered Species Act (1973) sets up rules for saving animal species in danger of dying out completely.

/ / / / / / / / / / / / Glue Foldable here / / / / / / / / / / / /

Check for Understanding

How do different levels of government protect the environment?

1. ______

2. ______

Describe two ways that recycling helps the environment.

3. ______

4. ______

List two things that make dealing with solid waste difficult for local communities.

5. ______

6. ______

Citizens and the Law

Lesson 1: Sources and Types of Law

ESSENTIAL QUESTION

How do laws protect individual rights?

GUIDING QUESTIONS

1. ***What is the purpose of laws?***
2. ***What early legal systems influenced the laws we live by today?***
3. ***What types of laws exist in the American legal system?***

Terms to Know

potential capable of being or becoming
code an organized statement of a body of law
common law law based on court decisions and customs
precedent an earlier ruling on which decisions in later, similar cases are based
statute law made by a legislative branch of government
lawsuit a legal action in which a person or group sues to collect damages for some harm that has been done
constitutional law branch of law dealing with forming and interpreting constitutions
case law law based on judge's decisions instead of legislative action
administrative law rules and regulations set by government agencies

What Do You Know?

In the first column, answer the questions based on what you know before you study. After this lesson, complete the last column.

Now...		Later...
	Why do we need laws?	
	Give some examples of laws in our country.	

Reading Check

1. How do laws help people live together peacefully?

____

____

Why We Have Laws

Laws are sets of rules. They allow people to live together in peace and help prevent violence. Laws explain which actions are allowed in a society and which will be punished. If you break the law, you can expect to be punished. Punishments are used to discourage **potential,** or possible, criminals from breaking the law.

Some laws are better than others. The table on the next page shows the four main qualities of good laws.

Lesson 1: Sources and Types of Law, *Continued*

Qualities of Good Laws			
Fair	**Reasonable**	**Understandable**	**Enforceable**
A fair law treats people equally. Fair laws do not make different rules for different groups of people.	To be reasonable, a law must not be too harsh. Cutting off someone's hand for stealing a loaf of bread would not be reasonable.	They must be easy to understand. Otherwise people might break them without realizing it.	Laws that are hard for police and other officials to enforce are not good laws.

Use the Graphic

2. What are the four qualities of a good law? Circle the answer in the text. Underline the explanation of each quality.

Explaining

3. About how long ago was the Code of Hammurabi written?

____

Making Connections

4. Explain the connection between the growth of the Roman Empire and the influence of its laws.

____

____

Explaining

5. Where did canon law come from?

____

____

____

Development of the Legal System

There were laws even in the earliest societies. It is thought that prehistoric people had rules about behavior. The earliest laws were not written, they were spoken. Over time, people began to write them down.

In about 1760 B.C. King Hammurabi (HA•muh•RAH•bee) of the Middle Eastern empire in Babylonia created the oldest written law. It is called the Code of Hammurabi. A **code** is an organized statement of a body of law. The Code of Hammurabi was written in a wedge shaped script called cuneiform. The code included laws related to the family, such as marriage and slavery, as well as business practices. It also set prices for goods and services.

The Israelites were a people who lived near the eastern Mediterranean coast. They followed a set of written laws also. These laws outlawed such acts as murder and theft. Many of these acts are still considered crimes today.

The ancient Romans developed a set of laws that were the most important in the Western world. The first Roman laws were published in 450 B.C. As the Roman Empire grew the laws spread to parts of Europe, Asia, and Africa. In A.D. 533 the ruler of the Byzantine (BIH•zehn•TEEN) Empire, simplified the laws and named it the Justinian Code. This code became part of the laws of the Roman Catholic Church. This part of church law is called canon law.

The Justinian Code was updated in 1804 by the French emperor Napoleon Bonaparte. He called it the Napoleonic Code. Napoleon spread his code to all the lands he conquered. The Louisiana Territory had been under French control before the United States bought it in 1803. Louisiana still has laws that were based on this code.

Lesson 1: Sources and Types of Law, *Continued*

FOLDABLES®

6. Place a three-tab Foldable along the dotted line to cover the text. Label the anchor tab *English Laws.* Label the three tabs *Common Law, Precedents,* and *Statutes.* Use both sides of the tabs to define each term.

Comparing and Contrasting

7. What is the difference between a *precedent* and a *statute*?

____

____

Reading Check

8. How are Roman law, the Justinian Code, and the Napoleonic Code related?

____

____

____

____

____

____

____

/ / / / / / / / / / / / / / /Glue Foldable here/ / / / / / / / / / / / / /

The most important source for American laws is English **common law.** Common law is law based on court decisions and customs instead of legal code. It began after the Normans of France took control of England in 1066. Judges were sent into the countryside to hear cases. These judges based their rulings on **precedents,** or the rulings given earlier in similar cases. This practice of following precedent became part of the common law. Common law is considered judge-made law.

The English blended Roman law and canon law into common law. Common law included the basic principles of individual rights, such as the idea that a person is innocent until proven guilty. Over time the English added to the common law by allowing Parliament to make laws. Laws made by a legislative branch like Parliament are called **statutes.** When English settlers came to North America in the 1600s and 1700s, they brought their traditions of common law and individual rights with them. They are a key part of the United States judicial system today.

Development of the Legal System

Code of Hammurabi 1760 B.C.
The earliest example of a written code.

↓

Israelites
They followed a written set of laws that outlawed acts such as theft and murder.

↓

Ancient Roman law 450 B.C.
The most important laws in the western world. Partly written by judges and adopted by the senate.

↓

Justinian Code A.D. 533
Roman law was simplified into an orderly body of rules.

↓

English common law after 1066
Law was based on court decisions, not a legal code; considered judge-made law.

↓

U.S. laws developed 1600s–1700s
Principles of English common law and individual rights became key parts of the basic laws of the new nation.

↓

Napoleonic Code 1804
Updated the Justinian Code to a new body of laws.

Lesson 1: Sources and Types of Law, *Continued*

Types of Laws

There are three basic types of laws. Earlier you learned about public laws. The chart below explains the other two types. They are criminal and civil laws.

Types of Laws	Definition
Criminal laws	rules against behaviors that can hurt people or property
Civil laws	rules governing disputes between people or groups

Criminal laws seek to protect public safety. These crimes are divided into two types:

1. *Felonies*–These are serious crimes such as murder and robbery. They have serious penalties.
2. *Misdemeanors*–These are less serious crimes such as vandalism. They usually involve a fine or jail time of less than one year.

Property crimes are the most common type of crime. They can be either misdemeanors or felonies. They do not involve force or the threat of force toward other people. Examples include shoplifting, identity theft, and setting a fire.

Civil laws handle arguments between people and groups. They often involve broken contracts. For example, if you order something from a store, but do not receive the item, the seller has broken a contract with you. You could sue them in court.

A civil case brought before a court is called a **lawsuit.** A lawsuit is legal action to collect damages, or money, for some harm that has been done. Individuals who think they have been wronged must file a lawsuit themselves. The government cannot bring such a case.

Military law is a set of statutes that people serving in the U.S. armed forces follow. Civilians who work for the military do not have to follow those laws. However, people serving in the military do have to follow civil laws. Military laws cover crimes such as disobeying a superior officer and desertion. If the crime is serious a person can end up at a court-martial. That is the court that tries people accused of breaking military laws.

Listing

9. List the three basic types of laws.

____

____

____

Analyzing

10. What is the purpose of criminal laws?

____

____

Identifying

11. Which is more serious, a felony or a misdemeanor?

____

Explaining

12. What is the most common type of crime? Give an example.

____

____

Identifying

13. A person accused of breaking military laws is tried at a ______________.

Citizens and the Law

Lesson 1: Sources and Types of Law, *Continued*

Visualizing

14. If you visualize the sources of law as a pyramid, which one would be at the bottom?

______

Reading Check

15. What is the most important source of law in the United States?

______

Identifying

16. A precedent is a ruling from a case used to judge later similar cases. Which type of law uses precedents?

______

FOLDABLES®

17. Place a Venn diagram Foldable along the line. Label the anchor tab *Laws.* Label the tabs *Past, Both,* and *Present.* Use the tabs to list facts about past and present laws and what they have in common.

Criminal and civil laws come from several main sources. These include:

- the United States Constitution
- state constitutions
- statutes
- case law
- administrative agencies

The Constitution is the highest law in the nation. If there is a conflict between it and one of the other sources of law, the Constitution is always followed.

Constitutional law deals with the structure and meaning of constitutions. It handles questions about the limits of government power. It also deals with individual rights.

A statute is a law written by a legislature. The U.S. Congress, state legislatures, and local lawmakers write statutes. Statutes control our behavior in many ways. For example, they set speed limits and minimum wages. Statutes are also the source of many rights, such as the right to a free public education.

Case law is law that is based on judge's decisions. Some cases brought to court cannot be decided based on existing statutes. In these cases judges look to precedent to make their rulings. These rulings have the same weight as laws.

Administrative law involves all the rules the executive branch makes as it does its job. The federal and state constitutions give legislatures the power to create administrative agencies. For example, Congress created the Federal Aviation Administration. Any orders this agency hands down to airlines have the same weight as other laws.

Glue Foldable here

Check for Understanding

List two purposes for laws in our society.

1. ______

2. ______

How did English law affect our laws today?

3. ______

Which type of law deals with individual rights?

4. ______

NAME ______________________ DATE ____________ CLASS ____________

networks

Lesson 2: The American Legal System

ESSENTIAL QUESTION

How do laws protect individual rights?

GUIDING QUESTIONS

1. ***What basic legal rights are provided to all Americans?***
2. ***What legal protections does the U.S. Constitution offer a citizen who is accused of a crime?***

Terms to Know

writ of habeas corpus court order that says police have to bring a prisoner to court to explain why the person is being held

bill of attainder a law that punishes a person without a trial or a fair hearing in court

ex post facto law a law that punishes a person for an action that was not illegal when it was done

due process following established legal procedures

presumption belief based on a likelihood

search warrant court order allowing police to search a suspect's home or business

exclusionary rule rule that says that evidence gained by police illegally may not be used in court

Miranda Warning list of rights that police must read to a person before questioning

double jeopardy putting a person on trial for a crime for which he or she was previously acquitted

proportion relation of one part to another, balance

bail money used as a security deposit to make sure a person returns for their trial

What Do You Know?

In the first column, answer the questions based on what you know before you study. After this lesson, complete the last column.

Now...		Later...
	How does the Constitution protect your rights?	

Basic Legal Rights

The U.S. Constitution includes many important protections for citizens. These protections prevent the government from using the law unfairly. One of the most important protections is found in Article I. It says that someone who is arrested has the right to ask for a **writ of habeas corpus** (HAY•bee•uhs KAWR•puhs). A writ is a court order. A writ of habeas corpus makes officials explain to a judge why they are holding someone in jail. The judge decides if their reason for holding the person is legal or not. This rule stops officials from putting people in jail unlawfully.

Reading Check

1. How does the Constitution protect you from unlawful imprisonment?

____

____

Lesson 2: The American Legal System, *Continued*

Mark the Text

2. Circle the main idea in the first paragraph.

Vocabulary

3. Explain the *due process* right guaranteed in the Fourteenth Amendment.

____

____

____

____

Identifying

4. Study the chart. Which amendment guarantees the right to trial by jury?

____

What is the source of the protection that requires police to bring a prisoner to court to have the charges against them explained?

____

____

Article I also prevents the government from delivering bills of attainder and creating ex post facto laws. A **bill of attainder** is a law that punishes a person without a trial. An **ex post facto law** punishes a person for doing something that was not illegal at the time it was done. *Ex post facto* means "after the fact."

The Constitution guarantees that the government respects individual rights as it carries out the law. After the Civil War, the Fourteenth Amendment gave civil rights to formerly enslaved people. This amendment says the states must treat all people equally under the law. It bans unequal treatment based on factors such as gender, race, and religion. It has been used to win rights for minorities and women.

The Fourteenth Amendment strengthened the Fifth Amendment right of **due process.** This right says that the government cannot take away our lives, liberty, or property without following the law. For example, a person has the right to a trial by jury.

The Rights of the Accused

The Constitution makes sure that people accused of crimes are treated fairly. It also makes sure they have a chance to defend themselves. These rights are based on the **presumption** of innocence. This means a person is believed to be innocent until proven guilty in court.

Constitutional Rights of the Accused

Source	Rights
Article I	habeas corpus; no bills of attainder; no ex post facto laws
Fourth Amendment	no unreasonable searches and seizures
Fifth Amendment	guarantees due process; no self-incrimination; no double jeopardy; guarantees grand jury in federal crimes
Sixth Amendment	right to counsel; right to know the accusations; right to a speedy public trial; right to confront witnesses; right to be tried by an impartial jury
Eighth Amendment	no cruel and unusual punishments; no excessive bail
Fourteenth Amendment	states must apply the law equally; guarantees due process

Lesson 2: The American Legal System, *Continued*

One right of the accused is found in the Fourth Amendment. It protects us against "unreasonable searches and seizures." That means an officer cannot search your home or take your property without reason. It says that police must get a **search warrant** from a judge before searching a person's home or property. A search warrant is a court document that allows a search. To get a search warrant, police must explain what they are looking for. They must prove that they have a good reason, or probable cause, for the search. If police find evidence without a warrant, that evidence cannot be used in court. This is known as the **exclusionary rule.** This is true in federal and state cases.

The Fifth Amendment protects the rights of the accused. Those rights are listed in the graphic organizer below.

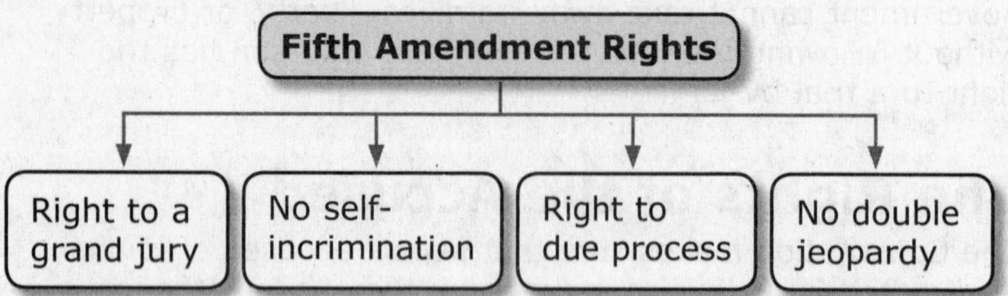

No self-incrimination means that a person has the right to remain silent. That means a person does not have to answer questions that might show they took part in a crime. This was decided in 1966 in the case *Miranda* v. *Arizona.* That year the Supreme Court said that police must issue the **Miranda Warning** to suspects.

A Miranda Warning tells suspects that

- they have the right to remain silent.
- anything they say may be used against them.
- they have the right to an attorney; if they cannot afford one, the court will provide one.

Double jeopardy means to be tried twice for the same crime. A person who was tried once and found not guilty cannot be tried again for the same crime.

The Fifth Amendment also says that an accused person can have his or her case brought to a grand jury. This is mainly used for federal crimes. A grand jury is a group of people who decides whether there is enough evidence to hold a trial. If the grand jury believes there is enough evidence, it indicts the suspect. This means the suspect is formally charged with a crime.

Reading Check

5. Explain why illegally obtained evidence cannot be used in court.

____

____

____

Prior Knowledge

6. Explain the Fifth Amendment's guarantee of due process.

____

____

____

Making Connections

7. In your own words, explain how the Miranda Warning protects the rights of people who are suspected of a crime.

____

____

Mark the Text

8. Underline the sentence that explains what a grand jury is.

Lesson 2: The American Legal System, *Continued*

Listing

9. List two rights of the accused found in the Sixth Amendment.

___

___

Paraphrasing

10. What is meant by the Eighth Amendment's guarantee that punishments should not be "cruel and unusual"?

___

___

___

FOLDABLES®

11. Place a two-tab Foldable along the dotted line. Label the anchor tab *Basic Legal Rights.* Label the two tabs *Articles* and *Amendments*. On both sides of the tabs, explain how each provides protection of basic legal rights.

Glue Foldable here

Some rights of the accused are found in the Sixth Amendment. It says a person has the right to be defended by a lawyer. It also promises that accused people

- have a right to know the charges against them.
- can question their accusers.
- have the right to be tried by an impartial jury.

An impartial jury is a jury made up of people who know no one in the case and have no opinion about it.

The Sixth Amendment also guarantees a speedy public trial. This protects people from being held in jail too long. It also means that trials should be open to the public.

Other rights of the accused are found in the Eighth Amendment. It prohibits, or does not allow, "cruel and unusual" punishments. This means that a punishment must fit the crime. For example, a life sentence in jail for shoplifting would be too severe. Some people believe that the death penalty is cruel and unusual punishment. In 1972 the Supreme Court ruled on this. The Court did not agree that it was cruel, but it did find that it was not applied equally to all persons. It targeted African-Americans and poor people. The Court said that the death penalty was being used in a way that was not constitutional. State death penalty laws were changed after this ruling.

The Eighth Amendment also says that a judge cannot set bail too high. **Bail** is money that a person gives the court in order to be set free from jail until the trial. It is like a security deposit. When the person shows up at the trial the money is returned. When setting bail, the judge looks at how serious the crime is and the criminal record of the accused.

Check for Understanding

List five basic legal rights that the Constitution guarantees to all American citizens.

1. ___

2. ___

3. ___

4. ___

5. ___

Lesson 1: Civil Law

ESSENTIAL QUESTION

Why does conflict develop?

GUIDING QUESTIONS

1. ***What is civil law?***
2. ***What legal procedures are followed in civil lawsuits?***

Terms to Know

contract a set of promises between agreeing parties that is enforceable by law
tort a wrongful act for which a person has the right to sue
negligence a lack of proper care and attention
plaintiff the person who files a lawsuit
defendant the person who is being sued
complaint a formal notice that a lawsuit has been brought
damages money ordered by a court to pay for injuries or losses suffered
summons a notice directing a person to appear in court to answer a complaint or a charge
respond to give a spoken or written answer
discovery a process by which lawyers check facts and gather evidence before a trial

What Do You Know?

In the first column, answer the questions based on what you know before you study. After this lesson, complete the last column.

Now...		Later...
	Why might you sue someone?	
	What happens when you file a lawsuit?	

Types of Civil Law

Civil law is the branch of the law that deals with disputes between people, companies, or the government. Such disputes take place when people think they have been harmed by someone else's actions. In civil law, court cases are called lawsuits. Most lawsuits involve one of four types of civil law. The types of civil law are contract law, property law, family law, and personal injury law.

One type of civil law involves contracts. A **contract** is an agreement between two or more parties to exchange something of value. A written contract is written out and signed by both parties. A contract is broken when one party fails to keep his or her promise. If that happens, the second party can sue.

Vocabulary

1. What is a *contract* and why are contracts important?

____

____

____

____

Lesson 1: Civil Law, *Continued*

Explaining

2. Give an example of a spoken contract.

Categorizing

3. Which branch of civil law would apply in a case in which one sister sues another over the possessions or property given to them after a family member dies?

Vocabulary

4. A wrongful act that causes injury to another person is called a ________. What is another name for this type of case?

Mark the Text

5. Underline the definition of *negligence*.

Not all contracts have to be written. Some everyday actions are contracts though no papers are signed. For example, when a restaurant takes your order for food, a contract is made. The restaurant has promised food. You have promised to pay for the food. That is an example of an oral, or spoken, contract.

Property law includes rules about the buying, selling, and use of land or a building. For example, suppose someone rents a house. The law says that the renter must take care of the house while living in it. The owner must keep the house in good shape for the renter's use. Arguments may arise over who should pay to repair, or fix, something that is broken. For example, if the roof leaks, it is the owner's duty to make the repair. But, what if the renter does not tell the owner the roof is leaking until there is major damage? Who should pay for the repairs then? If the owner and renter cannot agree, one might take the other to court.

Family law has to do with rules applied to family relationships. For example, suppose a married couple is getting a divorce. The way they split their property is a matter of civil law. So is the question of how to divide who will take care of any children they have. A court often decides disputes over such issues. Deaths in a family can also lead to property disputes. For example, people sometimes disagree on who should be given possessions or property when a family member dies.

Personal injury is another branch of civil law. These cases are also called torts. A **tort** is a wrongful act that causes injury to another person or damage to his or her property. For example, a person throws a ball and breaks a window. The flying glass cuts someone nearby. The injured person can sue the person who threw the ball to make them pay for the injury.

A tort may be intentional. This would be the case if the person threw the ball at the window on purpose. But suppose the thrower simply wasn't paying attention. Then the tort would be a result of **negligence** (NEH•glih•JUHNTS). Negligence is acting in a careless or reckless way. It happens when someone does something a reasonable person would not have done.

Lesson 1: Civil Law, *Continued*

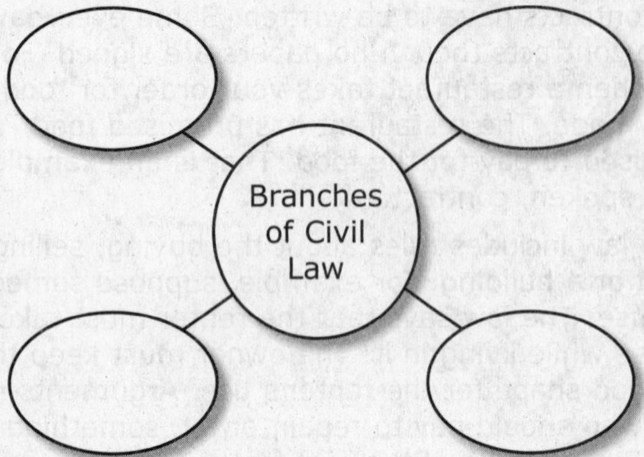

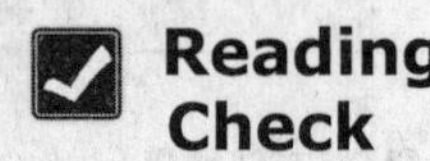

Identifying

6. Fill in the diagram with the four main branches of civil law that you just learned about.

Reading Check

7. Why do people file lawsuits?

____

____

Listing

8. List the steps in the civil legal process that happen before a case goes to trial.

____

____

Vocabulary

9. What is *discovery*?

____

____

Describing

10. Suppose a judge or jury rules in favor of the plaintiff. What happens next?

____

____

____

The Legal Process in Civil Cases

Every lawsuit begins with a plaintiff. The **plaintiff** is the person who brings the lawsuit. The **defendant** is the person being sued.

First, the plaintiff's lawyer files a complaint with the court. The **complaint** describes the wrong and the harm that was done. It usually asks the court to order the defendant to pay the plaintiff a sum of money, called **damages,** to repay the plaintiff for the loss. It may ask the court to order the plaintiff to take a certain action, such as honoring a contract.

Next, the court sends the defendant a **summons.** It tells the defendant that he or she is being sued. It tells the defendant when and where to appear in court.

The defendant's lawyer may **respond** to, or answer, the complaint by filing an answer to the charges. Then both lawyers gather evidence about the dispute. This step is called **discovery.**

At this point, if one side seems likely to win, the other side may offer to come to a settlement, or an agreement. If both sides can agree on the terms, then a settlement is reached. This can be done any time, even during the trial. But because trials are so costly, people usually reach settlements before trials start. Many civil cases never get to trial.

If the two sides do not settle, the suit goes to trial. First the plaintiff presents evidence. Then the defendant presents evidence. Each side sums up its case. Then the judge or a jury reaches a verdict, or decision, in favor of one party.

If the defendant wins, the plaintiff gets nothing. In fact, the plaintiff may even have to pay the defendant's court costs.

Lesson 1: Civil Law, *Continued*

Reading Check

11. What are *damages*?

____

____

____

Sequencing

12. Use the flow chart to write the steps in a civil lawsuit. Add more boxes if you need them.

FOLDABLES®

13. Place a one-tab Foldable along the dotted line to cover the Check for Understanding box. Label the anchor *Civil Law*. On both sides of the tabs, list five facts about civil law.

If the plaintiff wins and damages are involved, the judge or jury sets the amount of damages. Sometimes a judge or jury will also order the defendant to pay punitive damages. This type of damages is meant to punish. Sometimes the judge does not award damages. The judge may order the defendant to take a certain action. The defendant can appeal the verdict to a higher court. He or she may ask to have the verdict overturned or to have the damages reduced.

Steps in a Civil Lawsuit

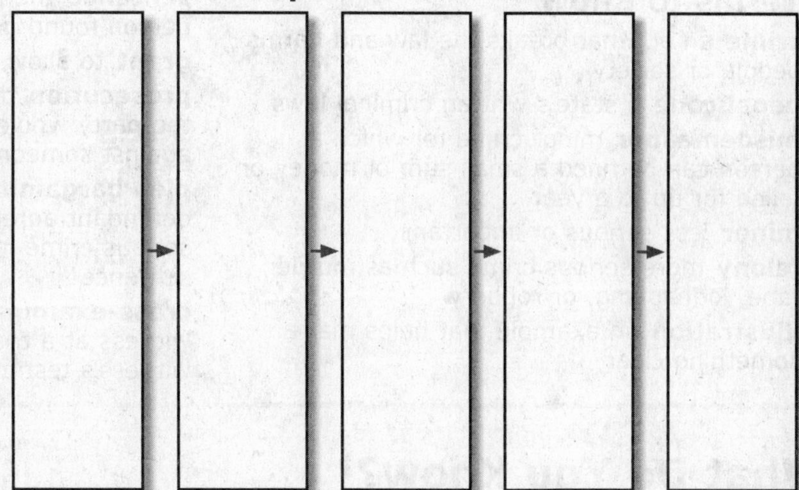

Glue Foldable here

Check for Understanding

What are the two types of torts?

1. ______________________

2. ______________________

Explain the difference between a complaint and a summons.

3. ______________________

____

____

____

Civil and Criminal Law

Lesson 2: Criminal Law

ESSENTIAL QUESTIONS

Why does conflict develop?
How can governments ensure citizens are treated fairly?

GUIDING QUESTIONS

1. ***What does criminal law involve?***
2. ***What are the legal procedures in a criminal law case?***

Terms to Know

crime an act that breaks the law and harms people or society
penal code a state's written criminal laws
misdemeanor minor crime for which a person can be fined a small sum of money or jailed for up to a year
minor less serious or important
felony more serious crime such as murder, rape, kidnapping, or robbery
illustration an example that helps make something clear
sentence the punishment given to a person found guilty of committing a crime
grant to allow
prosecution the government in the role of the party who starts the legal proceedings against someone accused of a crime
plea bargaining a process in which a defendant agrees to plead guilty to a less serious crime in order to get a lighter sentence
cross-examination the questioning of a witness at a trial to check or discredit the witness's testimony

What Do You Know?

In the first column, answer the questions based on what you know before you study. After this lesson, complete the last column.

Now...		Later...
	What is criminal law?	

Crime and Punishment

A **crime** is any act that breaks the law and harms people or society. The type of law that deals with crime is called criminal law. Criminal laws are rules for behavior. They outlaw things like stealing, damaging property, or attacking someone. All these actions are crimes.

Each state has a list of laws called a **penal** (PEE•nuhl) **code.** It describes every crime and the punishment that goes with it. The federal government also has a penal code. Examples of federal crimes are robbing a bank or committing terrorism. Most crimes break state laws. So, most cases are tried in state courts and most inmates are in state prisons. More serious crimes receive harsher punishments.

Vocabulary

1. How are *crime* and the *penal code* related?

____

____

____

Lesson 2: Criminal Law, *Continued*

Analyzing

2. Suppose someone uses a gun to steal $20 from a person. Is this crime a misdemeanor or a felony? Why?

Reading Check

3. What are the two ways of classifying crimes?

Listing

4. What purposes are served by a criminal sentence?

Vocabulary

5. What does the *prosecution* do?

Crimes are classified in different ways. There are two broad categories of crimes based on how serious they are. A crime can be a misdemeanor (MIHS•dih•MEE•nuhr) or a felony. A **misdemeanor** is a **minor,** or less serious, crime. A person can be fined a small amount of money or spend up to one year in jail. For example, stealing a $40 shirt from a store is a misdemeanor. A **felony** is a more serious crime. A person who commits a felony is punished by spending at least one year in prison. Robbing a store at gunpoint is a felony.

Crimes can be grouped as being against people or property. Crimes against people include things like assault and kidnapping. Crimes against people are seen as more serious than crimes against property because they cause harm to a person. Most crimes against people are felonies.

Crimes against property include things like theft and vandalism. An **illustration,** or example, of vandalism is if someone were to purposely throw a bucket of paint onto a neighbor's new car. If the value of what is stolen or damaged is less than $100, the crime is a misdemeanor. Otherwise it is a felony. It is also a felony if it involves the threat or use of force against a person.

Most penal codes set minimum and maximum penalties for each crime. Within those limits, a judge decides what **sentence,** or punishment, a person will serve.

Some prisoners are able to get paroled, or released early, after serving part of their sentence. Prisoners who are **granted,** or allowed, parole must report to a parole officer for the remainder of their sentence.

A prison sentence has a number of purposes. One is simply to punish. Another purpose is to protect society by keeping dangerous people locked up. A third is to serve as a warning to others not to commit crime.

A sentence can also be used to change a person's behavior. Many prisons have programs to educate and train prisoners for jobs. Learning new skills prepares criminals to become responsible citizens when they are released.

Criminal Case Procedure

In a criminal case, the government is always the plaintiff. That is, the government is the party that brings charges against a defendant. It is called the **prosecution.** This means that it starts the legal process against the defendant for breaking the law. During this process, the defendant's rights are protected by the Bill of Rights.

Lesson 2: Criminal Law, *Continued*

The diagram shows how the rules of due process are followed.

The Criminal Case Process

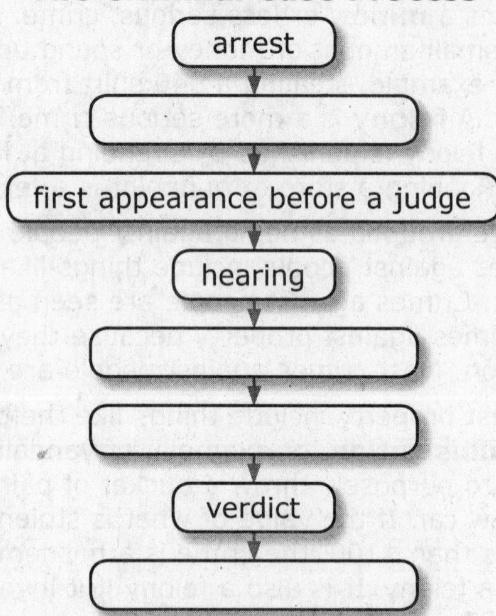

A criminal case begins when the police believe a crime has been committed. An arrest is made based on evidence. Police collect evidence to convince a judge to let them arrest someone for the crime. A judge issues an arrest warrant for the suspect. When the police make an arrest, they have to advise the suspect of their rights to remain silent and to have an attorney.

The suspect is then taken to a police station and a record of the arrest is made. This is called a booking. The police usually take a picture and fingerprints of the suspect.

Next, the suspect appears before a judge for a preliminary hearing. The judge explains the charges. The prosecution has to prove to the judge that there is probable cause—or a good reason—for believing the accused is guilty of the crime. If the suspect does not have the money for a lawyer, the judge appoints one. If the crime is a misdemeanor, the suspect pleads either guilty or not guilty. If the plea is guilty, the judge sentences the suspect. If the plea is not guilty, the judge sets a date for a trial.

If the crime is a felony, no plea is made. Instead, the judge sets a date for a hearing to learn more about the case. The judge also decides whether to hold or release the suspect. A judge may have a suspect post bail, an amount of money left with the court until the trial. Suspects can also be released until their trial.

Sequencing

6. The diagram shows how a criminal case proceeds. Fill in the empty boxes with the missing steps.

Identifying

7. What are the steps in a criminal case before a hearing or trial takes place?

____
____
____
____

Explaining

8. What do police have to advise suspects of when they arrest them?

____
____
____

Describing

9. What happens at a preliminary hearing?

____
____
____
____

Lesson 2: Criminal Law, *Continued*

Reading Check

10. Why are most criminal cases settled without going to trial?

____

____

Describing

11. What happens during cross-examination?

____

____

Drawing Conclusions

12. Why do you think judges consider a defendant's history when sentencing?

____

____

FOLDABLES®

13. Place a two-tab Foldable along the line. Label the anchor *Criminal Cases: Arraignment*. Label the two tabs *guilty* and *not guilty*. On both sides describe what each plea means.

When that happens, the suspect promises in writing to return to appear in court.

The next step is to indict, or charge, the accused with the crime. Many states have a grand jury do it. Some use a judge. The case is dismissed if there is not enough evidence.

If the case is not dismissed, the next step is the arraignment. For a felony, the suspect is formally charged and enters a plea of guilty or not guilty. The prosecution and defense lawyers begin **plea bargaining.** This is a form of compromise. The prosecution agrees to a less serious charge. The defendant agrees to plead guilty. Many criminal cases end with a plea bargain and never go to trial.

Defendants in a felony case can choose to be tried by a jury or a judge. In a jury trial, the lawyers choose a jury from a large group of citizens who have been called to serve.

The trial starts with an opening statement from each side. Then each side presents its case. Each side offers evidence and presents witnesses for questioning. This is called **cross-examination.** After their cases are given, each makes closing statements.

In a jury trial, the judge explains to the jury how the law applies. Then the jurors go into a room to review the case. To find a defendant guilty, the jurors must be convinced beyond a reasonable doubt. In other words, they must decide that there is no other reasonable explanation except that the accused committed the crime. In almost all states, all the jurors votes must be the same to decide the verdict. If a jury cannot agree, the judge will declare a mistrial.

A defendant who is found not guilty is set free. A guilty defendant is given a sentence by the judge. Judges take many things into account when sentencing. These include the defendant's criminal record and statements made by the victim's family. A person found guilty of a felony will often appeal the verdict to a higher court.

/ / / / / / / / / / / / / Glue Foldable here / / / / / / / / / / / / / /

Check for Understanding

Give an example of a misdemeanor and a felony.

1. ______________ **2.** ______________

What two conditions must be met for a jury to reach a guilty verdict?

3. ______________ **4.** ______________

NAME ______________________ DATE ______________ CLASS ____________

networks

Civil and Criminal Law

Lesson 3: The Juvenile Justice System

ESSENTIAL QUESTION

How can governments ensure citizens are treated fairly?

GUIDING QUESTIONS

1. ***How has treatment of young criminal offenders changed?***
2. ***What procedures are followed when a young person breaks the law?***

Terms to Know

rehabilitate to correct a person's behavior

emphasis weight or stress

juvenile delinquent a child or teenager who commits a crime or repeatedly breaks the law

minor of comparatively less importance

delinquent offender a youth who has committed a crime punishable by criminal law

status offender a youth charged with being beyond the control of his or her guardian

custody taking charge, or control, of someone in an official way

detention hearing the procedure by which a judge decides whether to charge a juvenile with an offense; like a preliminary hearing in an adult trial

adjudication hearing the procedure used to determine the facts in a juvenile case; like a trial in criminal law

disposition hearing the sentencing in a juvenile case

What Do You Know?

In the first column, answer the questions based on what you know before you study. After this lesson, complete the last column.

Now...		Later...
	Is it less serious when a youth breaks a law than an adult?	
	What happens when a youth breaks the law?	

Juvenile Justice

At one time, children in this country who committed crimes were tried and punished like adults. They were sent to adult jails. They often served long prison terms.

This began to change in the 1800s. People began to believe that juveniles committed crimes because their families did not teach them proper values. Reformers wanted a special court that would do the parent's jobs. Instead of punishing these children as adults, the court would **rehabilitate** (REE•uh•BIH•luh•TAYT), or correct, their behavior and teach them right from wrong.

Mark the text

1. Underline the text that tells how the treatment of children who committed crimes began to change in the 1800s.

Lesson 3: The Juvenile Justice System, *Continued*

Reading Check

2. What adult rights has the Supreme Court extended to juvenile offenders?

FOLDABLES

3. Place a two-tab Foldable along the line. Label the anchor *Juvenile Delinquents*. Label the two tabs *Delinquent Offenders* and *Status Offenders*. On both sides, define each term.

Identifying

4. What can a juvenile court do to help children who suffer from neglect?

Vocabulary

5. What is *custody*?

Glue Foldable here

The first juvenile court was set up in Chicago, Illinois, in 1899. Today, every state has a juvenile court system. The Supreme Court has ruled that children charged with crimes have the same legal rights as adults. They have the right

- to be told the charges against them
- to an attorney
- to cross-examine, or question, witnesses against them
- to remain silent when questioned

People continue to argue whether the goal of the juvenile system should be punishment or rehabilitation. In the 1990s, public opinion began to change. The **emphasis,** or weight, shifted back to punishment. Juvenile crime rates had quickly risen. The public wanted law and order. The legislatures took action by changing the laws. Now, in many states, it is easier to try young offenders in adult courts. Also, in most states, a juvenile charged with a felony can be tried as an adult. Most states consider anyone under age 18 to be a juvenile. In some states the age is 16.

Children and teens commit many crimes each year. Some crimes are **minor,** such as shoplifting. Other crimes such as armed robbery are more serious. A **juvenile delinquent** (JOO•vuh•NEYE•uhl dee•LIHN•kwuhnt) is a young person who commits a crime. There are two types of juvenile delinquents. **Delinquent offenders** are youths who have committed acts that would be crimes if done by an adult, like stealing a car. **Status offenders** have committed acts that would *not* be crimes if done by an adult. Examples include skipping school or running away from home. Status offenders do not listen to their parents or other adults; they cannot be controlled by them. For this reason, the court supervises, or takes control of, status offenders.

The Juvenile Court System

Juvenile courts handle two kinds of cases. They are neglect cases and delinquency cases. Neglect cases concern young people who are abused or not taken care of by their parents or guardians. A juvenile court can remove these children from their homes. The court places them with other families.

Delinquency cases concern young people who break the law. The legal process begins when the police take a young person into custody. **Custody** is to take charge, or control, of someone in an official way.

Lesson 3: The Juvenile Justice System, *Continued*

If the offense is not serious, the police may give the youth a warning and release them to a caregiver. They may also pass the case on to a social service agency.

Steps in a Juvenile Court Case	
Step	**What Happens**
1.	Police bring a young offender into confinement.
2.	A social worker reviews the case.
3. detention hearing	
4.	Evidence is presented; witnesses are questioned; the judge reaches a finding.
5. disposition hearing	

If the offense is serious or the youth has a prior, or past, record, the police may turn him or her over to the juvenile court. A social worker reviews the case and decides how it should be handled. This review is called intake. Some cases are dismissed during intake. Others are sent to adult court.

Some young people receive services such as counseling or drug treatment and do not have to go to court. This is called diversion.

Youths who are still in the system after intake face up to three hearings. The first is a **detention hearing.** This is like a preliminary, or first, hearing in an adult trial. The state must show that there is good reason to charge the youth with the crime.

Identifying

6. Fill in the missing boxes to show what happens in a juvenile court case.

Explaining

7. What happens during intake?

____

____

____

Defining

8. Some young offenders receive services and do not have to go to court. This is called

______________________.

Reading Check

9. What steps in the juvenile court system are similar to a trial and to a sentencing hearing in the adult court system?

____

____

____

____

Lesson 3: The Juvenile Justice System, *Continued*

FOLDABLES®

10. Place a Venn diagram Foldable along the dotted line to cover the Check for Understanding box. Label the anchor tab *Juvenile Court System*. Label the three tabs *Neglect Cases*, *Both*, and *Delinquency cases*. On both sides of the tabs, list two facts about neglect cases and delinquency cases. Then write what they have in common on the middle tab.

If the youth is charged, the next step is an **adjudication** (uh•joo•dih•KAY•shuhn) **hearing.** This is like a trial in an adult case. Each side has an attorney. Evidence is presented and witnesses are questioned and cross-examined. A judge's finding that the juvenile is delinquent is like a guilty verdict.

A **disposition hearing** is next. This is like a sentencing hearing for an adult. Some youths receive probation. They are allowed to stay free as long as they meet the conditions of the court for a set period of time. Examples of those conditions are doing community service or completing a drug treatment program. For youths who finish the conditions of probation without getting into more trouble, the charges are dropped and taken off their record.

For serious crimes, a youth may be sent to an institution for young offenders. Most delinquents serve from one to three years. In some states they can be held until age 18 or 21.

Glue Foldable here

Check for Understanding

Compare the treatment of youth offenders before the mid–1800s to how they are treated today.

1. ______________________________________

____

What two kinds of cases does the juvenile court system see?

2. ______________________________________

3. ______________________________________

Introduction to Economics

Lesson 1: What Is Economics?

ESSENTIAL QUESTIONS

Why and how do people make economic choices?
How do economic systems influence societies?

GUIDING QUESTIONS

1. ***What is scarcity, and how does it affect economic choices?***
2. ***What determines how societies make economic choices?***

Terms to Know

want things people would like to have
resource anything that can be used to make goods or services
economics the study of how people use limited resources to satisfy unlimited wants
scarcity not having enough resources to satisfy all one's needs and wants
individual a person
distribute to deliver
economic system a nation's way of producing the things its people want and need
traditional economy an economic system in which major economic decisions are based on custom or habit
market economy an economic system in which people and businesses own all resources and make economic decisions on the basis of price
command economy an economic system in which the government makes the major economic decisions
mixed market economy an economy in which businesses and individuals make the major economic decisions but in which the government also plays a role

What Do You Know?

In the first column, answer the questions based on what you know before you study. After this lesson, complete the last column.

Now...		Later...
	How do people fill their wants and needs when there are not enough resources?	
	What are economic choices?	

Our Wants and Resources

When people shop, they often want to buy more than they can afford. For example, Jayna is shopping for a new dress. She finds a dress she likes, but she also sees a sweater she wants. She does not have enough money to buy both.

Jayna must decide how best to use her money to satisfy her wants. **Wants** are desires that can be met by getting a product or a service. Most of us want many things. In fact, our wants are almost without limit.

Vocabulary

1. What are *wants?*

____

____

Lesson 1: What is Economics?, *Continued*

Examining Details

2. What resources would the owner of a pizza shop need? Name an example of each kind.

natural resources

____

labor

____

capital

____

Explaining

3. How are economics and scarcity related?

____

____

____

____

Reading Check

4. What is the basic economic problem faced by people and nations alike?

____

____

____

____

Wants can be either goods or services. Goods are things we can touch or hold. Dresses and sweaters are examples of goods. A service is work done for someone else. For example, the store clerk who rings up Jayna's purchase is performing a service.

Jayna must use her money to pay for her new dress. Money is a resource. **Resources** include everything that can be used to make or get goods and services. Economists talk about three kinds of resources, shown in the diagram below.

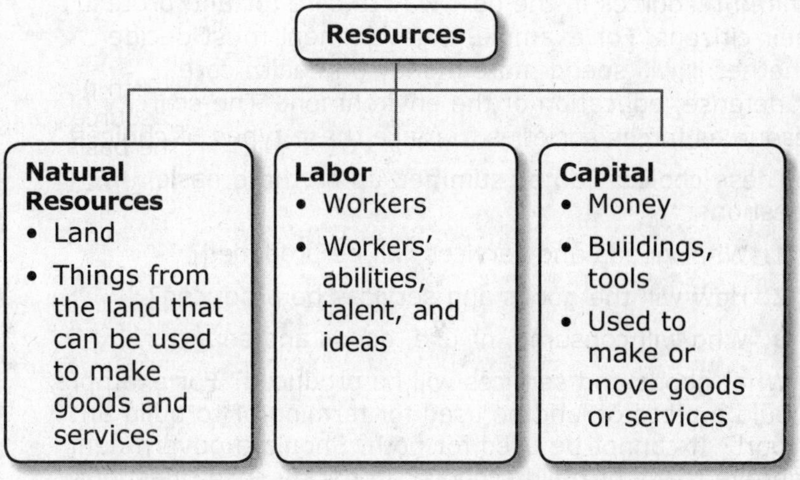

Resources

Natural Resources	**Labor**	**Capital**
• Land • Things from the land that can be used to make goods and services	• Workers • Workers' abilities, talent, and ideas	• Money • Buildings, tools • Used to make or move goods or services

Resources are limited but wants are not. This means we must make choices. **Economics** is the study of how people use limited resources to satisfy unlimited wants and needs.

It is not only individuals who have many wants. City, state, and national governments have wants, too. Sometimes there are not enough resources to satisfy, or meet, wants and needs. This is known as **scarcity.** In fact, no country has all of the resources it needs. Both individuals and governments are affected by scarcity. This makes scarcity the basic economic problem in the world. Economics looks at how people and governments deal with the problem of scarcity.

/ / / / / / / / / / / / / / Glue Foldable here / / / / / / / / / / / / / /

What Creates Scarcity

Limited resources	+	**Unlimited wants and needs**	=	**Scarcity**

Societies and Economic Choices

Individuals, or people, make economic choices all the time. So do countries. Nations must decide how to use their limited resources in the best way to care for and protect their citizens. For example, a government must decide whether it will spend more money on health care or defense, education or the environment. The scarcity of resources forces societies to make these types of choices.

These choices can be summed up by three basic questions:

1. What goods and services will be produced?
2. How will the goods and services be produced?
3. Who will consume, or use, goods and services?

What goods and services will be produced? For example, should a piece of land be used for farming or to build an airport? It cannot be used for both. Should a government improve roads or build schools? To decide such questions societies must think about their resources. A nation with good soil and a long growing season might use much of its land to grow crops.

How will goods and services be produced? For example, should food be produced on big factory farms or small family farms?

Who will get the goods and services? Societies must decide who gets goods and how much people can have. They have different ways of **distributing** goods. Should new cars go to public officials or to the highest bidder? Should new housing units be reserved for low-income people or should they be available to anyone?

Societies answer these questions in different ways. Every country has its own **economic system,** or way of producing the things people want and need.

5. Place a two-tab Foldable along the dotted line. Label the anchor tab *Economics*. Label the two tabs *Limited* and *Unlimited*. Use both sides of the tabs to explain what you know about limited resources and unlimited wants.

Reading Check

6. What determines the kind of economy a nation has?

____

____

Explaining

7. What must a society consider when deciding what goods and services to produce?

____

____

Mark the Text

8. Underline the words that tell you the meaning of *economic system*.

NAME ______________________ DATE ______________ CLASS __________

networks

There are three basic types of economic systems as shown in the chart.

The Three Types of Economic Systems	
Traditional Economy	Individuals own resources. Economic decisions are made based on custom and habit.
Market Economy	Individuals and businesses own resources. They make economic decisions based on prices.
Command Economy	The government owns resources. Government planners make economic decisions.

The first type is the **traditional economy.** People in a traditional economy base their economic choices on custom or habit. For example, a person whose parents and grandparents were farmers would also be a farmer.

Another type of economy is the **market economy.** In this system, people and businesses own the resources. They use them to produce goods and services. They answer the three economic questions based on price.

The third type of economic system is the **command economy.** In this system, the government owns the resources and decides what goods to produce. They also decide how much to produce and who is allowed to buy them.

The United States has features of all three types: traditional, market, and command. As a result, it is considered a **mixed market economy.** Businesses and people produce goods, and government makes rules for businesses to follow.

Identifying

9. Study the chart. In Country *X* a government planner has decided that half the nation's factories will make televisions. What type of economic system does Country *X* have?

____

____

FOLDABLES®

10. Place a two-tab Foldable along the dotted line. Cut each tab in half to form four tabs. Label the anchor tab *Types of Economies*. Label the four tabs *Traditional, Market, Command,* and *Mixed Market*. On both sides of the tabs, list one fact about each.

/ / / / / / / / / / / / / / Glue Foldable here / / / / / / / / / / / / / /

Check for Understanding

How is scarcity related to economic choices?

1. ______________________

How does a society's choice of economic system relate to the three basic economic questions?

2. ______________________

NAME ______________________ DATE ______________ CLASS ______________

networks

Introduction to Economics

Lesson 2: Economic Decisions

ESSENTIAL QUESTIONS

Why and how do people make economic choices?
How do economic systems influence societies?

GUIDING QUESTIONS

1. ***Why are trade-offs important in making economic decisions?***
2. ***How do costs and revenues influence economic decision making?***

Terms to Know

option a choice or alternative
trade-off giving up one option in order to get something of greater value
opportunity cost the loss of the next-best option when choosing to do one thing or another
fixed cost an expense that does not change no matter how much a business produces
variable cost an expense that changes depending on how much a business produces
vary to change
total cost the sum of all fixed and variable costs
marginal cost the additional expense of producing one more unit of something
revenue the money a business gets from selling a good or service
marginal revenue the additional income received from selling one more unit of something
benefit-cost analysis a comparison of the costs and benefits of a decision

What Do You Know?

In the first column, answer the questions based on what you know before you study. After this lesson, complete the last column.

Now...		Later...
	What is a trade-off?	

Trade-Offs

When you make a choice between two things you want to buy, you are making an economic decision. To make a good decision, you must think about the benefits and costs of each choice.

Once you choose you give up one **option** in favor of a better one. This is called a **trade-off.** Suppose you turn down a night out with friends in order to study for a test. You have made a trade-off with your time.

Businesses and governments also make trade-offs. A town might have to choose between building a new school or a new road. Trade-offs are made when money, time, and other resources are limited.

Reading Check

1. What is a trade-off in an economic decision?

____

____

Introduction to Economics

Lesson 2: Economic Decisions, *Continued*

Prior Knowledge

2. Why might governments have to make more trade-offs when economic times are hard?

____

____

Drawing Conclusions

3. What does it say about your choice if the opportunity cost is more valuable than your choice?

____

____

____

Vocabulary

4. What is *revenue*?

____

____

Explaining

5. Why would the cost of labor and supplies go up if Joe's stays open longer?

____

____

____

____

In making a trade-off, a person chooses one option over all others. The next-best use of your time or money when you choose to do one thing over another is called **opportunity cost.** For example, when you chose to study you gave up the chance to visit friends. Your opportunity cost is the fun you would have had with your friends.

Choices made by businesses and governments also have opportunity costs. A city might decide to spend money to improve a park rather than to fix sidewalks. The opportunity cost is the sidewalks that do not get fixed.

Opportunity costs are not always measured in money or things. One example for a business is the work time that is lost while employees are trained in a new computer program. If the training will improve employees' future work, then the opportunity cost is worthwhile.

Measuring Costs and Revenues

Business people have to make economic decisions every day. In order to better understand how those decisions are made, let us look at an example. Joe owns a restaurant called Joe's Seafood Depot. It is open from four o'clock in the afternoon to ten o'clock at night. Joe wonders if his restaurant would make more money if he kept it open longer every day.

In order to find out if it will be profitable to stay open longer, Joe has to figure out his **fixed costs** and his **variable costs.** His fixed costs, like rent and insurance, will not increase if he stays open a few more hours. But his variable costs will **vary,** or change. His variable costs include the money he pays his workers, his electric and gas bills, and the supplies he uses to produce his product. His **total costs** for running the business are the sum of his fixed costs and his variable costs.

Before deciding how many hours longer he wants to stay open, Joe will figure out his **marginal costs.** Economists define marginal cost as the increase in expense caused by producing one more unit of something. In Joe's case this additional unit is staying open for one more hour.

Once Joe knows his costs for staying open later he has to decide if he can make enough **revenue** to pay the costs and still make a profit. Revenue is the money Joe's customers pay him when they eat in his restaurant. The chart on the next page shows both the marginal cost and the **marginal revenue** Joe expects to make for each added hour he keeps his restaurant open.

Lesson 2: Economic Decisions, *Continued*

Marginal Cost and Revenue for Joe's Seafood Depot		
Added Hours	**Marginal Cost**	**Marginal Revenue**
1	$30	$70
2	$30	$60
3	$30	$50
4	$30	$40
5	$30	$30
6	$30	$20

Sometimes business people, like Joe, want to grow their business, serve more customers, and make more money. When trying to decide between different options, they will likely use a benefit-cost analysis. In Joe's case, he might be trying to decide if he should build an addition onto the Seafood Depot or perhaps open a second Seafood Depot in a neighboring town.

Benefit-cost analysis compares the size of the benefit with the size of the cost by dividing the two. This type of analysis helps businesses choose among two or more options. For example it will help a business choose between options A and B. If option A creates revenue of $100 at a cost of $80, the benefit-cost ratio is 1.25. We get the number 1.25 by dividing $100 by $80. If option B creates revenue of $150 and costs $90, the benefit-cost ratio is 1.67. In order to be profitable, businesses will choose the option with the higher benefit-cost number.

Business people also use another type of analysis to compare two options. It is called marginal analysis. Marginal analysis compares the additional benefit of doing something with its additional cost. If the additional benefit is greater than the additional cost, the choice is a good one.

Joe could use marginal analysis to help him decide how many more hours to stay open. Look at the Marginal Analysis For Joe's Seafood Depot graph on the next page. The graph shows that the marginal revenue of staying open one more hour is $70 and the marginal cost is $30. Because the benefit is greater than the cost, Joe will likely stay open at least one more hour and perhaps longer.

Examining Details

6. Study the chart. If Joe's stays open for five extra hours, how much revenue will he make in the fifth hour? Should he stay open that long?

____

____

Examining Details

7. Look at the Marginal Cost column. How much does it cost Joe to stay open each hour?

____

Mark the Text

8. Circle the two things that are compared in a benefit-cost analysis.

Reading Check

9. What two things are compared in a marginal analysis?

____

____

____

Lesson 2: Economic Decisions, *Continued*

? Analyzing

10. Examine the key on the Marginal Analysis for Joe's Seafood Depot graph. What two things are being graphed? Explain what happens when the two lines cross.

____

____

____

____

FOLDABLES®

11. Place a two-tab Foldable along the dotted line. Cut each tab in half to form four tabs. Write the title *Costs and Revenues* on the anchor tab. Label the four tabs *Fixed Costs, Variable Costs, Total Cost, Marginal Cost.* Write the definition of each on the reverse side of the tabs.

Glue Foldable here

When looking at marginal analysis, the rule is to continue doing something until the marginal cost is equal to the marginal revenue. For Joe, they are equal at five hours. Costs and benefits both equal $30. Then benefits go down.

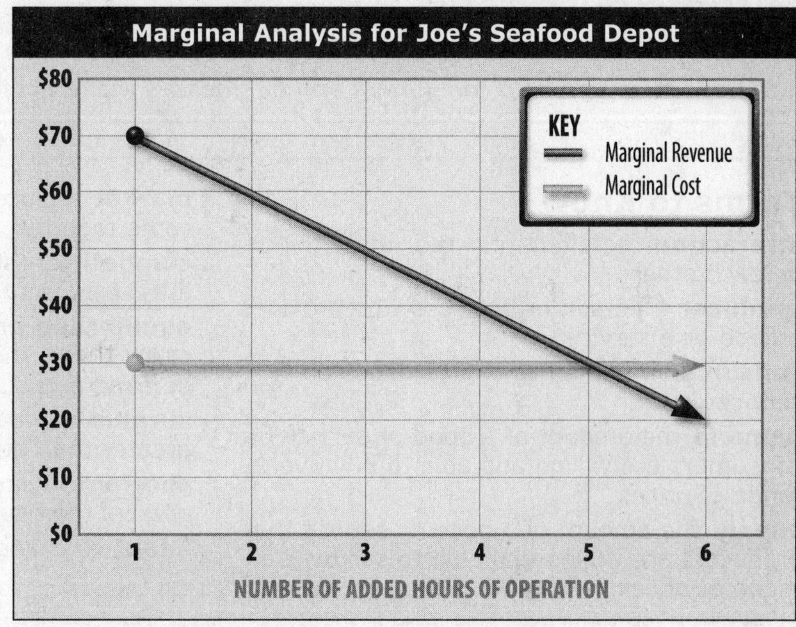

Marginal analysis even works for decisions that are not about money. It can apply to a decision about how long a nap should be! The benefits of the nap are highest during the first hour. After that they gradually decline.

The cost of taking a nap would be the opportunity cost of what you were not doing while you napped. The ideal length of your nap is the point at which the declining benefits equal the rising costs.

Check for Understanding

How are trade-offs and opportunity costs related?

1. _______________

____

Why is it important for a business to analyze costs and revenues before deciding to expand?

2. _______________

____

Introduction to Economics

Lesson 3: Demand and Supply in a Market Economy

ESSENTIAL QUESTIONS

Why and how do people make economic choices?
How do economic systems influence societies?

GUIDING QUESTIONS

1. ***How do demand and supply affect prices?***
2. ***How do prices help consumers and businesses make economic decisions?***

Terms to Know

interaction the effect of two or more things on each other
producer a person or business who provides a good or a service
consumer a person who buys goods or services
demand the amount of a good or service that consumers are willing and able to buy over a range of prices
supply the amount of a good or service that producers are willing and able to sell over a range of prices
market a place where buyers and sellers come together
competition struggle among sellers to attract buyers
equilibrium price the price set for a good or service in the marketplace at which demand and supply are balanced
surplus a situation in which supply is greater than demand
shortage a situation in which demand is greater than supply
adapt to change

What Do You Know?

In the first column, answer the questions based on what you know before you study. After this lesson, complete the last column.

Now...		Later...
	How does supply and demand work?	

Demand and Supply Make Markets

What makes prices go up and down? In a command economy, government officials set most prices. In a market economy prices are set by the **interaction** of demand and supply. **Producers** are the businesses that provide goods and services. **Consumers** are the people who buy them. Producers create supply and consumers create demand. In economics, **demand** is the amount of a good or service that people are willing and able to buy at a particular price.

Mark the Text

1. Circle the forces that set prices in a market economy.

Introduction to Economics

Lesson 3: Demand and Supply in a Market Economy, *Continued*

Explaining

2. What is the relationship between price and supply?

____

____

____

Describing

3. Study the charts. What happens to the demand for oil as the price rises?

____

How does an increase in the price of oil affect the supply of oil?

____

____

Drawing Conclusions

4. What does the demand schedule tell you about the relationship between the price per barrel and the quantity demanded?

____

____

____

____

This definition of demand has four key parts:

1. Amount—Demand measures how much of something consumers will buy. This amount changes as prices change.
2. Willing to buy—Consumers must want to buy the good or service or there is no demand.
3. Able to buy—Consumers also must be able to buy. Wanting an item without having the money to pay for it does not count as demand.
4. Price—Demand is tied to price. The amount of an item people are willing and able to buy is linked to its price.

Supply is the amount of a good or service that producers are willing and able to sell at various prices during a set time period. As the price of a product goes up, producers are willing to supply more. As the price goes down, they supply less.

The amount of a good or service that is supplied and demanded at each price can be shown in a schedule. The schedules below show how much oil consumers demanded and producers supplied at certain prices.

Demand Schedule for Crude Oil	
Price Per Barrel	**Quantity Demanded**
$10	50
$20	40
$30	30
$40	20
$50	10

Supply Schedule for Crude Oil	
Price Per Barrel	**Quantity Supplied**
$10	10
$20	20
$30	30
$40	40
$50	50

Economists use graphs to show how much of a good is supplied and demanded at each price. The data from schedules can be plotted on a graph. These graphs are called a demand curve and a supply curve. The graph on the next page shows the demand and supply curves for oil.

As you can see, the demand curve slopes down to the right. The supply curve slopes up to the right. They go in opposite directions. That is because as the price goes up, producers supply more, but consumers demand less. When prices are low, people demand more.

Lesson 3: Demand and Supply in a Market Economy, *Continued*

Demand and supply curves together show a **market.** A market is anywhere buyers and sellers of the same good or service come together. Markets need many buyers and sellers to work well. This **competition** keeps prices down. Competition is the sellers' struggle to attract buyers. If the market does not have enough sellers, prices may go too high. That is why U.S. laws ban monopolies.

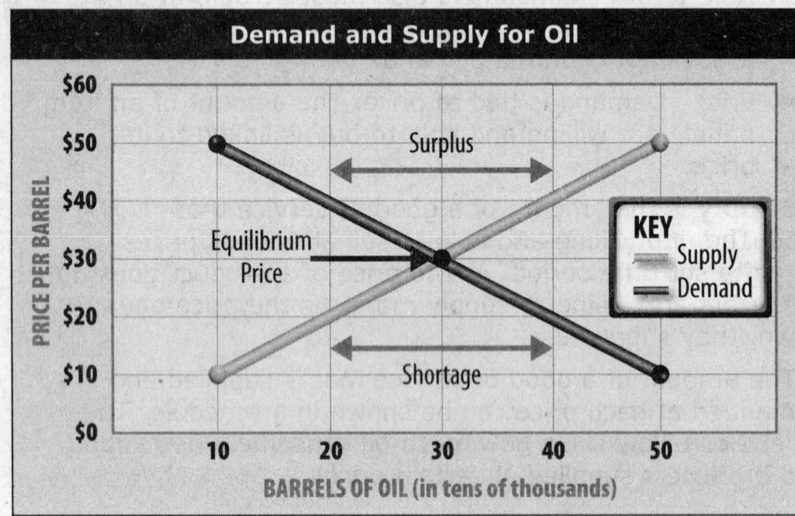

Markets are important in many ways. One major way is that they set prices. Look again at the graph. Note that the lines on the graph cross at one point. This point is the price set by the market. At this price demand and supply balance. This is the **equilibrium** (EE•kwuh•LIH•bree•uhm) **price.** At this price, consumers want to buy just as much oil as producers want to sell.

If the price of oil rises higher than the equilibrium price, producers will supply more. However, consumers will not buy more. This will result in a surplus of oil. A **surplus** occurs when supply is greater than demand. A surplus makes prices fall.

If the price of oil falls below the equilibrium price, the opposite will happen. There will be a shortage. A **shortage** occurs when there is not enough supply to meet demand. A shortage makes prices rise.

Drawing Conclusions

5. Explain how increased competition affects prices and why.

____

____

Examining Details

6. What is the equilibrium price of oil according to the graph?

____

Contrasting

7. What is the difference between a *surplus* and a *shortage*?

____

____

____

Describing

8. How do prices help determine for whom goods will be produced in a market economy?

____

____

____

Lesson 3: Demand and Supply in a Market Economy, *Continued*

Reading Check

9. What three changes will cause demand to rise?

____
____
____

Listing

10. List two factors other than price that affect supply.

____
____
____

Paraphrasing

11. Study the information in the table. Then use your own words to write a short paragraph describing the factors that affect supply and demand.

____
____
____
____
____
____

Price is not the only thing that affects demand. Other factors that change the demand for a good or service are

- The number of consumers. More consumers mean more demand. Fewer consumers mean less demand.
- Consumer income. If people have more money to spend, they buy more. Demand goes up. If people have less money to spend, they buy less. The equilibrium price decreases.
- Consumer preferences. If people decide they like a product, demand for it goes up. Demand goes down if consumers do not like it.

Supply is also affected by factors other than price. Two key factors are

- The number of suppliers. When more suppliers enter the market for a product, the supply increases. If some producers leave the market, the supply decreases. When this happens, prices go up. Since consumers have fewer choices, producers can charge more.
- The costs of production. If the costs of making a product go up, producers make less profit. This leads them to produce less. Supply goes down. When producers find a cheaper way to make something, they make more profit. They will supply more of it at all prices. Supply goes up.

Factors that Affect Demand and Supply

Demand	Supply
• Prices • Number of consumers • Consumer income • Consumer preferences	• Prices • Number of suppliers • Cost of production

Lesson 3: Demand and Supply in a Market Economy, *Continued*

The Economic Role of Prices

Prices play a key role in a market economy. First they help answer the three basic economic questions. These questions are *what* to produce, *how* to produce, and *for whom* to produce.

Businesses decide *what* to produce based on consumer demand. If a business cannot sell a product, the price falls. When the price falls, producers stop making the product. So prices determine what gets produced.

In the same way, prices determine *how* things are produced. Cars provide one example. Cars built by hand would cost too much. For this reason automakers use mass production to keep prices down. All businesses try to keep production costs down. This allows them to sell at prices consumers will pay.

Prices also answer the last question: *for whom* are goods produced? They are produced for those who have the money and desire to buy them at a given price.

In a market economy, prices also have other uses. They measure value. They send signals to producers and consumers about the value of a product or service. For producers the signals help them decide where to set prices. If consumers will not buy an item at a certain price, producers realize they should lower that price. For consumers prices signal what an item is worth. If no producer offers an item at the low price consumers want, then consumers must **adapt.** This means they must change their expectations about what they will have to pay.

Prices do not play the same role in a command economy. In this case government officials answer the three basic economic questions. Prices are not set by supply and demand. Instead, officials set prices based on their idea of the value of goods and services.

Check for Understanding

What happens to demand as prices rise?

1. ______________________________

How do prices help businesses decide what to produce?

2. ______________________________

____

Glue Foldable here

Reading Check

12. Are prices more changeable in a market economy or in a command economy? Why?

____

____

____

____

____

____

FOLDABLES®

13. Place a Venn diagram Foldable along the line. Write the title *The Role of Prices* on the anchor tab. Label the top tab *Demand*, the middle tab *Both*, and the bottom tab *Prices*. On both sides of the tabs, write about each and what they have in common.

The American Economy

Lesson 1: Gross Domestic Product

ESSENTIAL QUESTION

Why and how do people make economic choices?

GUIDING QUESTIONS

1. ***Why is Gross Domestic Product important to a nation?***
2. ***Why is GDP difficult to measure?***

Terms to Know

product item produced in an economy

Gross Domestic Product (GDP) the total market value of all final goods and services produced in a country in one year

output the amount produced

entrepreneur a person who starts a new business

transfer to move ownership to a new owner

GDP per capita the total amount of goods and services produced in a year divided by the population

standard of living quality of life measured by how well people are able to meet their needs and wants

What Do You Know?

In the first column, answer the questions based on what you know before you study. After this lesson, complete the last column.

Now...		Later...
	What do you think the Gross Domestic Product (GDP) is?	
	What factors does society have to think about when deciding how to use money?	

Visualizing

1. What is an example of a service that you might use?

____

____

Visualizing

2. What is a good you have bought recently?

____

Why GDP Is Important

The United States economy has many parts. Farmers grow crops, factories make many kinds of goods, and people buy goods. These are all part of the economy. An item produced, or made, in an economy is called a **product.** A product may be a good such as a video game, or a service such as a haircut. Goods are things that you can use. Bicycles, cell phones, and books are all goods. Services are jobs done for someone else for pay, such as babysitting.

The making of goods or providing of services are the activities that make up the **Gross Domestic Product (GDP).** GDP is the total market value of all the final products made in a country in one year. The United States has the world's largest economy. In 2010, the **output,** or amount of products produced, in the United States was about 15 *trillion* dollars ($15,000,000,000,000). That is about 20 percent, or one-fifth, of the output of the entire world.

Lesson 1: Gross Domestic Product, *Continued*

Making goods and providing services create income for people. When people get paid for their work, they earn income. GDP is a way to measure the income of the nation. GDP includes purchases made by consumers, businesses, and the government.

It takes many people to create a product. When a bicycle is made, the people who mine for the metal, create the frame of the bicycle, make the tires, and paint it are all paid. Then the people who fix parts of bicycles that break after they have been used are paid for their work.

People called entrepreneurs are very important to the economy. An **entrepreneur** (AHN•truh•pruh•NUHR) is a person who takes a risk and starts a new business. The new business may or may not succeed. The risk is rewarded if the business earns money.

An entrepreneur is a factor of production. Businesses bring together the other three factors of production. They are: natural resources (land, soil, forests, and mineral deposits); labor (factory workers, miners, and store owners); and capital (tools, buildings, and money). The diagram below shows which factors of production are used to make a bicycle.

Factors of Production

Natural Resources—metal for the frame, petroleum for the tires

Capital—tools, factory building

Labor—workers to gather the natural resources, designers, machine operators, workers to assemble the bicycle

Entrepreneur—one to manufacture the bicycle, another to open a bicycle shop, one to repair broken bicycles

Glue Foldable here

Measuring GDP

Think about how many goods and services are offered in your own community. How difficult do you think that may be to measure? Now try to imagine how many goods and services are provided in the whole country!

FOLDABLES®

3. Place a one-tab Foldable along the dotted line to cover the diagram. Label the anchor tab *Entrepreneur.* Then write two sentences explaining what entrepreneurs are and why they are important.

Explaining

4. Study the diagram. Who might earn an income when a new bicycle is produced?

___

___

___

Reading Check

5. Why does GDP represent income for all factors of production?

___

___

___

___

___

Lesson 1: Gross Domestic Product, *Continued*

Explaining

6. Why would a used book not be considered part of GDP, even though a new book is?

______

______

______

Listing

7. Give two examples of final goods and two examples of intermediate goods.

______

______

______

______

Defining

8. Based on the table, what must you know to find GDP?

______

______

Reading Check

9. What is the difference between GDP and GDP per capita?

______

______

Suppose a country produced only a small number of goods and services. The GDP would be much easier to calculate. Measuring the GDP of the United States is very hard because the total number of goods and services is huge. Before we can really understand how the GDP is figured out, however, there are other things we need to know.

GDP does not include all goods and services. It includes only *final* goods and services sold in the market. A final good or service is something that is sold directly to the user. A book is a final good. The ink and paper used to make the book are not final goods. They are not part of the GDP. *Intermediate* goods are goods that go into making a final product. The parts used to make a bicycle are intermediate goods. Used goods do not count, either. They were already counted when they were first sold. **Transferring** them, or reselling them, does not involve new production.

To find GDP, you must know the price of final goods and services and how many were sold. Multiply these two numbers, then add your answers. The table below shows an example of how to calculate GDP.

Calculating Gross Domestic Product (GDP)

Final Goods and Services	Price X	Number Sold =	Total
Game downloads	$5	20	$100
Books	$10	12	+ $120
Haircuts	$12	5	+ $60
		GDP	**$280**

This is a simple version of the kind of math economists use to figure out the GDP of a nation.

GDP tells how large a country's economy is. When we compare countries, it is better to measure **GDP per capita.** The phrase "per capita" means per person. It is best to compare countries using GDP per capita because countries have different populations and different size economies. This calculation gives the share of GDP each person would get if it were divided equally. To find the GDP per capita, you take the country's total GDP and divide it by the total population.

Lesson 1: Gross Domestic Product, *Continued*

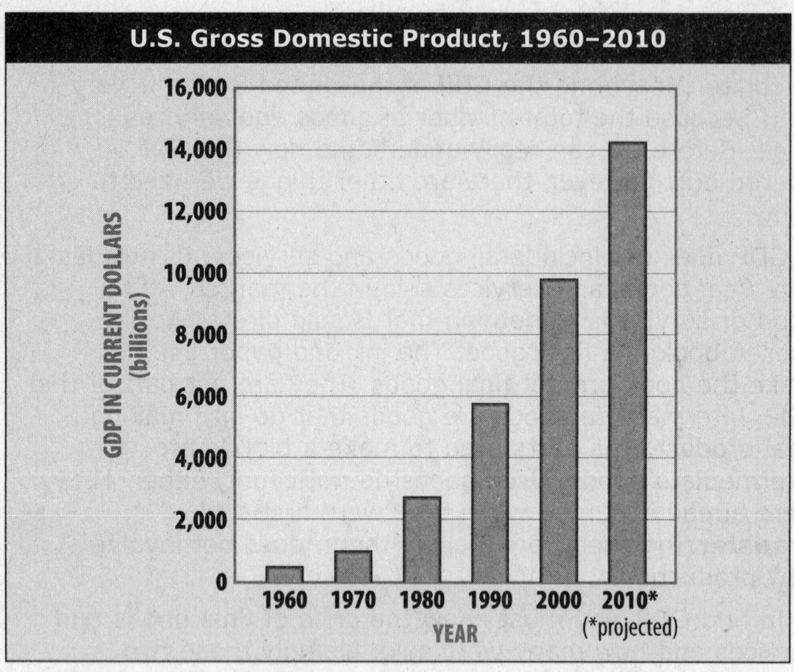

The **standard of living** is the quality of life of the people in a country. It is based on how well people are able to meet their needs and wants. The GDP does not measure the standard of living. If the GDP of a nation is high, it does not mean that the standard of living for all citizens is good. The higher the GDP per capita, the better the standard of living. Environmental conditions are also looked at when measuring the standard of living. Pollution lowers the standard of living. The United States has many laws to control pollution, but some other countries, such as China, do not.

Check for Understanding

Why is the GDP important?

1. _______________

What makes an entrepreneur decide to risk starting a new business?

2. _______________

What does GDP measure?

3. _______________

____

Glue Foldable here

Examining Details

10. Study the graph. In what year was U.S. GDP just below $10 trillion?

____

Comparing and Contrasting

11. How would the standard of living of a country with a high GDP per capita compare to that of one with a low GDP per capita?

____

____

____

FOLDABLES®

12. Place a two-tab Foldable along the dotted line. Label the anchor tab *GDP*. Label the top tab *What It Is* and write the definition of GDP on the reverse. Label the bottom tab *What It Represents* and write facts about what GDP represents on the reverse.

NAME ____________________ DATE ____________ CLASS ________

networks

The American Economy

Lesson 2: Economic Flow and Economic Growth

ESSENTIAL QUESTION

Why and how do people make economic choices?

GUIDING QUESTIONS

1. ***Why do resources, goods, and services flow in a circular pattern in a market system?***
2. ***How can nations create and promote economic growth?***

Terms to Know

circular flow model the circular flow of resources, goods, services, and money through the economy

sector category

factor market where factors of production are bought and sold

product market where businesses sell goods and services to buyers

comprise to be made up of

economic growth an increase in the output of goods and services over time

productivity a measure of how efficiently resources are used to create products

specialization when businesses and people focus their work on one product or service

division of labor breaking down a large job into smaller tasks, each of which is done by a different worker

human capital the knowledge, skills, and experience of workers

What Do You Know?

In the first column, answer the questions based on what you know before you study. After this lesson, complete the last column.

Now...		Later...
	Why are resources, goods, and services important to an economy?	
	How does an economy grow?	

Prior Knowledge

1. List all the factors of production.

____

____

____

The Circular Flow Model

It can be hard to understand what happens in a country's economy. Economists use models to help understand the economy. A model can be a graph or a diagram. The **circular flow model** is used in this lesson.

It shows how resources, goods and services, and money flow between businesses and consumers in a circular path.

Lesson 2: Economic Flow and Economic Growth, *Continued*

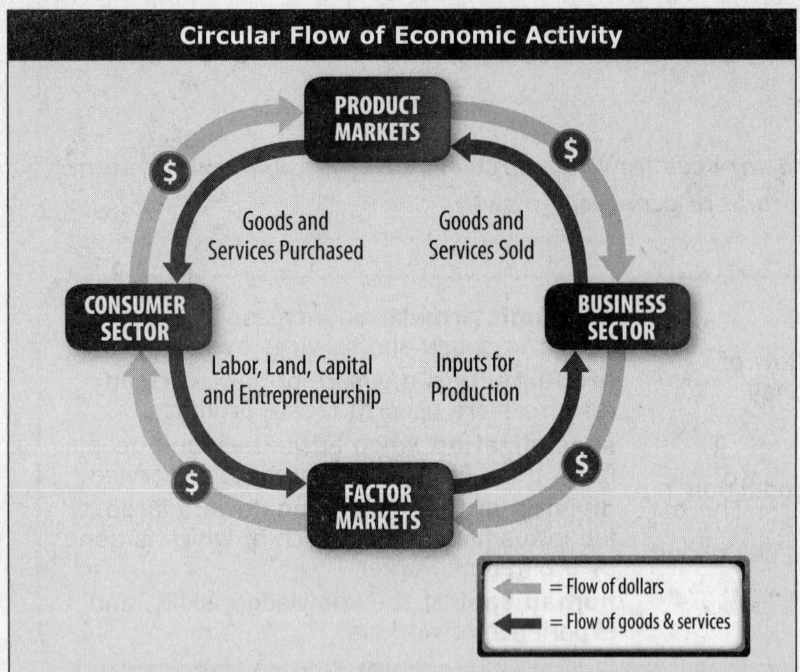

The model has four main parts. Two parts are markets where buying and selling take place. The other two parts are **sectors,** or categories. These show the two main groups of participants in markets. These are the people and businesses active in the economy.

Find the boxes on the diagram that show the two markets. They are the **factor market** and the **product market.** The factor market is where factors of production are bought and sold. When people go to work they are selling their labor in the factor market. Machines, tools, and natural resources such as oil are also part of the factor market. The product market is where businesses sell goods and services. An easy way to remember the product market is to think of it as one store where all goods and services are sold.

The consumer sector is made up of all the people who get paid and buy goods and services. Consumers, or buyers, take part in both the factor and product markets. Workers are paid for their time and skill. They sell their labor in the factor market. Then they use that money to buy goods and services in the product market.

The business sector includes companies that produce goods and services. Businesses sell goods and services in the product market. Businesses use the money they make to buy land, labor, and capital in the factor market.

Listing

2. Read the diagram. List the four main parts of the Circular Flow of Economic Activity model.

____

____

____

____

Identifying

3. A student works part time in a video game store. Which part of the circular flow model does this represent?

____

____

Identifying

4. Who is part of both the factor and product markets?

____

____

Mark the Text

5. Underline the words that tell you what the *consumer sector* is.

Lesson 2: Economic Flow and Economic Growth, *Continued*

Mark the Text

6. Underline the text that explains the direction money flows in the circular flow model.

7. Where and how have you participated in the product market?

8. Describe the two sectors of the economy that are not shown on the circular flow diagram.

Reading Check

9. How do people benefit from economic growth?

Look at the circular flow diagram on the previous page. You can see that money always flows in a clockwise direction. First, look at the loop that shows where the money goes. The money starts in the consumer sector, then moves through the product market to the business sector. The money then flows through the factor market back to the consumer. Next, look at the loop that shows the goods, services, and factors of production. It flows in the opposite direction.

The model shows what happens in real life. The money spent and the products bought flow in opposite directions. For example, think about what happens when you have to go to the store to buy milk. You go into the store with money. The cashier takes your money and gives you a carton of milk. Money flows in one direction, milk in the other. The model also shows that markets link consumers and businesses. Though you may never go into the factory that bottles the milk, you still interact with it when you buy the milk.

Two other sectors involved in economic flow are the government sector and the foreign sector. The government sector **comprises,** or is made up of, federal, state, and local governments. Governments buy products and services in the product market the same way consumers do. They also sell goods and services to earn income. For example, governments charge park entry fees, state universities charge tuition, and local bus systems charge fares. Governments also collect taxes.

The foreign sector is made up of the people and businesses from other countries that buy and sell goods in the United States. Americans buy more from other countries than we sell to them.

Promoting Economic Growth

Economic growth is an increase in the output of goods and services over time. Economists track economic growth in many ways. One way is by watching the changes in the GDP. When the GDP is higher than the previous year, the economy has grown. Government and business leaders try to promote economic growth. This growth raises our standard of living.

As you remember, the four factors of production are used to make goods and provide services. A country's natural and human resources are very important for economic growth. Natural resources are often in limited supply.

NAME ______________________ DATE ______________ CLASS ______________

networks

Lesson 2: Economic Flow and Economic Growth, *Continued*

For instance, there is a limited amount of land. Also, we could use up all the oil in the world or use wood faster than it can grow back.

For the economy to grow, the population also needs to grow or to become more productive. **Productivity** is a measure of how efficiently resources are used. Say a factory that has made 1,000 computers a week begins to make 1,200 a week without adding any new workers. This means productivity has increased.

Productivity usually improves when businesses and people focus on one product or service. This is called **specialization.** Specialization allows businesses and people to become experts at what they do.

Specialization leads to **division of labor.** Division of labor breaks down a large job into smaller tasks. A different worker does each task. Each worker can focus on his or her task and find ways to do it faster and better. This is one way that specialization increases productivity.

Businesses often try to increase productivity. They do this by focusing on their **human capital,** or workers. As workers gain training, education, and experience, their work improves. The productivity of the business increases. This leads to economic growth and a higher standard of living.

Check for Understanding

Through what two markets do resources, goods, services, and money flow in the U.S. economy?

1. ______________________

2. ______________________

List three things that businesses do to promote economic growth.

3. ______________________

4. ______________________

5. ______________________

Glue Foldable here

Prior Knowledge

10. Explain the difference between the GDP and the GDP per capita.

____

Vocabulary

11. What is the purpose of *division of labor*?

____

FOLDABLES®

12. Place a three-tab Foldable along the dotted line. Write *Economic Growth* on the anchor tab. Label the three tabs *Productivity Improves, Business Improves,* and *Workers Improve.* On both sides of the tabs, write one thing you remember about economic growth as it relates to each title.

The American Economy

Lesson 3: Capitalism and Free Enterprise

ESSENTIAL QUESTION

Why and how do people make economic choices?

GUIDING QUESTIONS

1. ***What makes capitalism a successful economic system?***
2. ***How is the history of capitalism associated with the Founders?***

Terms to Know

capitalism economic system in which private citizens own the factors of production and decide how to use them to make money

free enterprise economic system in which individuals and businesses are allowed to compete for profit with little government interference

voluntary exchange when buyers and sellers choose to take part in an exchange

profit the money left over from the sale of goods or services after all costs have been paid

profit motive the desire to earn money by creating and selling goods and services

competition the struggle between businesses with similar products to attract consumers

private property rights the right to own, use, and sell property

dispose to get rid of

incentive a reward offered to try to persuade people to take certain actions

laissez-faire economics belief that the government should play only a small role in the economy

What Do You Know?

In the first column, answer the questions based on what you know before you study. After this lesson, complete the last column.

Now...		Later...
	What is capitalism?	

Mark the Text

1. Circle the name for the system in which businesses compete without government involvement.

Capitalism in the United States

The U.S. market economy is huge. One reason it is so large is that citizens, not the government, make most of the economic decisions. Another word for this type of system is **capitalism.** Under capitalism, private citizens own the factors of production. They decide how to use them to make money. Our economy is also called a **free enterprise** system. In this type of system, businesses can compete with one another without the government getting in the way. Free enterprise has helped the U.S. economy grow to become the wealthiest in the world.

Lesson 3: Capitalism and Free Enterprise, *Continued*

Six features of a free enterprise system help make the U.S. economy work. As you read, fill in the chart below listing the six features of a free enterprise system and how each works.

Features of a Free Enterprise System	
Feature of U.S. Economy	**How it Works**
Economic Freedom	Americans choose how they will earn and spend their money.
	The place where buyers and sellers interact. Supply and demand drive the markets.
Voluntary Exchange	
Competition	
	People have the right to use or sell their property as they see fit. People get to keep the profits they make off their property. Therefore they are more likely to take care of or invest in their property.

The first is economic freedom. The American people are free to buy and sell the factors of production. They can choose how they will earn and spend their money. This freedom allows the economy to be more organized and productive.

The second feature is the market. The market is the place where buyers and sellers interact. Supply and demand drive the U.S. markets. Consumers like you demand products and services. Businesses supply them. In our economy buyers and sellers decide what those goods and services will be and who will use them. Though there can be problems in markets, over time they have proven to be the best way to bring buyers and sellers together. Markets encourage competition and set prices.

Paraphrasing

2. Complete the chart as you read the text. Then briefly summarize how the market works.

Explaining

3. Explain why property rights are important in a market economy.

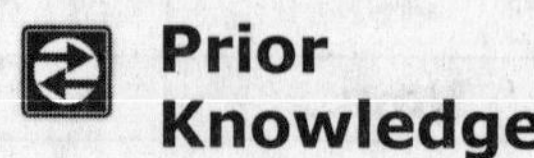

4. What is the main difference between an entrepreneur and a laborer?

Mark the Text

5. Underline the text that explains where buyers and sellers interact.

Lesson 3: Capitalism and Free Enterprise, *Continued*

Defining

6. What is the meaning of the term *voluntary*?

____

____

Listing

7. List the six main features of capitalism that contribute to its success.

____

____

____

____

____

____

Reading Check

8. Why do people risk their money to start businesses?

____

____

____

The third feature of capitalism is **voluntary exchange.** This happens when buyers and sellers choose to take part in an exchange. Buyers give up their money to gain a product. Sellers give up their products to gain money. Buyers and sellers both benefit.

The fourth feature is the profit motive. A desire to make money encourages a person to offer a product to buyers. The potential for **profit** leads entrepreneurs to take risks. Profit is the money left over from the sale of goods or services after all the costs of making it have been paid. The **profit motive** is the main reason capitalism succeeds. The profit motive is the desire to earn money by creating and selling goods and services. It also pushes people to invent new goods and services. The profit motive drives the economy.

Competition is the fifth feature of capitalism. Competition is when businesses that sell similar products try to attract consumers. Businesses that have lower prices usually win the most buyers. But if a business can offer a higher quality product, it may win the buyers over.

The final feature is **private property rights.** People in this country have the right to own and use their own property. They can also choose to **dispose** of, or get rid of, their property. A person cannot use property in a way that violates the rights of others, however. Private property rights give people the **incentive** to work because they are able to keep any profits they might earn. Incentive is the desire or drive to do something. These rights also motivate people to save, invest, and to take care of their property.

U.S. Private Property Rights

You have the right to own property and use it as you see fit.

This means you have incentive to

- ✓ work to buy property
- ✓ save and invest
- ✓ take care of your belongings

Lesson 3: Capitalism and Free Enterprise, *Continued*

The Origins of U.S. Capitalism

In 1776, Adam Smith published a book called *The Wealth of Nations.* Smith was a Scottish philosopher and economist. He believed that self-interest, or one's own well-being, makes people work. It also causes them to use resources wisely. He supported the idea that the market works best on its own, without government involvement.

Smith believed in **laissez-faire economics.** *Laissez-faire* (LEH•SAY•FEHR) is a French term. It means "to leave alone." In economics it means that the government should keep its hands off the marketplace. It should only make sure that competition is allowed.

Smith's ideas helped shape the ideas of many of the nation's founders, including Alexander Hamilton, Thomas Jefferson, and James Madison.

Check for Understanding

What are two benefits of private property rights?

1. ______________________

2. ______________________

List the two ideas about government found in Adam Smith's laissez-faire economics.

3. ______________________

4. ______________________

Glue Foldable here

Paraphrasing

9. How did the ideas of Adam Smith shape the history of the United States?

____

Reading Check

10. What role did Adam Smith believe government should play in the marketplace?

____

FOLDABLES®

11. Place a one-tab Foldable along the dotted line. Write the title *U.S. Capitalism* on the anchor tab. List four words or phrases you remember about the beginning of capitalism in the United States.

NAME ____________________ DATE ______________ CLASS __________

networks

Personal Finance

Lesson 1: Consumerism

ESSENTIAL QUESTION

Why and how do people make economic choices?

GUIDING QUESTIONS

1. ***What rights do you have as a consumer?***
2. ***What responsibilities do you have as a consumer?***
3. ***What steps can you take to be a successful consumer?***

Terms to Know

consumerism a movement to educate and protect buyers

redress payment for a wrong or loss

comparison shopping comparing prices of products at different stores

generic good a good that does not have a brand name but is similar to a more expensive, well-known product

warranty the promise of the person who made or sold the product to fix or replace it

distinguish to see the differences in

impulse buying buying that is unplanned and based on emotion

disposable income income left after all taxes have been paid on it

discretionary income income left after all taxes have been paid on it and that you can choose to spend

What Do You Know?

In the first column, answer the questions based on what you know before you study. After this lesson, complete the last column.

Now...		Later...
	What are consumer rights?	
	How do you make smart decisions about what you buy?	

Prior Knowledge

1. What is a consumer?

____

____

____

Consumer Rights

Have you ever seen a commercial for a new product on television? Should you believe everything it says about the product? What if the product is not good? What if it can hurt you? How can you protect yourself? You have certain rights as a consumer. These rights have been won partly through **consumerism,** a movement to teach buyers about what they buy. The movement also insists that manufacturers make better and safer products.

NAME ______________________ DATE ______________ CLASS ______________

networks

Lesson 1: Consumerism, *Continued*

The government first protected consumers in the late 1800s. In 1906, it created the Food and Drug Administration (FDA). The FDA guarantees the safety of food, drugs, and medicine sold in the United States. Eight years later Congress created the Federal Trade Commission (FTC). The FTC protects consumers from businesses that are dishonest and act unfairly such as selling a product that does not work.

In 1962 President John F. Kennedy proposed a consumer bill of rights. He did so because he believed that the average person could not be sure that products were safe. Over time, people found that the four basic rights did not give them enough protection. New rights were then added. The chart below shows the rights given to consumers in the consumer bill of rights.

The Consumer Bill of Rights

Consumers have the right to...	This means...
safety	products should not be harmful
information	consumers should have the facts they need to make good choices about products; they should be protected from dishonest information
choice	a variety of goods and services should be available to consumers and offered at competitive prices
a voice	consumers' interests should be considered when laws are being made
redress	consumers have the right to have problems fixed and receive payment for false claims, poor service, or harmful products
environmental health	consumers should not suffer harmful air, water, or soil conditions because of economic activity; they have the right to work in healthy and safe environments
service	consumers should be treated respectfully, have their questions and concerns answered, and have the right to refuse service
consumer education	consumers have the right to receive information that helps them understand the rights listed above

Critical Thinking

2. Explain the difference between the FDA and the FTC.

____

____

Identifying

3. Study the chart. If a consumer is the victim of a false claim, what does the Consumer Bill of Rights say they are entitled to?

____

Reading Check

4. What rights do consumers have?

____

____

____

____

____

____

____

____

Critical Thinking

5. What is the difference between a consumer right and a consumer responsibility?

____

____

____

____

Defining

6. Before buying a new computer, you check prices at three different stores and two online retailers. What is this called?

____

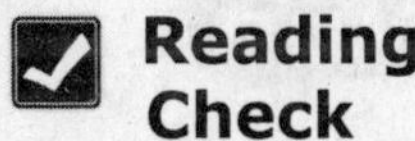

Mark the Text

7. Underline the three main responsibilities of a consumer.

Reading Check

8. What are some ways to be an informed consumer?

____

____

____

____

Consumer Responsibilities

Consumers have rights. They also have responsibilities. One responsibility is to make smart decisions about what you buy. One thing you can do is look for information about the products you want to buy. You can use consumer magazines and Web sites to learn about a product. These sources tell you what other buyers thought about the product.

Advertising gives buyers brief information about the goods and services being sold. However, ads may try to make you buy a product you do not need. Be aware that advertisers give you only the information that will make you want to buy the product. For example, they will not tell you if a product they are selling breaks easily.

Next, you must decide where to buy the product. Look at the prices at different stores. This is called **comparison shopping.** Check newspapers, store flyers, and Web sites. When visiting stores look at both name-brand and generic goods. A generic good does not have a brand name, but is similar to a more expensive and well-known product.

Another responsibility is to report any problems with a product. If you buy a product or service that does not work correctly, report the problem right away. Do not try to fix a broken product yourself. This may not be safe, and it could cancel the **warranty.** A warranty is the promise of the person who made or sold the product to fix or replace it if it breaks within a set time period after you buy it. If your product breaks, return it to the store. You can also contact the company to see if they will fix it or give you a new one. Keep a record of your attempts to get a product fixed. If the seller or manufacturer will not fix the problem, contact your state's consumer protection agency.

Consumers have the right to expect that producers and sellers will be honest. That means that consumers also have a responsibility to be honest with producers and sellers. A consumer should not try to return a product to the store if he or she broke it.

Making Purchasing Decisions

Can you think of a time you spent your money on something you wanted instead of something you needed? Were you happy with that decision? Making smart buying decisions first involves **distinguishing** between wants and needs. *To distinguish* means "to see the differences." A need is something you must have to survive. A want is something extra that you would like to have.

Lesson 1: Consumerism, *Continued*

You also must find out how much money you have to spend. The money you have left after paying taxes is your **disposable income.** Disposable income is used to pay for needs like food, clothing, and housing. It is also called **discretionary income.** That is because you can choose how you want to spend it.

Disposable Income

Have you ever seen something in a store window and thought, "I have to have that!"? How many times have you gone in to buy it? When deciding how to spend your money, it is important to avoid **impulse buying.** This is buying that is unplanned and often based on emotion.

There are many ways to avoid impulse buying. Before you shop, make a list of what you need. Buy only what is on the list. Think before you buy. Don't buy something extra right away; think about it for a while. Be careful with online buying. It is quick and simple, which makes it easy to overspend. Finally, set up a budget and stick to it.

When deciding how to spend your money, you have to think about opportunity costs. Remember that opportunity cost is the value of the choice you did not make. For example, if you want to buy new shoes, what else won't you be able to buy or do if you spend your money on the shoes? What opportunities will be lost? Are the shoes worth giving up these things?

Check for Understanding

Name two options to consider when comparison shopping.

1. ______________________

2. ______________________

What are two steps that you can take to help you make smart buying decisions?

3. ______________________

4. ______________________

Glue Foldable here

Examining Details

9. Susan lives in an apartment in town. What is the name for the income that she uses to pay her rent?

____

Listing

10. Fill in the table by listing three examples of what a person would buy with disposable income.

Reading Check

11. What is an example of opportunity cost?

____

____

FOLDABLES®

12. Place a two-tab Foldable along the line. Label the anchor tab *Consumer*. Label the other tabs *Rights* and *Responsibilities*. Write three facts about each.

NAME ______________________ DATE ______________ CLASS __________

Lesson 2: Budgeting Your Money

ESSENTIAL QUESTION

Why and how do people make economic choices?

GUIDING QUESTIONS

1. ***How can making a personal budget lead to financial responsibility?***
2. ***Why is it important to use credit responsibly?***

Terms to Know

budget a plan for making and spending money
expense money spent on goods and services
balance the money that is left after subtracting expenses from income
deficit a negative balance
data factual information used for reasoning
credit permission to pay later for goods or services obtained today
fee the cost of a service
interest the fee charged for borrowing money
loan money lent at interest
borrower person taking out a loan
annual percentage rate (APR) annual cost of credit; a percentage of the amount borrowed

What Do You Know?

In the first column, answer the questions based on what you know before you study. After this lesson, complete the last column.

Now...		Later...
	What should you include when making a budget?	
	What is credit?	

FOLDABLES®

1. Place a two-tab Foldable on the line. Make four tabs. Write *Budget* on the anchor tab. Write *Expenses, Balance, Surplus,* and *Deficit*. on the tabs and define each.

Using a Personal Budget

/ / / / / / / / / / / / / Glue Foldable here / / / / / / / / / / / / / /

Making a **budget** can help you make sure you have enough money to do the things you want to do. A budget keeps track of all the money you earn and spend. It is a useful tool to help you make sure you do not spend more money than you should.

The basic parts of a budget are the same whether you are a preparing an individual budget or the federal government's budget. The three parts of a budget are income, expenses, and the balance. The money you earn or other money you receive is your income. The ways you spend your money are called your **expenses.** The **balance** is the money that is left after you have paid your expenses.

Lesson 2: Budgeting Your Money, *Continued*

If you have more income than expenses, you have a surplus. If you have more expenses than income, you have a **deficit.** The goal is to keep a positive balance. Keeping a positive balance helps make sure you will have enough money to meet any emergency expenses or add to your savings.

Steps to Make a Budget

1. Make a list of all the money you spend for two weeks. Include food, clothing, entertainment, savings, and everything else. If there are some items that do not fit into any category (group), list them under extra expenses. Include impulse buying.
2. Make a list of all the money you earn for the same two weeks. List the sources of that money. They might include an allowance, pay from a job, or gifts.
3. Analyze your **data** (information). Subtract the total of everything you spent from what you earned. Did you have a surplus, deficit, or balanced budget? A balanced budget is one in which income equals expenses.
4. If you have a deficit at the end of the two-week period, you should look for ways to cut your spending or earn more money. If you have a surplus, you can increase spending or you can save the extra money.

Using Credit

Almost everyone needs to borrow money at some point. That includes businesses as well as people. The key tool for borrowing money is **credit.** Credit is money borrowed to pay for goods or services. Credit lets you buy now and pay later.

To understand credit, you need to know some key terms. They are listed in the box below.

Credit Mini-Glossary

- Lender—person or business that loans money for a fee, or cost
- Interest—the cost charged for borrowing money
- Loan—money lent for a fee
- Borrower—person taking out a loan
- Annual percentage rate (APR)—annual cost of credit; a percentage of the amount borrowed
- Credit rating—estimate of a borrower's ability to repay a loan
- Collateral—property, such as a house or a car, that a borrower offers to make the loan safe for the lender

Visualizing

2. Write a simple equation to show how to calculate your balance.

____

Paraphrasing

3. Write a few sentences describing how to make a budget.

____

____

Reading Check

4. What is a balanced budget?

____

____

____

Mark the Text

5. Underline the definition of *credit* in the text.

Prior Knowledge

6. How would borrowing money affect your budget?

____

____

____

NAME ______________________ DATE ____________ CLASS ________

networks

Lesson 2: Budgeting Your Money, *Continued*

Comparing and Contrasting

7. Study the table. What is the difference between a bank and a credit union?

____

____

____

____

Mark the Text

8. Underline the sentence that explains what you need to be approved for credit.

Comprehension

9. Explain what a down payment is and what types of purchases it is used for.

____

____

____

____

Identifying

10. What is the most common type of credit used?

____

There are many places where you can get credit. One such place is at stores that have their own store credit cards. The maximum credit amount will often be small, from $250–$1000. Once you use your credit card to make purchases, you will have to pay at least a small amount back each month. That amount includes some of the money you borrowed and the interest you owe on that money.

When you are an adult and need to buy a car or a home, you will be able to get higher amounts of credit from banks, credit unions, and other types of financial companies. To be approved for credit, you have to have a history of paying back the money you borrowed in the past. The table below list several sources of credit.

Sources of Credit	
Banks	Banks provide many services. They accept deposits, offer checking accounts, and make loans.
Credit unions	A credit union is a bank formed by a group with a common bond. That bond may be an employer, for example.
Finance companies	These businesses specialize in loans to individuals. They do not accept deposits. They charge a higher rate of interest than banks.
Stores	Many stores that sell items such as clothing, electronics, or furniture offer credit cards. They usually have low credit limits. A credit limit is the maximum amount a customer can borrow.

Loans for large purchases, such as cars or homes, require a down payment from the borrower. A down payment is a payment for part of the purchase price. The rest of the price is the amount borrowed. The amount borrowed is divided into equal loan payments, with interest added.

Credit cards are the most common type of credit. They are issued by banks, credit card companies, and stores. Credit cards allow you to borrow money to pay for goods and services. Credit cards set a limit on the amount of money you can borrow.

NAME ______ DATE ______ CLASS ______

networks

Personal Finance

Lesson 2: Budgeting Your Money, *Continued*

Here is how credit cards work. First you must apply for a card. The card issuer will check your credit rating. It will set a limit on the card based on what it thinks you can afford. Some companies do not charge interest if you pay the full balance each month. If you make your payment late, you can be charged a fee, and your interest rate could increase. Even without fees, credit card balances can add up quickly. This can ruin your finances.

Imagine you have purchased a $2,000 item with a credit card that charges 18 percent interest. If you pay only the minimum payment each month, it will take you more than 10 years to repay the credit card loan for the item. By then you will have paid $1,142 in interest. The $2,000 item will have cost you a total of $3,142.

The chart below shows benefits and drawbacks of credit.

Benefits	Drawbacks
• Person can buy now and pay later • Making payments on time teaches discipline • Requires analysis of finances, an important life skill	• Can cause financial trouble if a person borrows more than he or she is able to pay back • Makes things cost more because of interest

To be a responsible borrower, you have to make payments on time and not borrow more than you can afford. Also, before applying for credit, ask the following:

- What is the APR?
- Are there extra fees?
- How much time will I have to make payments?
- What are the penalties for late payments?

Glue Foldable here

Check for Understanding

Name two sources of credit.

1. ______ **2.** ______

What are two questions to ask before applying for credit?

3. ______ **4.** ______

Describing

11. Study the diagram. What is the main drawback of using credit cards?

______

______

Reading Check

12. What might happen if a lender gives you more credit than you are able to repay?

______

______

______

FOLDABLES®

13. Place a two-tab Foldable along the dotted line. Write *Credit* on the anchor tab. Label the two tabs *Loans* and *Credit Cards*. Write the definition of each on the front. Write facts about each on the reverse.

Lesson 3: Saving and Investing

ESSENTIAL QUESTION

Why and how do people make economic choices?

GUIDING QUESTIONS

1. ***Why is it important to save part of your income?***
2. ***What types of savings plans exist?***
3. ***How do investments in stocks and bonds promote long-term financial goals?***

Terms to Know

principal money deposited into a savings account on which interest is earned
access the freedom to use something
maturity the time at which you can withdraw funds from a CD
penalty fee for early withdrawal of funds
return the profit earned by an investor
stock a share of a company owned by an investor
dividend a portion of a company's earnings paid to shareholders
bond interest-bearing certificate of agreement between a borrower and a lender
mutual fund an investment company

What Do You Know?

In the first column, answer the questions based on what you know before you study. After this lesson, complete the last column.

Now...		Later...
	Why should you save part of your income?	
	What are savings plans?	
	What are some benefits of investing in stocks and bonds?	

Comparing and Contrasting

1. What is the difference between interest and principal?

____

____

____

____

Saving Money

Saving means setting aside some of your income so you can use it later. Saving lets you plan for long-term goals. Your long-term goal may be to buy a car or go on a vacation. You might also choose to plan ahead and save money for college.

Saving also allows you to be ready for an emergency. If your car breaks down, you will have the money to get it fixed.

One way to save money is to open a savings account at a bank. Banks pay you interest, which makes your savings grow. Interest is the payment people are given when they let the bank use their money. The interest you earn is added to your **principal.** Principal is the money that you deposit into your account.

Lesson 3: Saving and Investing, *Continued*

Saving money is also good for the economy. The banks loan your money to other customers. This money finds its way into your local community and helps it grow.

Checking accounts are used for money that you need easy **access** to for paying bills and buying things. Checking accounts pay little or no interest.

There are several ways to access the money in your checking account. They are shown in the chart below.

Accessing Checking Account Funds	
Checks • Can be used to pay bills or make purchases.	**Example:** You write a check to buy a shirt. The store sends your check to your bank. The bank then sends the money to the store from the funds in your account.
Debit card • Issued by your bank. Works like a credit card.	**Example:** When you buy something using a debit card, the money comes out of your checking account.
Electronic banking • Pay bills online.	**Example:** You use your online account to direct the bank to make a payment, which is automatically deducted from your account.

The biggest difference between a checkbook and a debit card is what happens if someone steals your card or checkbook. If someone writes a check for $500 without your approval, your loss is limited to $50 by law. The other $450 is a loss to the bank. If someone uses your debit card to charge $500 without your approval, your loss can be as high as $500. That is because the bank is not responsible for the misuse of your card. Banks have been encouraging customers to use debit cards instead of checks. One reason is the lower liability they face for debit card misuse.

Savings Plans

No matter how much you decide to save, it is always a good idea to have some kind of savings plan. There are many ways to save money. Opening a savings account is one way. One good thing about savings accounts is easy access to the money. No fees are charged for taking money out of the account.

Reading Check

2. For what sorts of emergencies might a person need savings?

____

____

Identifying

3. Study the chart. What are the ways used to access money in a checking account?

____

____

____

Mark the Text

4. Underline the words in the text that help you understand the meaning of the term *penalty*.

Now use this information to write a definition for *penalty*.

____

____

Lesson 3: Saving and Investing, *Continued*

Explaining

5. Why do longer-term CDs usually pay a higher interest rate?

____

____

____

Reading Check

6. Which type of account is more flexible, a checking account or a CD?

____

____

Identifying

7. Give an example of why it might be risky to invest in a company's stock.

____

____

Identifying

8. Study the chart. Finish these statements.

Original investments = _____.

Loss if company goes out of business = _____.

Another way to save is through a money market account. A money market account is like a savings account, but you usually have to deposit a larger amount of money than in a savings account. Another difference is the type of access you have to your money. In a money market account, access to your funds is limited. You can only make a set amount of transactions each month. A good thing about a money market account is that it pays more interest than a regular savings account.

You can also save with a certificate of deposit (CD). With a CD, you deposit money for a set length of time. This set time is usually several months or years. CDs with longer terms, or lengths of time, pay more interest than those with shorter terms. CDs also offer a fixed rate of interest. That means it will not change during the set length of time you have your CD. The interest is usually higher than on a savings account. The interest will be added to your principal when the CD reaches **maturity,** or comes due. If you take your money out early, you pay a **penalty.**

Stocks and Bonds

Savings accounts, money market accounts, and CDs are all useful ways to save money. However, the **return** they offer is usually low. Return is another word for the profit earned. Stocks and bonds usually have higher returns, but they also have risk. You may lose some or all of your money.

When people buy **stock,** they are buying part of a company. Stock is sold in pieces called shares. A person who owns stock is called a shareholder. The value of shares can go up or down. Share values usually go up when a company is making money and down when a company is not. You can sell your shares of stock at any time. The goal is to sell when the price is higher than what you paid for them. Then you will make a profit.

It is a risk to invest in stocks. You may not make a profit. If a company goes out of business, you can lose all of your money. The following example shows how this works.

Investing in the Stock Market	
Buy 10 shares of stock at $100 per share	Investment = $1000
Sell 10 shares at $110 per share	Profit = $100
Sell 10 shares at $90 per share	Loss = $100
Company goes out of business; shares are worth $0	Loss = $1000

Lesson 3: Saving and Investing, *Continued*

Some companies pay **dividends.** A dividend is a portion of the company's profit. Shareholders get an equal dividend payment for each share they own.

Bonds are money a person lends to a company or the government. When you buy a bond, you are lending money for a set length of time, usually 5, 10, or 20 years.

Companies sell bonds to raise money for new equipment, land, or to pay expenses. In return for borrowing money, the company will pay interest for a set number of years. Buying bonds is a risk. If the company does not do well, it may not be able to pay the loan back.

The U.S. government also issues bonds. They are said to be the safest of all investments.

A final type of investment is a **mutual** (MYOO•chuh•wuhl) **fund.** Mutual funds combine money from many people. The money is invested in a group of stocks chosen and managed by experts. The risk is lower because so many different stocks are owned. Stocks that go up in value can balance stocks that go down.

The government keeps track of many mutual funds. This is done using a measuring system called an index. The Dow Jones Industrial Average (DJIA) and the Standard & Poor's 500 (S&P 500) are the two most common indexes.

Check for Understanding

Why is it important to save part of your income?

1. ______

What are two of the safest ways to save money?

2. ______

3. ______

Give one example of a long-term investment.

4. ______

Glue Foldable here

Contrasting

9. What is the difference between making a profit on a stock and getting paid a dividend from a stock?

______

______

Reading Check

10. How does a mutual fund help reduce risk?

______

______

______

FOLDABLES®

11. Place a Venn diagram Foldable along the dotted line. Write *Profit on Money* on the anchor tab. Label the top tab *Saving Money,* the middle tab *Both,* and the bottom tab *Investing Money*. On the tabs, write facts about each. Then, on the middle tab, write what they have in common.

NAME ______________________ DATE ______________ CLASS __________

networks

Business in America

Lesson 1: How Businesses Are Organized

ESSENTIAL QUESTION

Why and how do people make economic choices?

GUIDING QUESTIONS

1. ***What are the advantages and disadvantages of a sole proprietorship?***
2. ***What are the advantages and disadvantages of a partnership?***
3. ***How is a corporation structured, and what are its advantages and disadvantages?***

Terms to Know

sole proprietorship a business owned and operated by one person

consult to ask advice or seek information

financial capital the money used to run or expand a business

liability legal responsibility for something such as an action or debt

partnership a business owned by two or more people

clarify to explain; to make something more understandable

corporation a business owned by many people but treated by law as a person

charter a government document giving permission to organize a corporation

board of directors a group of people elected by the shareholders of a corporation to act on their behalf

franchise a company that has permission to sell a suppliers goods or services in a specific area in exchange for a sum of money

nonprofit organization a business that does not intend to make a profit from the goods and services it provides

What Do You Know?

In the first column, answer the questions based on what you know before you study. After this lesson, complete the last column.

Now...		Later...
	What is a sole proprietorship?	
	What is a partnership?	

Mark the Text

1. Underline the the definition of *sole proprietorship*.

Sole Proprietorships

If you have ever made money doing yard work or babysitting, then you have had your own business. If you worked by yourself, you were a sole proprietor. A **sole proprietorship** (pruh•PREYE•uh•tuhr•ship) is a business owned by one person. It is also the most common form of business. It is often a small business serving a local community. For example, a local auto repair shop, ice cream shop, or dentist's office is likely to be a sole proprietorship.

Lesson 1: How Businesses Are Organized, *Continued*

The owner of this form of business is called a sole proprietor. Sole proprietors are their own bosses. They decide what products or services to sell. They make their own hours. They keep all profits. They do not have to **consult,** or ask, anyone when making decisions. These are advantages of a sole proprietorship.

There are also disadvantages. Sole proprietors often have trouble raising **financial** (fuh•NAN•shuhl) **capital.** This is money that is needed for a business to run and grow. Sole proprietors also have unlimited **liability** (LEYE•uh•BIH•luh•tee) for their business. Liability is legal responsibility. That means the owner has to pay all the business debts. It also means that if someone brings a lawsuit against the business and wins, the owner has to pay. Sometimes the owner's house or other personal property may be taken and sold to pay their debts.

Partnerships

/ / / / / / / / / / / / Glue Foldable here / / / / / / / / / / / / /

What if your business started to take up all of your free time and you wanted some of that time back? You could ask a friend to help you. In return you could give your friend a share of your business. This form of business is called a **partnership.** A partnership is a business that two or more people own and operate.

To form a partnership, two or more people sign a legal agreement called articles of partnership. This agreement explains what each partner will do in the business. It **clarifies,** or explains, how much money each will put in and how much of the profits each will get.

There are two kinds of partnerships, general and limited. In a general partnership, all the partners own the business. Every partner is responsible for managing the business and paying its debts. They are all called general partners.

A limited partnership has both general partners and limited partners. Limited partners own a part of the business. They provide the money needed for the business, but they do not help run it. They also share in the profits and have less liability than general partners. They are liable only for the amount of money they invested in the business.

The main advantage of a partnership is that the business can raise more money to grow. New partners can be added to bring in money. Each partner brings different strengths to the business. That gives it a better chance of success.

Reading Check

2. In a sole proprietorship, who receives all profits?

____

____

3. Place a two-tab Foldable along the line. Write *Partnership* on the anchor tab. Label the two tabs *General* and *Limited.* As you read, record what you learn about the two types of partnerships.

Vocabulary

4. What is a *partnership*? Give an example of a partnership.

____

____

Reading Check

5. What are the two types of partnership?

____

____

Prior Knowledge

6. Why is unlimited liability a disadvantage for a business owner?

______

______

______

Mark the Text

7. Underline the owners of a corporation in the chart. Then, circle the people who represent the owners.

Examining Details

8. How are a corporation's president and its stockholders related?

______

______

______

Critical Thinking

9. Employees are called the "backbone" of the organization. Why do you think this is said?

______

______

The main disadvantage for general partners is that each one has unlimited liability. For example, if a business has two general partners, each partner gets one-half of the profits. Then suppose the business falls into debt. One of the partners has no money. The other partner is responsible for the whole debt.

Corporations

The third form of business is the **corporation.** Under the law, a corporation is a legal body separate from its owners. It has the rights and responsibilities of an individual. It can own property. It can make contracts, sue, and be sued. It also pays taxes.

To form a corporation, a person or group applies to a state government for a **charter.** The charter describes the business and tells how much stock the corporation can sell. The chart below shows how corporations are organized.

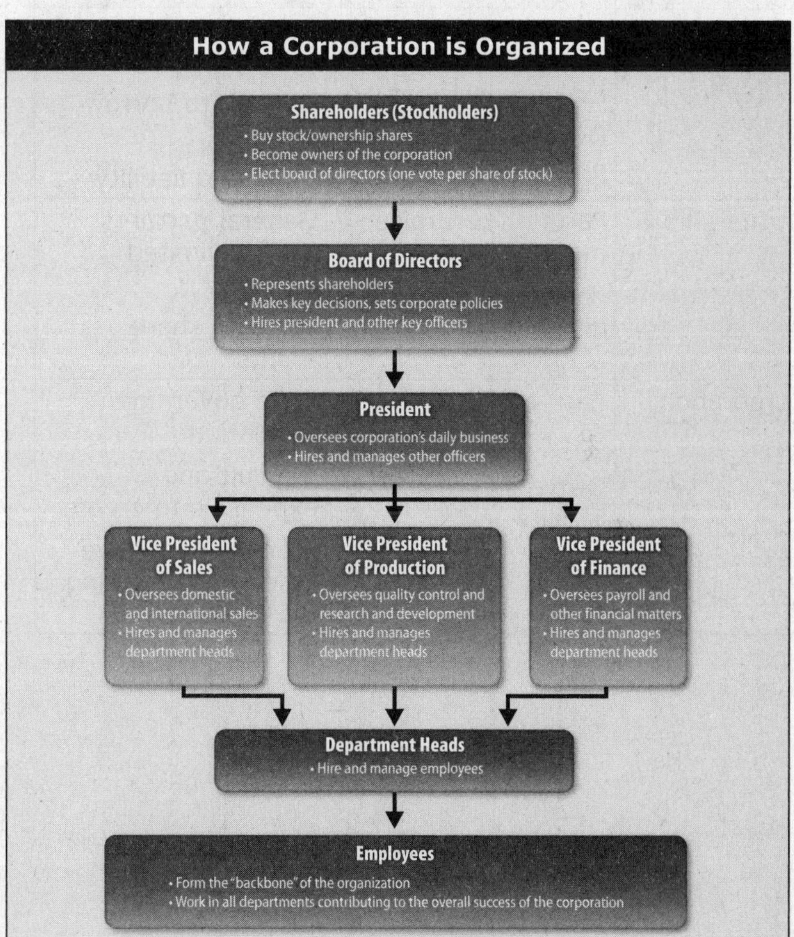

Business in America

Lesson 1: How Businesses Are Organized, *Continued*

There are advantages to a corporation. It is easy to raise money, because corporations can issue and sell stock, and it is easy to transfer ownership. Stockholders can sell their stock to other investors. Also, when a stockholder dies, the stock is passed down like other property. As a result, corporations have a long life. They also have limited liability. This means that if the business owes money, it is responsible for its debts, not the owners. The personal property of the owners cannot be sold to pay those debts.

Corporations also have disadvantages. They can be difficult and expensive to set up. They must follow more government rules than other businesses. They must also hold stockholders meetings once a year. All of those rules mean the actions of the company are watched more closely than other forms of business.

Form of Business	Advantages	Disadvantages
Sole proprietorship	Do not have to consult others before making decisions Owner keeps all profits	Difficult to raise money Difficult to borrow money Unlimited liability
Partnership	Partners can raise more money Partners have different strengths	General partners have unlimited liability Partners share profits
Corporation	Easy to raise money Have a long life Owners have limited liability	More government regulation Difficult and expensive to create Stockholders have little say in running the business

Mark the Text

10. Underline the three main advantages of corporations.

Reading Check

11. Who owns a corporation?

____

____

Visualizing

12. Study the information in the chart. Decide which form of business you would like to work with in the future. Then, draw an advertisement for that business. Make sure to illustrate the advantages of the form of business.

Lesson 1: How Businesses Are Organized, *Continued*

Paraphrasing

13. In your own words, how does a franchise work?

____

____

____

Identifying

14. What is the main disadvantage of owning a franchise?

____

____

Comparing

15. In what way is a nonprofit organization different from other forms of business?

____

____

FOLDABLES®

16. Place a one-tab Foldable along the dotted line. Write *Business* on the anchor tab. Then write four things about the structure and forms of businesses.

Glue Foldable here

Another way to set up a business is as a **franchise** (FRAN•CHYZ). The owner of a franchise pays a fee and part of the profits to a supplier. In return the owner of the franchise has the right to sell a certain product in a certain area. Many national fast-food restaurants and hotel chains are set up this way.

Owning a franchise has advantages. There is no competition from nearby sellers of the same product. Suppliers help franchise owners advertise and run the business. The main disadvantage is that a franchise owner does not have total control over his or her business. In all these forms of business, the goal is to make a profit.

A **nonprofit organization** is a different form of business. It provides goods or services without trying to make a profit. For example, the American Red Cross is a nonprofit organization.

One type of nonprofit is a **cooperative.** This is a group formed to carry on economic activity for the benefit of its members. There are many kinds of cooperatives. For example, a consumer cooperative buys goods in large amounts to keep costs down for its members. A farmers' cooperative helps its members sell their crops and livestock to large central markets where they can get better prices.

Check for Understanding

List the three basic forms of business organization.

1. ______________

2. ______________

3. ______________

Give an advantage and a disadvantage of each form of business.

4. ______________

5. ______________

6. ______________

NAME ______________________ DATE ______________ CLASS ______________

networks

Business in America

Lesson 2: Labor

ESSENTIAL QUESTION

Why and how do people make economic choices?

GUIDING QUESTIONS

1. ***What is the role of organized labor in the U.S. economy?***
2. ***How do labor and management work out agreements?***

Terms to Know

labor union a group of workers formed to improve wages and working conditions for its members

right-to-work laws state laws that forbid employers from forcing workers to join unions

circumstance situation

collective bargaining a process by which unions and employers negotiate the conditions of employment

strike when workers purposely stop working to force an employer to give in to demands

picketing a union method in which striking workers walk with signs that express their grievances

lockout when management closes a workplace to keep union members from working

injunction a court order to stop an action

option something that is chosen; a choice

mediation a situation in which union and company officials bring in a third party to help them reach an agreement

arbitration a situation in which union and company officials submit the issues they disagree upon to a third party for a decision

What Do You Know?

In the first column, answer the questions based on what you know before you study. After this lesson, complete the last column.

Now...		Later...
	How do workers and management solve problems?	

Organized Labor

An important part of any economy is its labor force. In the past 40 years, America's labor force has doubled in size. However, fewer workers are joining **labor unions.** A labor union is an organized group of workers that helps to make wages and working conditions better for its members.

One reason that fewer people are joining unions is that there are now fewer manufacturing jobs and more service jobs available. Fewer workers in service jobs join unions. More employers are also keeping unions out of their businesses.

Explaining

1. What are some of the ways labor unions help workers?

____

____

Lesson 2: Labor, *Continued*

Visualizing

2. Study the graph. What has been the trend in union membership over the last 25 years? Do you think this trend will continue in the future?

______

______

______

Reading Check

3. How does a trade union differ from an industrial union?

______

______

______

Making Inferences

4. How do you think right-to-work laws might affect union membership?

______

______

______

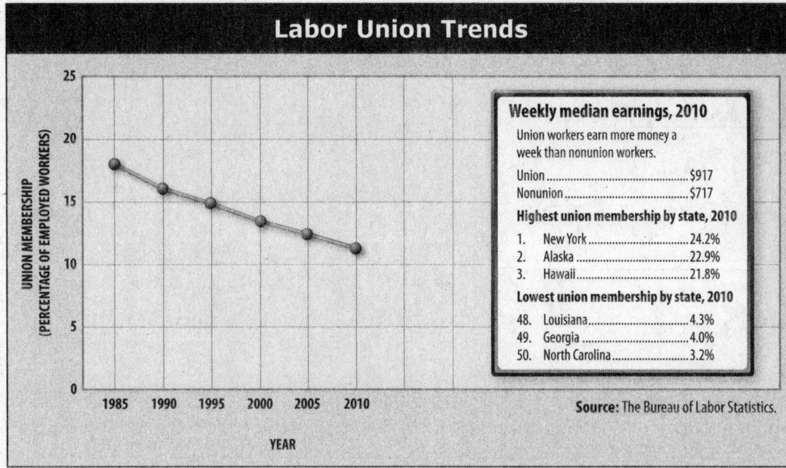

Today, there are more government workers than factory workers who belong to unions. The largest union is the American Federation of State, County, and Municipal Employees (AFSCME). Members of this union hold many different jobs. A few examples of these jobs are garbage collectors, school nurses, and prison guards.

There are two types of unions. In a trade union the members all work at the same craft or trade. For example, printers and bakers have trade unions. In an industrial union members do different types of work in the same industry. The United Auto Workers (UAW) is an industrial union. Its members work in the car industry.

Unions are organized. The basic unit of a union is the local. The workers in one factory or location form a local union. All of a union's locals form the national union. Most national unions belong to the AFL-CIO. This stands for the American Federation of Labor-Congress of Industrial Organizations. It is the country's largest labor group.

Workers in a workplace must vote to join a union. A federal agency watches these votes to make sure they are fair. That agency is the National Labor Relations Board.

One way that unions organize in the workplace is as a *union shop*. In a union shop the employer can hire anyone for a job. Shortly after starting the job, however, that person must join the union.

Many companies do not like union shops. In some states companies have convinced state governments to make them illegal. As a result, 22 states have **right-to-work laws** that ban, or outlaw, union shops.

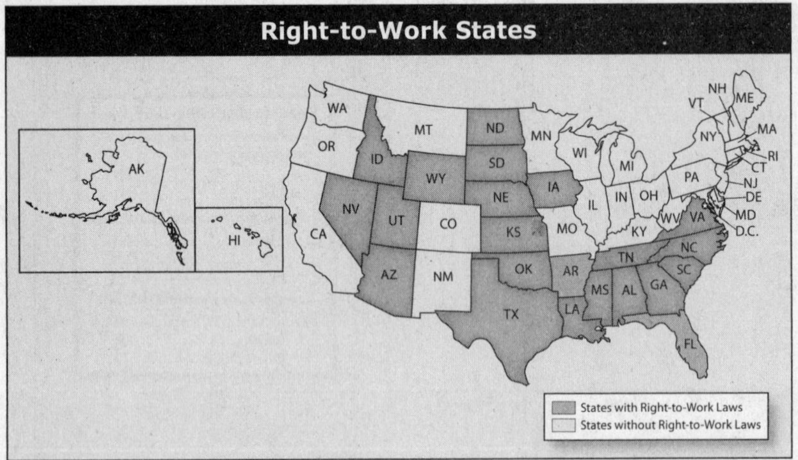

There are other **circumstances,** or situations, in which a worker does not have to join a union. Some states have a *modified union shop*. This means that workers can choose whether or not they want to join a union. Workers who join the union have to stay as members as long as they keep their jobs. Other workplaces have an *agency shop.* Workers in agency shops who do not join a union must still pay a fee to the union for representing them.

Labor Negotiations

The goal of a union is to get an employer to agree to what the workers want or need. This is usually done through **collective bargaining** (kuh•LEK•tihv BAHR•guhn•ihng). In this process union leaders and employers meet to work out the employees' contract. The contract states the workers' wages, hours, benefits, and conditions of work. Sometimes the union and the employer cannot agree. The unions and the employers have several tools to use to help them get what they want.

A union may call a **strike.** In a strike all union members refuse to work. The idea is that a company cannot survive without workers and will give in to the union's demands. Strikers often stand outside the workplace with protest signs. This is called **picketing.** It is meant to embarrass the company and keep other workers from working. Picketing also helps workers get support. Another tool is to convince people to stop buying the company's products.

Employers have tools to pressure the unions. A company may order a **lockout.** This keeps union workers out of the building and allows the company to hire replacements. It hopes the loss of income will force workers to stop the strike.

Examining Details

5. Use the details in the text and the map to explain the changing trends of labor unions in recent years.

____

____

____

____

Vocabulary

6. What is *collective bargaining*?

____

____

Critical Thinking

7. Why do you think picketing is a useful tool for workers when negotiating with employers?

____

____

Reading Check

8. What is the difference between a strike and a lockout?

____

____

Lesson 2: Labor, *Continued*

Examining Details

9. How might each party be involved in a court injunction?

unions ____________

employers ____________

federal government

____

Identifying

10. When does the government step into a labor dispute?

____

____

Identifying

11. Fill in the graphic organizer with facts about union bargaining goals.

FOLDABLES®

12. Place a two-tab Foldable on the line. Write *Unions* on the anchor. Label the tabs *Mediation* and *Arbitration.* On both sides, write facts about each term.

Companies and unions can ask the courts for an **injunction** (ihn•JUHNGK•shuhn). This is a court order to stop an action. For instance, a court can order a union not to strike. It can also order a company to end a lockout.

Some industries are important to the nation's economy and security. The federal government can ask for an injunction to prevent a strike or a lockout in these industries. In 2002 there was a disagreement between the port operators and the dockworkers on the west coast. The company locked out the workers for five months. President George W. Bush asked for an injunction to end the lockout. He said that the ports needed to be open for military operations. A judge granted the injunction.

Sometimes a strike threatens the nation's welfare so the government will step in. The president may order a "cooling off" period. During this time workers go back to work. The union and employer try to reach an agreement. In a crisis the government may even take over an industry while the two sides work to reach an agreement.

There are other **options,** or choices, available to unions and employers to reach an agreement. They may try **mediation** (MEE•dee•AY•shuhn). This involves bringing in a third party to help reach a compromise. They may also try **arbitration** (AHR•buh•TRAY•shuhn). In arbitration a third party decides on a solution. Both the employer and union agree in advance to accept its decision.

Glue Foldable here

Check for Understanding

How are mediation and arbitration different?

1. ____________

____

____

Lesson 3: Roles and Responsibilities of Businesses

ESSENTIAL QUESTION

How do economic systems influence societies?

GUIDING QUESTIONS

1. ***In what ways do businesses help their communities?***
2. ***How do businesses carry out their responsibilities to their consumers, owners, and employees?***

Terms to Know

social responsibility the duty that businesses have to pursue goals that benefit society as well as themselves

foundation an organization created by a person or a business to provide money for a specific purpose, especially for charity or research

crucial very important, especially for its effect on something

reveal to make something known

transparency the process of making business deals or conditions more visible

What Do You Know?

In the first column, answer the questions based on what you know before you study. After this lesson, complete the last column.

Now...		Later...
	How do businesses help their communities?	
	How do businesses meet their responsibilities to their consumers, owners, and employees?	

The Social Responsibility of Businesses

Does your school ever get help from a business? Take a look around to answer that question. Have you ever seen a car wash for your school being held on a business's property? Are your sports teams sponsored by local businesses? Are there business advertisements in the back pages of your school's theater programs or your yearbook? If you can answer "yes" to any of these questions, then a business has helped your school.

Businesses have many important roles in society. As producers they supply the food, clothing, and shelter that meet our basic needs. They also supply many of the things that make life enjoyable. Businesses also have a **social responsibility.** This is the duty to work toward goals that help others as well as themselves.

Each year American corporations give away about $14 billion. Some give away free goods and services.

Examining Details

1. Why do many businesses donate to causes? Give some examples of how businesses donate.

____

____

____

Vocabulary

2. What is a *foundation*?

____

____

Mark the Text

3. Underline some examples of how small companies help others.

Identifying

4. Study the charts. How much money did corporations give in 2009? Why do you think foundations gave more than corporations?

____

____

____

____

Reading Check

5. What are some of the good causes that American companies have donated to?

____

____

____

____

For example, some drug companies give medicines to people who cannot afford to pay for them. Other companies donate money to causes they support. For instance, Apple and the GAP give money to fight diseases around the world.

Wealthy business owners often set up **foundations.** A foundation is an organization set up by person or a company to give money for a specific purpose. They often support a charity or research. Bill Gates, the founder of Microsoft Corporation, started a foundation. It has given away about $23 billion. The money aids health and education programs around the world.

Corporations also set up foundations to support causes. The Wal-Mart Foundation plans to give away over $2 billion by the year 2015 to help stop hunger in the United States.

Business giving does not just come from big companies. About 75% of small companies give money to help others. Some professionals give free services to the poor or to nonprofit groups. These are just a few of the ways that businesses give to their communities. The charts below show the amount of money donated to charities in 2009.

2009 Contributions By Source	
Individuals	$227.4 billion
Foundations	$38.4 billion
Bequests	$23.8 billion
Corporations	$14.1 billion

2009 Contributions By Type of Recipient	
Religion	$100.95 billion
Education	$40.01 billion
Gifts to Foundations	$31.0 billion
Human Services	$27.08 billion
Public-Society Benefit	$22.77 billion
Health	$22.46 billion
Unallocated	$28.59 billion
International Affairs	$8.89 billion
Arts, Culture & Humanities	$12.34 billion
Environment & Animals	$6.6 billion
Foundation Grants to Individuals	$3.51 billion

Source: Giving USA 2010

Other Business Responsibilities

Businesses have a responsibility to many groups. Consumers are one group. Businesses are required to sell products that are safe. Their products must work as promised. Advertising must be truthful. Businesses must treat customers fairly.

Businesses are also responsible to their owners. This responsibility is **crucial,** or important, for corporations because the owners do not manage the company. Stockholders own a corporation and managers run it. These are two separate groups of people.

The law says that corporations must send out reports about their finances regularly. These reports **reveal,** or make public, the amount of money a company makes and spends. This is called **transparency.** Investors use these reports to make decisions about buying and selling stock in a company. It is illegal for corporations to give false information.

Businesses are responsible to their employees. Businesses have to provide a safe workplace. They also have to treat all workers fairly. They may not treat employees differently because of race, religion, color, gender, age, or disability.

Many companies provide benefits to their workers, such as paying for education or childcare. In 2010 Congress passed a health care reform law. It requires most businesses to provide health insurance to employees. These types of benefits help the company as well as the worker. Healthy, better-educated workers can be more productive.

/ / / / / / / / / / / / / /Glue Foldable here/ / / / / / / / / / / / / / /

Check for Understanding

Businesses have responsibilities toward what four groups?

1. ______ **2.** ______

3. ______ **4.** ______

Explain why it is important for a business to show responsibility toward its community.

5. ______

______

Vocabulary

6. Complete the sentences below with the words *crucial* and *reveal.*

It is ______ that I turn my report in on time to get a good grade.

The school held an assembly to ______ the winner of the reading contest.

Reading Check

7. Why is it important for corporations to publish financial information regularly?

______

______

FOLDABLES®

8. Place a two-tab Foldable on the line. Write *Responsibilities* on the anchor. Label the tabs *Business* and *Community.* Use both sides to explain the responsibilities businesses and communities have to each other.

NAME ______________________ DATE ______________ CLASS __________

networks

Government's Role in the Economy

Lesson 1: Government Involvement in the Economy

ESSENTIAL QUESTION

How does government influence the economy and economic institutions?

GUIDING QUESTIONS

1. ***What goods does government provide?***
2. ***How does government encourage or increase competition among businesses?***
3. ***How does government regulate business?***

Terms to Know

private good an economic good that, when consumed by one person, cannot be used by another

public good an economic good that is used by everyone, such as highways

externality an economic side effect

affect to impact; to have an effect on

monopoly a sole provider of a good or service

antitrust law law that prevents monopolies from forming and promotes competition

merger when two or more companies combine to form one business

natural monopoly a market situation in which the costs of production are low because a single firm produces the product

restore to bring back

recall removal of an unsafe product from store shelves

What Do You Know?

In the first column, answer the questions based on what you know before you study. After this lesson, complete the last column.

Now...		Later...
	What are goods and services?	
	What helps a businesses succeed?	
	How can the government protect consumers?	

Vocabulary

1. Give an example of a *private good* other than those given here.

____

Providing Public Goods

Most goods produced by businesses are **private goods.** Private goods have two features:

1. Private goods are items that people cannot have unless they pay for them.
2. Private goods can be used by only one person. If you buy a shirt, no one else can buy that exact shirt, for example. Food, clothing, books, and cars are examples of private goods.

Lesson 1: Government Involvement in the Economy, *Continued*

Public goods are different from private goods. People do not pay for public goods. More than one person can use public goods. Sidewalks are an example. If one person walks on a sidewalk, this does not stop others from walking on that same sidewalk. Public goods include many services that benefit people in their communities. Included are police and fire protection, public parks, and public libraries. Similarly, the entire nation is made safer by the armed forces.

Businesses do not often provide public goods. This is because it is hard to charge everyone who uses them. For example, how much should you be charged for using the sidewalk? How much for police protection? Instead, government takes on the responsibility for providing public goods. It pays for them with taxes and fees.

At times economic activities and the use of public goods cause side effects called **externalities** (EHK•STUHR•NAH•luh•teez). Externalities are positive or negative side effects of an action that **affects,** or impacts someone else.

Good highways are an example of a positive externality. Good roads make it cheaper for companies to transport goods. The goods can then be sold for lower prices. Lower prices benefit all consumers.

Externalities can also be negative. Pollution from cars is a negative externality. Even people who don't have a car can suffer from air pollution's negative effects, like having trouble breathing. One role of the government is to try to prevent negative externalities. This is why the government regulates auto exhaust.

Maintaining Competition

One goal of the government is to make sure there is competition in the marketplace. Markets are places where goods and services are sold. Markets work best when there are large numbers of buyers and sellers. If there is no competition, then only one supplier controls the market. This is called a **monopoly** (muh•NAH•pah•lee). With no competition a monopoly can charge any price it wants. Customers are forced to pay because they cannot get the product or service anywhere else.

To control monopolies, the government has passed **antitrust** (AN•tee•TRUHST) **laws.** A trust is several businesses banded together that threaten competition. Antitrust laws prevent trusts and work to keep competition in the marketplace.

Reading Check

2. How does government pay for public goods?

____

Explaining

3. Explain why most public goods come from government and not businesses.

____

____

____

Identifying

4. When one person buys cigarettes and smokes them in public, this exposes other people to secondhand smoke. What is this an example of?

____

____

Defining

5. What is a trust?

____

____

Lesson 1: Government Involvement in the Economy, *Continued*

Visualizing

6. If one person owns all the rental properties in a town, what is this called? How might it affect what people must pay to rent a house or apartment in that town?

______

______

Examining Details

7. Why does the government sometimes allow monopolies?

______

______

Reading Check

8. Why does government promote competition?

______

______

______

In 1890, the government passed the Sherman Antitrust Act. It bans monopolies and any business practices that prevent competition. In 1911, this law was used to break up the Standard Oil Company's monopoly on oil. In the 1980s, it was used to break up American Telephone and Telegraph's (AT&T) monopoly on telephone service.

In 1914, Congress passed the Clayton Antitrust Act. It banned specific business practices that limit competition. For example, the law no longer allowed one person to be on the board of directors of two competing companies. The law also gave the government power over some mergers.

When two or more companies combine to form one business, this is called a **merger** (MUHR•juhr). Mergers can threaten competition and lead to higher prices for consumers. If a merger goes against antitrust laws and threatens competition, the government can step in and stop it. This is the job of the Federal Trade Commission (FTC).

In addition to encouraging competition, the government also regulates other business activities. These include natural monopolies, product advertising, and product safety.

When a good or service is very expensive to produce, it can actually be cheaper to have one company produce it. This is called a **natural monopoly.** Many public services are delivered by natural monopolies. Natural gas is one example. Electricity is another.

The government sometimes allows these natural monopolies because they serve the best interest of the public. However, the company with the monopoly must agree to government regulation. Regulation might include setting prices or quality standards.

In recent years, governments moved to end natural monopolies to bring back, or **restore,** competition. This is called deregulating. Deregulation did not always lead to lower prices, though. As a result, many states are backing away from deregulation of natural monopolies.

Lesson 1: Government Involvement in the Economy, *Continued*

Providing Consumer Health and Safety

The government also plays a key role in protecting the public's health and safety. Federal agencies such as the Food and Drug Administration (FDA) oversee the safety of food, medical equipment, and many other things. The chart below shows some federal regulatory agencies and their work.

Selected U.S. Government Regulatory Agencies

DEPARTMENT OR AGENCY	PURPOSE
Consumer Product Safety Commission (CPSC)	Protects the public from risks of serious injury or death from consumer products
Environmental Protection Agency (EPA)	Protects human health and the natural environment (air, water, and land)
Federal Trade Commission (FTC)	Promotes and protects consumer interests and competition in the marketplace
Food and Drug Administration (FDA)	Makes sure food, drugs, and cosmetics are truthfully labeled and safe for consumers
Occupational Safety and Health Administration (OSHA)	Makes sure workers have a safe and healthful workplace

The Consumer Product Safety Commission (CPSC) aims to protect consumers from injury. If the CPSC decides a product is unsafe, it issues a **recall.** This means the product must be removed from store shelves. The manufacturer must make the product safe. It can also offer a substitute product or refund the customer's money.

Check for Understanding

Describe the government's role in providing goods.

1. ______________________________

____

What major laws have been passed to prevent monopolies and trusts? What is the overriding goal of these laws?

2. ______________________________

____

Glue Foldable here

Reading Check

9. What is the role of the FDA?

____

____

Explaining

10. Why might the government regulate a meatpacking plant?

____

____

FOLDABLES®

11. Place a three-tab Foldable along the dotted line. Label the anchor tab *"How does government…"*. Label the three tabs *handle competition, provide public goods and services*, and *regulate business*. On both sides of the tabs, list one fact about each.

Government's Role in the Economy

Lesson 2: Measuring the Economy

ESSENTIAL QUESTION

How does government influence the economy and economic institutions?

GUIDING QUESTIONS

1. ***Why is it important to measure an economy's performance?***
2. ***What are other signs of an economy's health?***
3. ***How is the stock market a measure of the economy's performance?***

Terms to Know

real GDP Gross Domestic Product after adjustments for inflation

business cycle alternating periods of economic growth and decline

indicate to signal

recession a time of declining economic activity lasting six months or longer

depression state of the economy with high unemployment, severely depressed real GDP, and general economic hardship

enormous very large

unemployment rate the percentage of people in the civilian labor force who are not working but are looking for jobs

fixed income income that does not rise even though prices are going up

inflation long-term increase in the general level of prices

bear market a time when stock prices fall for a substantial period

bull market a time when stock prices rise steadily

What Do You Know?

In the first column, answer the questions based on what you know before you study. After this lesson, complete the last column.

Now...		Later...
	Why is a nation's economy important?	
	What is the stock market?	

Visualizing

1. What image can you think of to illustrate the ups and downs of the economy?

____

____

Economic Performance

Many people and groups want to know how the economy is doing. Prices are the signals that help people, businesses, and the government make economic decisions. Prices are a key part of a market economy, but they can show information about the Gross Domestic Product (GDP) that may be misleading.

For example, if a country has a bigger GDP in one year than it had the year before, we may think that the economy has grown. But that may not be true.

Lesson 2: Measuring the Economy, *Continued*

A country's GDP grows only *if* the increase is due to a higher rate of output, or production, and not because prices of products have gone up. Simply put, a GDP grows only if the nation produces more, not if products cost more. For this reason, economists cannot depend on the GDP alone. Instead, they use a measurement called the real GDP.

Real GDP is the GDP after the changes caused by price increases have been removed. It is basically the same thing as GDP in an economy where prices do not change. It is a better measure of an economy over time than GDP.

Measuring real GDP is important. Government leaders want to know if their policies are working. Investors want to know where to put their money. Consumers want to plan future purchases. Growth in real GDP **indicates,** or signals, a healthy economy. In a healthy economy, jobs are produced and people have opportunities.

The economy does not grow at a steady rate. It goes through ups and downs. This series of ups and downs is the **business cycle.** The graph below shows a business cycle.

Model of the Business Cycle

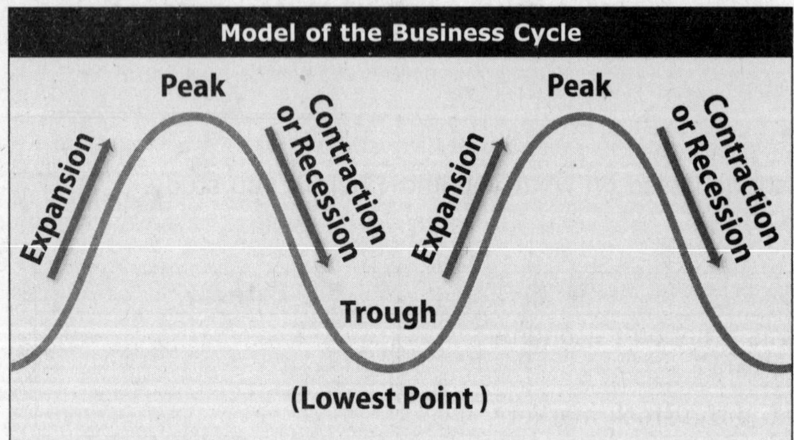

Business cycles have two parts.

1. The cycle starts at a peak and continues until the next peak. The peak is the point where real GDP stops going up and starts to go down.
2. Real GDP will eventually stop going down and start to rise again. The economy recovers. The point where GDP stops going down is called a trough. The trough is the lowest part of the business cycle.

If real GDP is low for more than six months the economy is in a **recession** (rih•SEH•shuhn). Recessions normally last less than a year. The recession of December 2007 to June 2008 was longer. This was the longest recession since the 1930s.

Glue Foldable here

Analyzing

2. If real GDP is going down, what part of the business cycle is the economy in?

____

____

Mark the Text

3. Underline the definition of a business cycle in the text.

Reading Check

4. What does a peak on a business cycle graph mean?

____

____

FOLDABLES®

5. Place a three-tab Foldable along the dotted line. Write *Economic Highs and Lows* on the anchor tab. Label the three tabs *expansion, recession,* and *depression.* On both sides of the tabs, record facts that you learn about each.

Lesson 2: Measuring the Economy, *Continued*

Vocabulary

6. Use the definitions of *recession* and *depression* to explain the similarities and differences between the two.

____

____

____

Mark the Text

7. Underline the definition of *unemployment rate* and the definition of *civilian labor force.*

Making Inferences

8. If the unemployment rate is going up, is the economy doing well or doing poorly? Explain why.

____

____

____

Reading Check

9. What does inflation do to purchasing power? Why?

____

____

Periods of expansion tend to be longer than declines. Most recent expansions last from 6 to 10 years. The new peak can be even higher than the one before.

A **depression** is a period of severe economic decline. A recession may turn into a depression if real GDP continues to go down rather than turning back up. The U.S. has had one major depression. It was called the Great Depression, and began with the stock market crash of 1929.

The fall in real GDP was **enormous.** Between 1929 and 1933, prices fell by about one-third. One in four Americans were out of work. Many banks closed and many stocks became worthless.

As a result of the Great Depression, new government programs were put in place to protect people financially. Because of these safeguards, many economists believe a depression of this size will never happen again.

Other Measures of Performance

In addition to real GDP, economists have other ways to tell how the economy is doing. One way is by tracking the number of people who have or do not have jobs. Economists are mostly interested in the civilian labor force. *Civilian* means people outside the military. The civilian labor force is made up of all of the people 16 and older who are either working or are looking for work.

The **unemployment** (UHN•ehm•PLOY•muhnt) **rate** is the number of civilians who are out of work and looking for a job. A low rate indicates a healthy economy. A high rate indicates a troubled economy. The unemployment rate rises during recessions.

Economists also look at prices. If prices stay level, consumers and businesses are better off. This is especially important for people who are retired and on a **fixed income.** A fixed income stays the same each month.

When prices remain stable, money keeps its value. When prices go up, money loses value. For example, suppose an ice cream cone that usually costs a dollar doubles in price. Now you need twice as many dollars to buy the same ice cream cone. The higher price means that your dollar buys less.

A long-term increase in prices is called **inflation** (ihn•FLAY•shuhn).The chart on the next page shows how inflation affects the economy. The government tracks inflation using prices of about 400 products that make up the consumer price index (CPI). The CPI shows the rate of inflation.

Lesson 2: Measuring the Economy, *Continued*

How Inflation Affects the Economy

Economic Indicators

The health of the economy is measured by real GDP, the unemployment rate, and prices. Another measurement is the stock market.

The price of a company's stock is set by supply and demand. Supply is the number of stocks available. Demand is the number of stocks investors want to buy. Changes in a company's profits can change the demand for a stock. If the demand for stock changes, its price changes too. Economists look at overall changes in stock prices.

Indexes like the DJIA and the S&P 500 show investors' attitudes about the future. A "**bear market**" is when stock indexes are going down. It can sometimes signal a coming recession. A rising stock market is called a "**bull market.**" Bull markets are a good sign that the economy is doing well.

Another way to measure economic growth is the Leading Economic Index. This index combines data from ten sources. It uses the S&P, the number of hours worked in manufacturing, the number of building permits issued in the previous month, and other data. This combined average is more accurate.

The index is called "leading" because real GDP generally follows it. If the leading index goes down, real GDP usually goes down soon after. If the leading index goes up, real GDP usually goes up. The Leading Economic Index is a very good tool for predicting the future of the economy.

Check for Understanding

Give an example of a group that wants to know how the economy is doing and why they need this information.

1. ______________________________________

____

Describe how stock prices can show the overall health of the economy.

2. ______________________________________

Glue Foldable here

Identifying

10. Which is better for the economy, a bear market or a bull market?

____

____

Reading Check

11. What is the Leading Economic Index?

____

____

FOLDABLES®

12. Place a two-tab Foldable along the dotted line. Cut the tabs in half up to the anchor tab to make four tabs. Label the anchor tab *How is the economy doing?* Label the four-tabs *real GDP, unemployment rate, prices,* and *stock market*. On both sides of the tabs, list one fact about each.

NAME ______________________ DATE ____________ CLASS ________

networks

Government's Role in the Economy

Lesson 3: The Government and Income Inequality

ESSENTIAL QUESTION

How does government influence the economy and economic institutions?

GUIDING QUESTIONS

1. ***What factors influence income?***
2. ***In what ways does government help those in poverty?***

Terms to Know

attain to gain, achieve

potential possible; capable of being

welfare money or necessities given to the poor

Temporary Assistance for Needy Families (TANF) welfare program paid for by the federal government and run by the individual states

workfare aid programs that require people who are receiving welfare to do some work for their benefits

compensation payment to unemployed or injured workers to make up for lost wages

What Do You Know?

In the first column, answer the questions based on what you know before you study. After this lesson, complete the last column.

Now...		Later...
	What can you do to make sure you have a job that pays well in the future?	
	How do your community leaders help people in need?	

Mark the Text

1. Underline the three things that play a role in how much income people have.

Explaining

2. What are the economic consequences of dropping out of high school?

____

____

Income Inequality

The United States is a wealthy nation. Not all Americans are wealthy though. Some have high incomes, and others are quite poor. People's incomes are different for many reasons. Education level, family wealth, and discrimination each play a role.

Education is one key to income. That is why the government wants Americans to graduate from high school and go on to college. A person with a college degree can earn quite a bit more income than a person with a high school diploma.

When teens drop out of high school they harm the nation's economy. Having a poorly educated workforce hurts our country's ability to compete with other nations. The level of education a person **attains,** or achieves, influences his or her income. The more education a person has, the greater his or her **potential,** or possible, income.

Lesson 3: The Government and Income Inequality, *Continued*

People without high school diplomas normally earn lower wages and have higher rates of unemployment.

The government tries to encourage people to go to college. Some programs help students from low-income families and students with disabilities prepare for college. The government also offers low-cost loans and grants to help pay for college.

Family wealth is also a factor that affects income. People born into wealthy families often have better educational opportunities than those who do not. They also may be able to join an established family business. Many inherit wealth from their parents.

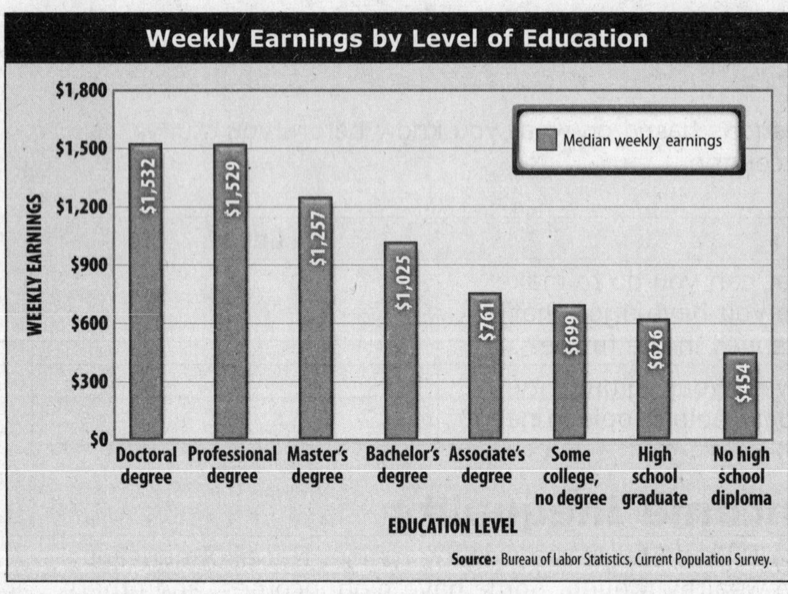

Discrimination also affects income. Women and minorities may face discrimination that keeps them from getting jobs they are qualified for. They may also have trouble getting promotions and earning higher salaries.

Congress has passed laws to help protect people from discrimination. These laws are shown in the chart on the next page. People can use the courts to enforce these laws.

Listing

3. What three factors affect income?

____

____

____

Reading Check

4. How does education affect income?

____

____

____

____

Making Connections

5. How can increasing opportunities for education and preventing discrimination help the economy?

____

____

____

____

____

Lesson 3: The Government and Income Inequality, *Continued*

Identifying

6. What does the Civil Rights Act do and when was it passed?

____

____

____

____

Making Inferences

7. How does the Lilly Ledbetter Fair Pay Act help protect the rights of women in the workplace?

____

____

____

Vocabulary

8. Define *welfare* and give one example of a welfare program.

____

____

Program: ____________

Reading Check

9. What is the purpose of poverty guidelines?

____

____

Antidiscrimination Laws		
Law	**Year Passed**	**Content**
Equal Pay Act	1963	Requires men and women to be given equal pay for equal work.
Civil Rights Act	1964	Bans discrimination on the basis of gender, race, color, religion, and national origin.
Equal Employment Opportunity Act	1972	Strengthens the government's ability to enforce the Civil Rights Act.
Americans with Disabilities Act	1990	Gives job protection to those with physical and mental disabilities.
Lilly Ledbetter Fair Pay Act	2009	Allows workers who face gender discrimination to sue employers.

Poverty

In a recent year, more than 40 million Americans lived in poverty. This means they did not earn enough income to pay for basic needs such as food, clothing, and shelter. Nearly 44 million people in this country fell into this category in 2009. Millions found themselves there as a result of the recession that began in 2007.

Both federal and state governments give welfare to struggling families. **Welfare** is money or necessities given to the poor. Welfare programs began in the United States during the Great Depression of the 1930s.

The government uses income guidelines to decide if an individual or a family can receive this help. The guidelines are based on how much it costs to buy enough food, clothing, and shelter to survive.

A short-term form of help is **Temporary Assistance for Needy Families (TANF).** TANF is paid for by the federal government, but is run by the states. The program began in 1996. It replaced another welfare program that had begun in the 1930s. The new program has stricter rules. These rules are intended to encourage participants to find jobs quickly.

Lesson 3: The Government and Income Inequality, *Continued*

In many states TANF programs require people to work in order to get help. These programs are called **workfare** (WUHRK•FAYR). The work often involves community service. Those getting the aid may also be required to go to job training or education programs.

Unemployment insurance provides **compensation** (KAHM•puhn•SAY•shuhn) for workers who lose their jobs. Compensation is temporary payment to make up for lost wages. Workers who have been hurt on the job can receive workers' compensation. It includes wages and medical expenses.

Identifying

10. Which group of people is the unemployment insurance program meant to help?

____

____

/ / / / / / / / / / / / / Glue Foldable here / / / / / / / / / / / / /

Check for Understanding

Describe the ways in which the government tries to improve economic opportunities for individuals.

1. ______________________

____

____

How does the government try to help those in poverty?

2. ______________________

____

____

____

FOLDABLES®

11. Place a Venn diagram Foldable along the dotted line. Label the anchor tab *Government Programs.* Label the first tab *Economic Opportunities*, the middle tab *Both,* and the last tab *Poverty Aid.* On the reverse tabs, list facts about each and then list what they have in common.

NAME ______________________ DATE ____________ CLASS ________

networks

The Government and Banking

Lesson 1: Money

ESSENTIAL QUESTION

How does government influence the economy and economic institutions?

GUIDING QUESTIONS

1. ***What gives money value?***
2. ***What do financial institutions do?***

Terms to Know

medium a way to carry out an action

barter to trade a good or a service for another good or service

coin piece of metal used as money, such as a penny

currency money, both coins and paper bills

electronic money money in the form of a computer entry at a bank or other financial institution

deposit the money that customers put into a financial institution

funds money

commercial bank financial institution that offers full banking services to both individuals and businesses

savings and loan association (S&L) financial institution that traditionally loaned money to people buying homes

credit union nonprofit service cooperative that offers banking services to members only

deposit insurance government-backed program that protects bank deposits up to a certain amount if a bank fails

What Do You Know?

In the first column, answer the questions based on what you know before you study. After this lesson, complete the last column.

Now...		Later...
	Where does the value of money come from?	
	What is a financial institution?	

Reading Check

1. What are the three functions of money?

____

____

All About Money

Money is anything that people use in exchange for goods. It can include objects such as stones, salt, shells, gold, or silver. Money has value because it performs three functions.

The Three Functions of Money

1. Money is a medium of exchange. A **medium** is a way to do something. Money is a way to exchange, or trade, goods and services. Without money, people barter. To **barter** means to trade goods or services directly.

Lesson 1: Money, *Continued*

2. Money is a store of value. This means it is a way to hold wealth. You can hold money until you are ready to use it.

3. Money is a measure of value. You can get an idea of an item's value by knowing how much money it costs. For example, a ring that costs $100 has more value than one that costs $10.

An object must have four characteristics in order to work as money.

The Four Characteristics of Money

1. *Portable.* It must be easy to carry around.

2. *Divisible.* It must be easy to break down into smaller amounts. That way it can be used for both large and small purchases. Strings of beads worked for some societies because beads could be removed to make smaller payments.

3. *Durable*. Money changes hands many times. Whatever is used must be able to last for a long time.

4. *Limited supply*. If money were easy to make, everyone would make it. Then it would become worthless.

Money can take different forms. The diagram below shows the forms we use in the United States.

/ / / / / / / / / / / / / / Glue Foldable here / / / / / / / / / / / / / /

Coins: Pieces of metal like pennies or dimes

Paper money: Rectangular pieces of high-quality paper

Money

Electronic money: Computer entries at financial institutions

Comparing

2. Chocolate coins share many characteristics with metal coins. What characteristic makes chocolate coins hard to use as money?

____

____

FOLDABLES®

3. Place a one-tab Foldable on the line. Label the anchor *Money*. Use both sides to explain why we need money to get the things we need and want.

Identifying

4. Study the graphic. What form of money is a person accessing when he or she uses online banking?

____

Listing

5. List the three forms of money used in the United States.

____

____

____

Lesson 1: Money, *Continued*

Analyzing

6. How do features of U.S. currency such as the security thread limit the supply? Why is it important to make sure the supply is limited?

____

____

____

____

Mark the Text

7. Study the graphic. Circle the three security features you think are most effective for preventing counterfeiting.

Vocabulary

8. Fill in the blank with the correct term. Banks take the __________ made by customers and use them to make loans.

Explaining

9. How do banks make money on loans?

____

____

Currency is another name for the objects we use as money, such as coins and paper bills. The government prints the paper bills using special paper and printing to make it difficult to counterfeit, or make illegally. The image below points out some of the special parts of U.S. paper currency.

Features of U.S. Currency

Financial Institutions

Many people and businesses store their money in a financial institution such as a bank. The money that a person puts into a financial institution is called a **deposit**. A deposit can be made using paper money, coins, checks, or electronic money. Some workers have their pay automatically deposited into their bank accounts. The deposit decreases the **funds,** or money, in the employer's account and increases the money in the workers' accounts.

Banks take the deposits made by customers and lend that money to other people and businesses. Banks charge interest and other fees for these loans to make money. They also pay interest on deposits to attract customers. Banks charge high interest rates on loans and pay low interest rates on deposits. That way they make a profit and stay in business.

The Government and Banking

Lesson 1: Money, *Continued*

Financial institutions are businesses that store money for and loan money to other businesses and individuals. The diagram below shows that there are three types of financial institutions.

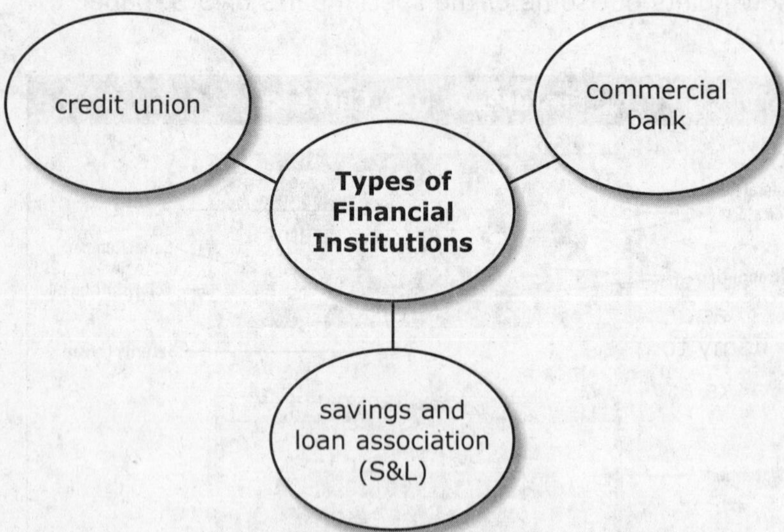

Another kind of financial institution is a **commercial bank.** A commercial bank provides full banking services to people and businesses, such as checking accounts, savings accounts, and loans. Commercial banks are the biggest and most important part of the financial system.

Another kind of financial institution is a **savings and loan association (S&L).** At one time S&Ls mainly loaned money for buying homes. Now they work like commercial banks. The biggest difference is that most S&L customers are people rather than businesses.

A third kind of financial institution is a **credit union.** A credit union is a nonprofit cooperative business. People who work in the same industry or company, or belong to the same labor union form one. This kind of institution accepts deposits, makes loans, and offers other banking services. You must, however, be a member of the credit union to use the services.

Defining

10. What is a financial institution?

____

____

Reading Check

11. What are the three main types of financial institutions?

____

____

____

Contrasting

12. Explain the difference between a commercial bank and a S&L.

____

____

____

Paraphrasing

13. Write a sentence explaining what a credit union is in your own words.

____

____

____

____

The Government and Banking

Lesson 1: Money, *Continued*

Defining

14. What is the FDIC?

____

____

Making Inferences

15. What is the reason for deposit insurance and government regulation of the banking industry?

____

____

____

____

FOLDABLES®

16. Place a two-tab Foldable along the dotted line. Label the first tab *Types of Money* and the second tab *Types of Financial Institutions*. On the tabs list as many types of each as you can remember.

Glue Foldable here

Money deposited in a financial institution is safe. This is because the government backs every bank and S&L with **deposit insurance.** This insurance protects customers' money if the bank goes out of business. The Federal Deposit Insurance Corporation (FDIC) insures the commercial banks and S&Ls. The program for credit unions is the National Credit Union Share Insurance Fund (NCUSIF). Both programs cover deposits of up to $250,000.

The government began insuring deposits in 1933 as a result of the Great Depression. During that time, depositors began to mistrust the banks and started pulling all their money out. This caused banks to go out of business. The government started the FDIC after these bank failures so that people would have more trust in banks and put their money in them. That trust allows the economy to grow.

Banks are also regulated, or watched over, by federal and state governments. A bank must have a government-issued charter to go into business. To get the charter, the government checks the bank's finances to make sure it has enough money. The government also makes sure the people who will run the bank have the knowledge to do it well. After the charter is issued, government officials continue to watch the bank. They make sure that it follows the law and is in good financial condition.

Check for Understanding

Does electronic money have all the features necessary to serve well as money? Explain.

1. ______________________

____

List three functions that financial institutions perform.

2. ______________________

3. ______________________

4. ______________________

NAME ______________________ DATE ______________ CLASS __________

Lesson 2: The Federal Reserve System

ESSENTIAL QUESTION

How does government influence the economy and economic institutions?

GUIDING QUESTIONS

1. ***What is the structure of the Federal Reserve System?***
2. ***What are the functions of the Federal Reserve System?***

Terms to Know

central bank a bank from which other banks can borrow money; also the place where the government does its banking business

Federal Open Market Committee (FOMC) most powerful committee on the Fed, which makes decisions about he money supply

monetary policy changing the money supply to affect the cost of credut, economic growth, and price stability

manipulate to make changes to something to produce a desired effect

open market operations (OMO) the buying or selling of government bonds and Treasury bills

discount rate the interest rate that the Fed charges on its loans to financial institutions

reserve requirement the amount of a deposit that banks have to keep on hand or deposit in their Federal Reserve district bank

distribute to give out

What Do You Know?

In the first column, answer the questions based on what you know before you study. After this lesson, complete the last column.

Now...		Later...
	What is the Federal Reserve System?	
	What does the Federal Reserve do?	

The Fed's Structure

In the early 1900s, the United States faced hard economic times. Banks could not make new loans. Many people thought that a **central bank** would fix this problem. A central bank is a bank for banks. It can loan money to banks.

The government required banks with a national charter to give money to create the central bank. The banks would have stock in the new bank. Stock is a share of the ownership of a business. The new central bank was created in 1913. It was named the Federal Reserve System. This system is sometimes called "the Fed."

Explaining

1. Why was the Fed created?

____

____

____

Lesson 2: The Federal Reserve System, *Continued*

Listing

2. List the main functions of the Federal Reserve.

___

___

___

Examining Details

3. According to the chart, what does the Board of Governors oversee?

___

___

___

___

Identifying

4. According to the chart, what banks are members of the Federal Reserve?

___

___

Reading Check

5. How many district banks are in the Fed?

___

___

The Fed has many important functions. It manages our money and watches over commercial banks. It is the government's bank, and it helps keep the U.S. economy healthy. The chart below shows how it is organized. At its top is the Board of Governors. The Board of Governors has seven members. One of the seven is the Chairman of the Board of Governors, who advises the president about economic policy.

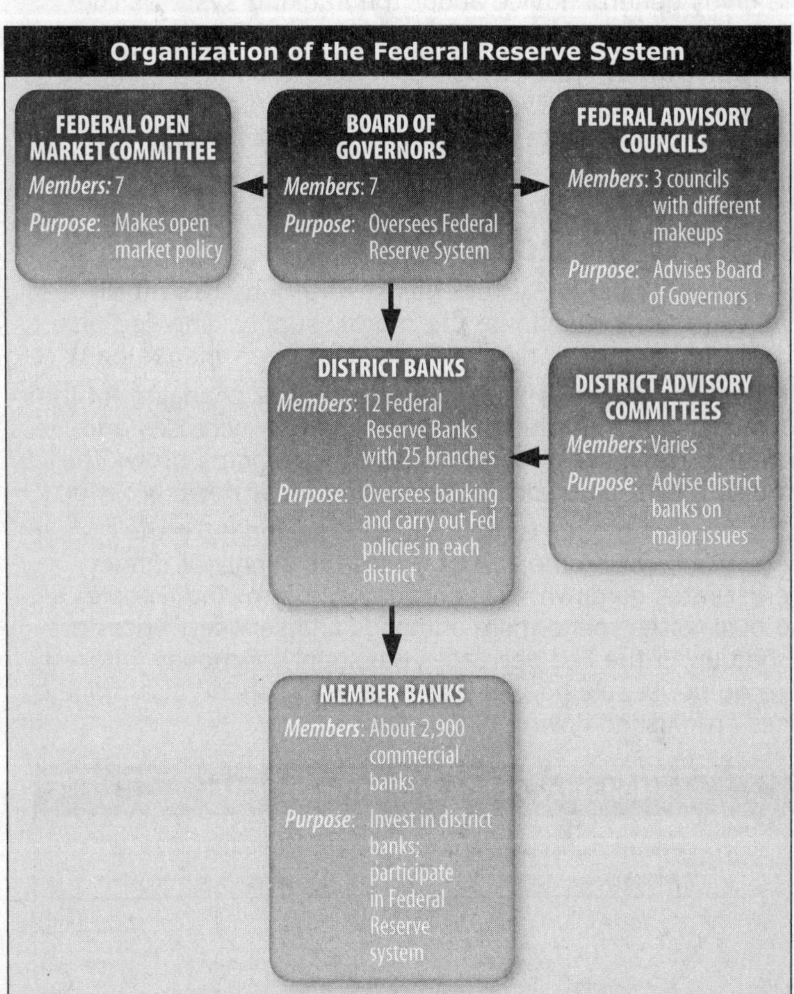

Board of Governors The president and the Senate choose the board members. They serve for 14 years. This long term length makes sure board members are fairly free of influence from elected officials as they do their jobs.

District Banks There are 12 Federal Reserve districts in the United States. Each district has one main Federal Reserve Bank and several branch banks. These banks carry out the policies set by the Board of Governors.

Lesson 2: The Federal Reserve System, *Continued*

A nine-member board of directors runs each district.

Councils The Federal Reserve System also includes several councils. One of the most important is the **Federal Open Market Committee (FOMC).** This committee manages the country's money supply. This ability gives the council a lot of power over the economy.

Three councils give advice to the Board of Governors. One gives general advice about the banking system. The other two councils focus on consumers and S&Ls.

Member Banks About 2,900 commercial banks belong to the Federal Reserve System. Most of them are national banks. Some are state banks, which do not have to join the Fed.

What the Fed Does

The Federal Reserve System has several jobs. Its most important job is managing the money supply. The Fed also watches over banks and serves as the government's bank.

Monetary policy is the **manipulating,** or changing, of the money supply to help the economy. The Fed increases and decreases the money supply to help the economy grow. The Fed also tries to keep prices from going up or down too much.

The price of money is the cost of borrowing it, or the interest rate. When the Fed increases the supply of money, interest rates go down. This encourages borrowing. People and businesses spend more on goods and services. Prices are pushed up. If the Fed decreases the supply of money, interest rates go up. People borrow less money and spend less money. Prices are pushed down.

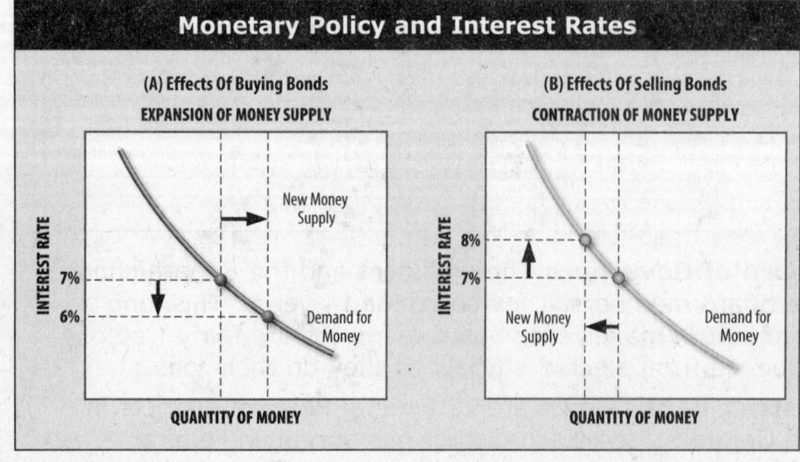

Vocabulary

6. What is the job of the FOMC?

Reading Check

7. Why does the Fed regulate monetary policy?

Visualizing

8. Draw an arrow to show how increasing the money supply affects interest rates.

Draw an arrow to show how decreasing the money supply affects interest rates.

Synthesizing

9. When the Fed wants to increase the amount of lending banks do, does it try to shrink or to grow the money supply? Explain why.

Lesson 2: The Federal Reserve System, *Continued*

Listing

10. List the three tools the Fed has for increasing or decreasing the money supply.

Paraphrasing

11. Write a sentence explaining the *discount rate* in your own words.

Making Inferences

12. Why does the Fed make sure banks keep a reserve when they loan money?

The Fed has three tools to control the money supply. The first is called **open market operations (OMO).** It includes the buying and selling of government bonds and Treasury bills. Bonds and bills are the way the government borrows money from the public.

Open Market Operations	
GOAL: **Grow** the money supply.	**GOAL:** **Shrink** the money supply.
ACTION: FOMC **buys** bonds from investors.	**ACTION:** FOMC **sells** bonds to investors.
SHORT-TERM RESULTS: Investors gain funds which they deposit in banks.	**SHORT-TERM RESULTS:** Investors pay for bonds with money they withdraw from banks.
LONG-TERM RESULTS: Money supply grows; banks have more money to lend; interest rates **drop**.	**LONG-TERM RESULTS:** Money supply shrinks; banks have less money to lend; interest rates **rise**.

The Fed's second tool is the discount rate. The **discount rate** is the interest rate banks pay to borrow money from the Fed. To grow the money supply, the Fed lowers the discount rate. This encourages banks to borrow money and lend it out. To shrink the money supply, the Fed raises the discount rate. This discourages borrowing.

The Fed's third tool is the reserve requirement. The **reserve requirement** is the amount of a deposit a bank must keep on hand. When the Fed increases the reserve requirement, banks hold on to more money. As a result they have less money to lend. When the Fed decreases the reserve requirement, banks have more money to lend.

The Fed also regulates banks. It writes regulations, or rules, that lenders must follow. Regulations cover many areas, including rules about making the terms of a loan clear to consumers. The Fed also has many other regulatory responsibilities.

Lesson 2: The Federal Reserve System, *Continued*

Another important job of the Fed is to take care of our currency. The U.S. Bureau of Engraving and Printing prints paper money. It then sends the bills to the Fed. The Fed keeps the currency safe and **distributes,** or gives it out, to banks as needed. Banks send bills that are worn out to the Fed to be replaced with new bills.

The Fed is the government's bank. When people pay their taxes, the money is sent from the U.S. Treasury to the Fed. The Fed also holds other money that the government receives. The government can write checks whenever it needs to make a purchase or payment. Federal checks are taken out of an account at the Fed.

Check for Understanding

What are two major jobs of the Fed?

1. ______________________

2. ______________________

How can the Fed use the reserve requirement to change the money supply?

3. ______________________

____

Glue Foldable here

FOLDABLES®

13. Place a two-tab Foldable along the dotted line. Label the anchor tab *Federal Reserve.* Label the two tabs *Decreasing Reserve* and *Increasing Reserve*. On both sides of the tabs, write what happens to the money supply when the reserve is increased or decreased.

The Government and Banking

Lesson 3: Banks and Banking

ESSENTIAL QUESTION

How does government influence the economy and economic institutions?

GUIDING QUESTIONS

1. ***What purpose do banks serve in the economy?***
2. ***How has banking become safer, faster, and more efficient over the years?***

Terms to Know

savings account an account that pays interest on deposits and allows withdrawals
certificate of deposit (CD) a timed deposit that states the amount of the deposit, maturity, and rate of interest paid
period a stretch of time
money market account type of savings account that pays interest and also allows check writing
checking account an account from which deposited money can be withdrawn at any time by writing a check

What Do You Know?

In the first column, answer the questions based on what you know before you study. After this lesson, complete the last column.

Now...		Later...
	What kinds of accounts do banks offer to customers?	
	Who chartered the first banks in the United States?	

Identifying

1. What are two types of accounts used for saving money?

____

____

Mark the Text

2. Underline the benefits of CDs. Circle their drawbacks.

Banks in the Economy

Banks offer many types of accounts. Some are used to save money. Others are used to pay bills and buy goods and services. Savings accounts and certificates of deposit are used for saving money. Most **savings accounts** pay interest and allow people to make withdrawals. The interest payments are meant to encourage people to keep their money in the bank and add to it.

A **certificate of deposit (CD)** pays more interest than regular savings accounts. However, it has a fixed term. This means that you must keep your money in the account for a set **period,** or length of time, if you want to get the higher rate of interest. You will get a lower interest rate as a penalty for taking your money out early.

A third type of account is a **money market account.** This account is like a checking and a savings account combined. It pays interest, but also allows the customer to write checks. There are special restrictions. Some banks set the number of withdrawals that are allowed, and some demand a minimum balance for this type of account.

The Government and Banking

Lesson 3: Banks and Banking, *Continued*

Money deposited in a **checking account** can be taken out at any time by writing a check, using a debit card, or making an electronic payment. People use checking accounts to pay bills and buy things. Some checking accounts pay interest, but it is usually lower than that offered by other types of accounts.

In addition to offering accounts, banks also make loans, or lend money. People and businesses sometimes need to borrow money from a bank. They do this by getting a loan. To get a loan the borrower and the bank (the lender) must agree to loan terms. This agreement includes the amount borrowed, the interest rate, and the time in which the loan needs to be repaid.

A loan's **terms** include information about the loan's

- **purpose**
- **amount**
- **rate of interest**
- **length**

New technology has introduced new forms of banking. People can now do their banking using the telephone, cell phone, automated teller machine (ATM), and the computer without ever having to go to the bank itself. Internet banking allows people to check account balances, monitor transactions, and pay bills. Some banks allow people to make purchases with a swipe of their cell phones rather than by check or credit card.

How Banking Has Changed

Banking has changed over the years. One of the first changes happened in 1791 with the First Bank of the United States. It was founded to collect money, make payments, and make loans for the national government. Some leaders feared that the Bank would become too powerful. They limited its charter to 20 years, then it went out of business.

During the War of 1812, it became clear that the government needed a bank from which it could borrow money. The Second Bank of the United States was created in 1816 and lasted until 1836.

Reading Check

3. What are the different ways that savings and checking accounts are used?

____

____

Defining

4. Study the chart. What is a bank loan and what are loan terms?

____

____

____

Explaining

5. Why was the charter of the First Bank of the United States limited to 20 years?

____

____

Paraphrasing

6. Describe the U.S. banking system between the War of 1812 and the start of the Civil War.

____

____

____

____

Lesson 3: Banks and Banking, *Continued*

Examining Details

7. What problems led to the demand for a uniform paper currency?

___

___

___

Describing

8. Why was the new Federal Reserve unable to stop the Great Depression?

___

___

___

Making Connections

9. How does the Banking Act still affect banking?

___

___

___

Mark the Text

10. Fill in the diagram with the event that caused the government to create the 1933 Banking Act.

From the 1830s to the 1860s, states took over the job of supervising privately owned banks. The states did not have enough control. Banks at that time were making loans using their own paper money. These banks printed too many notes, leading to a large supply of money which caused inflation. Demand arose for a uniform paper currency that was acceptable anywhere without risk.

The federal government passed the National Bank Act in 1863. Under the new law, the national government began issuing charters to banks. The national banks were better funded and regulated. They all used the same currency backed by U.S. government bonds. These changes helped bring some order to the banking industry.

Despite these improvements, the banks still had problems. Congress created the Federal Reserve System in 1913 to try to fix the banking system. Banks were placed under one main power: the Federal Reserve. The country was divided into 12 districts. Each district has one main Federal Reserve bank and several branch banks. The problem was that the districts did not cooperate with each other. This made it hard for the Federal Reserve to stop the Great Depression, which began in 1929.

As you read earlier, thousands of banks failed during the Great Depression. Many people began to panic. They then tried to take their money out of banks at the same time. The banks that did not have enough money failed and closed. These bank closures caused more people to panic and more banks to fail. Many people lost all their money.

To stop the panic, President Franklin D. Roosevelt closed all the banks for four days in 1933. He sent inspectors to see which banks had enough money and which were about to fail. Only healthy banks were allowed to reopen. Congress then passed the Banking Act of 1933.

U.S. Banking Legislation

Lesson 3: Banks and Banking, *Continued*

This law created deposit insurance and gave the Federal Reserve more power. A second law in 1935 made this power even greater. The changes gave the Board of Governors more power over the district banks. This central control helped the Fed to be more united.

These actions kept the banks running smoothly until the 1980s. Then a crisis hit savings and loan associations (S&Ls). Many had made risky loans that were never paid back. Hundreds of S&Ls failed. In 1989 Congress made the FDIC larger so it could cover S&Ls. The FDIC began to watch over them more closely.

Then in 2007 the economy went into a deep recession. Many banks had been making risky loans for years. So many banks were in danger of failing that the entire financial system was in crisis. In 2008 the Federal Reserve and the U.S. Treasury loaned trillions of dollars to financial institutions and troubled companies to stop the crisis. The plan worked, but the recovery was slow.

Check for Understanding

What role do banks play in the economy?

1. ______________________________

____

____

List two twentieth-century changes that made banking safer.

2. ______________________________

3. ______________________________

Glue Foldable here

Reading Check

11. How did the changes after the S&L crisis make the banking industry safer?

____

____

____

Analyzing

12. How did massive loans from the Fed and the Treasury prevent many banks and other companies from failing?

____

____

FOLDABLES®

13. Place a two-tab Foldable along the dotted line. Write the title *Banks* on the anchor tab. Label the two tabs *Banks Succeed* and *Banks Fail*. Use the space on both sides of the tabs to describe what happens to a community when banks are successful or when they fail.

NAME ______________________ DATE ____________ CLASS ________

networks

Lesson 1: The Federal Budget: Revenues and Expenditures

ESSENTIAL QUESTION

How does government influence the economy and economic institutions?

GUIDING QUESTIONS

1. ***How does the federal budget reflect choices?***
2. ***How do state and local revenues and expenditures differ from those of the federal government?***

Terms to Know

exceed to go beyond or become bigger than
fiscal year any 12-month period chosen for keeping accounts
transmit to send
mandatory spending federal spending required by law that does not need approval from Congress each year
discretionary spending federal spending that must be approved by Congress each year
appropriations bill legislation that determines spending for specific programs for the coming year
intergovernmental revenue money that one level of government receives from another level of government
sales tax a tax paid by consumers when they buy a good or a service
subsidize to aid or support with money
entitlement program a government program that makes payments to certain people to help them meet their needs
property tax a tax on the value of land and property owned by someone

What Do You Know?

In the first column, answer the questions based on what you know before you study. After this lesson, complete the last column.

Now...		Later...
	How does the federal government pay for the services it provides?	

Making Inferences

1. What can you do if your expenses are higher than income?

____

____

Understanding the Federal Budget

A budget is a spending plan for the future. To make a personal budget, you figure out all of your income for a certain period. Then you figure out all of your expenses for the same period. If your expenses **exceed,** or are more than, your income, you need to find ways to spend less or to make more money.

The federal government does basically the same thing. Each year it makes a budget for the coming **fiscal** (FIHS•kuhl) **year.** A fiscal year is any 12-month period used for keeping accounts. The federal government's fiscal year begins on October 1 and ends on September 30.

Financing the Government

Lesson 1: The Federal Budget: Revenues and Expenditures, *Continued*

The budget is named for the calendar year in which it ends. For example, the budget for fiscal year (FY) 2015 covers the period from October 1, 2014, to September 30, 2015.

The president and Congress both work on the budget. The diagram below shows how they do this. First, the president **transmits,** or sends, a budget message to Congress. It states how much money the president wants to spend on every federal program.

/ / / / / / / / / / / / / Glue Foldable here / / / / / / / / / / / / /

The Federal Budget Process

STEP 1	STEP 2	STEP 3
President sends Congress a budget message that: • estimates revenue and expenses; • indicates spending priorities; • states plans for taxes.	House and Senate pass budget resolutions that outline spending and taxes for the next five years. Caps on spending are set for areas controlled by committees of Congress.	House and Senate pass bills authorizing spending, which cannot exceed limits set in Step 2.

A committee reviews the president's message. Then it writes a plan called a budget resolution. The resolution sets limits on spending in certain areas. It says how much total revenue the government will collect. The budget resolution goes to the full House and Senate for approval.

The federal budget has two different kinds of spending. **Mandatory spending** is spending that is set by law. It does not need to be approved each year. An example is Social Security. **Discretionary** (dis•KREH•shuh•NEHR•ee) **spending** is spending on budget choices that are made and approved each year. It can go up or down from year to year. An example is spending on defense.

Congress passes a number of **appropriations** (uh•PROH•pree•AY•shuhnz) **bills.** These bills list how much the government will spend on specific programs. These bills start in the House and are then approved by the Senate. Spending cannot exceed the limits in the budget resolution.

After each bill is passed by the House and Senate, it is sent to the president. The president can sign it into law or veto it. If the bill is vetoed, Congress has two choices. It can either rewrite the bill or override the veto.

The finished federal budget has two parts—revenues and expenditures. Revenue is the money a government collects to use for its spending. The biggest source of revenue is personal income tax. People pay this tax on the money they earn.

Reading Check

2. How is making a federal budget similar to and different from making a personal budget?

____

____

____

FOLDABLES®

3. Place a two-tab Foldable along the dotted line to cover the text. Label the anchor tab *Federal Budget*. Label the two tabs *Revenue* and *Expenditures*. On both sides of the tabs, write facts about the federal budget as you read.

? Comparing

4. What is the difference between *mandatory spending* and *discretionary spending*?

____

____

____

____

Identifying

5. Where does most federal revenue come from? What does the government spend the most money on?

____

Visualizing

6. Study the graphs. What percentage of its budget did the federal government spend on Medicare?

____

Contrasting

7. How is budgeting different for states than for the federal government?

____

____

Identifying

8. What is intergovernmental revenue?

____

____

____

The following graphs show the federal budget for FY 2011. Most revenue comes from personal income taxes and payroll taxes. Defense and Social Security are the two biggest expenses. Note the category called "interest on debt." This is the interest the government must pay on the money it has borrowed.

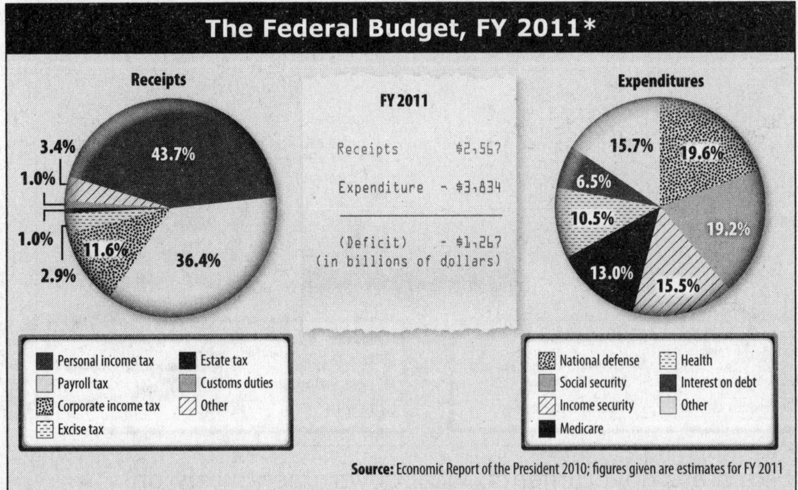

Budgeting for State and Local Governments

State and local governments also make budgets. In almost all states, the law says that state and local governments cannot spend more money than they take in. They must balance their budgets and cannot borrow to make up for too little revenue.

The graphs on the next page show state budgets for FY 2011. They show that state governments get most of their money from **intergovernmental revenue.** This is money that one level of government gets from another. The states get money from the federal government.

Another large source of money for states is sales taxes. Consumers pay **sales tax** when they buy a product or service. Most states have sales taxes. Most also have a personal income tax.

On the spending side, public welfare is the largest category. This refers to programs to help people with little money with basic health and living conditions. Most of this spending is on states' shares of funding for **entitlement programs.** These are called "entitlements" because the law sets the requirements, or rules, for the programs. An example is the Medicaid program. Medicaid helps people get health care.

Lesson 1: The Federal Budget: Revenues and Expenditures, *Continued*

Education is also a large spending category. Some state education money goes to help local governments. Some is used to **subsidize** (SUHB•suh•DEYEZ) college for young people. To subsidize means to help pay for.

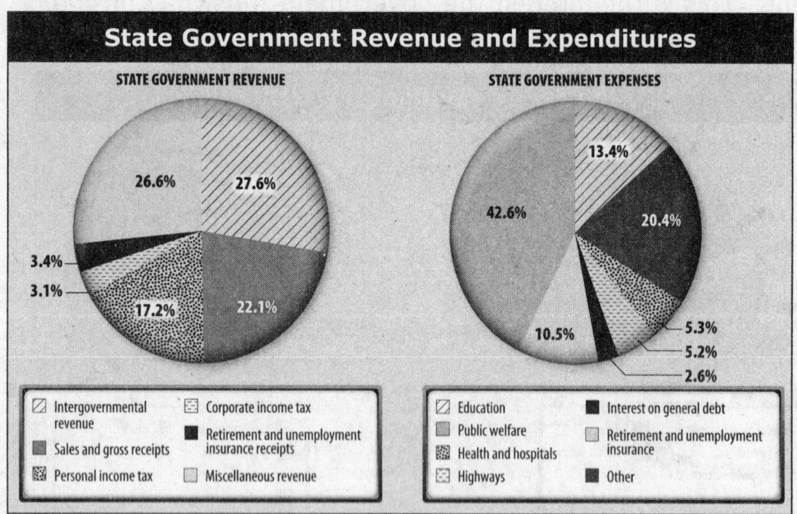

Like state governments, local governments rely on intergovernmental revenue. Local governments get money from state governments. This money is their largest source of revenue. They also collect **property taxes** to raise money. These are taxes on the value of the land and buildings people own. Property taxes are a large source of income for local governments. Some local governments have sales or income taxes too. Traffic fines and permit fees also bring in revenue for local governments.

Local governments provide many of the services people depend on. This is where most local spending goes. Education is the largest portion of local spending. Other services include police and fire protection, libraries, water service, sewage, trash collection, and street repair.

Glue Foldable here

Check for Understanding

What is the biggest source of revenue for local governments? For state governments?

1. _______________ **2.** _______________

How do the federal government and state governments differ when it comes to balancing a budget?

3. _______________

Reading Check

9. What is the biggest spending area for state governments? What is the largest local government expenditure?

____

Identifying

10. What services are provided by local governments?

____

FOLDABLES®

11. Place a three-tab Foldable along the dotted line. Label the top tab *Federal,* the middle tab *State,* and the bottom tab *Local*. On the tabs, write how each level of government gets revenue.

NAME ______________________ DATE ______________ CLASS __________

networks

Financing the Government

Lesson 2: Fiscal Policy

ESSENTIAL QUESTION

How does government influence the economy and economic institutions?

GUIDING QUESTIONS

1. ***What do governments do when the budget does not balance?***
2. ***How does the government try to influence the economy?***

Terms to Know

balanced budget a budget in which expenditures and revenue are equal

predict to say what will happen in the future

budget surplus a situation in which a government collects more revenues than it spends

budget deficit a situation in which a government spends more than it collects in revenues

debt money borrowed and not yet paid back

achieve to attain

fiscal policy the government's use of spending and taxes to help the economy grow

automatic stabilizer any economic feature that works to increase or preserve income without other government action

What Do You Know?

In the first column, answer the questions based on what you know before you study. After this lesson, complete the last column.

Now...		Later...
	How and why does the government try to fix an unbalanced budget?	

Describing

1. What are some reasons that it is difficult for governments to balance their budgets?

____

____

____

____

Surpluses and Deficits

Making a government budget is easier than following one. Budgets are made based on what officials **predict,** or think is going to happen in the future. Their predictions can be wrong. Unexpected events such as natural disasters can happen that cause spending to increase. Revenues can go down when the economy slows.

Governments try to balance their budgets. A **balanced budget** is one in which revenue and spending in a year equal each other.

When a government collects more money than it spends, it has a **budget surplus.** Governments often save budget surpluses to use as a reserve. This reserve is spent to balance the budget in years when revenues are low.

Financing the Government

Lesson 2: Fiscal Policy, *Continued*

When a government spends more money than it collects, it has a **budget deficit.** In all states except Vermont, the law says that the state must have a balanced budget. If spending exceeds revenues, the state cannot borrow money to make up the difference. It has to cut spending, raise taxes—or both.

The federal government does not face the same limits. It can and often does have a budget deficit.

To make up the difference between what the government spends and what it collects, the federal government borrows money. It does this by selling bonds. A bond is a contract to repay the cost of the bond, plus interest, at a future date. Most government bonds are repaid in 10 to 30 years. A person who buys U.S. savings bonds is lending the government money. The government also sells Treasury bills. The government repays Treasury bills in one year or less.

Borrowing to cover budget deficits puts the government in **debt.** Debt is money that has been borrowed and not yet paid back. Being in debt means owing money. For each year the federal government has a deficit, its total debt goes up. The line graph below shows that the federal government's debt has been growing for many years.

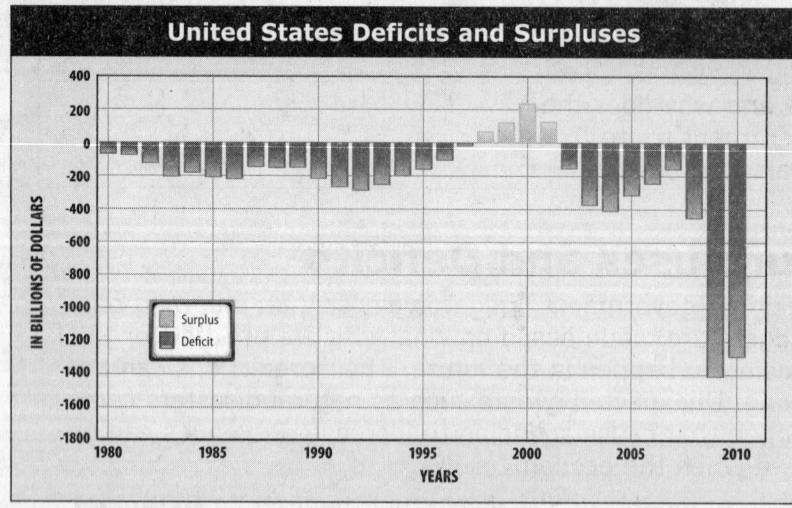

The federal debt is expected to keep growing in the future. This growing debt has some negative effects:

- *The interest on the debt is costly*. Interest payments are a large part of the federal budget. As the debt grows, so does the interest.

Contrasting

2. How is a budget surplus different from a budget deficit?

____

____

Analyzing Cause and Effect

3. Why does the federal debt continue to grow?

____

____

Reading Check

4. For the most part, has the federal government had a balanced budget, a surplus, or a deficit over the last two decades?

____

Visualizing

5. When was the last time the United States had a surplus?

____

Summarizing

6. What are some possible effects of the federal debt?

Listing

7. What are the federal government's goals for the economy?

Vocabulary

8. What is *fiscal policy*?

Reading Check

9. Under what conditions does the federal government use fiscal policy? Why?

- *Federal borrowing can slow down the economy.* Many Americans buy government bonds. Bonds are a way to save for the future. Buyers plan to get their money back with interest later on. But people who save for the future have less money to spend now. Less spending means slower business growth.
- *Federal borrowing can cause interest rates to rise.* When the government borrows money, it leaves less money for others to borrow. This can cause the price of borrowing to go up.
- *Long-term debt could cause investors to lose confidence in the government.* People might begin to see the federal government as a bad investment. They could force the government to pay higher interest rates.

Managing the Economy

For much of U.S. history, the federal government did not take an active role in the economy. That changed during the Great Depression in the 1930s.

Banks and businesses collapsed. Millions of people were out of work. President Roosevelt stepped in to help the economy recover. He started government programs to give people jobs and increase their income.

In the late 1940s Congress set official goals for the economy. The goals were to:

- keep people working
- keep producing goods
- keep consumers buying goods and services

The federal government has two tools it can use to **achieve,** or reach, these goals. One is monetary policy. The Federal Reserve is in charge of monetary policy.

The other tool is **fiscal policy.** This is how the government uses taxes and spending to reach economic goals. The government spending by President Roosevelt is an example of fiscal policy.

When the economy is shrinking or growing too slowly, fiscal policy is used to help it grow. The government spends more and taxes less. By spending more money, the government increases demand for goods and services. If demand increases, businesses will produce more. As a result, they may hire more workers.

Lesson 2: Fiscal Policy, *Continued*

By cutting taxes, the government takes less of people's earnings. People keep more money. Economists think that if people have more money, they will spend it. This spending increases demand.

The government usually takes these steps when the economy slows down or enters a recession. A plan to spur the economy by spending more and taxing less is called an economic stimulus. For example, in 2009 Congress passed a stimulus plan to help the country during a deep recession.

Fiscal policy can be hard to put into practice. Many leaders do not agree with spending money when the government is already in debt. That makes it hard to agree on how much to spend and on what programs. Fiscal policy is slow, and its effects are hard to predict. The economy is complex, and a program may not always be strong enough to have the desired effect.

For these reasons, the federal government prefers to use programs called **automatic stabilizers.** These programs help the economy automatically, without other action from the government. The two most important automatic stabilizers are unemployment insurance and the progressive income tax system. Both are always in place. They begin to work as soon as the economy slows down.

For example, when people lose jobs in a recession, they start getting unemployment insurance payments. This program pays unemployed people an income while they look for new jobs. They spend the income and help keep the economy from slowing further.

The federal income tax also works as a stabilizer because it is a progressive tax. When people lose their jobs, their income goes down, so they pay a lower percentage of their income in taxes. This partly makes up for the loss of income. When they go back to work, their income grows. They are then taxed at a higher rate. This helps the government to lower the deficit caused by the recession.

/ / / / / / / / / / / / / Glue Foldable here / / / / / / / / / / / / / /

Check for Understanding

Explain what a government might do if its budget is not balanced.

1. ______________________

List two problems that federal debt can cause.

2. ______________ **3.** ______________

Identifying

10. What are the drawbacks to fiscal policy?

____

____

____

Mark the Text

11. Underline the definition of *automatic stabilizers* in the text.

Vocabulary

12. Why are unemployment insurance and the progressive income tax known as *automatic stabilizers*?

____

____

____

FOLDABLES®

13. Place a Foldable along the line. Write *Government* on the anchor tab. Label the tabs *Budget Surplus* and *Budget Deficit*. List two facts about each.

International Trade and Economic Systems

Lesson 1: Why and How Nations Trade

ESSENTIAL QUESTION

Why do people trade?

GUIDING QUESTIONS

1. ***Why do nations trade with one another?***
2. ***How does a nation's trade balance affect its economy?***

Terms to Know

import to buy goods from another country
export to sell goods to other countries
comparative advantage ability of one country to produce an item more efficiently than another country
protectionism the use of tactics that make imported goods more expensive than domestic goods
tariff a tax on an imported good
quota a limit on the amount of foreign goods imported into a country
free trade the lack of trade restrictions among countries
integrate to join many parts together into a functioning whole
balance of trade difference between the value of a nation's imports and its exports
exchange rate the value of a nation's money when compared to other nations' money

What Do You Know?

In the first column, answer the questions based on what you know before you study. After this lesson, complete the last column.

Now...		Later...
	Why is it important to trade with other nations?	

Vocabulary

1. Explain the difference between an *export* and an *import*.

____

____

____

Trade Between Nations

Nations do not always have the resources they need to make the things their people want. To solve this problem of scarcity, nations trade with one another. They trade food, goods, services, and natural resources. Nations **import,** or bring into the country, goods produced in other nations. They **export,** or sell to other nations, goods they produce. For example the United States does not produce enough oil to meet its needs. To solve this problem, the U.S. imports oil from other countries.

The main reason countries trade is because of **comparative advantage.** Comparative advantage is the ability to produce something at a lower *opportunity cost* than another country can.

Lesson 1: Why and How Nations Trade, *Continued*

An example will explain how this works. Suppose that two countries, A and B, can produce only two goods, bread and bicycles. The opportunity cost of making one bicycle is the bread each country cannot produce while its resources are being used to make a bicycle. Country A can produce one bicycle or 10 loaves of bread. Country B can produce one bicycle or 15 loaves of bread. Country A has a lower opportunity cost. It has the comparative advantage in producing bicycles.

A country's factors of production—natural resources, labor, capital, and entrepreneurs—usually decide its comparative advantage. China is a good example of this. China has a huge labor force. Most of these people earn low wages. This means that labor in China costs less than labor in many other countries. As a result, China has a comparative advantage in making goods that need lots of labor to produce. The United States and Brazil have a large amount of farm and ranch land. This gives them a comparative advantage in farm exports. They lead the world in farm exports.

Some less advanced economies produce only one product for export. These economies are called single resource economies. The danger of this is that if the price for that product goes down, the product makes less money, and the nation's economy goes down, too.

Most people look for low prices when they shop. To give people the low prices they are looking for, many U.S. stores sell goods made in countries such as China. It costs less to make most goods in China than it costs to make them in the United States. Goods that cost less to make can be sold for lower prices. Lower prices are good for consumers, but not always for companies. When people buy cheaper products imported from other countries, U.S. manufacturers may lose money. This sometimes causes them to produce less, lay off workers, or even shut down.

When trading with another country hurts a nation, that nation may turn to protectionism. **Protectionism** means using tactics, or methods, to keep goods made at home cheaper than imported goods.

Prior Knowledge

2. Define *opportunity cost* and give an example of one.

____

____

____

____

Vocabulary

3. Give two examples of countries that have a comparative advantage in producing something. Name the country and the product.

____

____

____

____

Paraphrasing

4. Paraphrase the paragraph that explains why the size of China's labor force is a comparative advantage.

____

____

____

____

International Trade and Economic Systems

Lesson 1: Why and How Nations Trade, *Continued*

5. Place a two-tab Foldable along the line to cover the text. Write *Trade Barriers* on the anchor. Label the two tabs *Tariff* and *Quota.* On the front define each term. On the reverse, write an example of each.

Reading Check

6. Why do nations sometimes impose tariffs?

____

Visualizing

7. Do quotas keep prices at home higher or push prices down? Draw an arrow to show your answer.

____

Comparing and Contrasting

8. What is the relationship between trade barriers and free trade?

____

____

/Glue Foldable here/

The two most common kinds of trade barriers are tariffs and quotas. The diagram below shows this.

Trade barriers
- Tariff—import tax raises price of imported goods.
- Quota—limits quantities of imported items to keep prices higher at home.

A **tariff** is a tax on imports. This tax raises the price of imported goods. This makes them more costly than they would otherwise be. Tires are one example. Recently, many U.S. tire companies had to shut down because tires made in China cost less money. To help U.S. tire makers, President Obama placed a tariff on tires from China. This raised the price of Chinese tires.

A **quota** limits the amount of an item that is allowed to enter a country. The United States has placed quotas on sugar imports for years. Limiting sugar imports helps keep prices higher for sugar made at home.

A third way the government tries to help U.S. producers is with subsidies. A subsidy is a payment the government gives to help a domestic producer. The United States and other nations pay subsidies to farmers. These payments help farmers keep their prices competitive. These methods to limit imports have a major drawback. In exchange for protecting jobs, the prices of goods go up.

Many economists do not like trade barriers. They think barriers do more harm than good. Many countries try to have few or no trade barriers. This is called **free trade.** When countries try to increase trade, they join with trading partners and set up areas of free trade called free trade zones.

In 1994 the United States, Canada, and Mexico joined together to create the largest free trade zone in the world. Under the North American Free Trade Agreement (NAFTA), the three countries agreed to remove most trade barriers. Since then, trade among the three nations has more than tripled. This increase in trade has brought lower prices and a greater variety of goods to consumers in all three countries. Many companies hurt by these imports lost sales, however, and had to close factories. As a result, thousands of jobs have been lost.

Lesson 1: Why and How Nations Trade, *Continued*

The benefits of free trade encouraged 27 European nations to **integrate,** or join, their economies. They formed the European Union (EU), one of the largest economies in the world. Most EU nations use the same currency, the euro. Using the euro makes trade easier. The EU also creates a large free trade zone. Goods, services, and workers can travel freely among EU nations. Other free trade zones include the African Union (AU) and the Asia-Pacific Economic Cooperation (APEC).

The World Trade Organization (WTO) helps regulate international trade. The WTO has 153 member nations. It makes trade rules and settles disagreements between members. One of its goals is to help countries that are trying to build their economies.

Balance of Trade

The difference between the value of a nation's imports and the value of its exports is its **balance of trade.** If a nation exports more than it imports, it has a *trade surplus*. If a nation imports more than it exports, it has a *trade deficit.* The example below shows a country that has a trade surplus of $30 billion.

$100 billion (value of exports)	–	$70 billion (value of imports)	=	$30 billion (positive balance of trade)

Trade deficits can slow down an economy. If a country imports more than it exports, production slows and jobs may be lost. It also leads to debt. When a country's exports are low, it must borrow money from other countries to pay for the goods it imports. A trade deficit can also make a country's currency, or money, go down in value.

The value of one currency when exchanged, or traded, for another is its **exchange rate.** The value of one currency to another is set by supply and demand.

Mark the Text

9. Underline the sentences that describe the role of the WTO.

Vocabulary

10. What is the term for the difference between the value of a nation's imports and exports? What phrase is used when a nation's trade is not in balance?

____

____

Prior Knowledge

11. How might other countries' trade barriers affect a nation's balance of trade? Why?

____

____

Reading Check

12. What is the exchange rate?

____

____

____

NAME ______________________ DATE ______________ CLASS __________

Lesson 1: Why and How Nations Trade, *Continued*

Paraphrasing

13. Paraphrase the paragraphs that explain how the value of a nation's currency can decrease and how that affects its exports.

____

____

____

____

____

____

____

FOLDABLES®

14. Place a two-tab Foldable along the line. Write *Balance of Trade* on the anchor tab. Label the first tab *Trade Surplus* and draw an up arrow next to it. Label the second tab *Trade Deficit* and draw an arrow going down next to that. On the tabs, write one fact about each term.

Glue Foldable here

Suppose the United States wants to import goods from Japan. Japan's currency is the yen. The United States must sell dollars and buy yen to buy Japanese goods. Selling dollars makes more dollars available in the markets where currency is bought and sold. The larger supply of dollars drives down the value of dollars, and thus the dollar itself. This is how heavy imports can hurt a nation by lowering the value of its currency.

The lower currency value might not be all bad. It should help the country to export more. Because its currency is worth less than before, its goods are cheaper for other countries to buy.

Check for Understanding

For what two reasons does the United States import goods and services?

1. ______________________

____

2. ______________________

____

What is a trade surplus and why is it good for a nation's economy?

3. ______________________

____

NAME ______________________ DATE ______________ CLASS ____________

networks

Lesson 2: Economic Systems and Development

ESSENTIAL QUESTION

Why and how do people make economic choices?

GUIDING QUESTIONS

1. ***What characteristics do market economies share?***
2. ***Who makes the basic economic decisions in a command economy?***
3. ***Why do most countries have a mixed economy?***
4. ***What kinds of challenges do developing countries face?***

Terms to Know

privatization the process of changing from state-owned businesses, factories, and farms to ones owned by private citizens

mixed economy a system combining characteristics of more than one type of economy

orient to tend toward a certain direction

developed country a country with a high standard of living and high levels of industrialization and per capita income

developing country a country with low per capita incomes in which a large number of people have a low standard of living

What Do You Know?

In the first column, answer the questions based on what you know before you study. After this lesson, complete the last column.

Now...		Later...
	What is a market economy?	
	Why might a mixed economy work best for some countries?	

Market Economies

There are different kinds of economies. All decide *what* to produce, *how* to produce it, and *for whom* to produce it. The type of economic system a society uses is decided by how it answers these questions. In a market economy, the individuals are the ones who provide the answers.

In market economies, the people, not the government, make economic decisions. The people own and decide how to use the factors of production. Those factors are natural resources, capital, labor, and entrepreneurship. No central power runs the economy.

In a market economy, prices are determined by supply and demand. Supply is the amount of a good that is made. Demand is the amount of a good consumers want.

One trait of a market economy is individual freedom. For a market economy to work, people must be free to own property and control their own labor. Another characteristic is high GDP per capita.

Reading Check

1. Who owns the factors of production in a market economy?

____

____

____

____

____

Lesson 2: Economic Systems and Development, *Continued*

Prior Knowledge

2. Explain the difference between the GDP and GDP per capita.

____

____

Mark the Text

3. Finish the chart with the characteristics of a market economy.

Examining Details

4. List two positive and two negative characteristics of market economies.

____

____

____

____

Reading Check

5. What is the government's role in a command economy?

____

____

____

The GDP per capita is the total value of goods produced in a country, divided by the country's population. It is the best way to measure economic success.

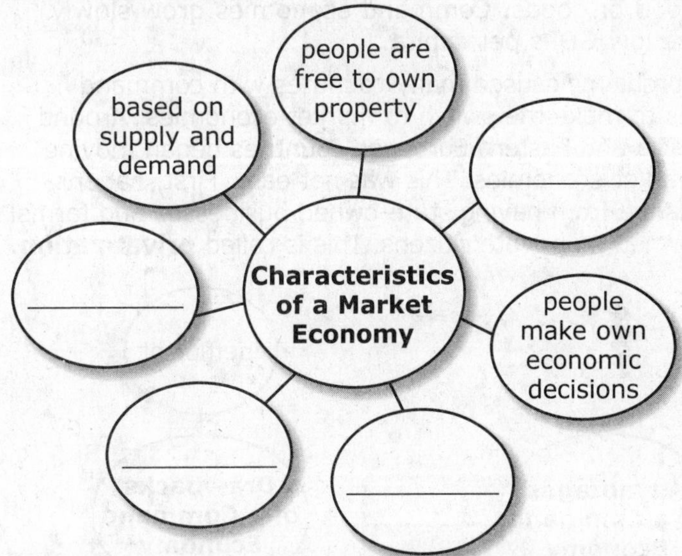

Market economies do have some drawbacks.

- They do not grow steadily. Sometimes the economy rises and sometimes it falls.
- They are profit-driven—the main goal of most businesses is to make money, so the workers may not have good working conditions or fair pay.
- They can result in negative externalities, harmful side effects that affect third parties. Pollution is one example.

Command Economies

Another type of economy is called a command economy. People in a command economy have little say as to how the economy should work. The government owns the factors of production. It also decides, or commands, what is produced, how it is produced, and for whom it will be produced. It even sets wages and prices. Under this system, the government controls the supply of goods.

Command economies have planning agencies with a lot of power. They decide how different parts of the economy will work. This system is called a command system because the government tells producers what to do. It is also called a central planning system.

Lesson 2: Economic Systems and Development, *Continued*

Command economies have pros and cons. Central planning helped the Soviet Union's economy rebuild quickly after World War II. But it also can mean that there is not enough food or goods. Command economies grow slowly. They have low GDPs per capita.

These problems caused many countries with command economies to make the switch to market economies. Around 1990, Russia and Eastern European countries began moving toward market economies. This was not easy. First, nations had to change from having state-owned businesses and farms to ones owned by private citizens. This is called **privatization.**

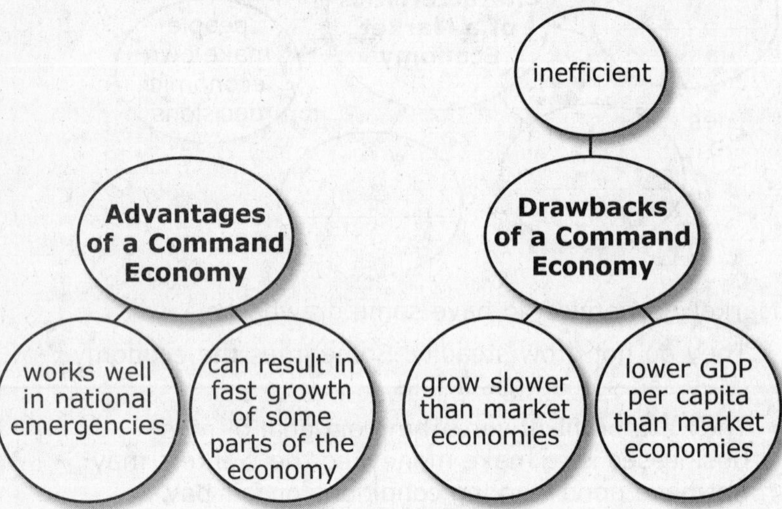

Newly private businesses had to learn to be more efficient, or organized. Some countries are still waiting for their economies to improve.

China started using some features of a market economy in the 1970s. China has been successful. Both its GDP and GDP per capita have grown. China's economy is now one of the largest in the world. This major benefit does come with some problems. One is pollution. Another is a growing gap between income groups.

Mixed Economies

Mixed economies combine parts of a market economy with parts of a command economy.

Most countries have mixed economies. Both the market and the government are important in this type of economy.The United States has a mixed economy.

Prior Knowledge

6. How are shortages in a command economy related to supply and demand?

____

____

____

____

Vocabulary

7. Explain what the word *privatization* means in economic terms.

____

____

____

Mark the Text

8. Find and underline the phrases that identify consequences of China's economic reforms.

Identifying

9. What types of economies are combined in a mixed economy?

____

____

Lesson 2: Economic Systems and Development, *Continued*

Reading Check

10. What are signs that the United States does not have a pure market economy?

Contrasting

11. Explain the difference between *developed countries* and *developing countries*.

Here, private citizens own the factors of production and make the economic choices. This means the U.S. economy is market-**oriented**, or directed by the market. At the same time, the government does play a role. It provides some goods and services, such as public schools and roads; it encourages competition; and regulates, or watches over, businesses. For example, the government has passed laws that set a minimum wage for workers and make sure products are safe.

Developed and Developing Countries

Countries that have a high standard of living and a lot of industry are called **developed countries.** Only about 35 countries are considered developed. Examples include the United States, Canada, Japan, and Germany.

Other countries have started taking steps to become developed countries. These nations are building their export businesses to help their economies grow. They are called *newly industrialized countries.* China and India are examples.

Countries that are not very productive and have low GDP per capita are called **developing countries.** They are struggling to develop market economies. The diagram below shows some things that get in the way of that goal.

One thing that gets in the way of development is high population growth. Often when a country's population is growing fast, the economy cannot keep up.

Lesson 2: Economic Systems and Development, *Continued*

Each person then gets a smaller and smaller share of what the economy is making. The country's GDP per capita goes down.

Some countries have too many trade barriers. The barriers sometimes protect poorly run, unproductive businesses.

A country's location can make it hard for its economy to grow. Landlocked countries cannot use ocean trade routes that make trading much easier. They have difficulty getting their goods to other nations.

Wars are another obstacle. They ruin resources and destroy lives. Productivity goes down and people face a shortage of food, health care, and education. As a result, countries have more difficulty investing in their economies.

Many developing countries have large debts. These countries borrowed large amounts of money to help their economies grow. Their economies did not grow fast enough to pay the loans back. Now they have to use too much of their income to pay off their debt.

Finally, government corruption is a problem in some countries. Leaders have stolen money that was meant to help their nations' economies and their people.

Reading Check

12. How do trade barriers hurt development?

____

____

Defining

13. Use context clues to determine the definition of *landlocked.*

____

____

How does being landlocked affect a nation's economy?

____

____

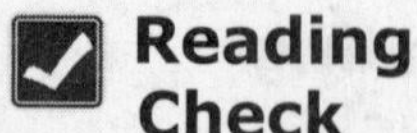

14. Place a Venn diagram along the dotted line. Write *3 Types of Economies* on the anchor. Label the tabs *Market Economy*, *Mixed Economy*, and *Command Economy*. On the tabs, write about each, and explain how a mixed economy is a combination of the other types.

/ / / / / / / / / / / / / / Glue Foldable here / / / / / / / / / / / / / /

Check for Understanding

Name two characteristics of a market economy.

1. ______________________

2. ______________________

What is the major difference between a market and a command economy?

3. ______________________

____

____

List two challenges faced by developing countries.

4. ______________________

5. ______________________

NAME _______________ DATE _______________ CLASS _______________

networks

The United States and Foreign Affairs

Lesson 1: Global Interdependence and Issues

ESSENTIAL QUESTION

Why and how do nations interact with one another?

GUIDING QUESTIONS

1. ***Why do nations depend upon one another?***
2. ***What are some consequences of global interdependence?***

Terms to Know

global interdependence the reliance of people and nations around the world on one another for goods and services

trade war economic conflict that occurs when one or more nations put up trade barriers to punish another nation for trade barriers it erected against them

stable not subject to major changes

deforestation the mass removal of trees from large areas

ethnic group a group of people who share the same national, cultural, or racial background

terrorism the use of violence or the threat of violence to make people behave a certain way

refugee a person who has unwillingly left his or her home to escape war, famine, or natural disaster

What Do You Know?

In the first column, answer the questions based on what you know before you study. After this lesson, complete the last column.

Now...		Later...
	Why do nations trade?	
	What issues affect the whole world community?	

FOLDABLES®

1. Place a one-tab Foldable along the line. Write *Global Interdependence* on the anchor tab. Write the definition and examples of things nations trade on the tabs.

Global Interdependence

Glue Foldable here

People and nations around the world depend on one another for goods and services. This is called **global interdependence.** Countries trade things they have for things they do not have. This exchange of goods and services involves both rich and poor nations. Rich nations buy raw materials and local products from poor nations. Poor nations buy technology, medicine, and other goods from developed countries.

Global trade works because nations have different resources. One country may have advanced technology but few natural resources. Another may have natural resources but little technology.

Lesson 1: Global Interdependence and Issues, *Continued*

Yet another country may have a large labor force but not enough food to feed its people. These differences encourage trade between nations.

The United States exports many goods. It sells wheat, aircraft, computer software, video games, and much more. The United States also imports many goods. One major import is oil. The United States imports more than half of the oil it uses every day.

Sometimes nations cooperate on trade issues. One example is the European Union. This group of 27 European nations has ended most trade barriers among its members. The North American Free Trade Agreement (NAFTA) is another example. It is an agreement among the United States, Canada, and Mexico. The goal of these agreements is to promote free trade.

Global Issues

Global interdependence has led to increased trade and prosperity in many parts of the world. People usually have more choices when trade increases. Prices usually go down also. Increased trade has costs as well as benefits. Workers, for example, can lose jobs due to international trade. One reason is that some companies hire workers in other countries that have low labor costs.

Nations sometimes try to protect their industries from imports produced in countries with cheaper labor. They do this by putting up barriers to trade. A trade barrier is any government policy that limits trade among nations. One type of trade barrier is the tariff. A tariff is a tax on imports. Tariffs raise the price of imported goods. These barriers have a cost though. Tariffs may help home industries, but they hurt consumers by raising prices.

Other nations may respond with trade barriers of their own. Sometimes tariffs lead to trade wars. A **trade war** is an economic conflict that occurs when one or more nations put up trade barriers to punish another nation for its trade barriers against them. Trade wars raise prices and reduce choice for everyone.

Reading Check

2. What is global interdependence?

____

____

____

Identifying

3. What is one major U.S. *import?*

____

Mark the Text

4. Underline the words that tell you what a *trade barrier* is.

Paraphrasing

5. Briefly explain what a trade war is. What are some causes and effects of a trade war?

____

____

____

____

____

Lesson 1: Global Interdependence and Issues, *Continued*

Listing

6. Look at the graphic. List four things developing countries lack.

Visualizing

7. Draw a diagram to show interdependence between Venezuela and the United States.

Reading Check

8. Why do nations sometimes disagree?

Identifying

9. What are two possible results of deforestation?

Economic inequality among nations is a major global challenge. Nations have grown at different rates, widening the wealth gap between rich and poor.

Nations that have grown wealthy because their economies are doing well are called developed countries. They generally have a high GDP per capita.They usually have governments that are **stable,** or not likely to change much. The United States and Germany are examples of developed countries.

Developing countries have low GDP per capita and low rates of growth. Many factors contribute to these problems. Some struggle with political unrest and conflict. Haiti is one example of a developing country. It is the poorest nation in the Western Hemisphere. The diagrams below show the challenges faced by developing nations.

Developing Countries

Sometimes nations disagree. Nations have different forms of government and different views about the world. The United States and Venezuela are one example. The two nations dislike each other's economic policies. They trade with each other in spite of this. Venezuela needs money from the United States. The United States needs oil from Venezuela. Economic interdependence can sometimes, but not always, force nations to cooperate.

The environment is another global concern. As nations have developed their industries they have hurt the environment. The removal of trees from large areas, known as **deforestation,** leads to flooding and mudslides. Since trees absorb carbon dioxide, their destruction has led to higher levels of it in the air. Many experts believe that burning oil, gas, and coal has helped cause climate change.

Lesson 1: Global Interdependence and Issues, *Continued*

One way to help the environment is through conservation. Conservation means using resources carefully. It also means limiting bad effects of human activity. For example, conserving gasoline helps reduce air pollution.

People disagree about conservation. Supporters say it will help save the environment, prevent climate change, and help prevent health problems. Critics say that conservation drives up the costs of goods and services. Developing nations struggle to balance concern for the environment with the need for economic growth.

Today's world faces other challenges as well. Tension over immigration is one such problem. Immigrants are people who move to a new country in search of better lives. When large groups move, they place added demands on resources in their new country. This can cause tension within nations. Differences among religious and **ethnic groups** can make such problems worse. An ethnic group is a group of people who share a common national, cultural, or racial background.

Other global issues today are the threat of war and **terrorism.** Terrorism is the use of violence or the threat of violence to make people afraid and to force people–or governments–to behave in a certain way.

When wars, natural disasters, or famine force people to leave their homes, they are called **refugees.** Millions of refugees need help from the nations of the world. In addition many people in the world do not have enough food, clean water, or health care. Nations must cooperate with one another in order to meet these challenges.

Identifying

10. Give an example of conservation.

____

____

____

Defining

11. People who move to another country in search of better lives are called

______________________,

while those who are forced to leave by famine, war, or natural disaster are called

______________________.

FOLDABLES®

12. Place a two-tab Foldable along the dotted line. Write *Global Community* on the anchor tab. Label the two tabs *Who is in it?* and *What is it?* On the reverse tabs, answer each question about the global community.

/ / / / / / / / / / / / / Glue Foldable here / / / / / / / / / / / / / /

Check for Understanding

Why does global interdependence increase trade?

1. ______________________

____

Name four challenges faced by the global community today.

2. ____________ **3.** ____________

4. ____________ **5.** ____________

NAME ______________________ DATE ____________ CLASS __________

networks

The United States and Foreign Affairs

Lesson 2: The United States and International Organizations

ESSENTIAL QUESTION

Why and how do nations interact with one another?

GUIDING QUESTIONS

1. ***What is the purpose of international organizations?***
2. ***How do international organizations help people?***

Terms to Know

diplomat a representative of a country's government in meetings with other countries

non-governmental organization (NGO) international organization that is not connected to any government

prisoner of war person captured by opposing forces during a war

neutral taking no side or part in a conflict or disagreement

What Do You Know?

In the first column, answer the questions based on what you know before you study. After this lesson, complete the last column.

Now...		Later...
	What is an international organization?	
	What do international organizations do?	

The Purpose of International Organizations

Nations join together for many reasons. One is to help a country in times of trouble. When a natural disaster strikes one nation, the world community tries to help. Nations send food, water, medical aid, and equipment. Nations also join together to deal with issues that affect the entire world. These include

- environmental problems,
- fights between countries
- trade and economic issues

Nations try to solve problems by talking directly with one another through **diplomats.** Diplomats are officials who represent their countries. They often meet to discuss issues and find solutions.

Countries also form organizations to address international problems. These are called governmental organizations. Diplomats from each member country meet regularly to discuss problems. Sometimes they agree about what to do to solve a problem. Sometimes they disagree.

Listing

1. List some reasons that nations join together. What common issues do they share?

____

____

____

____

Mark the Text

2. Underline the words that tell you the meaning of the term *diplomat*.

The United States and Foreign Affairs

Lesson 2: The United States and International Organizations, *Continued*

Each member nation gives part of the money needed to run a governmental organization. They agree to follow the rules of the organization and support its decisions.

Some governmental organizations have a single purpose. For example, the North Atlantic Treaty Organization (NATO) was formed to defend its members. Other governmental organizations have many goals. The goals of the United Nations include promoting peace, building schools, and improving health care.

Governmental organizations can change the world. For example, the European Union (EU) set up a common unit of money for most of its members. The euro is now a standard currency, which makes it easier for nations to trade. At times, group efforts are less effective. Terrorism persists, although all international organizations condemn it.

Some international organizations are not connected to any government. These are called **non-governmental organizations (NGOs).** NGOs are founded by people who see a need or want to work for a cause such as fighting hunger or poverty. NGOs usually rely on volunteers and donations.

Sometimes governmental organizations and NGOs work together. After the earthquake in Haiti in 2010, many organizations worked together to help provide relief.

NGOs can do things that governments cannot. They may be able to get aid into countries that would not accept help from groups connected with governments. The International Committee of the Red Cross (ICRC), for example, serves people in need on both sides in a war.

Nongovernmental Organizations (NGOs)

NGO	REGION	AREA OF CONCERN
Amnesty International	Worldwide	Human Rights
CARE International	Worldwide	Poverty, Education, Economic Development, Health
Doctors Without Borders	Worldwide	Health, Disaster Response/Relief
Hunger Project	North America	Hunger
International Committee of the Red Cross	Worldwide	Human Rights, Public Health, Disaster Response/Relief
MacArthur Foundation	Worldwide	Human Rights, Economic Development, Peace, Education, Environment
MAP International	Worldwide	Health, Disaster Response/Relief
Nature Conservancy	Worldwide	Environment

Identifying

3. What does "NATO" stand for? What is the purpose of this organization?

Contrasting

4. How do the finances of governmental and non-governmental organizations differ?

Reading Check

5. What is one success and one failure of governmental organizations in recent times?

Use the Graphic

6. Look at the table. Circle the areas of concern for the NGO CARE International.

Lesson 2: The United States and International Organizations, *Continued*

Identifying

7. What is the main goal of the United Nations? Which parts of the UN are connected to this goal?

____

____

____

____

Visualizing

8. Study the chart. Then on a map or globe, locate the five permanent members of the U.N. Security Council. Then list them below.

____

____

____

____

Describing

9. What does the World Trade Organization do?

____

____

International Organizations

There are many international organizations at work today. A few of the most important are discussed below.

The United Nations One of the most important international organizations is the United Nations (UN). It was formed at the end of World War II and has 192 member nations. The main goal of the UN is to keep peace among nations. It also works to fight poverty and protect human rights. The following chart shows some of the most important parts of the UN.

Organization of the United Nations

Part of United Nations	Membership	Purpose
General Assembly	All 192 UN member nations	Main meeting of UN
Security Council	5 permanent: United Kingdom, China, France, Russia, U.S.; 10 temporary: elected to 2 year terms	World peace and security
International Court of Justice (World Court)	15 judges elected by General Assembly, Security Council	Settles disputes between nations
Other UN councils	Various nations	Economic issues, social justice, public health

North Atlantic Treaty Organization Another important international group is the North Atlantic Treaty Organization (NATO). NATO has 28 member nations in Europe and North America. They have pledged to work for peace and to defend one another in times of war. NATO has at times sent soldiers to crisis situations around the world. This happened in Afghanistan in 2001 and Iraq in 2003.

World Trade Organization The World Trade Organization (WTO) has over 150 member nations. Its goal is to arrange trade agreements and settle trade disputes. The WTO works to remove trade barriers. Its decisions are usually made by consensus. Consensus is general agreement. Some people believe that the WTO favors developed nations. Others think that it ignores concerns about the environment. WTO members disagree with these opinions.

Lesson 2: The United States and International Organizations, *Continued*

World Health Organization The World Health Organization (WHO) is part of the United Nations. It fights disease around the world. It does this through improving health guidelines and studying public health issues. The efforts of this group have helped teach people about diseases such as the HIV virus, and reduce other diseases such as polio.

Peace Corps The Peace Corps is a volunteer organization run by the U.S. government. Its original goal was to help Americans and people from other nations understand each other. Nearly 8,000 American volunteers work in countries all over the world. Some work on public health projects such as providing clean water. Others teach or help with local business development.

International Committee of the Red Cross The International Committee of the Red Cross (ICRC) provides aid to victims of war. The ICRC works to protect those who are not part of the fighting. It also tries to make sure that **prisoners of war** are treated well. Prisoners of war are people captured during a war. The ICRC stays **neutral.** This means it does not take sides during a war. Most nations respect the efforts of the ICRC and allow it to do its work.

Many other international organizations, both governmental and non-governmental, exist throughout the world. They work on many issues of global importance.

Prior Knowledge

10. In our world of global interdependence, which organization(s) discussed here might become even more important? Why?

____

____

____

Reading Check

11. What are some main goals of international organizations?

____

____

FOLDABLES

12. Place a one-tab Foldable along the dotted line. Write *International Organizations* on the anchor tab. Write the definition on the front of the tab. On the reverse, list three international organizations.

/ / / / / / / / / / / / Glue Foldable here / / / / / / / / / / / /

Check for Understanding

List three ways that nations work together in international organizations.

1. _______________

2. _______________

3. _______________

Give an example of one international organization that helps people and explain how it does so.

4. _______________

____

NAME ______________________ DATE ______________ CLASS __________

networks

The United States and Foreign Affairs

Lesson 3: The United States and World Affairs

ESSENTIAL QUESTION

Why does conflict develop?

GUIDING QUESTIONS

1. ***What are human rights?***
2. ***Why does conflict among nations occur?***
3. ***Why has the United States engaged in conflict in recent years?***

Terms to Know

culture the ideas, customs, art, and beliefs of a people or group

universal worldwide, or applying to all

human right a protection or a freedom that all people should have

repression preventing people from expressing themselves or from freely engaging in normal life

genocide the attempt to kill all members of an ethnic group

communism a one-party system of government based on state ownership and control of property and industry

weapon of mass destruction (WMD) a weapon that can kill or harm large numbers of people and damage or destroy large areas

What Do You Know?

In the first column, answer the questions based on what you know before you study. After this lesson, complete the last column.

Now...		Later...
	What are human rights?	
	How can disagreements about politics lead to international conflict?	

Reading Check

1. What are human rights?

____

____

____

Human Rights

Differences exist between people around the world. Beliefs, cultures, languages, and governments are all different. **Culture** means the ideas, skills, art, and customs of a people. All people around the world have many things in common as well. Everyone wants to be safe and to have enough to eat. Everyone wants a place to live. These ideas are **universal.** This means they apply to everyone.

These shared desires form the basis for the concept of human rights. A **Human right** is a basic freedom that all people should have. Those rights include food, safety, shelter, protection under law, and freedom of thought. These ideas have inspired people around the world. They have shaped events such as the American Revolution. They continue to affect the world today.

Lesson 3: The United States and World Affairs, *Continued*

Soon after the United Nations was formed, its members agreed on a list of people's basic rights. In 1948 it adopted the Universal Declaration of Human Rights. This declaration defined the rights that all people should have.

The Declaration has 30 articles. Article 1 says that all people are born free and have equal rights. Article 2 says that no one should be treated differently due to things such as race, sex, or religion. These two articles form the basis for the other rights. The chart below shows a partial list.

Universal Declaration of Human Rights
People should be . . .
free from arrest without cause
free from slavery and torture
free from forced marriages
People should have . . .
equal protection under law
the right to own property
the right to move about freely
the right to take part in government
equal pay for equal work
the right to a decent standard of living
the right to medical care

Unfortunately some governments do not protect their people's rights. Some rulers use **repression** to stay in power. Repression means preventing people from expressing themselves or from freely living a normal life. These rulers often deny their citizens basic human rights and protections.

Some nations do not uphold the right to freedom of ideas and the press. China, Iran, Saudi Arabia, and North Korea limit people's ability to get information. North Korea does not allow its people to criticize the government.

Conflict between ethnic groups has led to war and genocide. **Genocide** is the attempt to kill all members of an ethnic group such as the Jews in WWII. In the 1990s, millions of people were killed in East Africa due to ethnic conflict in Rwanda and Burundi. Since 2003, there has been ethnic conflict in the Darfur region of Sudan, in Africa.

The U.S. government tries to promote human rights. It protests governments that take away people's freedoms. Sometimes it refuses to trade with such countries.

The UN Human Rights Council reports on human rights issues around the world and suggests possible actions. The UN Security Council can refer cases of human rights abuse by governments to the International Criminal Court for trial.

Describing

2. What did the United Nations do in 1948 in response to human rights abuses?

____

____

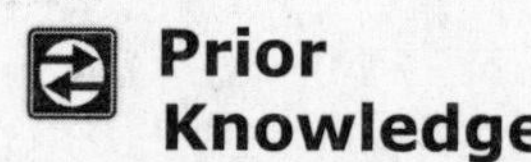

Prior Knowledge

3. Study the chart. Which of these human rights do you recognize from the U.S. Constitution?

____

____

____

Mark the Text

4. Circle the names of the nations that do not allow freedom of the press.

Identifying

5. What does the U.S. government do to try to promote human rights?

____

____

____

Lesson 3: The United States and World Affairs, *Continued*

Describing

6. Describe how NGOs such as Amnesty International and Human Rights Watch work for human rights around the world.

____

____

____

____

Comparing and Contrasting

7. What two types of governments opposed one another during the Cold War?

____

____

Reading Check

8. Did the policies of the United States during the Cold War advance or hold back human rights?

____

____

____

Many non-governmental organizations (NGOs) also work for human rights. Amnesty International and Human Rights Watch campaign around the world to end human rights abuses. They bring abuses to the world's attention by publishing reports that identify countries that violate rights. This puts pressure on governments that disobey international human rights laws.

Democracy, Liberty, and Conflict

How much a nation respects human rights depends on its type of government. Democratic nations usually protect human rights better than non-democratic nations do. There were few democracies in the world in the early 1900s. Since then many nations have become democratic. About 60 percent of nations are democracies now. The United States has made the spread of democracy a goal of its foreign policy for many years.

During World War II the United States, Great Britain, and the Soviet Union were the Allied Powers. After the war the Allies split into two camps. On one side were the United States and Western Europe. These nations were democracies with market-based economies. The Soviet Union and Eastern Europe were on the other side. They practiced communism. **Communism** is a system of government in which one party is in control. The government owns the property and industry. People living under communist governments do not have many of the freedoms that people in democracies have.

The Soviet Union came to control most of Eastern Europe. The United States and its allies tried to keep communism from spreading further. A bitter struggle developed. This clash of ideas was known as the Cold War because not much actual fighting took place. At times, however, violence did occur.

In its fight against communism, the United States sometimes supported rulers who abused human rights. Chile and Iran were not democratic, but the United States supported them because they opposed communism.

The Cold War ended with the collapse of the Soviet Union in 1991. New democracies emerged, but progress has slowed. The struggle for human rights continues. Many people in the world are still not free.

Lesson 3: The United States and World Affairs, *Continued*

Governments in large parts of South America and Africa restrict human rights. North Korea, China, and Cuba still deny their citizens freedom of speech and of the press.

New threats to peace have emerged, such as terrorism. Groups such as al Qaeda and the Taliban use terrorist attacks to try to impose their beliefs on others.

Recent Conflicts

On September 11, 2001, terrorists attacked the United States. Almost 3,000 people died. The United States responded in several ways.

The government set up the Department of Homeland Security. Its three main goals are to

- stop terrorist attacks on the United States
- reduce the threat of terrorist attacks
- help with recovery from attacks or natural disasters

Another response was the Patriot Act of 2001. This law gave the government new powers to fight terrorism. This included the power to search financial and phone records secretly. Some people disliked the law. They said it gave the government too much power and infringed on the right to privacy and freedom from unreasonable searches. As a result, Congress made some changes to the law.

U.S. War on Terrorism

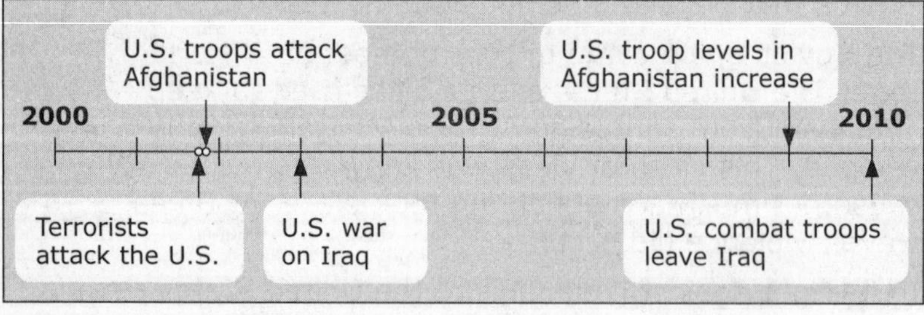

The United States also responded to the September 11th attacks with military force. Wars in Afghanistan and Iraq followed. Afghanistan's rulers, the Taliban, were supporting al Qaeda, who was responsible for the September 11th attacks. The Taliban refused to hand over the leader of al Qaeda, Osama bin Laden, to the United States. In October 2001 the U.S. military attacked Afghanistan.

The United States quickly defeated the Taliban, but al Qaeda's leader Osama bin Laden escaped. In the years following, little progress was made toward democracy. The Taliban returned again and again.

Examining Details

9. What new threats to human rights began after the end of the Cold War?

____

____

Listing

10. List the three main goals of the Department of Homeland Security.

____

____

____

Visualizing

11. Study the time line. For about how many years were there combat troops in Iraq?

____

Reading Check

12. What have been the biggest foreign policy challenges for the United States since 2000?

____

____

Lesson 3: The United States and World Affairs, *Continued*

Mark the Text

13. Underline the two reasons that the U.S. attacked Iraq in 2003.

Paraphrasing

14. What one major reason has caused the United States to engage in conflict in recent years?

____

____

FOLDABLES®

15. Place a two-tab Foldable along the dotted line. Write the title *Human Rights* on the anchor tab. Label the tabs *Democracies* and *Non-Democracies*. Use the space on both sides of the tabs to describe what attitude each group has toward human rights. How does each group treat people?

President Obama sent more troops to Afghanistan in 2009 to stop the Taliban from taking control. In May 2011, U.S. forces captured and killed bin Laden hiding out in Pakistan, but fighting continued in Afghanistan.

U.S. troops were also sent to Iraq. After the attacks of 2001, President George W. Bush feared that terrorist groups might get **weapons of mass destruction (WMDs).** A WMD is a weapon that can harm or kill large numbers of people. Leaders believed that Iraq's dictator Saddam Hussein might give WMDs to terrorist groups.

The United States attacked and defeated Iraq's army in 2003, removing Hussein from power. No WMDs were found. American troops stayed to help set up a democracy. This proved difficult. Rebel groups attacked U.S. troops and their allies. Violence between different ethnic and religious groups flared. In 2008, the addition of more U.S. troops helped calm the violence.

It was not until 2010 that President Obama took U.S. combat troops out of Iraq. Some soldiers stayed to help the country continue to set up a democratic government.

The United States continued to face challenges in the world. Iran's efforts to build a nuclear weapon were a serious concern. Iran was also suspected of helping terrorist groups. Some groups in Pakistan were suspected of the same thing. Conflict continued between Israelis and Palestinians. Other nations around the world were torn by conflicts. Terrorism, the new weapon of global warfare, played a role in of them.

/ / / / / / / / / / / / / Glue Foldable here / / / / / / / / / / / / /

Check for Understanding

Why do nations and people continue to fight for human rights?

1. ______________________

____

List two ways that differing political views led to conflict between nations during the Cold War.

2. ______________________

3. ______________________

Identifying

1.

2.

Instruction and Templates

Table of Contents

For each kind of Foldable®, you will find an instruction page followed by several template pages.

Notebook Foldables®

Using Foldables® in the *Reading Essentials and Study Guide* will help you develop note-taking and critical-thinking skills.

One-Tab

Folding Instructions

1. Cut out the template found on the following pages.
2. Fold the anchor tab over the information tab.
3. Glue the anchor tab to your workbook according to the instructions in the lesson.

Tip: Multiple Foldables® can be glued on top of each other by gluing anchor tabs on top of anchor tabs. This would make a small book on the page.

One-tab Foldable® glued onto a two-tab Foldable® to make a study book.

Title:

Title:

Title:

Title:

Title:

Title:

You can position a Foldable® three ways.

horizontally

vertically

Cut out your Foldable® along the dotted line.

Title:

Title:

Title:

Title:

Title:

Title:

You can position a Foldable® three ways.

horizontally

vertically

Cut out your Foldable® along the dotted line.

Title:

Title:

Title:

Title:

Title:

Title:

You can position a Foldable® three ways.

horizontally

vertically

Cut out your Foldable® along the dotted line.

Title:

Title:

Title:

Title:

Title:

Title:

You can position a Foldable® three ways.

horizontally

vertically

Cut out your Foldable® along the dotted line.

Title:

Title:

Title:

Title:

Title:

Title:

You can position a Foldable® three ways.

horizontally

vertically

Cut out your Foldable® along the dotted line.

Notebook Foldables®

Using Foldables® in the *Reading Essentials and Study Guide* will help you develop note-taking and critical-thinking skills.

Two-Tab

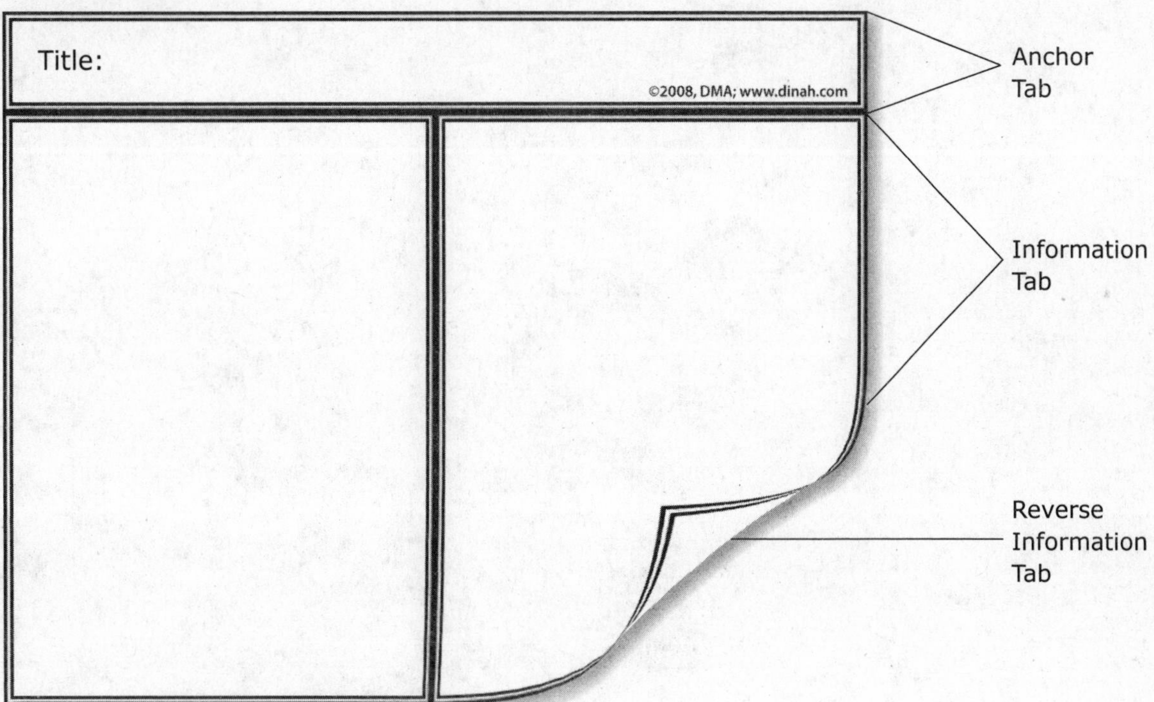

Folding Instructions

1. Cut out the template found on the following pages.
2. Fold the anchor tab over the information tab.
3. Glue the anchor tab to your workbook according to the instructions in the lesson.

Tip: Multiple Foldables® can be glued on top of each other by gluing anchor tabs on top of anchor tabs. This would make a small book on the page.

One-tab Foldable® glued onto a two-tab Foldable® to make a study book.

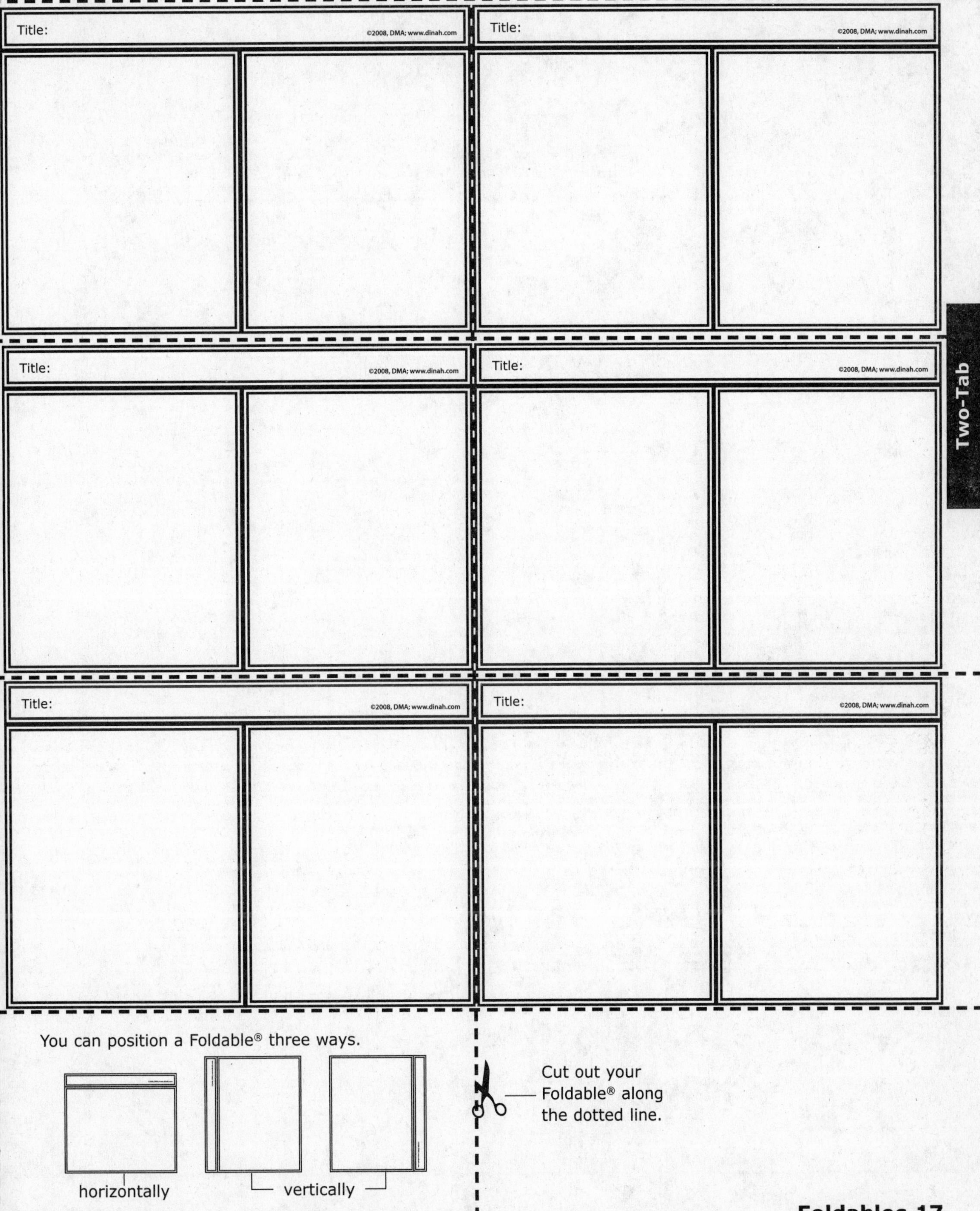

You can position a Foldable® three ways.

horizontally

vertically

Cut out your Foldable® along the dotted line.

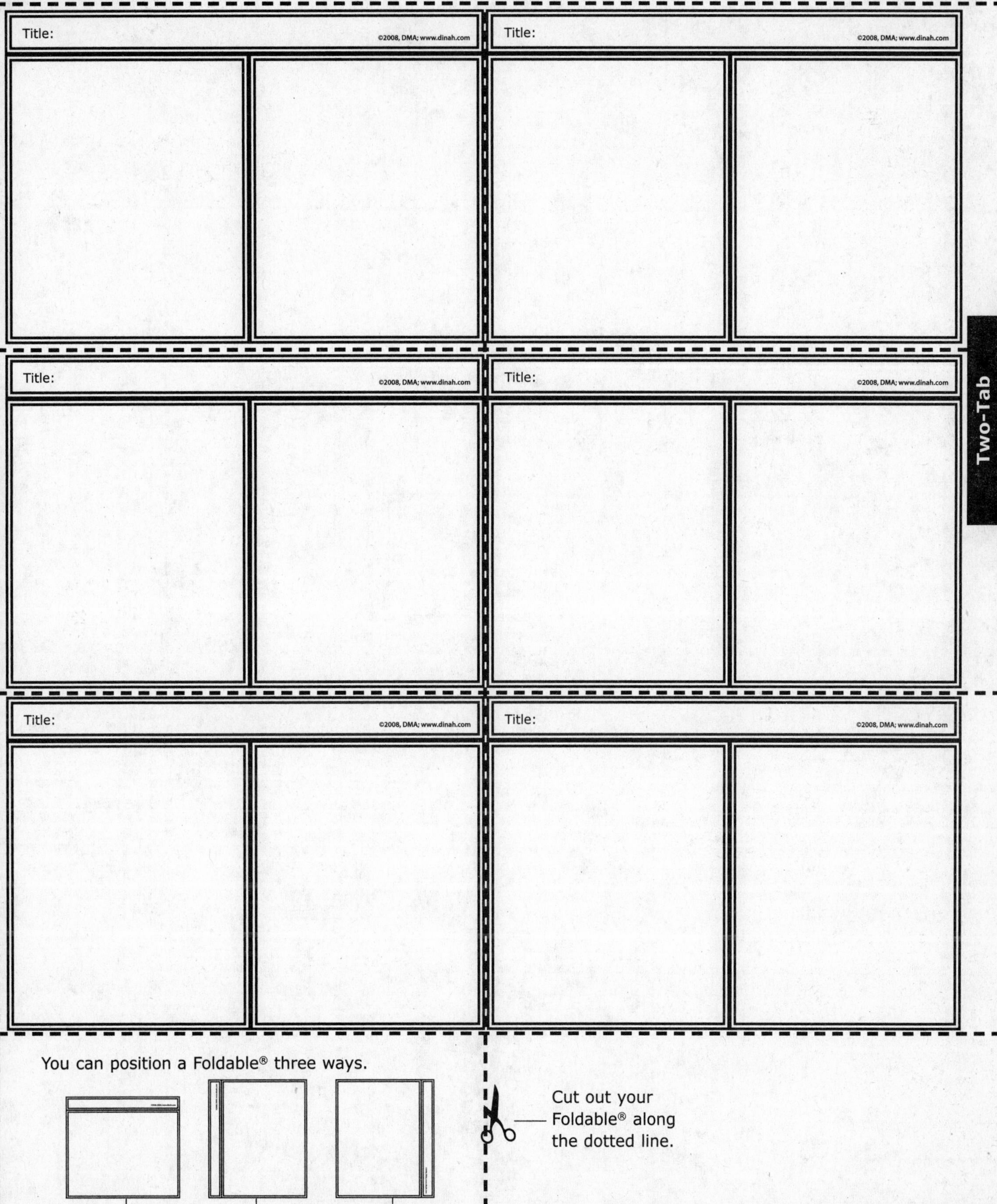

You can position a Foldable® three ways.

horizontally

vertically

Cut out your Foldable® along the dotted line.

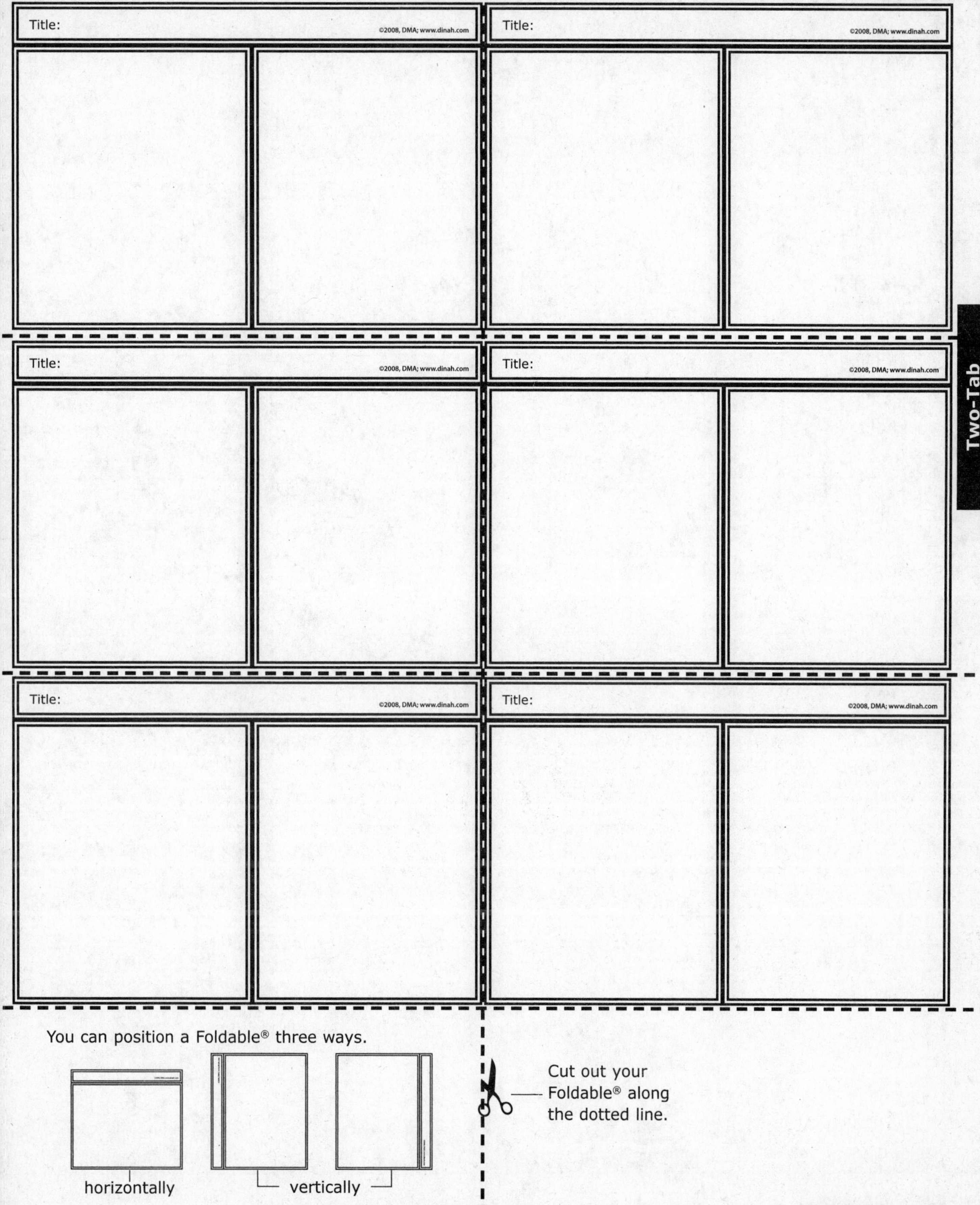

You can position a Foldable® three ways.

horizontally

vertically

Cut out your Foldable® along the dotted line.

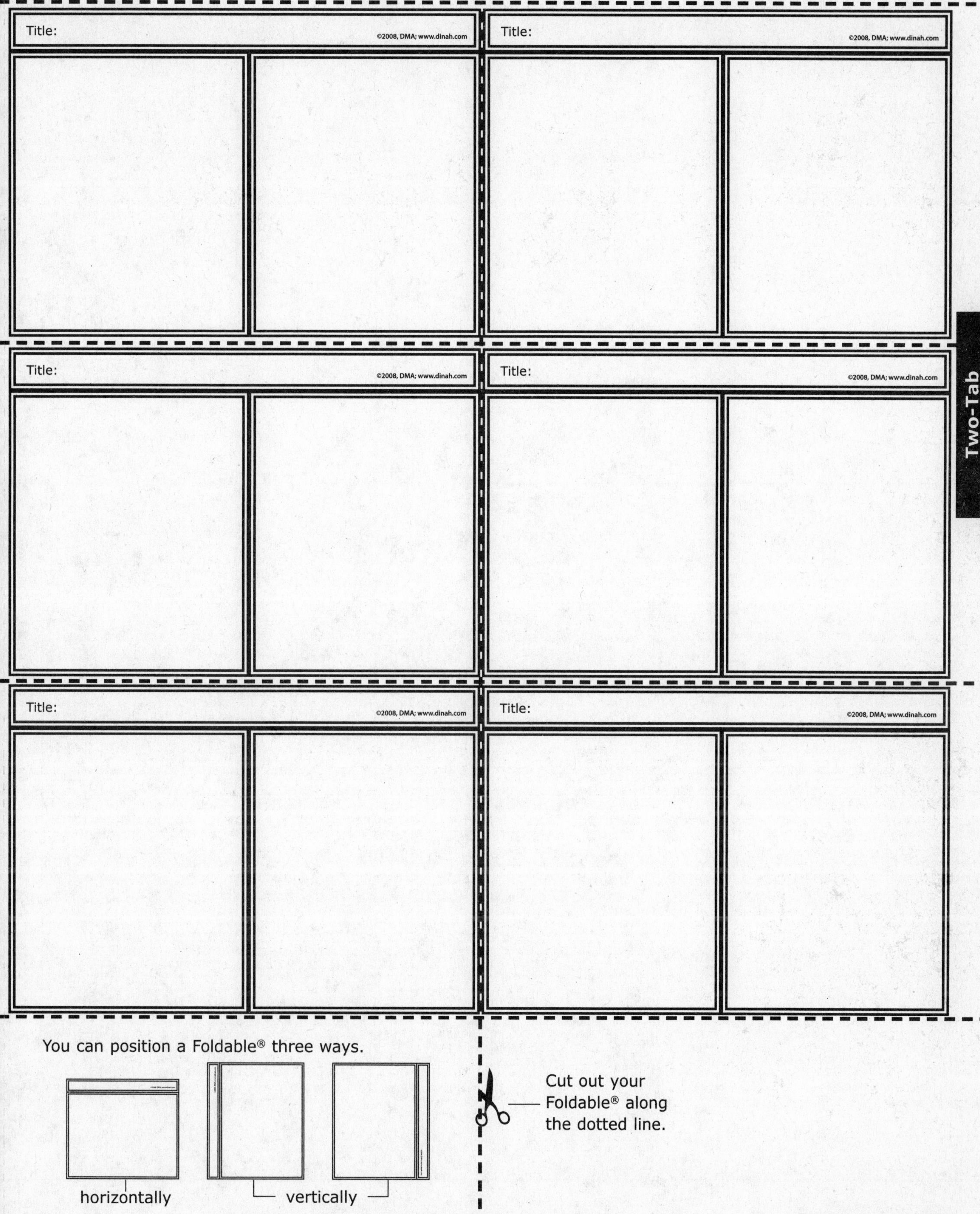

You can position a Foldable® three ways.

horizontally

vertically

Cut out your Foldable® along the dotted line.

Title:

Title:

Title:

Title:

Title:

Title:

You can position a Foldable® three ways.

horizontally

vertically

Cut out your Foldable® along the dotted line.

Title:

Title:

Title:

Title:

Title:

Title:

You can position a Foldable® three ways.

horizontally

vertically

Cut out your Foldable® along the dotted line.

Title: ©2008, DMA; www.dinah.com

Title: ©2008, DMA; www.dinah.com

Title: ©2008, DMA; www.dinah.com

Title: ©2008, DMA; www.dinah.com

Title: ©2008, DMA; www.dinah.com

Title: ©2008, DMA; www.dinah.com

You can position a Foldable® three ways.

horizontally

vertically

Cut out your Foldable® along the dotted line.

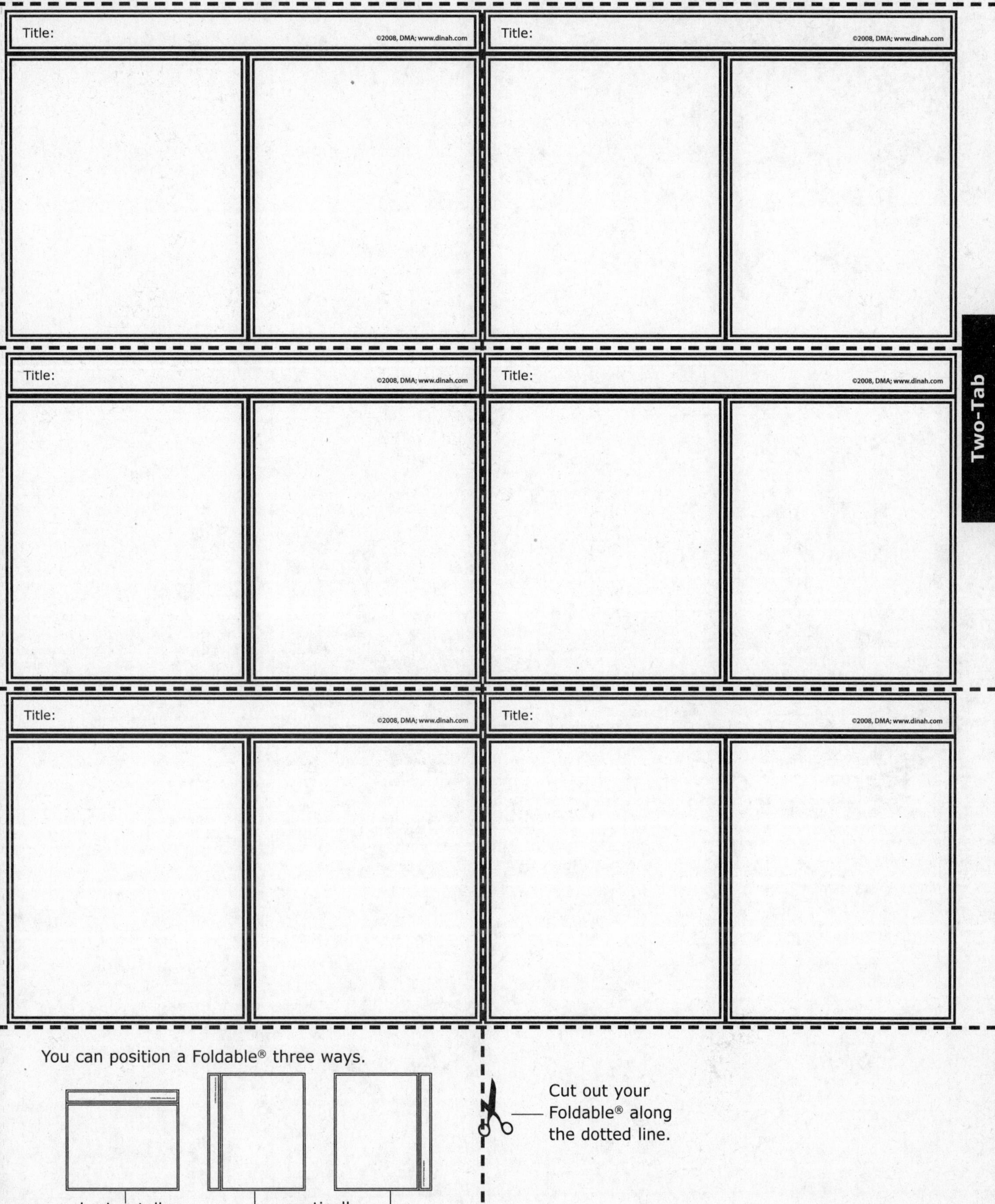

You can position a Foldable® three ways.

horizontally

vertically

Cut out your Foldable® along the dotted line.

FOLDABLES® by Dinah Zike

Notebook Foldables®

Using Foldables® in the *Reading Essentials and Study Guide* will help you develop note-taking and critical-thinking skills.

Three-Tab

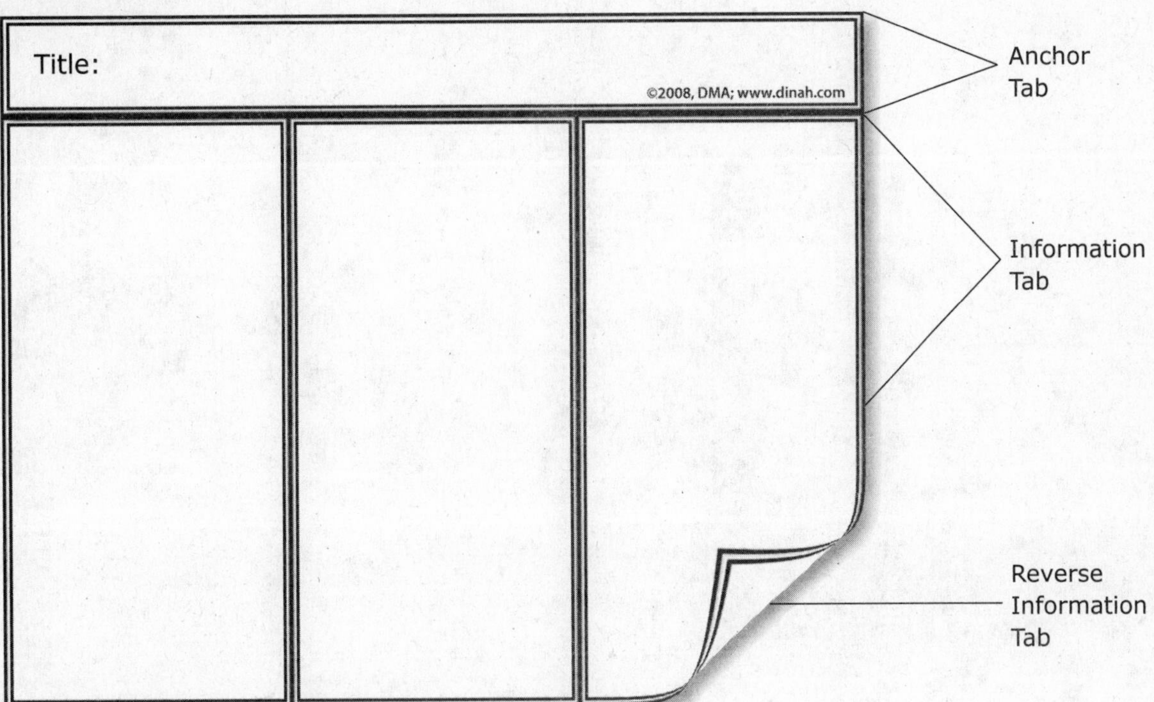

Folding Instructions

1. Cut out the template found on the following pages.
2. Fold the anchor tab over the information tab.
3. Glue the anchor tab to your workbook according to the instructions in the lesson.

Tip: Multiple Foldables® can be glued on top of each other by gluing anchor tabs on top of anchor tabs. This would make a small book on the page.

One-tab Foldable® glued onto a two-tab Foldable® to make a study book.

Title: ©2008, DMA; www.dinah.com

Title: ©2008, DMA; www.dinah.com

Title: ©2008, DMA; www.dinah.com

Title: ©2008, DMA; www.dinah.com

Title: ©2008, DMA; www.dinah.com

Title: ©2008, DMA; www.dinah.com

You can position a Foldable® three ways.

horizontally

vertically

Cut out your Foldable® along the dotted line.

Title:

Title:

Title:

Title:

Title:

Title:

You can position a Foldable® three ways.

horizontally

vertically

Cut out your Foldable® along the dotted line.

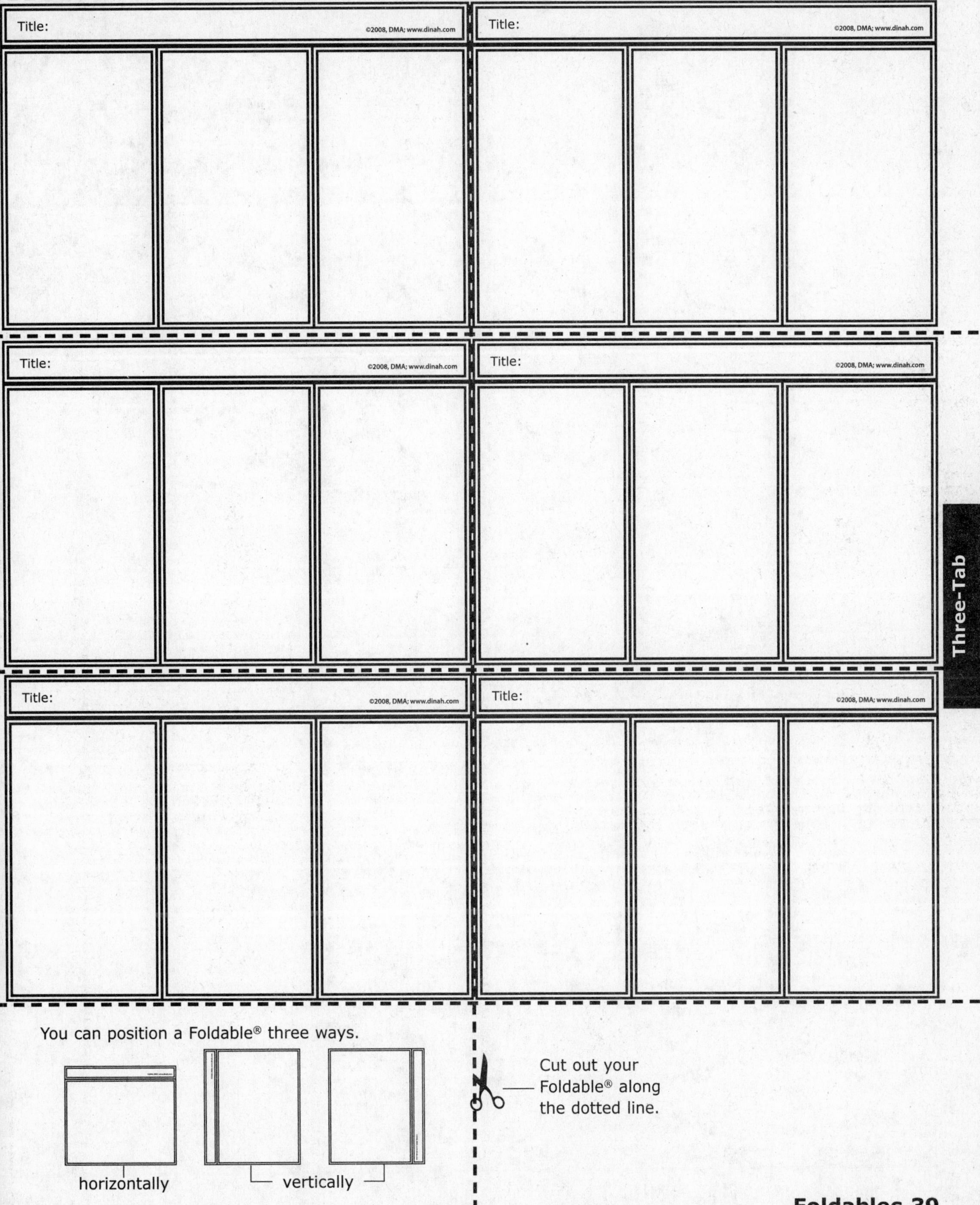

You can position a Foldable® three ways.

horizontally

vertically

Cut out your Foldable® along the dotted line.

FOLDABLES® by Dinah Zike

Notebook Foldables®

Using Foldables® in the *Reading Essentials and Study Guide* will help you develop note-taking and critical-thinking skills.

Venn Diagram

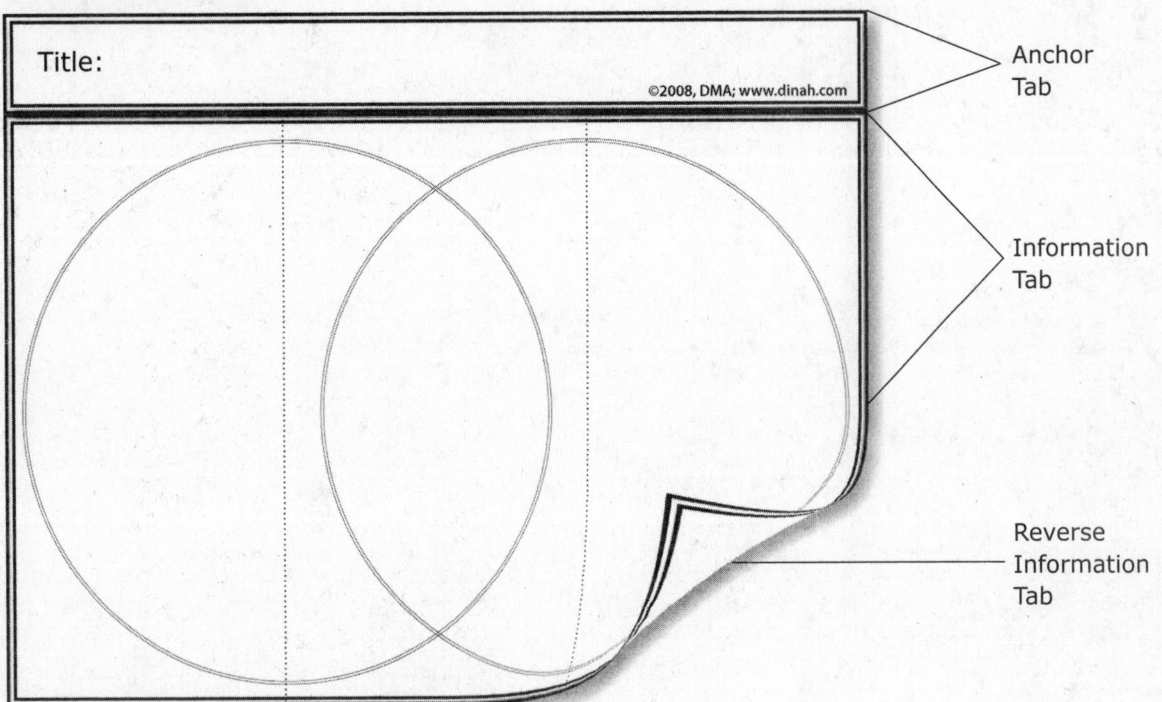

Folding Instructions

1. Cut out the template found on the following pages.
2. Fold the anchor tab over the information tab.
3. Glue the anchor tab to your workbook according to the instructions in the lesson.

Tip: Multiple Foldables® can be glued on top of each other by gluing anchor tabs on top of anchor tabs. This would make a small book on the page.

One-tab Foldable® glued onto a two-tab Foldable® to make a study book.

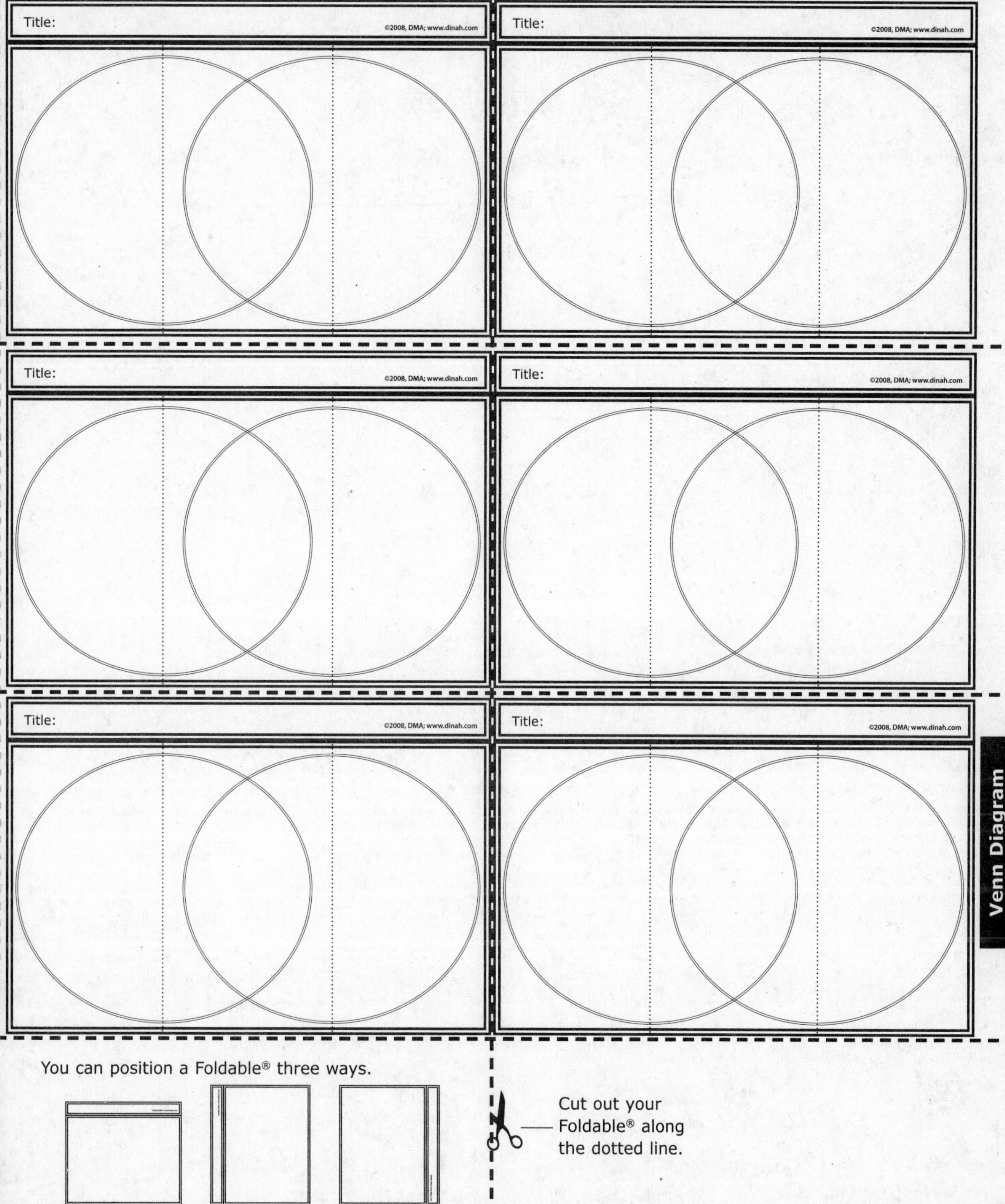

You can position a Foldable® three ways.

horizontally vertically

Cut out your Foldable® along the dotted line.

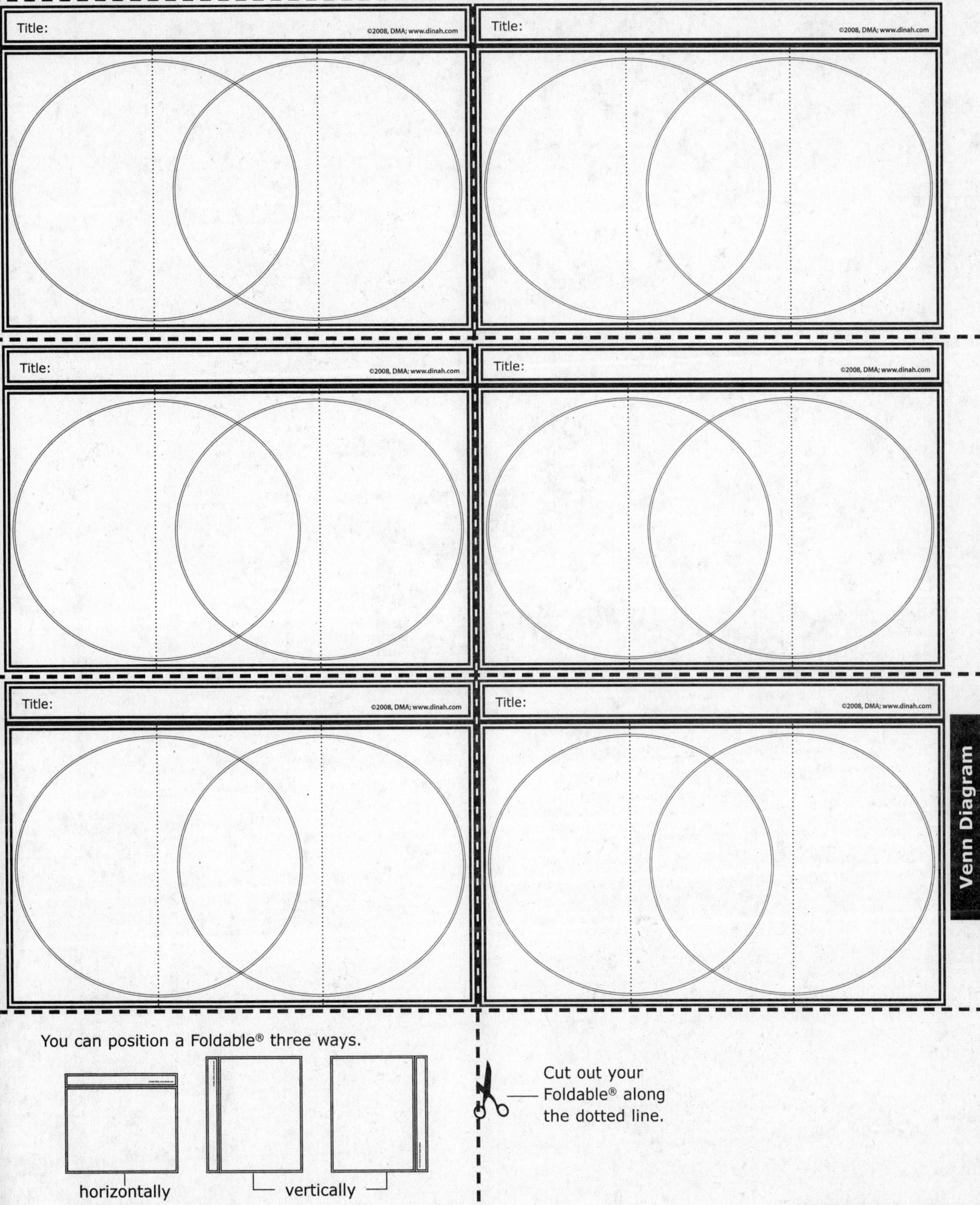

You can position a Foldable® three ways.

horizontally

vertically

Cut out your Foldable® along the dotted line.